Seize *work* the ^ Day

Using the
Tablet PC
to Take Total Control of Your Work and Meeting Day

By Michael Linenberger

New Academy Publishers
San Ramon, California

Although the author and publisher have made every effort to ensure the accuracy and completeness of information contained in this book, we assume no responsibility for errors, inaccuracies, omissions, or any inconsistency herein. Any slights of people, places, or organizations are unintentional.

First printing 2004

International Standard Book Number: 0-9749304-0-7

Library of Congress Control Number: 2004100616

ATTENTION CORPORATIONS, UNIVERSITIES, COLLEGES, AND PROFESSIONAL ORGANIZATIONS: quantity discounts are available on bulk purchases of this book for educational, gift purposes, or as premiums for increasing magazine subscriptions or renewals. Special books or book excerpts can also be created to fit special needs. For information, please contact New Academy Publishers, PO Box 577, San Ramon, California 94583.

The following trademarks appear throughout this book: Microsoft, Windows, Windows XP, Microsoft Windows XP Tablet PC Edition, Microsoft Office, Excel, Word, PowerPoint, Microsoft OneNote, Microsoft Windows Journal, Adobe Acrobat, FranklinCovey, FranklinCovey TabletPlanner, FranklinCovey PlanPlus for Microsoft Outlook, Mindjet MindManager, ScanSoft PaperPort Pro 9 Office. eBinder is a trademark of Agilix Labs. Weekly Compass is a registered trademark of FranklinCovey, Inc.

Contents at a Glance

Table of Contents

PART TWO: Seven Key Work Management Activities

Chapter 10 Manage Your Power Documents   363

Chapter 11 Brainstorming on the Tablet PC 429

Chapter 12 Mark Up and Edit Using the Tablet PC Pen 467

Chapter 13 Better Presentations 499

Chapter 14 Goal Setting on the Tablet PC 517

To Hong

Acknowledgments

Deep thanks go to the following individuals for their assistance in the preparation of this book: Rachel Anderson, Ron Baumanis, Gordon Burgett, Rob Bushway, Jaron Farr, Dennis Rice, Mark Shelley, Hobart Swan, Heidi Olsen, Amy Petty, Craig Pyle, Sarah Williams, W. Frederick Zimmerman. Special thanks go to Ruth Flaxman and Linda O'Connell for their excellent copy editing and proof reading. And to the organizer and community at TabletPCBuzz.com: keep up the great forum site; what an excellent place to learn the ins and outs of the Tablet PC.

About the Author

Michael Linenberger has been a technology professional for over 20 years. Michael served most recently as Vice President of Technology for Connection to eBay, an Accenture Service. Before that Michael was a management and technology consultant in the San Francisco office of Accenture, advising and managing projects for clients such as: eBay, Sun Microsystems, Cisco, Applied Materials, UPS, Adecco, and others.

Before Accenture, Michael led the technology department at U.S. Peace Corps.

Foreword

The Tablet PC has been more a quest than a product for many years. Represented in times past as "Pen Computing" and other names, it has been many times tried and failed. Why has it failed in the past? A combination of bad timing, bad implementation and other factors have all contributed to the lack of success of a worthy goal. So why is a Tablet PC a viable product today? Simply put, the world is ready for it, and the technology is here. The meeting of minds between computer hardware and software companies and those consumers actively using technology on a daily basis has presented the "call to arms" for this technology. The work day today for many people is a mobile one. Gone are the days when the majority would go to work at one place and be able to effectively carry out their workload. People are on the move, and that is where the Tablet PC makes a hugely valuable contribution to daily work efforts, above and beyond even the notebook PCs available today. The Tablet PC can go where no computer has gone before, and go quickly and efficiently, and with the added personalization of your own handwriting. It is time for the tablet.

In over 20 years of working as a computer professional, I have read many books, both technical and business professional. What I have generally found is that each type of book meets a certain percentage of my needs. But what most authors neglected to realize was that my needs were partially in both areas, technical and business. The book you hold in your hands does realize that pertinent fact. Make no mistake; this book is not just a computer "how-to" book. It is about business, and how to do it better utilizing a new technology tool. There is a mixture of the absolute technical details presented in such a way as to make it understandable to nontechnical people, but there also is a higher level of learning available that addresses the business needs of the professional worker today. The author's many years of executive and IT professional experience, combined with an obvious understanding of the Tablet PC itself, will provide you with an excellent source as you take this journey. In addition, he offers many unique yet tried tips on general task and time management developed throughout a long professional and technical career. Coverage of and suggestions for how to organize your meetings and related processes are excellent, not just for the individual, but for how the Tablet can contribute to the efforts of the entire team as a facilitation tool.

As with any new product, the Tablet PC and related software are not ready, "out of the box" to make you productive. This book will break it down for you in an organized manner from the start to help you become productive quickly. Of particular note are the coverage of Microsoft OneNote and Frank-linCovey's Tablet Planner and PlanPlus products. Mr. Linenberger has covered these products and their use on a Tablet PC like none other has before. There is not a great deal of information available on the use of these relatively new products, but they are covered in a most complete manner in this text.

Each day I assist users with this new tool as a Microsoft MVP (Most Valued Professional) for the Tablet PC, and many of the questions I see daily are answered here. Whether you have purchased a Tablet PC, or contemplating doing so, this will be a valuable resource. As you turn each page of this book, open your mind to new ways of achieving your workday goals, meetings, and tasks, and let the Tablet PC and applications change the way you work as you learn to "Think Ink." When you first begin to lay ink on that Tablet PC screen, you will be transformed. Once you realize the value in the new breed of Tab-let PC Applications, you will wonder to yourself, "How did I ever do without this tool?"

A word of caution here. If you use this book wisely, your daily productivity could increase, and your work day may end earlier. Oh my, what WILL you do with that extra time each day?

Good luck on your "inking" journey.

Dennis V. Rice, MCP, MCSA, MCSE, Microsoft MVP – Tablet PC Platform
January 2004
drice@saliantech.com

Seize the *work* Day
∧

Using the
Tablet PC
to Take Total Control of Your Work and Meeting Day

Introduction

Have you ever wished for a solution to a near out-of-control work day? If you are like I once was, you have often longed for a way to get and stay ahead of your work load. You have felt frustrated by hours of meetings that leave you little time to complete tasks during the day—by having to work late, night after night, to catch up on those responsibilities. You have felt frustrated by losing track of, or losing time for, commitments you have made. Frustrated by an avalanche of e-mails you cannot get to, by important documents you cannot find.

And you probably sense that if you *did* have a solution to these problems, a way to take back control, that you would finally have time to think *strategically* about work rather than tactically. That instead of focusing on putting out fires, you could be building solutions to avoid those fires. That you could "seize the work day," with confidence that all was on track and with sufficient time and energy to pursue new initiatives. And just maybe you could leave work a bit earlier each day.

And if you are like me you may have looked to new workflows and supporting technology-based solutions like the Palm or Pocket PC PDAs, and found them useful but woefully lacking for this problem. Or maybe you tried and gave up on desktop solutions like Outlook's task management approach. You have probably found that neither your desktop computer, nor your laptop, have the software, functionality, mobility, nor ease-of-use needed to really solve these problems.

If this describes you, this book is for you. In this book you will see that a properly configured Tablet PC set up and used correctly, and applied to appropriately matched workflows, really can be the solution to these problems. You'll see that the Tablet PC really *does* enable you to "seize the work day."

What This Book Contains

First, in Chapter 1, I will describe why the Tablet PC is such an important solution to the problems described above. Using the Tablet PC to adopt intelligent task management techniques, and to leverage meeting time, is key, and that is described in some detail in that chapter.

Then, throughout the book, I will teach you how to choose, configure, and use a Tablet PC with the specific intention of getting your work day under control.

I will take you through my strategies and recommended application usage of the Tablet PC with major work management activities in mind. I'll take a very personal approach to helping you succeed with the Tablet PC. I'll give detailed use approaches that have worked for me and that will work for you. I'll introduce you to new ways to use software you know, and to new software you don't know.

Choosing, Configuring, and Using the Tablet PC

Part One will focus on choosing and configuring the Tablet PC. It will discuss the different types of Tablet PCs. It will show you how to set up your Tablet PC so that it is easy, efficient, and unobtrusive to use in a work management setting, in ways that are often different from the setup recommended by other Tablet PC books.

If You Are New to the Tablet PC, Learn Basic Usage

And the book will get you started on using the Tablet PC for the first time. Chapter 3 is a Getting Started tutorial on the Tablet PC, in case you are just opening the box of this new tool.

You Will Learn How to Configure the Tablet PC as a PDA

Unfortunately, out-of-the-box, the Tablet PC is not configured so that you can use it as easily as you would a PDA. In Chapters 2 and 4 you will learn how to choose and configure the Tablet PC to maximize its effectiveness and possibly even replace your PDA. I will then show you throughout the book how to utilize the Tablet PC like a PDA on steroids, automating and organizing many of the work management tasks you now do inefficiently.

Learn to Configure and Use the Tablet PC as a Full Windows XP Computer, for Use in an Office Setting

In this book I'll show how one key to success with the Tablet PC is to configure it so you can also use it easily as your desktop computer. That way all your work is with you when you grab the Tablet PC and run to a meeting. In Chapter 4 I'll walk you through the configuration steps needed to enable this.

Prepare for Your First Meeting

Learning how to use the Tablet PC to leverage your low-performing meeting time is probably the most important thing you will learn in this book. However, it is very difficult to walk into that first management level meeting with a Tablet PC under your arm instead of your pen, paper notebook, and paper files. Difficult, that is, if you do not know how to pull this off effectively. Your Tablet PC needs to be ready, and you need to be ready, both in ways that aren't intuitively obvious. Throughout the book you will learn how to get ready for that first meeting, and all meetings beyond that.

Learn Strategies for Using Digital Ink and Text

I will explain why those few pundits that claim handwriting recognition on the Tablet PC is not quite ready for prime time are wrong, by discussing the strategies and best practices on when it is appropriate to use digital ink only, and when it is appropriate to convert digital ink to text. Chapter 5 looks at those strategies and when to apply them.

Use the 80/20 Rule

And it does not take a lot of effort to get ready. I am taking the perspective of a busy manager with limited time or inclination to figure out a new piece of technology. The book does not take the perspective of a die-hard computer user. I will in all cases focus on the 80/20 rule—80 percent of the value of the Tablet PC will be gained by focusing on only 20 percent of the possible features available. I will show you only high-value features and avoid the low-value frills that clog so many how-to books on computers and computer software. And, by the way, I will assume that you are not particularly technology savvy. And while this book may look thick, consider most of Part Two as optional. You pick and choose which software you need, and study those chapters.

Automating Seven Key Work Management Activities

All of Part Two focuses, one chapter at a time, on the seven key activities that lead to the benefits described at the start of this chapter. These are the activities that when used at appropriate times will boost your meeting and work productivity sky-high. I'll discuss in detail why those activities are so important. I'll discuss recommended software to automate those activities, and then show you how to use the software and how to work them into your work day. Note that in most cases I will show and instruct you on multiple possible software choices. You will be able to choose from several software packages, based on your preferences. Here are the activities covered in Part Two:

Task Management

Chapters 6 and 7 discuss in great detail the software choices for task management, and how to use that software to get ahead of your avalanche of tasks. Covered are leading theories on task management, my best practices in applying these theories to the Tablet PC, and the software choices to automate them. You are trained in use of that software, and in workflows that optimize your effectiveness.

Chapter 7 also focuses on how to get ahead of your out-of-control e-mail inbox.

Note Taking

Being able to find meeting notes for previous meetings quickly can make or break your success during a subsequent meeting. The pace of the modern business meeting is such that if you do not have information at hand when an important issue is being decided, your input is passed over.

The Tablet PC makes taking notes in your handwriting as easy as doing so on paper, and it makes retrieving the notes light-speeds faster than ever possible with paper. Chapters 8 and 9 discuss note-taking tools and how to use them.

Managing Your Power Documents

What are power documents? They are key documents that you use over and over again at work. Imagine if you could have all key documents available instantly when you needed them. The Tablet PC makes this possible, and this is discussed in Chapter 10.

Brainstorming on the Tablet PC

The Tablet PC offers a unique capability to increase your brainstorming tool choices. No longer are you limited to a white board or a blank sheet of paper. Chapter 11 shows you the tools available and how to use them.

Mark Up and Edit Documents Using the Tablet PC Pen Interface

The Tablet PC offers a unique opportunity for those who edit work. The ability to mark up documents in digital ink, and send those marked documents electronically, is incredibly useful. Chapter 12 focuses on the markup capabilities available.

Making Better Presentations

The Tablet PC enables improvements in your presentation capabilities during both the creation and the presentation stages. In Chapter 13 I show ways to create PowerPoint presentations faster than you imagined were possible, and how to leverage the Tablet PC during a presentation to enhance your audience's experience.

Goal Setting and Planning

There is something very personal and inspiring about using the Tablet PC in pen mode. Doing so lends itself to the state of mind needed to accomplish meaningful goal-setting activities. This, combined with good computer-based goal setting and planning tools, can jump start this activity that so many of us postpone. Chapter 14 shows you how.

In Conclusion, a Fun Ride Is Ahead

So get ready for a fun ride, you're about to be introduced to a tool, a friend really, which I predict will be at your side every moment of the working day for the foreseeable future. A tool that, once you are through the lessons of this book, you will not believe that you have lived without.

PART ONE: Why and How

Chapter 1 Seize the Work Day

Boost Your Work Management Effectiveness

If you manage your own work or the work of others, you will find that the Tablet PC operated by Windows XP Tablet PC Edition will help you tremendously. This book will tell you why and show you how.

The Tablet PC can help you:

- get your work totally organized

- turn the meetings you attend or give into more productive events

- facilitate seven key work management activities you do, such as task management, note taking, and document management—all of which will help you be more productive with your work

The net result? You will find yourself getting your work day under control in ways you never imagined. Your personal productivity will jump dramatically. And most importantly, with the recovered time, you can if you choose start to devote time for those things that are really important: strategic thinking, skills improvement, goal setting—and perhaps leave work earlier for a change.

In my role as a management consultant and as a technology VP for one of the "big-four" consulting firms, Accenture, I have never seen a more powerful piece of technology for getting the average knowledge worker's or manager's work day under control. I have used the Tablet PC consistently, since shortly after its release in 2002, managing work in an executive setting. I have spent nearly two decades studying and applying technology to business automation. Based on all this experience I am going to show you how to use the Tablet PC in ways that will lead to very welcome gains in your work productivity.

Who Can Benefit?

Whether you manage your own work or others', I'm going to assume you do three things repeatedly:

- work on countless tasks either on your own or in teams, tasks assigned to you by yourself or by others

- assign, or delegate, tasks to others

- attend meetings where you present or collect information and participate in decision making—meetings where I am sure you feel you are wasting valuable time

All of these things lead to work scenarios where the Tablet PC configured and used correctly will make a huge difference in your ability to get your work organized and completed more quickly.

Don't get me wrong, the uses of the Tablet PC go well beyond the above activities. Students, doctors, attorneys, graphic workers, mobile workers, among others, all can benefit greatly from the Tablet PC format. However the greatest potential value of the Tablet PC is for people who manage typical, daily, at-the-office work.

Get Totally Organized

Peter Drucker in his book *The Effective Executive* identifies five practices a work manager can do to become truly effective:

- manage time effectively

- focus on results and goals

- focus on strengths

- focus on high priority tasks

- learn how to make good decisions

I will show how the Tablet PC can directly improve your effectiveness with: managing time, goals, and task priorities. Chapter 11, on brainstorming, will assist in making good business decisions. And beyond this you will learn skills that assist indirectly in all five practices.

Tablet PC–Based Time and Task Management

Managing time and tasks effectively is probably the most important skill you can improve on as a work manager. Mastering that skill will:

- teach you to use your time effectively

- give you tools for effective delegation and follow up

- help you get projects under control

- increase your sense of accomplishment

- convince your superiors that you have your responsibilities managed

- free up time to focus on more important activities

- help you leave work earlier each night

The reason the Tablet PC works so well in boosting your task management capabilities is because it puts powerful PC-based task management tools within your reach right when you need them most: in the midst of work and meeting activities. And it does this with a pen interface that is easy to use, and that lends itself to instant input and updating of tasks, even amidst the combat of the busy day. And you have all the advantages of a full-strength Windows XP system; you are not limited by a PDA-sized tool. It's this combination of ease of use, ubiquitous at-hand availability, and full-strength computer automation that finally makes task management an achievable discipline for the average knowledge worker or manager. The Tablet PC is the technology that makes this practical.

In this book you will learn software and methods of task management that when exercised on the powerful Tablet PC will take your work-task control to new levels. With these task management approaches you will experience dramatic increases in productivity.

- You will learn what task management software to use and how to use it on the Tablet PC.

- You will eliminate the "everything is a fire" mentality by learning how to track which tasks need to be done at what time and which can wait. You will learn how to determine when you can leave guilt-free at the end of the day. And you will do this all from your Tablet PC, wherever you are.

- You will learn how to accomplish tasks more efficiently and get them done more quickly, freeing up time on your schedule.

- You will learn Tablet PC–based methods of effective delegation and follow up that really work, so that you can actually get tasks off your list.

- And, most importantly, you will learn how to use the Tablet PC to execute task activities during the free cycles in the meetings where tasks are assigned, so that you can leave the meeting virtually free of nagging follow-up activities.

Other Skills to Get You Totally Organized

And in addition to task management, you will learn other key skills to help you get totally organized:

- Note-taking and retrieval approaches on the Tablet PC that will "save your skin" in countless business situations because you can find recorded information nearly instantly.

- How to manage what I call power documents in an electronic binder for instant access, to increase your work effectiveness and control.

- Tablet PC advantages for presentation creation, document editing, brainstorming, and goal setting.

These are all additional skills that you can learn to boost your work management effectiveness and organization ability.

Boost Your Meeting Productivity

Of all the levers we will cover that the Tablet PC can push to reach the goal of increased productivity for the average knowledge worker, none is more important than the power of the Tablet PC to allow you to leverage meetings more effectively. As a result, you will earn back much of the time you lose in meetings.

The ability to do many if not all of the things listed above during spare cycles in a meeting is what grabs back so many hours of unproductive time in your day, and truly allows you to leave work earlier. And the ability for you to make meetings more productive rewards not only you, but your whole team.

Reclaim Your Lost Meeting Time

If I had a nickel for every poorly utilized minute of meeting time I've spent in my career I'd be a rich man. I'm sure you feel that way too. The Tablet PC gives back to you that lost effectiveness. Having a Tablet PC with you in a meeting (configured per the recommendations in this book) does this by:

■ Allowing you to effectively and discretely use slow or dead segments of meetings for productive work related to the meeting, at the time that needed actions are fresh in your mind.

■ Allowing you to follow up on meeting action items, while still in the meeting session, while action intentions are clear and enthusiasm is high.

■ Allowing you to have all key documents at-hand during meetings, documents that will make your meeting time much more effective.

■ Allowing you to record and find notes from previous meetings in ways that will provide essential information during the meeting, making the meeting more productive.

■ Giving you new tools to use within working meetings that will make those group-based tasks much more efficient.

The result? I now rarely walk out of meetings muttering to myself "and now to get back to real work," or, "when am I going to get these tasks organized so I can leave tonight?" The satisfaction of having reclaimed low productivity meeting time is enormous. The satisfaction of leaving work on time for a change is even better.

How Does the Tablet PC Do This for Meetings?

The first bullet above is by far the most important point. Having a properly configured Tablet PC with the right software in a meeting allows you to leverage your meetings enormously. It allows you to effectively and discretely use slow or dead segments of meetings for productive work related to the meeting, at the time that needed actions are fresh in your mind. I cannot overemphasize how important this is.

Ten Productive Things to Do with a Tablet PC in a Meeting

Per this point, here is a list of the productive meeting-related things I now do discreetly, on my Tablet PC, using the spare cycles available during most meetings (each of these I cover how to configure for and do, in later chapters):

- Create, prioritize, and assign tasks from action items identified during the meeting right in my Tablet PC–based task management system.

- Set date-driven reminders to follow up on deadlines discussed or set in the meeting.

- Update the status of tasks in my task list indicating progress made in the meetings.

- Find notes, documents, files, and e-mails relevant to the meeting at hand, as needed to accomplish follow-up tasks right in the meeting.

- Create or update key documents in my electronic binder to refer to the next time these meeting topics come up.

- If needed, convert portions of handwritten meeting notes to text for subsequent distribution.

- Create, and if wireless is available, even send e-mails to staff to follow up on important action items from the meeting.

- Create a brainstorm document of possible solutions for problems raised in the meeting, incorporating the best thinking from the meeting.

- With optional wireless access, pull up the web page for a product or company being discussed in the meeting, and communicate the researched information to the meeting at the moment it's needed.

- And if the meeting is really dead, the Tablet PC also allows you to spend time on nonmeeting-related e-mails and other work documents, and even "research" the web, all while waiting for the meeting to come back to a topic relevant to you.

Note that all of these activities are only possible if you have configured your Tablet PC correctly; this is the topic of the next chapters.

Why Not Just Use a Laptop? Why the Tablet PC?

For all these tasks described above, you may wonder, "Couldn't I just use a laptop to do the same?" Unless you are in a working meeting where the focus of the meeting is on completing computer tasks, the answer is a resounding no. Using a Tablet PC during a typical management meeting is totally different from using a laptop. It's the difference between night and day. The difference between success and failure. Here's why.

- **Discretion**: Nothing is more distracting than, during a management-style meeting, having a meeting participant typing away on a laptop. In contrast, working with a Tablet PC in your lap appears no different from what you would be doing with a pen and notepad in your lap. This is particularly true if you use, as recommended later in this book, an executive-style portfolio case that makes your Tablet PC resemble an executive notepad portfolio.

- **Communication barriers**: Placing a laptop with the screen flipped up in front of you on a conference room table creates a physical barrier between you and others in the room. This is literally a barrier to communication. The Tablet PC is normally on your lap, and out of sight. Or it is flat on the desk like a writing pad.

- **Personal effectiveness**: Research shows that if you use both hands to accomplish a task, a much larger percentage of your brain becomes engaged in that operation. Typing with both hands tends to totally engage your brain in the typing activity and makes you visibly less tuned-in to the meeting. In contrast, writing with one hand during a meeting is second nature to most of us. The brain stays mostly engaged in the meeting activities. We all can take notes and participate in a meeting at the same time. Using a Tablet PC in a meeting is little different from this.

- **Eye contact**: Related to the above point, and for the same reasons, many users have reported that it is much easier to maintain periodic and consistent eye contact with others in a meeting when using a Tablet PC versus using a laptop. This has a dramatic affect on the perception of others that you are engaged and personable. Lack of eye contact also limits your ability to read body language of others, adding to your distance from the meeting.

But You Also Have Your Computer, Don't You?

And with all the above said, guess what? You also have your primary work computer with you in the meeting, booted and ready for action. The point here is that occasionally, due to the course of activities in the meeting, you really *do* need access your regular computer, and with permission of all the meeting participants. Say the topic of the meeting hinges on the contents of a Word document that was distributed a few days earlier and is suddenly now being discussed, and the meeting is at a standstill because no one has a copy of it. You can now look for it (or an Excel spreadsheet, or any other computer-based document) discreetly or otherwise. All the participants in the meeting want to know what's in that document.

Have you ever tried to wait for someone to fish out and boot up their laptop in a meeting and find a document? It's like watching paint dry. However due to all the other uses of the Tablet PC, your computer is in the meeting room booted and ready to refer to at that time.

So in effect this is a bonus. Built into that mobile PDA is your full-fledged computer with all the things you may need it for occasionally in random meetings, and it is powered on nearly all the time since that is how you use the Tablet PC. And since all Tablet PCs come with an attached or detachable keyboard, those times when you really do need a laptop your fully powered laptop is there and ready. We'll cover more in Chapter 4 how to configure your Tablet PC as your active desktop and laptop computer.

Maintaining a Management Appearance

And assuming you're using the executive portfolio case I describe more fully in the hardware and software chapter (Chapter 2), it does all this without making you look like a computer technician carrying a laptop everywhere you go. To all casual observers, you're carrying a writing pad between meetings.

Why Meetings Are Such a Ripe Opportunity

Why is it so important to start leveraging your meeting time to increase your productivity? First, I am amazed at the reduced expectations that most organizations have regarding the productivity of meetings. It's almost as if meetings are approved rest periods in which the participants are allowed to leave their best work habits behind and instead just drift with the banter and flow of the meeting, not expecting any real outcome.

But even with a culture of proper meeting leadership where meetings are driven to meet clear outcomes, most participants, while the meeting is being led for them, shift into second or third gear contributing only small amounts here and there.

This of course is the cost side of the equation of what often can be a positive net outcome. The potential value of meetings is huge. When needed, the best contributions of multiple minds can be directed toward guiding future expenditures of valuable resources. Take the hourly cost of a small number of key managers during a short but important direction-setting meeting. Now compare that to the potentially huge cost of a large number of their subordinates all working for weeks in the wrong direction. Here the potential value of meetings is apparent.

But even with effectively run meetings with justified goals, we've all experienced this: we participate in a meeting in which good decisions are made with much enthusiasm and with the positive guidance of group consensus. Then we leave the meeting, not returning to the meeting actions we promised ourselves until say, the end of the day, or worse, until several days later if ever. At that point rigor mortis has set in. The ideas are no longer fresh, the clarity of the group vision has clouded over, and, perhaps worst, the enthusiasm is gone. At that moment, dragging ourselves into action mode toward the decisions made in the meeting is near impossible. No wonder so many meeting participants gain a reputation for lack of follow-up, and no wonder so many meetings gain a reputation of leading nowhere.

The gap that needs closing here is that we all have come to accept that the typical meeting must be held away from our key work tools: our desk, our files, our computer, and communications with our staff. It is impractical to have them present, and it would be distracting if they were there. And so we have come to accept that while in meetings we are present only for decision making, and that our follow-up actions are only appropriate once back at our desk, back at our "command post," even if days may pass before we get there.

Bring Your Command Post with You—Seize the Moment

But now, the Tablet PC gives you the tool necessary to discreetly take a simplified version of your command post with you into meetings, allowing you to effectively engage in follow-up and direction-setting activities while they are immediate in your mind, and while you have free mental cycles during the less engaged portions of the meeting.

And not only while the follow-up activities are fresh in your mind, but while the enthusiasm and energy and group guidance inherent in the meeting decisions are at their peak, there in the meeting. This is the time to seize the moment and set meaningful actions into motion.

A "Controversy"

There is a bit of controversy around the Tablet PC currently. A number of business and PC pundits have, upon cursory examination, declared that the Tablet PC is not yet a really useful tool. There are a lot of favorable reviews too, but when I read the negative reviews, and even some of the positive reviews, I could not help but think, "These guys are missing the point."

I'll get to that point in a minute, but first, note that the first time I saw Tablet PC I came to the same conclusion. Waiting for a flight, I chanced upon an airport kiosk set up courtesy of Microsoft to show off the Tablet PC during the initial product launch. Being in the technology business, I had wanted to see, touch, and play with one of these Tablet PCs. I had some time to kill, and here was my opportunity. However, within about five minutes of using the Tablet PC at this kiosk, I reluctantly concluded that these Tablet PCs were not ready for the kind of work management activities I routinely do.

Sky-High Productivity

In spite of that mixed experience, about a month later on a whim and sight unseen, I bought one through the mail and urged myself to use it in my management job. At about the two- or three-week point after that purchase, after a lot of experimentation and optimizing, my productivity curve crossed well into the positive and it has been going sky-high ever since.

So the point is the Tablet PC may be a bit confusing and not particularly impressive until you learn it, and until it is tuned and optimized for your work. What I discovered through some experimentation (experimentation which due to this book you can avoid) is that there are easy ways to fine-tune the Tablet PC usage and to add applications, which when combined, will lead you to dramatic productivity gains in your work management activities. I'll save you from that experimentation and show you what I've learned.

One way to think of this book is as a time management book for the Tablet PC. You can learn logical, effective habits and applications on a Tablet PC that, like time management techniques applied to your activities, will make your work activities productive, and that will put you well ahead of the rest of the pack.

The Tablet PC: a Manager Productivity Revolution

Managers have been partially left out of the computer revolution.

Sure, managers use e-mail, type their own documents, and create presentations. But if you look at the productivity gains that the computer has brought to industry in general, management has not benefited as greatly.

This is because management skills are largely soft skills, and not the easiest skills to automate. If you think of the computer successes in various industries what comes to mind? Probably financial systems, manufacturing and warehouse systems, ERP-based transactional systems, and more recently supply chain and CRM or customer support systems. But what about you, the average work manager? Do you really feel like you've automated your core management tasks?

The Ultimate PDA

To me, the Tablet PC is like a PDA on steroids when applied correctly to work management tasks. It's a PDA that finally fulfills all the promises of a PDA, and goes way beyond those. This is in contrast to how most reviewers look at the Tablet PC: as merely a laptop computer with a pen input.

This distinction is important. The key is that with a properly configured Tablet PC, work managers finally have a PDA with access to powerful applications that truly help in his or her daily management tasks. It's also a PDA with a screen large enough to do real work, with storage large enough to never run out, and with a processor powerful enough to never slow down. The fact that this PDA is also a fully functional Windows XP computer is in some ways merely icing on the cake (and quite cost effective too).

As this book will show, the Tablet PC when used properly gets us much closer to the goal of automating daily management activities. It represents a source of a much-needed work management productivity revolution.

Chapter 2 Choosing the Tablet PC and Software

Choosing Your Tablet PC

As of the writing of this book, there were nearly ten Tablet PCs on the market, and if you have not yet purchased your Tablet PC, you have some decisions to make. From one perspective, virtually any of these Tablet PCs will do the job for you, because all of the Tablet PCs are manufactured to specifications enforced by Microsoft. And so other than whether a keyboard is permanently attached or not there's not extensive variability between the functionality of the models. That said, based on my months of experience using the Tablet PC in a corporate environment, I have strong preferences on the hardware variables that are there, and I'll share those with you. Some of these hardware variables represent deal breakers for me, and may for you too, so if you have not yet bought your Tablet PC I recommend you read this chapter before purchasing. I'm not going to provide a deep comparative study of each of the different Tablet PCs. Rather, I'm going to tell you what hardware features and configurations have worked for me, and which ones I recommend you choose when picking a Tablet PC for work management.

Tablet PC Choices

Basic Hardware Choices: Slate versus Convertible versus Hybrid

If you've done any sort of research on the Tablet PC models available, you probably know that there are two basic types: the slate and the convertible. Briefly, the slate (see Figure 2-1) has no permanently attached keyboard and the convertible does (see Figure 2-2). The advantage of the slate is its lighter weight and thinner form factor. The advantage of the convertible is that you can quickly convert between a Tablet PC form factor and a laptop form factor.

In between these two major types are various hybrids. For example the HP Compaq Tablet PC TC1000 and TC1100 have a removable keyboard that allows it to act like a slate or like a convertible (see Figure 2-5). Motion Computing, which makes its own brand of slate tablet and also makes the Gateway slate tablet, offers an optional clip-on keyboard/screen-cover which allows their slate line to act like a convertible as well. The Electrovaya SC-2000 reportedly has a similar capability.

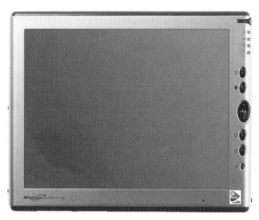

Figure 2-1. Motion Computing specializes in slate Tablet PC's with 12.1-inch screens. Its M1300 is well reviewed.

Figure 2-2. Acer was one of the first Tablet manufacturers to make a convertible model. Shown here is the widely used TravelMate C110 with a 10.4-inch screen.

Availability of Portfolio Case Drove My Purchase Decision

For using a Tablet PC in a management setting my preference is a slate or hybrid model, and the sole reason is that these easily fit into a portfolio case. If you're uncertain what I'm talking about when I say a portfolio case, think of one of those dark leather padded notepad covers that some executives bring to meetings to take notes with or keep their calendars in. Comparable portfolio cases are made for the slate style Tablet PCs and they make the Tablet PC look like a writing notepad or daily planner (see Figure 2-3).

Figure 2-3.   Using a portfolio case makes carrying your Tablet PC look more businesslike in professional and management settings.

If you follow my recommendations in this book, you will be bringing your Tablet PC to all your meetings both internal and external. And in this world of first impressions, I recommend that you make the introduction of the Tablet PC into your work life as tech-free in appearance as possible. When you walk across a room or a corporate campus, you will appear to be holding nothing more than a paper or planner portfolio. And when using your tablet with someone sitting across a table from you, they will, at least initially, think you are taking notes on paper. The idea is not to totally conceal your Tablet PC, but rather to avoid distracting a meeting, especially at the beginning when first impressions are made.

You need to decide what is appropriate for you within your own organization and within your job category. Many organizations, particularly technical ones, have no bias against technically orientated managers. But many do. I have worked in organizations where bringing a new unusual piece of technology into a client meeting would not be appropriate, it would be considered too distracting. So if you have any apprehensions about being sized-up as a "tech-guy" in meetings, decide now to use a portfolio case and buy a slate or hybrid that supports one. And for those times you are inevitably "discovered," a slate tablet inside a slim black portfolio case has a very sophisticated, professional look to it (at least you will be credited as someone with good taste).

Portfolio cases also provide moderate protection for your tablet from bumps and short falls. If you do not carry a briefcase around your office (most don't), the portfolio will help guard against some transport accidents.

Side Note: While portfolio cases are also available for some of the convertible models, they tend to make the whole package feel and appear very bulky, and those who have used both usually report preferring the slimmer form factor available by using a slate or hybrid Tablet PC with a portfolio case.

More Thoughts on Slates, Convertibles, and Hybrids

Buying a convertible may seem like a safer decision. After all, if your experiment with the Tablet PC does not work out for you, and you end up rarely using it in the tablet mode, you also end up with a good laptop. However for me the decision against getting a convertible, after months of slate use, turned out to be a good one. This is because I found I rarely used my Tablet PC in laptop mode even though I could easily do so by attaching my detachable keyboard. As you'll see in the chapters ahead, my use-strategy is as follows:

- When I'm at work sitting at my desk I use an external keyboard and monitor attached to the tablet.

- At work in meetings, I use the pen interface only. Using a keyboard in a meeting is usually not appropriate (see Chapter 1 for a discussion about this).

- And at home using my tablet I find I rarely do extended typing on a keyboard, so the handwriting mode (or speech recognition) is just fine for the little input I normally need to do. I enjoy being able to relax on a couch with the tablet in my lap doing fairly casual computer work with only a pen, something a slate/hybrid is ideal for.

It's nice to know that I can plug in a keyboard and use the tablet as a laptop if I need to, but I rarely do. So I am happy that I am spared the extra weight of a permanently attached keyboard.

One other point about a convertible: keep in mind that with a convertible you can only use the keyboard with the tablet screen in *landscape* mode. Some of the hybrid approaches (such as the optional clip-on keyboard used by Motion Computing) also allow you to attach the keyboard with the tablet in *portrait* mode.

All that said, for some work styles the convertible is the right choice. For example in writing this book, my work habits have changed. While this entire book was written using speech recognition on my tablet, I've also recently set up an external keyboard and monitor at my home office for when speech recognition just isn't appropriate (editing for example). So if your work includes extensive editing, consider how you will make a keyboard available. If such editing sessions are at times when you are between offices, and cannot take the time to fish out and clip on a detached keyboard, then the convertible make may make sense.

But for the model job description I am writing for (used mostly for office work, alternating between meetings, desktop, and some at-home work), the slate should serve you well. The advantages of a slate in that setting outweigh the disadvantages. And I suggest you commit yourself to the goals of this book, rather than compromise.

Figure 2-4. Fujitsu has a long history of making pen-based computers. Its Stylistic line (shown here is the ST5000D) is a popular and well-regarded slate Tablet PC.

Using on Airplanes

One important consideration when choosing between a slate, convertible, and hybrid is ease of use on a plane. It is unlikely that speech recognition will work on a noisy airplane, and so if you need to enter extensive text while on an airplane, a keyboard will be required. Many slates with external keyboards require you to prop up the slate with some easel-like device, to use it as a monitor while typing. The limited tray space on the normal airplane seat makes doing this difficult. In this case a more traditional laptop configuration is desirable, and a convertible tablet could have an advantage.

Note however that many hybrids have solved this problem. For example the HP Compaq Tablet PC TC1100, the Electrovaya SC-2000, and the Motion Computing slates all have detachable keyboards (either standard or as options) that actually hold and support their tablets just like a laptop. See Figure 2-5 for an example of one such arrangement. Consider this requirement when choosing other slate or hybrid brands.

Researching Tablet PC Models and Manufacturers

See the Appendix for links to product pages for the major Tablet PC manufacturers. At the time of this writing, of the manufacturers in that list, the following offered slate or hybrid models: Motion Computing, Fujitsu, Viewsonic, HP/Compaq, Gateway, Electrovaya, Tatung, and NEC.

Figure 2-5. The HP Compaq Tablet PC is one of the best selling lines. The TC1000 is a hybrid with a detachable keyboard that supports the tablet like a laptop.

Screen Size, Resolution, and Readability

The other major hardware decision regards screen size. The two common formats are 10.4 inches and 12.1 inches. I started out with a 12.1-inch screen and cannot imagine using a smaller one. While the smaller units are lighter and do make the portfolio look a bit more like a regular notepad or organizer, the larger units are not bad in appearance, nor are they heavy. And for me the larger screen makes a huge difference in usability.

As you become proficient at using handwriting for text recognition, you will find that your proficiency is dependent upon clear and somewhat larger handwriting. A larger screen gives you more room to rest your palm as you write, and more room to make strokes, all of which I and others feel are helpful to create this clear handwriting. And, just in general, larger screens are easier to work with on any computer. Keep in mind that I am advocating you use your Tablet PC as your primary computer as well, so keep it easy to use when away from your desk by getting a large tablet screen.

Side Note: Regardless of screen size, screen resolution is identical on nearly all Tablet PC makes and models: XGA (1,024-by-768). Exceptions are noted below.

All this said there are plenty of Tablet PC users who *do* report being satisfied with a 10.4-inch screen size. They like the smaller form factor (see Figure 2-6) and say writing on the 10.4-inch screen is just fine. And if you have a petite physical frame, a 12-inch tablet can look huge in your hands as a portfolio. If you are still trying to decide, I recommend you look at both sizes. Lift them, write on them, and then make the decision.

Figure 2-6. The NEC Versa LitePad is among the smallest and lightest of the slate Tablet PCs. It has a 10.4-inch screen, weighs only 2.2 pounds, and is only 0.6 inches thick.

Pushing the upper limits on size and weight are two new Tablet PC models. One from manufacturer Acer is the recently released convertible (Acer C300) with a 14-inch screen and a full size keyboard. It also has an optional built-in CD/DVD drive. This computer weighs 6.2 pounds so think carefully about whether this would be practical for carrying around between meetings. The other is the Gateway M275XL, also a convertible with a 14.1-inch screen and internal optical drive, weighing in at 5.7 lbs. Unfortunately at the time of this writing, these larger screens are usually limited by digitizers that only accept XGA (1,024-by-768) resolutions in tablet mode, so the existence of a larger screen can be a bit deceiving; the images may just be magnified when in tablet mode. Larger resolutions are on the way in other new models, so if you are considering a very large monitor Tablet PC like this, check the resolution specification. Note also that a portfolio case for one of these is going to look more like a briefcase. Given these issues my current recommendation is to stick with the 12.1-inch screen.

One more point on resolution. A recently released Tablet PC convertible by Toshiba (the Portege M200, see Figure 2-7) uses a 12.1 inch screen with the larger SXGA+ resolution (1,400-by-1,050) while in Tablet mode. This is a first for any Tablet PC. Such a resolution provides more total digital screen real-estate (but also makes items on the screen appear smaller).

Also note that screen brightness and readability at other than direct viewing angles varies greatly among the tablets. The HP Compaq TC1100 is among the best of the 10.4-inch screen line. The Electrovaya SC-2000 is a 12.1-inch slate known for its very bright screen. Motion Computing and Fujitsu offer special screens designed for outdoor readability and improved viewing angle.

Figure 2-7. The Toshiba Portege M200 convertible line offers one of the highest resolutions for a tablet while in tablet mode.

Availability of Standby and Hibernation

Also important is to be sure to get a Tablet PC that enables you to easily use the Windows standby and hibernation modes for power management. And you need to be able to map these power modes to the on/off switch on the unit. All current models should now support these requirements.

You'll see in an upcoming chapter on configuration recommendations that standby and hibernation are critical to effective use of the Tablet PC, and that the ability to map standby to the physical on/off switch is also very important. Hibernation has been somewhat problematic for laptops configured with Windows operating systems in the past. However, with many of the Windows XP laptops and particularly with the Tablet PC, it is now essentially problem-free. That said, in at least one Tablet PC (an early release of a Fujitsu model) hibernation did not work; this has reportedly been corrected.

Battery Life

Another consideration for Tablet PC selection is battery life. You'll need to judge your own work patterns when weighing various model selections. In my work environment I often end up with three one-hour meetings booked back-to-back. This means that I cannot easily drop the tablet off at my desk for a period of recharging, and so the battery needs to last longer than three hours. Three to four hours is the upper limit for most tablet PCs and many handle much less. However if you need more you might want to take a look at the Electrovaya line, which advertises up to a whopping sixteen hours on some models (though five to nine hours is more typically reported on the newer models). This Canadian company uses its own special line of high capacity batteries, and its recent SC-2000 model has gotten good reviews in the press. (See Figure 2-8).

Figure 2-8. Electrovaya Scribbler SC-2000 is a well reviewed tablet with an unusually long-lasting five to nine hour battery. It also has a prop-up attachable keyboard that helps this slate tablet act more like a convertible.

RAM and Hard Drive

You'll see in the chapters ahead that I advocate keeping four or five key pieces of software open simultaneously. Given this and the relatively high RAM requirements for Windows XP, I recommend a minimum of 512 MB of RAM. I have no scientific analysis to prove this is the minimum, but people who do know agree with this assessment of the RAM needs of Windows XP.

Regarding hard disk space, it seems that all new computers these days come with at least 20 gigabytes. At first I thought that would be more than sufficient for my work management needs. Just for a little insurance I got 40, and recently looked at my hard drive space and noticed I only had 25 GB left. Since I have only installed a moderate amount of software, I now feel that 40 GB is the minimum you should get on a Tablet PC. If you also intend to use your tablet for collections of digital photos or MP3 audio files, then the more hard disk space the better.

Built-In Wireless Networking

You *will* be using wireless networking with your Tablet PC; I guarantee it. While there may be no wireless network available in your office at the moment, it is too compelling a feature to not plan ahead for. At a minimum assume you will have a wireless network in your home soon if not already, and you will be using your tablet with it there. And many business organizations are installing wireless as we speak.

Wireless is an option on any machine that has a PC Card slot. Simply adding a wireless PC Card into that slot will enable this capability. However most of the tablet models available today include wireless capability built-in to the tablet itself. This way the PC Card slot does not need to be consumed by full time use of the wireless card. I recommend you get a Tablet PC with built-in wireless networking so that you can keep your PC Card slot open for other uses. And the "b" wireless standard should meet your needs ("g" is better).

Pressure-Sensitive Screen

A lower priority consideration is this: most models of Tablet PC are built with a pressure-sensitive screen that optionally allows you to vary the width of your ink strokes based on how firmly you push down on the pen. If you intend to do any sketching on your tablet, this is a nice feature. Look in the specifications of the Tablet PC you are considering for a reference to a Wacom digitizer; this is a pressure-sensitive digitizer.

Accessories You Need

Portfolio Case

Throughout this book you'll see me mention several times the value of hiding your Tablet PC inside a portfolio case (see Figure 2-3). For the uses that I advocate, using the Tablet PC in a work management setting, I consider this to be a requirement. The culture at your organization may vary, but if you agree this is important, before purchasing your Tablet PC make sure your selected

Tablet PC seller also sells a matching, high-quality, and well-reviewed portfolio case and purchase it along with your Tablet PC. The one I have also has a place for business cards and loose pieces of paper inside the folding cover.

External CD or DVD Drive

I know of only two Tablet PC models that come with a CD or DVD drive built in (Acer C300 and Gateway M275XL, both mentioned above). With the Tablet PC, these drives are almost always in an external device, and in most cases are purchased as an optional accessory. This is one accessory you need to get; otherwise you'll have no way to install CD-based software.

Docking Station

Nearly all Tablet PC models include the option to purchase a docking station that allows you to use your laptop more easily as a desktop computer. Laptop users are probably familiar with this accessory. What a docking station does is combine the signals from all the cables plugged into your computer into one docking port. This makes short work of attaching and detaching your tablet from desktop peripherals when you run to and from meetings. And some docking stations provide a well-designed method to prop up your slate Tablet PC to use as a vertically oriented monitor. (See Figure 2-9.)

Figure 2-9. A docking station for the Motion Computing slate, with external keyboard and CD/DVD drive attached.

In the chapters ahead I recommend you use your tablet also as your main desktop computer, so this peripheral is very useful provided it meets all your needs. However most docking stations do not allow you to dock while the Tablet PC is inside its portfolio case, and getting the tablet in and out of some portfolio cases may be a bit too clumsy to consider doing five or ten times a day. My first portfolio was like that; in contrast the portfolio case I use now is very quick to get in and out of. So I recommend this: purchase your portfolio case first and see if it truly allows easy egress. If it does then purchase the docking station next. If not, and the portfolio is important to your work, opt to plug and unplug the few needed cables one at a time whenever you leave and return to your desk. The cable ports on the Tablet PC are very easy to get at and this is usually not too clumsy or time consuming.

Unfortunately the makers of my tablet (Motion Computing) do not currently offer what would be the best solution for my usage patterns: a "port replicator." This is like a docking station but doesn't prop up the tablet (I use only an external monitor when docked, so don't need the prop-up capability). They have a smaller form factor and so should overcome any portfolio limitation. I notice that some of the other Tablet PC manufacturers do sell these.

External Monitor, Keyboard, and Mouse

Even a 12-inch screen is in my opinion inadequate for long periods of desktop use. Rather I recommend purchase of an external monitor that attaches to the tablet when you return your tablet to your desk. LCD monitors are relatively inexpensive these days and will allow you to enjoy some extra desk space. A traditional CRT monitor will work fine as well.

When choosing your tablet and the external monitor, one thing to keep in mind is how large a screen resolution your Tablet PC's built-in video system enables; the larger the resolution the better. I was surprised with the large resolution of the video system built in to my tablet. It easily supported a 17-inch monitor at very high resolution. So by adding a larger monitor I didn't just magnify the information on my screen, but actually added much more usable computer screen space.

Also keep in mind that since your tablet runs on Windows XP you can set up multiple monitors that display different portions of your computer desktop space, effectively creating a much larger total monitor space. So you may want to consider using the external monitor at the same time as your built-in Tablet PC monitor. If you decide to do this a docking station will definitely help.

And one more point about the external monitor. Depending on which Tablet PC you get, and whether you decide to take advantage of the larger screen resolution when plugging into an external monitor, you may need to change a number of monitor settings every time you switch between using the built-in tablet monitor while away from your desk and the external monitor while at your desk. Convertibles are usually able to handle this easily, and I have re-configured an existing button on the edge of my Motion Computing slate to switch monitors quickly. You will find more discussion on this in the Con-figuration chapter (Chapter 4).

Keyboard and Mouse

Also purchase an external keyboard and mouse for use at your desk. Even if you have a convertible Tablet PC it does not make sense to limit yourself to a laptop-sized keyboard for long-term desktop work. Make sure you get a key-board and mouse that are USB based; none of the current tablets support the old style connectors (although a docking station might). And try to find a set that together only consumes one USB port. This is common with wireless combination units and with units where the mouse plugs into the keyboard.

Extra Pen, Battery, and Battery Charger

Order an extra pen at the same time that you order your Tablet PC. Other-wise, if you lose your pen and have to wait to order or go buy another one, you are really stuck. And keep both the main pen and the spare somehow at-tached to your Tablet PC. The Motion Computing model has a pen slot built into the body of the computer, and the portfolio case has a pen slot as well. So what I do is leave the original pen in the tablet body slot and never use it. Rather I use my second pen inside the portfolio case slot as my primary pen, and only if I leave that behind somewhere do I resort to using the pen in the body slot as a backup.

Figure 2-10.   Wacom pen with eraser end.

If you get a Tablet PC model that supports pressure sensitivity, note that these models usually also support an eraser button available on the reverse end of the Wacom digitizer pens (see Figure 2-10). This allows you to (with some software) flip the pen around and erase your ink strokes just like using a pencil and paper. While the pressure sensitivity works with the standard tablet pen, if you want to use the eraser-end feature you need to purchase an optional Wacom pen with the eraser button at the reverse end. If you are going to get a second pen anyway, you might consider getting one of these. However you need to buy these pens directly from Wacom (see Appendix for source). I use one, but I use the eraser inconsistently since not all applications support it. This is purely an optional purchase.

If you get tired of packing your battery charger every time you leave the office with your tablet, consider buying an extra battery charger that you can leave at your desk. Note that an extra one often comes with a docking station. You may also want to consider buying a second battery to carry, in case your first one runs out while away from your charger. That said, the battery life on my tablet is nearly three and a half hours and so I have not yet needed to do this. Furthermore, changing batteries is a rather clumsy operation to execute in the context of a meeting. So if you have a choice, opt for longer battery life rather than relying on an extra battery.

Speech Recognition Headset

If you want to use the speech recognition capabilities of the Tablet PC, you'll need to purchase a microphone and speaker headset that has been designed for speech recognition. You can buy these in electronic stores for about $40 or less, a typical example being the Labtech line. Look for a reference to applicability to speech recognition on the package before purchasing. However I found spending a little more on a very high-quality speech recognition headset is a worthwhile investment, due to increased recognition accuracy. A highly regarded premium line is the Andrea brand, some models of which include an active noise reduction system which I have found is far superior to the passive noise reduction systems found in less expensive models. The Andrea model I have is the ANC-750 (see Figure 2-11) which you can find online for around $60 or $70. You will have to decide whether to get the USB models or a model with the traditional microphone and speaker plugs. I like the traditional one since I have more uses for my few USB ports. But if you use external speakers for music, you better get the USB model and buy an external USB hub if needed.

Figure 2-11. The Andrea ANC-750 speech recognition headset with active noise reduction.

Software to Buy

To achieve the boost in work management effectiveness that I discuss in this book you will need to buy some additional software for your Tablet PC. I have a recommended set in mind, and I call that set the manager-effectiveness software. This is software that when used together with the Tablet PC will greatly boost your work management effectiveness.

Microsoft Outlook

First, I assume that you're working in an office environment that has standardized on Microsoft desktop products, including Microsoft Outlook. Ninety percent of corporate America has done so, so I think this is a safe assumption. Outlook is key for much of the management productivity approaches that I convey in this book. If Outlook is not your current corporate e-mail standard, you may want to get it anyway for its scheduling and task management capabilities. These are the capabilities of Outlook that I focus on in this book. Nearly any version of Outlook will do, but I am particularly fond of the latest release: Outlook 2003. In fact in Chapters 7 and 8 I focus on a few Outlook features that are only available in Outlook 2003. If you intend to use FranklinCovey PlanPlus for Outlook, as I recommend below, Outlook 2000 is the minimum supported version.

FranklinCovey Software

FranklinCovey has released two integrated packages for the Tablet PC. Both enable four of the seven fundamental work management functions that I recommend you automate on your Tablet PC. Those four functions are task management, note taking, document management, and document markup. I strongly recommend that you choose one of these two packages as the core of your management-effectiveness software suite, even if you do not intend to use the package for all four of these functionalities. And in case you are wondering, I have no connection with the FranklinCovey organization; I just like their software.

FranklinCovey TabletPlanner 3.0

You'll find throughout this book references to a software package called FranklinCovey TabletPlanner. Designed from the ground up to be used on a Tablet PC, the software makes extensive use of digital ink throughout all of its functionalities. As a result it lends itself well to those times when typing is not possible. It also does a good job of imitating the paper versions of Franklin-Covey personal organizers.

The compromise of TabletPlanner is that its database resides separate from Outlook and so if you're already committed to Outlook within your enterprise for your calendaring, task management, or contact management you'll need to constantly synchronize between these two software packages. There are mixed opinions among TabletPlanner users as to the effectiveness of doing this synchronization. I tried using an early version of TabletPlanner and quickly gave up. I then switched to the other FranklinCovey product, PlanPlus for Outlook and found it perfect for my needs. Since then FranklinCovey has released an update to TabletPlanner (version 3.0) which fixes many of the issues that I and others had with the software, and so I've also reviewed TabletPlanner 3.0 throughout this book. I encourage you to decide for yourself by downloading a trial copy of TabletPlanner 3.0 and seeing if it meets your needs; many users find it quite good. Still, as you'll see, my original recommendation remains: use the FranklinCovey PlanPlus in combination with Outlook.

FranklinCovey PlanPlus 2.0 for Microsoft Outlook

Outlook, extended with PlanPlus 2.0, is the centerpiece of my recommended approach for you as a work manager to get control of your work life. The high value of this combination will be made clear in Chapter 6 on task management, where use of the software is discussed in detail. Its core advantage over TabletPlanner is full integration into the Outlook database, which gives you:

- the ability to use your enterprise Outlook system for managing your schedule, tasks, and contacts without the need for periodic synchronization, and

- the ability to take advantage of many advanced features of Outlook which are not available in TabletPlanner.

The downside compared to TabletPlanner is that you need to use the Tablet PC Input Panel to input your tasks and appointments. That said I decided early on that I am satisfied using the input panel for tasks because I like my task list to always be in text format. More on this in the task management chapter, Chapter 6.

In case you would like to first prove its value to your work routine, the trial version of this software is available as a free download from the Franklin-Covey website, listed in the Appendix.

MindManager for the Tablet PC

Read Chapter 11 on brainstorming on the Tablet PC and consider downloading a trial copy of MindManager for the Tablet PC. While the software is unusual, I use it nearly every day and find it highly effective.

Microsoft OneNote

I suggest you consider purchasing the new Microsoft OneNote software. While Windows Journal or the PowerNotes features of the FranklinCovey software will probably meet your needs for note taking, Microsoft OneNote as a more advanced note-taking tool is really very impressive. You may want to start out with Windows Journal (which comes free with all Tablet PCs) and then make the Microsoft OneNote purchase later. Some Tablet PC manufacturers (including Motion Computing) are now shipping OneNote preinstalled on their new tablets with their minimal software packages. So if you are currently shopping for a Tablet PC, inquire about that as an option.

Adobe Acrobat Standard Edition and PaperPort Pro 9 Office (Optional)

One of the document management approaches I recommend is creating an electronic binder. As you'll see in Chapter 10 there are a number of approaches to this. The FranklinCovey packages provide a solution. The approach I used required the purchase of Adobe Acrobat Standard Edition. Another approach is to use PaperPort Pro 9 Office. After reading that chapter you decide which software meets your needs, and consider these two packages.

Chapter 3 Getting Started

Using Your Tablet PC for the First Time

If you just bought a Tablet PC, you should spend at least a little time just playing with it. Don't try to do any serious work, rather just get a feel for doing digital-ink-based writing, using the pen to draw small sketches and operate menus. Enjoy it. Get used to holding it in your hand or on your lap while working on it. In a low stress environment, become handy with the unit. In this, the first part of getting familiar, don't focus too much on conversion of digital ink to text; it may just get you frustrated at first. Later in this chapter I'll take you through some lessons on text conversion, so you can get properly introduced.

Basic Skills

Windows XP Tablet PC Edition

The Tablet PC can be thought of as an improved laptop that runs an extended version of Windows XP. This extended version is called the Windows XP Tablet PC Edition.

The fact that the Tablet is an extension of Windows XP means that you do not lose anything from Windows. If you know how to use a Windows XP laptop, you are mostly there. All you need to learn now are the pen-based tools that have been added. If you have used earlier versions of Windows, but not XP, there are a few new things to learn for Windows, nearly all of which are covered here in the book.

Turning On and Booting Up Your Tablet PC

Like any other laptop, the Tablet PC has a power switch that starts the computer and boots the Windows operating system. So start this computer just like you would a laptop.

However, remember that while all laptops come with attached keyboards, many tablets don't, but rather have the keyboard unplugged by default when shipped. My Motion Computing Tablet PC had a small (paper) note attached to it when I unwrapped it telling me to make sure that I plugged in the keyboard before I started up my Tablet PC for the first time. There are some first launch configuration activities that various vendors may require when you launch the computer for the first time and that Windows XP requires. Many of these expect you to type, so having your keyboard plugged in at your very first launch is recommended. You can detach it right after that if you'd like.

In general, follow the manufacturer's instructions when starting your Tablet PC for the first time.

And when you are done using your tablet, turn it off using the Start menu shutdown command, just as you would a desktop. In Chapter 4 we will introduce better approaches.

Most other custom configurations I will also save until Chapter 4, but there are a few you may want to do now, such as setting up for left-handed use and calibrating the screen.

Left-Handed Users

If you are left handed you may want to set up your computer for left-handed control. This affects the accuracy of handwriting recognition and how menus are positioned. You change this configuration within the Tablet and Pen Settings control panel. There are two ways to open this utility. The first is to use an icon in the System Tray (these are the small icons in the lower right corner of the Windows XP taskbar). The icon looks like this (see Figure 3-1):

Figure 3-1. System tray icon for the Tablet and Pen Settings control panel (magnified).

Or you can access this through the Windows XP Control Panel. To do this, open the Windows Start menu and find the words "Control Panel" along the right side. Open it and then within the Control Panel window, find the icon for Tablet and Pen Settings and double-click it. Some computer manufacturers also install a shortcut to this within the All Programs menu.

Opening this utility exposes a multitab window. Select the Settings tab and set the hand preference there.

Screen Calibration

If the cursor under your pen does not seem to line up well with the tip of your pen, you may need to calibrate your Tablet PC screen. On the same Settings tab described above you will find a button called Calibrate. Click that button and follow the instructions. Do this once for each tablet orientation (landscape and portrait). You may need to repeat the calibration routine a number of times during the first weeks of usage, as you get used to the pen.

Using the Pen like a Mouse

The first thing you should learn is that you should use your pen like you would a mouse. (See Figure 3-2.) This is pretty basic stuff, and if you have already gotten a feel for using the pen as a mouse on the Tablet PC then skip this section.

Figure 3-2.   When in tablet mode, the pen replaces the mouse for all menu and selection activities (Acer Tablet PC shown).

However if this is new to you, think of the pen as having a magnet inside its tip. When you get the tip to within about half inch of the screen surface, the screen detects the presence of the pen and places the mouse cursor on the screen underneath the tip. You don't even need to touch the screen. Moving your pen just above the screen is like moving your mouse across the screen with no buttons pushed.

Single-Click

When you do touch the screen with the tip, think of that as corresponding to clicking the left mouse button on a traditional computer. So if you touch the screen briefly, think of that as a single left click. For example touch the pen tip to the Start menu button in the lower left corner of the screen now, and you'll see the Start menu opens just as though you had left-clicked a mouse on it.

For now when handling the pen, try to avoid touching the button on the side of the pen; we'll get to that in a moment.

Double-Click

Tapping the pen tip twice on the screen corresponds to double-clicking the mouse. Try this now to launch any application that may be on your desktop, such as Internet Explorer. Don't worry if you currently have no Internet connection, we are not browsing the Internet right now. Keep Internet Explorer open for a moment and note that you can use the pen to open menus. How would you open a menu with a mouse? You would move the mouse cursor over to the menu, click once briefly, and move the mouse down to the menu selection you're seeking. With a pen you do essentially the same: with the pen about a half inch above the screen move the pen tip over to the File menu of Internet Explorer, tap once and then lift the pen tip in place slightly off the screen. You'll see the menu open and as long as you keep the pen tip approximately in place, the menu will remain open. Now move the pen tip, again slightly off the screen, down the menu selections, and each menu selection will highlight as you move over them, just like moving a mouse over the menu. To select a menu item, tap the pen tip once on that menu item.

For now let's close Internet Explorer by clicking the pen tip once in the close box (the X box) in the upper right corner of that application.

Right-Click

A slightly more difficult operation is to learn how to right-click with the pen. Right-clicking of course is the way to bring up an in-context menu with a brief list of actions that may apply to whatever you are doing in your application at the moment. If you are not accustomed to right-clicking on your current computer, don't worry, this is not a required action for most applications.

There are two ways to right-click with the pen. The first is to tap and hold the pen tip to the Tablet PC screen for a few seconds without moving it. This is my preferred method. After about two seconds you'll see a small starburst form around the cursor at your pen tip, and then a small image of a mouse with the right mouse button darkened will appear. This sequence of images is an attempt to communicate to you that you have just done the equivalent of right-clicking your mouse button.

Once you lift the mouse slightly, the in-context menu will appear and you can select one of the menu items by tapping once on it with your pen tip.

Side Note: If you do not see the above behavior when pressing and holding the pen, go now to Chapter 4 and find the section titled Turning Off the Pen Button, and follow the instructions there to configure your Tablet PC.

The other way to right-click is to press the small button on the pen shaft. I really don't like this method, because I keep accidentally hitting that button when I don't intend to and end up right-clicking at odd times in my tablet usage. So I have disabled this button for right-clicking; disabling the button is covered about midway through Chapter 4.

Writing with the Pen

Let's get started with writing by taking a very brief first look at Windows Journal. By the way, you should plan on using Windows Journal as your default application for learning nearly everything pen oriented. There's a reason why nearly every book and article about the Tablet PC starts out by teaching you how to use Windows Journal. That's because Windows Journal is a simple and versatile application that highlights the best aspects of the Tablet PC.

Basic Windows Journal

Windows Journal comes free and installed with all Tablet PCs. But first you have to find where under the Start menu the launch icon for Windows Journal is located, which varies across tablet manufactures. First try looking on the desktop of the computer for an icon. If it is not there, next click the Start menu, and then click the All Programs button in the lower left portion of the Start menu. With some tablets, Windows Journal is listed directly in the All Programs list. With most tablets, however, you need to first go, within the All Programs list, to the Tablet PC group, click once there, and choose Windows Journal from the short list of Tablet PC applications. Also under that list should be an entry for "Tablet PC Tutorials"; I'll have you work through some of those tutorials a little bit later, but remember where they are.

Wherever you find it, tap twice on the Windows Journal icon, and you'll see the default Windows Journal screen. This user interface is the essence of simplicity. A blank notepad-looking page appears ready for you to start writing. (See Figure 3-3.)

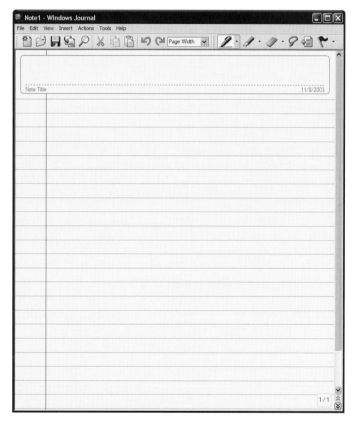

Figure 3-3.   A blank Windows Journal page ready for note taking.

Let's do some writing. Just place your pen tip anywhere on the lined portion of the writing area of the screen and you'll see that instead of a standard Windows arrow cursor, a small black dot appears. This represents the tip of an actual writing pen and tells you that you are ready to start writing.

Let's write your name: use the pen just like you would an ink pen on a piece of paper. The first-time user may expect to have to place a cursor on the page as in a word processing program, but that's not how Windows Journal works.

Think of this as a drawing program; you can start drawing anywhere on the page.

For your first writing use cursive handwriting, or print, whichever you like. You'll see ink-like writing appear on the paper; this is digital ink. There is no great magic here, but get used to feeling the pen as it moves across the screen of your computer. It's a bit more slippery then a normal piece of paper, and because it has a different feel it may take a small amount of practice to prevent you from creating some wild pen strokes.

Write some more, anything; copy some text out of this book if you like, or write any thoughts you might have in mind. Keep practicing writing; keep moving down the page adding more text until writing with the pen in ink feels second nature. Ignore mistakes for now.

Getting Used to Writing on a Glass Screen

One thing you'll need to get used to is where you rest your palm as you write. Because of the slippery nature of the pen tip on glass, keeping control of the pen tip during writing is easier if you have your palm firmly planted on the glass and hold the pen tip at a comfortable distance away from your palm. You'll probably find yourself moving your palm more often when you write with the Tablet PC than when you write on paper, otherwise your writing can get a little wild.

If you make a mistake, you can erase the strokes with the eraser tool. Let's do this now: in the toolbar at the top of the page, the fourth icon from the right is a pink bricklike icon. This is supposed to represent the physical appearance of a chalkboard or whiteboard eraser (although I've never seen a pink whiteboard eraser before!). Tap once on that icon now, and note that the cursor icon changes. It most likely changes to the following icon:

or it may look like this:

We'll cover the differences between these two eraser types within the note-taking chapter (Chapter 8). For now use whichever type appears for you by default.

Now pass your pen over some of your ink and you'll see it disappear like magic.

To get back to the Pen tool, tap once on the Pen icon, which is the sixth icon from the right in the toolbar at the top of the window.

These two tools will be your most-used tools in Windows Journal and in many other applications as well, so get used to what they look like and accustomed to finding them quickly.

Now let's do some simple drawing (you need to get back to the Pen tool to do this).

But first let's start a new Windows Journal document. Click on the left-most icon on the toolbar. This creates an entirely new Windows Journal document.

Adding Pages to a Document

If you just want to add additional pages to the current document, rather than create a new document, click on the downward-pointing chevron icon in the lower right corner of the window.

Unlike word processors, which automatically add additional space as you type, in Windows Journal you have to explicitly add pages as you get to the bottom of each page.

In keeping with the business orientation of this book, let's quickly create an org chart for your organization. Create something like the sketch below. (See Figure 3-4.)

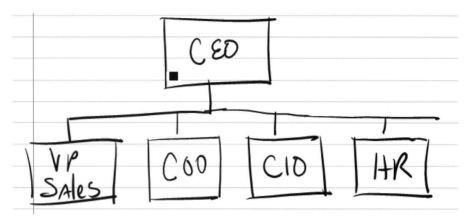

Figure 3-4. You can draw and write on a Windows Journal note page.

Now let's draw a simple process chart (create a new document again if you are out of note space). On the left side of the page, draw the project management process chart below. (See Figure 3-5.)

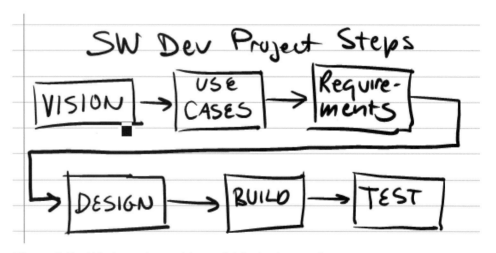

Figure 3-5. Windows Journal is useful for brainstorming.

Now Let's Take a Peek at Some More Advanced Features of Windows Journal

Draw one more rectangle to the right of the last square on the process chart. And before you enter text into the rectangle, click on the Selection tool icon (also called the Lasso tool).

Now, draw an imaginary circle well outside and around the new rectangle but not touching any of the other objects on the page. You'll see a series of dots appear as you draw, forming that imaginary circle. (See Figure 3-6.)

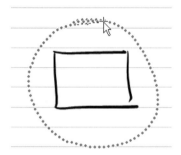

Figure 3-6. Using the Lasso tool to select an object.

When you close the circle, lift your pen slightly off the screen; the circle will disappear, and your square will now change in appearance. (See Figure 3-7.)

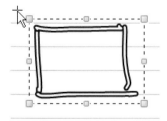

Figure 3-7. A selected object in Windows Journal.

The lines of your rectangle now appear doubled. This is just a convention to indicate that your rectangle image has been selected. You'll also see a dotted-line box around your rectangle. When you place your pen above the screen well inside that dotted box you'll see the cursor has changed into the following four-arrow cursor icon:

Place your pen on the screen now inside the box and move the pen tip about. You should see the rectangle move about your screen as well, following your pen; this is how you move objects within Windows Journal.

Tap and drag one of the small blue squares that surround your rectangle and you can resize your sketched rectangle.

And one last thing. With the rectangle still selected, lift your pen off the screen and tap on the Actions menu at the top of the screen, and tap the last item in the menu: Change Shape To and choose Square from the submenu. Note that your hand-drawn rectangle has now been converted to a perfect clean rectangle. (See Figure 3-8.)

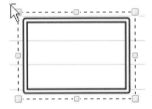

Figure 3-8.   Windows Journal can change rough shapes into perfect shapes.

Next, we'll show you how to convert your handwriting to text, something you might want to do if you're going to truly clean up this process flow document. Later we'll show you how to send these drawings to colleagues inside of an e-mail. Being able to quickly draw business sketches, clean them up, and send them off for review is a powerful tool of Windows Journal.

Converting Handwriting to Text in Windows Journal

Okay, we're finally ready to test the ability to convert handwriting to text. Each application, by the way, approaches this somewhat differently. We'll focus here just on how Windows Journal does it; later we will cover more generalized methods of handwriting conversion.

Do this: anywhere on a Windows Journal page, using your handwriting, write the following text very smoothly and cleanly (I purposely put a mistake in the spelling in the figure below, you'll see why in a moment, but make your spelling accurate):

Staff Meeting

Now using the Selection tool that we used earlier (the Lasso tool) draw an imaginary circle around that text so that it is highlighted. (See Figure 3-9.)

Figure 3-9. The first step of text conversion is to select the text with the Lasso tool.

Now choose from the Actions menu the second choice down, which is Convert Handwriting to Text...

You'll be presented with the following dialog box (see Figure 3-10):

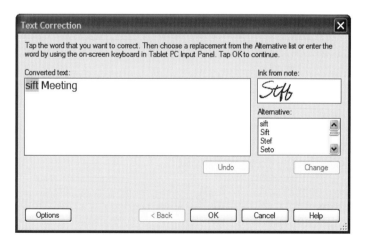

Figure 3-10. Windows Journal gives you a chance to correct text conversion errors.

This is the Windows Journal way of letting you review and if needed correct your converted text prior to accepting the conversion. In my sample with a mistake, highlighted in green are words that Windows Journal suspects it may have converted wrong. For each highlighted word (one at a time) Journal will display on the upper right side of the dialog box the original digital ink that corresponds to the selected word, and then below that, possible alternative word choices.

Do not worry if Windows did not interpret your handwriting correctly, and let's not make any corrections now, because you may need to use the Tablet PC Input Panel to do so, and we have not reviewed using that yet. For now, click OK and the following window will appear (Figure 3-11):

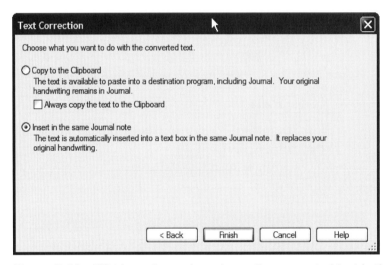

Figure 3-11. Windows Journal can leave the converted text in the document or copy it to the Clipboard for pasting into other applications.

Choose the second menu item: Insert in the same Journal note, and click the Finish button. You'll next see your handwriting converted to text and selected as a large text box. (See Figure 3-12.)

Figure 3-12. Converted text copied back into Windows Journal.

By the way, this is one of the few irritating points Windows Journal has: it always creates an oversized text box no matter how small the amount of text is. So the next thing I usually do is resize the text box to just surround the text itself (to do this, click and drag the blue box in the lower right corner of the text window). And finally, your next step is to move the text to some more logical placement on the page. Just click anywhere within the text box, and when you see the four arrow cursor appear, drag the text wherever you like.

Tablet PC Input Panel

Now it is time to learn a more generalized method of handwriting conversion. This is by using the Tablet PC Input Panel. The Tablet PC Input Panel is a capability built in to the Tablet PC operating system, which allows you to use your pen to enter text into any Windows application, whether the application is Tablet PC enabled or not.

Note that as of June 2004 the Tablet PC Input Panel described below is due to be updated. If you are reading this book after receiving that update, the steps below may not match what you see on your tablet. If they do not, refer to my website to download a free update to this chapter: (www.seizetheworkday.com).

The input panel is activated by clicking on the small keyboard and pen icon located just to the right of the Start button in the lower left corner of your Tablet PC screen.

 Click here to open the Tablet PC Input Panel

Click on this small icon and the Tablet PC Input Panel will open, either in Keyboard mode (see Figure 3-13)

Figure 3-13. Keyboard mode of Tablet PC Input Panel

or in Writing Pad mode (see Figure 3-14). The actual size and shape of your Input Panel may look different.

Figure 3-14. Writing Pad mode of the Tablet PC Input Panel.

You choose between the two modes by clicking on the tabs in the lower right corner of the panel.

In either mode, to use the input panel, first start the application that you want to enter text into, make it the active window, click the cursor in that window where you want the text to appear, and then start using the Tablet PC Input Panel to enter text.

Let's try this out. First we need to open an application that accepts text. Tap on the Start menu, click on the All Programs button, and if you have it installed, choose Microsoft Word. If you do not have Microsoft Word installed, use Notepad instead, which is under All Programs, under the Accessories group.

With either of these two applications open, and your cursor within a writing portion of a new document, let's start practicing using the keyboard portion of the Tablet PC Input Panel. If needed, open the Tablet PC Input Panel, click on the Keyboard tab, and now tap on individual keys to cause the text to appear in your application. This is pretty simple stuff, slow, but simple. You'll use the keyboard portion of the Tablet PC Input Panel primarily as a correction mechanism when your handwriting recognition is not accurate. Don't even consider using this keyboard as a primary mode of text input, it's just way too slow.

And now for using the Writing Pad, where we finally do real handwriting recognition. Ensure once again that the Microsoft Word or Notepad application is active, and a document is open, and the cursor is in a writing portion of the document window. Click on the Writing Pad tab of the Tablet PC Input Panel. Referring to Figure 3-14, you'll see that there is a large blank area on the left side, ready for you to handwrite into. Go ahead, using cursive text, write the words: "Buy low, sell high." After a pause, you'll see the words converted into text and inserted into your document. And hopefully, the words were converted correctly. If not, use the pen to select the incorrect text, and the keyboard tab on the Tablet PC Input Panel to make corrections.

Tips for Accurate Handwriting Conversion

- Obviously, the more clearly you write, the more accurate the conversion.

- I find that cursive writing converts much more accurately than hand-printed text.

- Leave clear open spaces between each word.

- Keep the writing horizontal.

- You'll find that some letters must be written a certain way to be recognized. For example, I find the cursive letter "I" when written as a word is difficult for the Tablet PC to recognize. If I print it, the recognition is more often correct. You'll learn over time which letters are difficult in your handwriting.

- And finally, see Chapter 5 on Digital Ink Strategies for a complete discussion of best times to use ink with the Tablet PC.

Time to Take the Tutorials

By now you have a rough idea on how to use the Tablet PC for basic input. It's now a good time to take the computer-based tutorials that came with your Tablet PC.

Open the Start menu, choose All Programs, choose the Tablet PC group, and launch the entry called "Tablet PC Tutorials." The following screen will appear. (See Figure 3-15.)

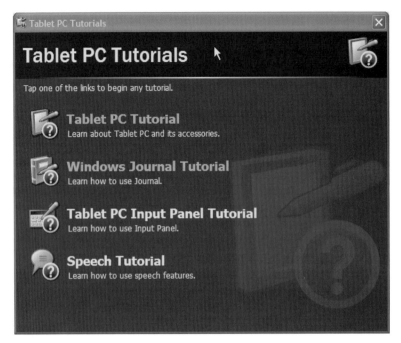

Figure 3-15. Tutorials window.

Clicking on any one of these four tutorials will start a series of screens that will train you in usage of the Tablet PC, repeating some of what we just went over and going into more depth in these and other areas. I recommend that you take the first three of these four tutorials now. Save the speech tutorial until after you have used the Tablet PC for a while.

Chapter 4 Configure Your Tablet PC for Success

Two Modes of Configuration

The key to work management effectiveness, particularly if your role includes lots of meetings, is to use your Tablet PC both as your desktop computer and as your mobile PDA.

As a Desktop

When you stand up to go to a meeting and pick the Tablet PC off your desk, you need to take access to all your daily work and references with you. You need a mobile command post with access to all your files, key documents, and software. All your work tools should be readily available.

I have found that the only effective way to accomplish this is to use your Tablet PC as your primary desktop computer. Make it your one workstation that you work on at your desk and that goes everywhere you go. No second computer or server-based files that are out of sync, no separate PDA. Rather, make your Tablet PC the one place for all your work. All new Tablet PCs are powerful enough to do this and with a little configuration you can take advantage of that.

As a PDA

You need to be able to do the following nearly as fast as on a PDA: turn the Tablet PC on and off, get to your task list, your e-mail, your schedules, your contacts. And beyond traditional PDA functions, all the manager-effectiveness software and functions I describe throughout this book need to be at hand nearly instantly, whether at your desk or in a meeting.

Real Life Work Scenario

Here's my routine every day when I come into work: I take the Tablet PC out of my briefcase and immediately plug in the power and peripheral cables, which are all waiting on my desk from the night before. This takes about five seconds. I then boot up my Tablet PC and once fully booted switch the display to my external monitor. I then place the Tablet PC on the back of my desk. At this point, the Tablet PC is just like any desktop computer with an external monitor, external keyboard, and mouse. Anybody who walks by assumes I've got a standard Windows XP desktop computer in use; and for all intents and purposes, I do.

At my desk I then do my morning routines which usually start with checking my Outlook schedule and task list, reprioritizing tasks as needed, checking and respond-

ing to urgent e-mails, and then starting any tasks that I can fit in before my first morning meeting. All just like a normal desktop computer.

When it is time for my first meeting, I switch back to my tablet screen. I then unplug the cables, and if the meeting is a long distance away, flip the power switch on my Tablet PC which has been configured to place my Tablet PC into standby mode. All this takes about five seconds.

I carry the Tablet PC under my arm into my meeting. Remember it looks just like an executive portfolio and anyone I am meeting for the first time does not notice a difference. I generally do not bring anything else with me – no paper, no notepad, sometimes even no pen. After I am comfortably seated, I flip open and fold back the portfolio case cover, place the tablet on my lap, and sit back ready for taking meeting notes or referring to important documents.

My tablet is configured such that when it launched that morning all my key applications opened automatically: Outlook and FranklinCovey PlanPlus for e-mail, schedule, and task management, my Adobe Acrobat binder document with all my key documents in it, AOL Instant Messenger, and Windows Journal (or Microsoft One-Note) for note taking. So to start note taking in the meeting I merely need to click on the task bar entry to bring Windows Journal or OneNote to the front and start writing. If I need to refer to some previously received e-mails during the meeting I merely bring up the Outlook application and read the e-mails as if I were back at my desk. The same with Outlook tasks, contacts, or appointments.

Once the Tablet PC is configured correctly, this routine of moving the Tablet PC on and off the desk when moving to and from meetings quickly becomes completely second nature. The Tablet PC becomes an effortless and essential part of everyday work life. And all Tablet PCs are designed to enable this "grab and go" capability. You do not need to turn the tablet off or put it in standby as you jump in and out of meetings; you can unplug from your peripherals (or undock) and run with the tablet still on. There are some configuration steps needed to make this work effortlessly, which I show in this chapter.

Do This All at Once?

You may be reluctant to jump right in to a full desktop switch, particularly if you are new to the Tablet PC and not yet convinced of its high value. This is understandable as the conversion can take some effort, and it will, as you adjust to the change, distract some from your regular business activities. So if you like, do this transfer in phases: use your Tablet PC for only one activity for a week or two, perhaps note taking in meetings. Just know that you will only experience a fraction of the business value of the Tablet PC until you finish the full conversion.

I do suggest this, however: do not install any important new software on your Tablet PC until you have made the conversion. You will see why in a moment.

When you *are* ready to take the plunge, follow the configuration details below. You will be amazed at the leap in work-management effectiveness you will reach when you do.

In this chapter we will cover first how to configure your Tablet PC for desktop use, and then cover additional configurations to make it truly effective when used within meetings.

First, Configure the Tablet as Your Desktop Computer

Making a Tablet PC an effective desktop computer is not difficult. As mentioned earlier, it probably means having an external monitor, full size keyboard, and mouse on hand for those times when you are working long hours at your desk.

And it also means working a bit with your IT department to get your Tablet PC configured for your network and your e-mail system. Note that it is good to wait until this network configuration is done before installing new software and before making customized settings on your Tablet PC. The reason is that your IT department may have naming and user account conventions that they will ask you to implement on your Tablet PC when they add your Tablet PC to the office network. All the settings and software installations that you made on your Tablet PC before the new user account was created may not be easily accessible after creating your new account.

How This Will Look on Your (Physical) Desk

So how does this desktop usage work and what do you do when you need to take the Tablet PC with you to meetings? I mentioned in the hardware and software chapter (Chapter 2) that a docking station is recommended if you can accept the appearance on your desk, and if the use of the docking station is consistent with your portfolio cover approach. Let's cover both approaches.

Without Docking Station

When you're using your Tablet PC at your office desk without a docking station, you'll have the following cables plugged into your Tablet PC:

- your Tablet PC power cable

- an external monitor cable

- keyboard and mouse (USB)

- network cable (unless you're lucky enough to have wireless networking in your office)

You will be working on the external keyboard and monitor, and the tablet itself will be sitting at the back of your desk, out of sight. When you leave to go to a meeting, just pull the cables out and go.

This is how I worked at my company. When I left for a meeting I just left the cable-ends loose on the back of the desk and plugged them back in when back from meetings. All cables are hot swappable, meaning they can be plugged in and out while the tablet is running.

Side Note: Some USB devices may have problems with hot swapping. For example my HP scanner has issues. Some users have reported same with certain USB keyboards.

With Docking Station

Using a docking station makes things a bit easier, as long as it's consistent with your portfolio cover approach. All the cables are attached permanently to the back of your docking station and you merely insert the tablet into the station slot. With no cables to plug in and remove every time you run to a meeting and return, things are a little faster. Assuming you do use an external monitor, some docking solutions (HP) also switch the monitor feed back to the tablet when you pull the tablet out, which saves a few steps as well (more on that later in this chapter).

One question you need to answer if you do use an external monitor is should you also keep your tablet monitor active when it is in the docking station? My preference is no, to completely replace my screen with the external monitor, because I wish to keep my Tablet PC a bit less obvious, and it is simpler. If you take this approach, the docking station may be sitting behind your monitor, out of sight. Read the section below about configuring an external monitor, however, because there are valid reasons to use both together.

Dealing with Your IT Department to Configure Your Tablet PC for Connection to Your Enterprise Network

The first step to making your Tablet PC operational as a desktop computer at your workplace is to configure the tablet's network settings so that it will work on your corporate network. I'm going to assume that you work in an organization with an established computer network, e-mail system, file sharing system, and network printers. And I'm going to assume that you have an IT department that supports this network and the computers on it.

If No IT Department

If by chance you are in a smaller organization with no IT department and you do all your own computer configurations, my best recommendation is to refer to a good Windows XP book for network configuration instructions. The Tablet PC configures essentially the same as any other Windows XP machine for network purposes, including wireless setup.

There's more to attaching to your corporate network than merely plugging a network cable between your Tablet PC and the network jack on your cubical wall, or turning on the wireless network switch on your Tablet PC control panel. While I could walk you through in this book the various ways to configure a Windows XP machine for network use, it is almost certain that your corporate approach will have several significant twists to the configuration steps depending upon standards used within your corporate network. So to do this successfully your IT department will need to step in to assist.

In fact since for network configuration purposes the Tablet PC is no different from any other Windows XP computer, you can and should just hand the Tablet PC over to your IT Department and ask them to do the network configurations for you. Tell them you want to make it your new desktop computer but that you'll also be using it as a laptop. When you do this, there are a couple of possible complications that you will want to ask your IT department about before starting:

- Are outside computers allowed on your network?

- Will they do custom configurations?

- Will they grant administrative privileges?

Are Outside Computers Allowed on Your Network?

There is a chance that your IT department may initially refuse to allow you to add your computer to the network. It is not an unusual policy to disallow nonstandard or privately owned computers onto a corporate network. If you find this applies in your company, my advice would be to do the following: argue that adding your Tablet PC to the network will serve as a test of this new form of computing, a test which the IT department can learn from. Computer staff always want to learn and play with new hardware and they may enjoy the chance to try out a Tablet PC. If however after a little negotiation they still resist, you may need to go "over their head" and get clearance through your departmental leadership. Argue for approval based on a productivity business case; you can find business case data on the Microsoft website.

Will Your IT Department Do Custom Configurations?

One reason your IT department may object to installing your Tablet PC as your main desktop computer is that it represents added work for them. Many IT departments have created a "standard hard disk image" that they merely copy onto new computers as they are deployed to cubicles. This image includes a preconfigured operating system and all enterprise-licensed software. It makes installing new computers onto desktops a much easier task for your support group, and prevents them from needing to do custom configurations on new computers as they come in the door. The ability to use an image-based approach to computer installation is dependent upon having a standard hardware platform with predictable configuration requirements that match the standard image. Without a doubt, configuring a Tablet PC using this standard image installation approach will not be possible. And so configuring your Tablet PC *will* represent additional work for the IT department. Be ready to deal with this objection in your negotiations. Some favor swapping may be needed to pull this off. To soften the blow, you could offer to do all the software installations yourself, and just ask them to configure the network.

Administrative Privileges

Tell your IT department that as part of their network configurations you need to retain access to administrative privileges on your Tablet PC. You need this access so that you can install additional software later. However the standard network policy may be to deny administrative access. If you bought this Tablet PC with your own funds point this out when seeking this approval. Also point out that you have a number of other software packages that you need to install beyond the standard corporate package, and you intend to install these yourself.

The main reason for a policy such as this is to keep software off the network which may compromise network security. This is a reasonable goal, so offer to clear all packages with the IT department before you make any installations.

Bend the Rules if Necessary

If you know you're likely to lose some or all of the above battles, you may want to avoid the approval route and instead see if you can find someone in your organization technically savvy enough to configure your computer onto the network without drawing attention from the enforcement side of your IT department. In this case, your Tablet PC will probably sit discreetly next to your standard-issue desktop. You may want to discreetly swap the monitor cables without telling anyone, or install a "KVM" switch which allows you to share the keyboard and monitor between the two computers.

Other Considerations to Raise with Your IT Department

Can they configure Windows XP?

Be sure your IT department understands that this is a Windows XP operating system. Many organizations have not standardized yet on Windows XP (favoring Windows 2000 or NT) and your computer support group may need to locate specific staff who are familiar with it.

Wireless networking

Be sure to tell your IT department that your Tablet PC has wireless networking built in just in case a wireless access is in fact available for your enterprise network. Wireless networks are still considered to be somewhat of a security risk within large organizations and so it is likely that none is available; in that case you'll need to use the wired network jack on your Tablet PC. However if an officially sponsored wireless network is operating within range of your desk, and particularly in range of your conference rooms, do everything you can to get permission to access your corporate network through that wireless network. This will come in very handy when using your Tablet PC in meetings.

While there may be no officially sponsored wireless network, many IT departments set up unofficial or rogue wireless networks that have access to all network services but whose presence is not advertised. You may need to do some favor swapping to convince your IT department to let you use that network. Pay the price whatever it is; trust me, it's worth it.

Engaging the keyboard and mouse

Don't even consider having the IT department do their configuration work on your tablet while it is in pen mode. Rather, engage the keyboard and mouse mode on your Tablet PC before handing it to them. If they have never worked with the Tablet PC before, engaging this mode may be confusing, so do it for them.

Swap out old computer

You may be asked to turn in your old desktop, and you should consider that a fair trade. Just try to keep the monitor, keyboard, and mouse, since you will want to use those (however they need to be USB-based to be usable; if not, buy your own). And don't forget to move your files off the old computer before you let them take it away; more on this last point later.

Standard software

Be sure to confirm with your IT department that they will also install your organization's "standard desktop software" on your Tablet PC so that you have access to all the same software you had on your desktop computer. And if you purchased additional nonstandard software for your desktop for specialized purposes, don't forget to reinstall that on your Tablet PC after the network configuration is done.

Additional software

Your IT department may insist upon installing some additional software on your computer such as antivirus software or license tracking software. This is a fair request and you should agree to this.

Special Outlook configuration

You are also going to want to configure your tablet's Microsoft Outlook so that it is usable off the network. This is so that when you have your Tablet PC with you in a meeting you can still access your stored e-mails, schedule, contacts, and the like. Be sure to make that clear to your IT department because there are extra Outlook configuration steps needed to accomplish this, and these steps are normally not configured on desktop computers. We will review those below in case this is new to your IT department. This is something you can configure yourself if your IT department is not familiar with the steps.

Network Configuration Checklist

Here is a checklist of things your IT department should do to configure your Tablet PC for your network. A professional IT department, if they agree to place your Tablet PC on the network, should do all these things without being asked. It does not hurt to go over this checklist with them just to be sure you are in agreement on your goals.

- Configure your Tablet PC for connection to your enterprise network, which may include adding your computer to the domain of your organization's network.

- Configure for access to the Internet over your enterprise network, including adding appropriate DNS settings.

- Configure printer settings so you can print to your enterprise network printers.

- Configure access to any file shares that you may have previously been using over the network.

- Install and configure Microsoft Outlook so that you can access your firm's mail server over the network and use your Microsoft Outlook in offline mode.

Once the network configurations are complete, you or your IT Department should install and configure all other software you are going to need to work effectively at your organization with the Tablet PC as your primary desktop computer. This may include a standard software suite your organization uses. It may include software you have purchased separately.

Transferring Files from Your Desktop Computer

Once all your key standard desktop software is installed, you'll still need to find the documents and data files on your previous desktop and transfer them to your Windows XP Tablet PC. If possible copy your files to a CD before swapping. If that's not possible, the best way to transfer files is to have both your old desktop and your new Tablet PC on the network at once and then use one of two methods:

- Copy your files from the old desktop to a central file server temporarily and then from the central file server to your Tablet PC. Your IT department should be able to show you how to access a file server on your enterprise network where you can create a folder and copy all your files temporarily. Just remember to delete those files when you're finished with your transfer.

- Or if you feel strongly about duplicating all the custom settings from your previous computer, use the Files and Settings Transfer Wizard that comes with Windows XP. I've never used this so I cannot give you first-hand advice, but I understand that it does the best job of transferring the various configurations stored throughout your computer, many of which you may have forgotten you've made. It requires that the two computers can see each other on the network (something not always allowed within enterprise networks) and it will require you to insert the Windows XP CD into the CD ROM drive of the old computer so that the utility can run from there also. My advice however is to skip this approach and rebuild your settings as you become accustomed to the Tablet PC; many of the tablet settings will be different anyway.

There are other approaches as well, including direct cabling between the two computers. Brainstorm with your IT department to reach the best solution.

Breaking-In Period for Your Desktop Configurations

It is almost certain that in setting your tablet up for desktop use and in transferring your files, you will have forgotten to install some software or forgotten to transfer some files that you need. So, ideally, plan on spending a week or two to become fully productive using your Tablet PC as your desktop computer. Don't attempt to make this transition during your busiest week of the year.

Also, even if you have agreed to trade in your existing desktop computer, try to keep this existing desktop around for a week or so. Almost certainly you'll discover files that you failed to transfer, or you'll discover settings that you need to look up on your old computer. So you'll want to have your old computer on hand.

Monitor Approaches for Your Desk

As stated earlier, I recommend you use an external monitor with your Tablet PC when it is at your desk. If you do not attach an external monitor you'll need to use the monitor on your Tablet PC. With a slate computer this means propping the Tablet PC up on your desk so that you can view the monitor vertically. With a convertible you can do the same or allow the laptop style keyboard to hold up the monitor. The laptop keyboard is of course redundant in this case since you'll be using an external keyboard.

Assuming you're using a slate or hybrid Tablet PC inserted into a portfolio case, propping this up on your desktop to use as a monitor looks a little odd. I used it as such for a week or so before I finally attached an external monitor and was much happier when I did.

Virtually any external monitor will work. Many support higher resolutions than your Tablet PC monitor can display, but which are probably available on your tablet's built-in graphics subsystem. Try to acquire a 17-inch or larger monitor, just to make your work life easier. I prefer an LCD monitor to preserve desk space but a normal CRT monitor will work fine as well.

Attaching an External Monitor

Your Tablet PC almost certainly has an external monitor port. Plug the monitor into your already booted Tablet PC and power up the monitor. Your Tablet PC may at this point attempt to find and load a driver for this external monitor. If so, follow the screen commands, and note you may need to provide a CD to load the driver (although this is unlikely because most needed drivers come preloaded on Windows XP). If you are using a docking station the monitor plugs directly into that; follow manufacturer instructions in that case.

Modes of External Monitor Use

If you have ever used an external monitor or projector with a Windows XP laptop then you know that there are three modes in which you can use an external monitor:

- **Mirror mode**: The external monitor and Tablet PC display are turned on both at the same time, and the external monitor displays exactly what is shown on your Tablet PC screen, at the same resolution.

- **External monitor mode**: The Tablet PC display shuts off and only your external monitor displays an image. In this mode you can set the resolution to be higher than the maximum resolution of your Tablet PC screen, which is a good thing. It is also simpler to use. Perhaps most important, if you are concerned about appearances, it allows you to discreetly place the tablet at the back of your desk.

■ **Extended desktop mode**: The Tablet PC and external monitor are on at the same time, but represent different portions of a large virtual computer desktop. This is handy because it increases the workspace available to view and work in, which is a very valuable asset. But it is a mode I do not use because I prefer not to display a docking station nor have my Tablet PC propped up and displayed on my office desk.

Switching Between the External Monitor and the Tablet PC Monitor

When you grab your tablet to run to a meeting, and when you return, you will need to manually adjust settings on your tablet to switch monitors; on most tablets this does not happen automatically (on some models it does if you use a docking station). There usually are three or four different ways to manually switch between these modes. Which one to choose depends upon the software that came with your Tablet PC. It also depends on whether your Tablet PC is a slate or a convertible, and it depends on whether you are using a docking station or not.

Complicating this action is the fact that you will probably be using your external monitor at a higher resolution than your tablet screen can handle, so your setting change may also require a change to your screen resolution.

Working out the best strategy will save you time when jumping in and out of meetings. Here are the common methods to switch monitors on the fly.

Function key

If you are accustomed to using a projector with a laptop, you probably are familiar with using a specially labeled function key at the top of your laptop keyboard to switch your monitor between the three modes. If you are using a convertible Tablet PC this function key may be available to you; read your instruction manual. If not you should be able to map the monitor switching command to a key combination. With a slate you do not have access to this key. And in any case this key normally only switches which monitor is active; you may still need to change the resolution using the methods below.

Software-based tablet dashboard

For slate users, the easiest way to switch between monitors is to use some sort of specialized software-based control panel that probably came installed on your Tablet PC. The Motion Computing M1300 has such a control panel called the "Dashboard" that combines a number of hardware configuration controls into one easily accessed software control panel (see Figure 4-1). A command on this dashboard can be used to switch between monitor modes (look in the middle portion of the control panel for the entry External Display).

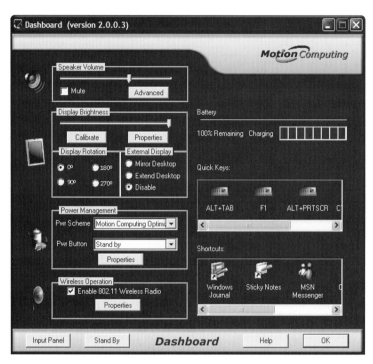

Figure 4-1. Monitor modes are selected in the middle portion of the Motion Dashboard, under "External Display."

This solution does not work for me because the one monitor mode I need, external monitor mode, is not available in the Motion Dashboard. It also does not give you control over screen resolution.

Windows XP control panel display settings

The third way to switch monitor modes is to use the Windows XP Control Panel from the Start menu. Open the Start menu (lower left corner of your screen) and find the entry for the Control Panel about halfway down the right side of the Start menu. Open it, and within the Control Panel window find the Display icon and go to the Settings tab of the window that opens. (See Figure 4-2.) There you can change where the video image is directed and the resolution of the screens. Unfortunately there's no way to save multiple settings, so switching between modes takes a few more mouse clicks to accomplish. This may cause you to fumble a bit when doing it repeatedly, so the next solution is recommended instead.

Figure 4-2. Settings tab of Display Properties control panel.

Intel® Extreme Graphics control panel

The fourth way to switch monitor modes (and the approach I use) is to use a software control panel provided by the video display manufacturer that drives the video monitor on your Tablet PC. Many tablets use a built-in Intel® Extreme Graphics controller (HP tablets do not). Tablets that do use this come preinstalled with a handy piece of software that allows you to take full control of monitor usage on the machine. Hopefully your Tablet PC has this or a similar piece of software. I access popup controls for this software via the Intel® Extreme Graphics icon in the System Tray (the System Tray holds the small icons in the lower right-hand corner of the Windows XP taskbar).

That icon came preinstalled on the M1300 and may have come on your tablet as well. Clicking that pops up the following control menu (see Figure 4-3).

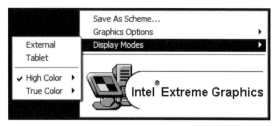

Figure 4-3. Popup control menu for Intel Extreme Graphics.

Use this software to direct the video image to your external monitor and to increase the resolution of the monitor. The nice feature of the Intel® Extreme Graphics software is that you can create a number of different settings optimized for the monitor and then save those settings to what's called a "scheme," which you can then give a name to. I created two of them, one called "External" and one called "Tablet." These scheme names then become listed within the popup menu that appears when you click on the Intel® Extreme Graphics taskbar icon and choose the Display Modes menu (see Figure 4-3). When you select a particular scheme, all the settings saved with that scheme are invoked at once. That includes target monitor, resolution, refresh rate, and color density. This saves time and confusion when you quickly switch between a disconnected tablet mode and a desktop-connected external monitor mode. You create the schemes by first configuring your monitor settings the way you like using the popup control menus, and then using the Save As Scheme... command shown in the figure above.

If your Tablet PC does not come with similar software, try the following add-on software which offers a similar solution: UltraMon from realtimesoft.com.

Map Your Tablet Monitor Mode to a Tablet Button

No matter which of the above approaches you use, owners of slate and hybrid models should consider mapping the command to activate your tablet screen to one or more of your tablet hardware buttons on the edge of your tablet. This is to save you from the following scenario. As you know with most tablets, before you pick your tablet off your desk, you should switch the video feed back to your tablet screen. This is usually not automatic, particularly if switching from external mode (some models, like the HP TC1000 when used with a docking station, *will* change the monitor selection automatically). But what if you forget? What if you grab your tablet off your desk while it is running, pull the monitor cable (or undock) and forget to first switch the display back to your tablet screen? You will arrive at the meeting with a black screen and no quick way to switch it on (convertible owners have a keyboard way to switch this and will be okay). Your only recourse if you have a slate is to do a forced shutdown (hold power button in off position for about 5 seconds) and then turn the computer back on. You risk losing data doing this, and you have to wait for a full reboot. If you've configured your power switch to standby (discussed ahead) this is faster but still a pain.

But all this is so much easier if you have the monitor command mapped to a physical tablet hardware button. I am a bit amazed that any slate or hybrid tablet ships without such a configuration by default. If your tablet, like mine, does not have such a pre-set button, you will need to configure it yourself. And once configured you will probably use this hardware button approach instead of using any of the above software techniques even in non-emergency situations, because it's a lot easier.

Below I will show you how to do that mapping using the Intel® Extreme Graphics controls, and using the Tablet and Pen Settings control panel. Note that this is probably one of the more complicated things I will teach you within this book, so you may want to come back to this later. When you do, set aside about one-half hour to study and do it.

About mapping the tablet hardware buttons

This is the first time we have discussed the hardware buttons on the edge of your tablet, and the first time we have discussed the fact that you can reconfigure some of those buttons. All tablet hardware buttons and button combinations come by default mapped to some action, some of which you may use often (scrolling or changing screen orientation for example), but most of which you will probably never use. Many of these you can reconfigure.

There are relatively few urgent reasons to do this reconfiguration, but the above monitor-switching issue is one case where reconfiguration is *very* useful. Imagine starting a meeting and discovering your tablet screen was frozen in the off position! For this exercise you will need to pick a configurable hardware button combination you know you will never use and change it. There are software equivalents to all the mapped actions, so you really do not lose any capability by changing the default configuration.

All Tablet PCs have this remapping capability. You can map these hardware buttons either to launch an application or to invoke keyboard combinations as if you had a keyboard plugged in. The latter is what you need to do in this case since that is what the Extreme Graphic utility expects.

There are two steps to do this, which I will describe below in detail, but list here briefly. First, you will configure the Enable Notebook command, which is part of the Extreme Graphic software, to be invoked by a keyboard combination. What this does is give you a keyboard shortcut to the command that turns the tablet monitor on. But since slate owners often carry no keyboard, that alone won't help. So the second step is to configure a tablet hardware button to invoke those keyboard strokes for you. These two modifications together solve the problem. Here are the details on those two steps.

Configuring the Extreme Graphics, Enable Notebook command

1 Open the Start menu, open the Windows XP Control Panel, and then open the Intel® Extreme Graphics control panel. Select the Hot Keys tab (see Figure 4-4).

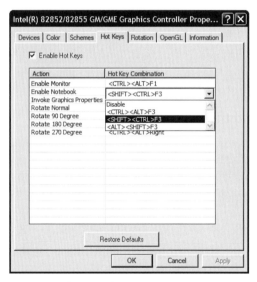

Figure 4-4.   Intel® Extreme Graphics control panel tab for setting keyboard Hot Key equivalents to monitor controls.

2 The action of interest is the second one down: Enable Notebook. Either leave it as assigned, or click on the current Hot Key Combination entry on the right, and pick another keyboard combination from the drop-down menu as shown in the figure above. Notice that there are only three keyboard combinations that you can choose from and they all include a function key. Write down what you choose; and also write down the other two choices that you did not choose (you'll see why in a moment). Click OK to close the window and save the setting.

Mapping to a tablet hardware button

Next you need to configure one or more of the tablet hardware buttons to invoke this keyboard combination when the button is pressed. In order to accomplish this configuration step you need to have a physical keyboard plugged in temporarily. The Tablet PC Input Panel cannot be used for configuration in this case because function keys are not available on the input panel keyboard.

Side Note: If you for some reason cannot get your hands on a physical keyboard, you can use the special Windows XP On-Screen Keyboard. To do this, open the Start menu, choose All Programs, Accessories, Accessibility, On-Screen Keyboard. Function keys are available on that virtual keyboard.

Here are the tablet hardware button configuration steps:

1 Open the Tablet and Pen Settings control panel. There are two ways to open this utility. The first is to use an icon in the System Tray (the System Tray holds the small icons in the lower right corner of the Windows XP taskbar). The icon looks like the image in Figure 4-5. Or you can find the Tablet and Pen Settings control within the Windows Control Panel. Some computer manufacturers also install a shortcut to this within the All Programs menu.

Figure 4-5. System Tray icon for the Tablet and Pen Settings control panel.

2 Opening this utility exposes a multitab window. Choose the Tablet Buttons tab (see Figure 4-6). On that tab you will see a scrolling list that lists on the left all the available tablet hardware buttons and button combinations, and on the right the actions they are currently mapped to. Choose one of the Tablet Button choices that you do not mind reconfiguring. In considering this I decided that I did not want to lose any of the existing single button commands, so I picked a two-button command: the Fn + Esc Key Button (the fifth one down). The plus sign in that list means you hold two buttons down at once to activate the command; Fn stands for the function button. If you are confused which tablet hardware buttons these written descriptions correspond to, note that this control panel window is designed to show you pictorially, in the upper portion of the window, which buttons on your tablet you select. These graphics change as you pick different Tablet Buttons in the lower scrolling list. Try it.

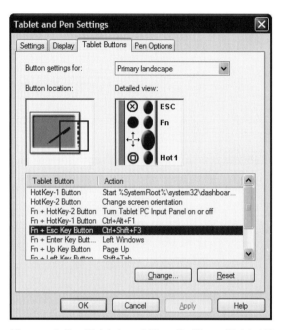

Figure 4-6. Tablet and Pen Settings Tablet Buttons control panel, for remapping the actions associated with tablet hardware buttons.

3 Once you select one from the Tablet Button column and are ready to change it, click the Change... button near the bottom of the window. This opens the dialog box in Figure 4-7.

4 Open the drop-down menu at the top of this dialog and pick Press a Key or Key Combination from the list. This is a long list and that choice may be hard to find. It's in about the middle of the list. Once selected, click within the Keys field at the dialog box bottom to select whatever the current contents are (or it may be currently blank).

Figure 4-7. Change Tablet Button Actions dialog box.

5 Now type on your keyboard the keyboard combination you wrote down
earlier. Once you type them the combination should appear written out in
the Keys field (see Figure 4-7 above for example). On my system, for some
reason, some of the key combinations would not "take"; what I mean by
that is that all the keys I typed would not be displayed in the Keys field;
only two would show. You cannot leave it that way, so you need to find a
combination that *will* completely take. This is why I had you write down
all the Extreme Graphics keyboard choices earlier; if the first one you
picked does not take, try the other ones on the list you wrote down earlier; one should work. When you find one that is accepted, click OK, and
then OK again to save your changes. If the one that "took" is different
from the first one you wrote down, remember to repeat step 1 (go back to
the Extreme Graphics control panel) and choose that new key combination there and save the change.

That should complete the steps. Now test your configuration; test this on your
Tablet PC with your external monitor plugged in and active. Find the hardware buttons on the tablet edge, and assuming you used the same
combination I did, hold down the *function* button (labeled on my tablet with a
black dot) and hit the *escape* button (labeled with an X). Your external monitor
should turn black, and your tablet monitor should turn on. If not, investigate
the above steps and determine where you went wrong.

From now on when you run to a nearby meeting with your tablet still on,
switching monitors should be a breeze.

While not urgent, you may consider also doing a similar configuration to do
the reverse, to switch your external monitor on. Note, however, that controlling resolutions may be difficult in that configuration; I leave that exercise to
you.

Configuring Outlook for Off-Network Use

Now that your Tablet PC is configured to be your primary work computer on the office network, let's also configure Outlook on your Tablet PC so that your Outlook data is available offline. The reason for doing this is that unless you have a wireless network in your office, you must disconnect from your network when you take your Tablet PC to meetings. Yet while at the meeting, much of the work that I advocate you do there requires you to have access to your most recent Outlook data. This requires Outlook to be configured for offline work. And even if your workplace has a wireless network, you'll find that the wireless network is often out of range, or you may wish to work at home.

Using Outlook in Offline Mode

Configuring Outlook for offline use is not something specific to the Tablet PC, but a general feature of Outlook. It is useful if you ever plan to use any computer disconnected from your corporate network. This style of configuration is commonly used with laptops.

First of all, I am assuming you are using Microsoft Outlook with a corporate Exchange server somewhere on your network. This is a very standard e-mail approach and probably the one most commonly used in corporate America. If rather than this your organization is using Outlook to access a POP mail server over the Internet (something a very small organization might do to save costs), then you can probably skip this section. That's because Outlook, when accessing POP mail, is used in essentially the same manner while both online and offline, and no special configuration is necessary.

Again though, assuming you're using the Exchange server approach, unless your organization is accustomed to configuring laptops for use both on and off your corporate network, your IT staff may not have created an offline configuration within Outlook when they set you up.

Here is some background for why this configuration is necessary.

You may be aware that all of the Outlook data you access in your day-to-day work is stored on a central Microsoft Exchange server. This server is something your IT department has set up for your entire organization, and it is remote from your desktop computer. So all of your e-mail, contacts, schedule items, tasks, and other Outlook data exist only on this central network server, and under normal circumstances this data is inaccessible when your computer is disconnected from your network. So your goal is to find a way to get this data synchronized onto your Tablet PC, so that you can access it when you are unplugged from the network.

Outlook Has Three Possible Offline Approaches

This concept of offline use of Outlook is a bit confusing because Outlook really has three offline approaches. The first, and possibly the most common, approach is the use of what are called Personal Folders.

Personal Folders (.pst)

With the Personal Folders approach you create a set of folders that are stored on the hard drive of your computer into which you can move Outlook items from the server. The folders are displayed right within your Outlook application folder hierarchy. In your list of Outlook folders they appear below your Exchange folders, under a master category called Personal Folders. The common use for Personal Folders in an Exchange server environment is to create a place to move old e-mail when cleaning your central server Inbox, once your server Inbox becomes too full. Most IT organizations have limits on the amount of e-mail that staff are allowed to store on the server, and IT departments will enforce these limits by automatically cleansing and deleting old e-mail from your server mailbox. If you wish to save that old e-mail and clean your server mailbox so you don't have mail automatically deleted, the personal folder approach is the way to do this. About once a week I manually move my oldest e-mail from my Exchange server Inbox folder to my Personal Folders Inbox folder, just for this purpose. You'll see Personal Folders also referred to as the ".pst" file in help files, since that's the extension Outlook adds to that file when it is created.

One nice side benefit of Personal Folders is that since they are stored locally, they are accessible while offline. In theory this could work as a synchronization method. But in practice it is not a practical way to consistently access up-to-date server data offline because you need to remember to manually copy all individual entries from the Exchange server folders to the Personal Folders every time they change. So using this approach as you get new e-mail, you must remember to drag that e-mail from the Exchange Inbox folder to your personal Inbox folder before you unplug from your network and generally this is not practical. And if you often refer to sent messages, the same process would be needed.

Side Note: With some help from a technical resource, you may be able to write Outlook rules to do this copying automatically upon receipt of new mail and sending of messages, and thus use Personal Folders as an effective offline mode. Better though is the next solution.

Outlook Offline Folders (.ost)

The better solution for off-network work with Outlook 2002 is to create what Microsoft calls Outlook offline folders. These are hidden Outlook folders which when configured are stored in a file with an ".ost" extension. This file is very similar to your .pst file, except that it does not display separately in your Outlook folder hierarchy, but rather exists hidden within the Outlook file system and is only accessible automatically by Outlook. And most importantly, with .ost offline folders, synchronization can be scheduled to occur automatically. I cover how to configure this below.

The downside to this solution is that every time your network status changes (for instance if you do not have a wireless network in your office, and you disconnect your network cable as you grab your tablet off your desk and run to a meeting) you will need to quit Outlook and restart it in order to use it. While this takes only a few seconds it is annoying to have to do, and you will often forget to do this when you return to your desk. I have worked for hours at my desk not realizing I was not getting e-mail due to forgetting to restart Outlook after returning from a meeting. You'd think there would be a better solution, and there is: Exchange 2003 and Outlook 2003.

Cached Exchange Mode for Exchange 2003 and Outlook 2003

If you are lucky enough to be using Exchange 2003 and Outlook 2003 then you can take advantage of a third mode called Cached Exchange Mode. It is much better than configuring offline folders in the 2002 versions. The reason it is better is because it does not require you to quit and restart Outlook when you switch from working online to offline and back. Rather it works transparently and automatically behind the scenes as your network status changes. Online and offline functionality kick in automatically, and when back online, subsequent synchronization happens automatically.

To configure this setting, first check with your IT department to confirm they are using Exchange 2003. If so, from within your Outlook 2003 client, choose Tools, E-mail Accounts, View or Change Existing E-mail Accounts, then select your Exchange account and click Change, and then check the box marked Use Cached Exchange Mode.

This is by far the easiest solution, and a reason to encourage your IT department to upgrade to Exchange 2003 if they have not done so.

Configuring Outlook for Offline Mode

Most readers are probably in an organization still using Outlook 2002 or earlier and so you will need to manually configure offline folders; you will need to use the .ost approach mentioned above. Here's a high level summary of how this is configured and used for Outlook 2002; the approach is similar in other Outlook versions.

■ First you must tell Outlook and Exchange that you want to create the .ost file, and where on your hard drive to store it.

■ Once the file is created, you then need to synchronize your Exchange folders with your local .ost file. You can either do this manually, or better, schedule automatic synchronization events. I configure Outlook on my Tablet PC so that synchronization occurs every 15 minutes and whenever I quit Outlook.

■ And finally, how do you access this offline data when you are in fact offline? When you launch Outlook and you are unplugged from the network, Outlook will go into offline mode, and your standard views of Inbox, calendar, contacts, will all automatically point to the .ost offline data. If you write e-mails while in offline mode, once back on your network, those e-mails will be sent upon synchronization. Note again that you will need to restart Outlook in order to switch back to online mode.

The steps below are fairly generalized. You may need to get assistance from technical staff because some steps may take added attention to fit with the specifics of your Tablet PC. These three major steps are labeled A, B, and C.

A. Create an Offline Folder (.ost) File

1 On the Tools menu, click E-Mail Accounts, click View or Change Existing E-mail Accounts, and then click Next.

2 In the Outlook Processes E-mail for These Accounts in the Following Order list, click Microsoft Exchange Server, and then click Change.

3 Click More Settings.

4 Click the Advanced tab, and then click Offline Folder File Settings.

5 In the File box, you should see a file path with a filename Outlook.ost. If so, click OK (if not, you may need assistance with the rest of this step).

B. Specify Any Added Folders You Want to Be Available for Offline Use

The Inbox, Outbox, Deleted Items, Sent Items, Calendar, Contacts, Tasks, Journal, Notes, and Drafts folders are automatically made available offline when you set up offline folders, so this should cover all standard Outlook folders. To use any other Exchange-based folders offline, if for some reason you have some, you must specifically enable them for offline use. Folders like PlanPlus notes folders may have been set up on the server, so these are candidates.

Also remember if you add more server-based folders later (again PlanPlus users take note) you need to come back to the above steps and add them to your list of folders available offline.

C. Setup Synchronization

1 On the Tools menu, point to Send/Receive Settings, and then click Define Send/Receive Groups.

2 In the list, click the All Accounts group.

3 To automatically synchronize all folders at specified intervals while you're online, select the Schedule an Automatic Send/Receive Every [x] Minutes checkbox, and then enter a number between 1 and 1440. (I set mine for 15 minutes.)

4 To synchronize all folders after every online Outlook session, select the Perform an Automatic Send/Receive When Exiting checkbox (recommended).

Configuring Your Tablet PC for Use as a PDA

Assuming you have configured the Tablet PC for a desktop as described above, and have now used it for a number of days as such, it is now time to finish configuring your tablet to be as easy to use as a PDA. These are the remaining configurations and self-study activities needed to leverage the key meeting-enabled activities I described in the first chapter. And you may even find as I did that you can discard your handheld PDA once your Tablet PC is configured this way.

Of all the activities for the Tablet PC these last ones are perhaps the most important to get right before starting to use your Tablet PC in meetings. Why? I am assuming you are at least partially concerned about your appearance while performing in meetings. If so, note that all it takes is one or two major missteps in a meeting while fumbling with your new unfamiliar Tablet PC and you may stop bringing the Tablet PC to future meetings. So take the time to do the following configuration and training steps. In this last section we are going to cover the following:

- installing and learning the additional software needed to be fully productive in meetings

- configuring for standby and hibernation power modes

- loading up the Startup folder and the Start menu

- turning off the pen button (optional)

- learning to use the Tablet PC Input Panel most effectively

- learning to use the Write Anywhere tool (optional)

- configuring and getting proficient with screen orientation

- setting some backup strategies

Installing and Learning the Additional Software Needed to Be Fully Productive in Meetings

Now that Tablet PC is configured for use on the corporate network, you can start installing the other Tablet PC software packages that we have been discussing and that will allow you to use the Tablet PC effectively at work. These packages are not part of your standard enterprise software suite and so you will probably need to install them yourself. Your new corporate network user account will be the default user for these software packages, which is why we waited till now to have you install them.

Later chapters go over each of the software packages; you may want to install them one at a time as you hit each chapter. Those chapters will teach you how to use the software. This will be a gradual process as you introduce new software into your work and meeting day, and become proficient with each package. Some of this software, like task management software, you can and should practice with outside of meetings, and only start using in meetings once proficient. Others like note taking you can probably start using in meetings pretty quickly without fumbling too much. Take your time and make the transition smoothly. Once you are up to speed you will be using your tablet for everything and will leave all your paper tools behind. That's when your productivity will really jump, so it's worth working toward that goal.

There's no particular trick to installing software on the Tablet PC; simply treat your tablet as any other Windows XP computer. You will as mentioned earlier need to have administrative privileges to install software. Also note that this may be the first time you have a need to use the optional CD or DVD drive with your tablet, so make sure you have this handy and know how to plug it in and operate it. It is also best to have your keyboard connected when you install new software.

Configuring How You Turn Your Tablet PC On and Off

This is an important topic and so I am going to give this a bit of added attention.

One of my requirements for the use of a Tablet PC in a busy work environment is the ability to turn it on and off quickly. If I am truly to make effective and efficient use of this tool, I cannot be forced to wait anything near the two to five minutes that my current desktop computer requires every time I boot it. Rather my vision is for a PDA-like capability: near instant on, instant off.

That said, as I was considering using a Tablet PC, I could not imagine a Windows-based computer having anything like this speed of control. A flawless implementation of the old laptop *standby* capability was my only hope, but I had long ago given up on using standby with laptops since standby never seemed to work correctly. I had found that when using standby either the laptop or the individual software would crash on resumption from standby.

If you've had similar experience with standby and gave up using it there's good news here: standby has been greatly improved on Windows laptops in recent years, and virtually all Tablet PCs have standby capability implemented flawlessly. The reason: accurate and fast operation of standby is a requirement within the Microsoft Tablet PC specification that manufacturers are required to meet. Manufacturers are now required to use only drivers that are compatible with standby. Standby now works.

By configuring a proper combination of standby and hibernation you can create a strategy that achieves nearly instant on and off capability in nearly all situations. As someone who plans to use the Tablet PC in a fast-paced work environment, you need to understand how to effectively use these modes.

Understanding and Configuring Standby and Hibernation Power Modes

If you have used Windows laptops running solely in battery mode before, you know that you're constantly in a struggle to get your work completed before your laptop battery runs out. There's nothing more frustrating than having your laptop shut down due to lack of battery charge while in the middle of work.

You will find that making use of battery-saving strategies is particularly important when using the Tablet PC in meetings. This is because you will in the context of meetings be consistently switching from working on your Tablet PC for a few minutes at a time, to long periods of no Tablet PC work while you are paying attention to the meeting, and back again, over and over. And leaving your Tablet PC fully powered during consecutive meetings will most likely drain your batteries before your last meetings are done.

Standby and Hibernation Defined

Standby is a mode that shuts down the screen and various other power-consuming components of the laptop or Tablet PC, such that power consumption drops quite considerably, reportedly to only a few percent of full power use. Recovering from standby on a Tablet PC takes only two to three seconds, so this is a quite valuable mode to use to save power and recover system use quickly. You normally use standby if you know that you will not be using your computer for anything short of a few hours.

Hibernation in contrast is a mode in which the contents of your random access memory (RAM) are copied to your hard drive and your computer is then fully powered down. When you power the computer back on, the opposite of this occurs: the previous contents of RAM are read from your hard drive back into RAM and your computer is placed back into its original state from when you first entered hibernation. All running programs and open files are available as before hibernation, ready for use. Recovering from hibernation can take up to 20 or 30 seconds. Not bad when compared to a full system boot up, but certainly not as good as standby. But since zero power is consumed during hibernation it is a good mode for long-term system non-use.

If you're unfamiliar with using standby and hibernation, you may be tempted to just fully shut down your tablet when you wish to save power. If so, you need to get past this old laptop habit. My strategy, which I hope you will adopt, is that in the middle of the day, even if I'm unplugged from power, I almost never shut down my Tablet PC but rather use standby and hibernation exclusively. The problem with shutdown of course is that a full shutdown requires considerable time during the shutdown and during the reboot later, and so if you are only pausing your work for a few minutes a shutdown is not practical. However it's these short pauses that happen so often in meetings and that often extend to tens of minutes. You need to take advantage of these to extend your battery life.

And even if you expect not to need to use your Tablet PC again for hours (say at the end of a long meeting), shutting down can lead to various system housekeeping messages asking among other things whether you want to save open documents. Your computer will not shut down until you attend to them. And the need to attend to these messages can cause a smooth shutdown and rapid meeting exit to be nearly impossible. With standby and hibernation that housekeeping is avoided.

So again, your power-off strategy should be to use standby and hibernation exclusively throughout the day. You need to feel as comfortable putting your Tablet PC into standby as you do turning your PDA off. Let's learn a little bit about the right strategy to use with standby and hibernation.

Accessing Standby and Hibernation

Clearly, you've seen the references to standby and hibernation on the Shut Down dialog from your Start menu (see Figure 4-8).

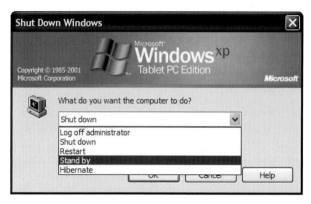

Figure 4-8. The Shut Down dialog is one way to access Standby.

This is *not* how we're going to do it; it's way too cumbersome a method to use twenty times a day. Rather, you should program the power switch on your Tablet PC to implement standby. Let's cover the full strategy.

Strategy for Using Standby, Hibernation, and Shutdown

The details of my power-off strategy are actually very simple: when I want to power down either for a brief or a long period of time I always switch into standby, period. And I've configured the physical power switch on the tablet so that instead of shutting down the tablet, it goes into standby mode. So flipping the power switch is always my action, whether I am powering down for 5 minutes or 5 hours. Very simple. You will see why this works in a moment.

I almost never enter hibernation mode directly. And I almost never fully shut down my Tablet PC during the day. And you only need to configure this setup once, and then you can forget about it.

Safe for standby

Note that I don't need to worry about power consumption during standby eventually draining the battery and leading to a premature power loss (and a resulting loss of data within open applications). This is because I've also en-sured that the power management schemes are set such that after a certain time of non-use, standby automatically converts into a hibernation state (mine is set to a two-hour delay before switching to hibernation). Remember, the hibernation state consumes no power and you can leave your Tablet PC in that state indefinitely. This automatic cutover to hibernation is a default factory setting anyway for my Tablet PC. You should ensure that your tablet is similarly configured.

With this power-off strategy, you never need to first decide how long your tablet will be in non-use as you go to power down. Whether you are in the middle of a meeting and think you will only be pausing for ten minutes, or you are leaving work at the end of the day. No matter what the situation, just flip the power switch and the optimum power-off strategy is automatically in place. This approach greatly simplifies your use of the Tablet PC at work, and it removes all hesitation from flipping the switch on your Tablet PC at the end of a brief segment of work. And it will greatly extend the battery life on your tablet.

Using the Power Switch

Even after configuring your power switch to function as above, turning your computer back on is always the same operation: flipping the power switch; that part does not change. The Tablet PC will figure out whether it needs to resume from standby, resume from hibernation, or launch from shutdown.

And if you need to do a full emergency shutdown of your computer, you can always hold your power switch in the off position for about 5 seconds; this turns off your computer completely (but may lose unsaved data).

Setting Power Configurations

Power switch

The simplest method to configure your power switch is to use the dashboard that came with your Tablet PC, if you have one. For example, configuring the physical power switch on the M1300 is done very simply via the Motion Computing dashboard. Look in the middle of the dashboard shown below under power management and you'll see that the power button is set to "stand by." (See Figure 4-9.) This is not a factory default setting for most Tablet PCs so you'll need to find the equivalent configuration method for your tablet and set it accordingly.

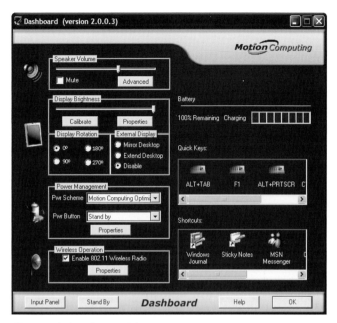

Figure 4-9. Power Management controls are accessed in the middle left portion of the Motion Dashboard.

If your Tablet PC does not have this simplified control, you need instead to use the Windows XP Power Options Properties control panel to configure the switch. From the Start menu choose Control Panel (right middle of start menu), and then find the Power Options icon and open it. Go to the Advanced tab (see Figure 4-10). Near the bottom of this tab you will see a control labeled: When I Press the Power Button on my Computer. Set that to read "Stand by."

Figure 4-10. Advanced tab of Power Options Properties control panel.

Standby to hibernation cutover

And regarding the time delay for when standby automatically cuts over to hibernation, you also access those settings from the Power Options control panel, this time from the Power Schemes tab; choose that tab now. (See Figure 4-11.)

It may take a little study to understand how this tab works, but the only setting here we really care about is in the lower right corner where you see the phrase "After 2 hours." Reading the labels in the upper and left margins of this configuration box will show you that this causes the system to hibernate after two hours of non-use when running on batteries. So if your tablet is in standby for two hours, at that point the system will go into hibernation mode. Make sure your tablet is configured in a similar way; just be sure the word "Never" is not selected here. Once this is done, you can start safely using standby as your primary power-off strategy.

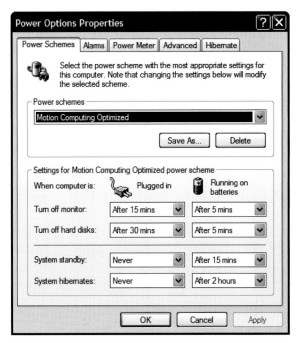

Figure 4-11. Power Schemes tab on the Power Options Properties control panel.

The additional settings on this panel are less important for our strategy, and you need not understand them fully. I suspect the default settings that came with your Tablet PC are adequately close to these. That said you may find it interesting to understand the rest of the settings as they help explain what may be puzzling behavior on your tablet during non-use.

Here's how this works: this setup is actually a multilevel cascading power-saving scheme. Reading from the top, again for batteries only (the right column) you will see that after five minutes of non-use the monitor and hard drive will shut off (which saves a moderate amount of power). After fifteen minutes of non-use the system will go into standby (which saves a much greater amount of power). And after two hours of non-use the system will go into hibernation: zero power consumption.

You may also notice there's a similar but less severe cascading power saving scheme for when the computer is plugged in. This is in place solely so you can save on your electric bill and perhaps reduce wear and tear on your computer.

Do All Tablet PCs Support This Power Strategy?

Unfortunately no. As of the date of this writing, some older models of the Fujitsu Tablet PC, if not updated with recent fixes, may still have trouble with hibernation. Presumably this is because some of their hardware drivers did not interact reliably with the hibernation state. I have not heard of any, but it's possible that other brands may have similar limitations. So if you're still in shopping mode for your Tablet PC, check this specification carefully prior to purchase.

Configuring Your Start Menu and Startup Folder

You may want to return to this section after you have worked through Part Two and selected the software you will install.

To reach our goal of using your Tablet PC nearly as simply as using a PDA, you should configure rapid access to your key applications. Having quick access to the manager-effectiveness software is critical to success in meetings with the Tablet PC. If you are forced to search through your All Programs menu under the Start menu for a key piece of software to launch while using your tablet in a fast-moving meeting, you may end up deciding the Tablet PC is too cumbersome.

To avoid using the All Programs menu, I am going to show you how to configure a number of standard Windows XP capabilities. These are fairly easy to implement, but for some reason, in the desktop world very few users take the time to learn them. With desktop use, these are not so critical. But with your Tablet PC they become essential to enabling smooth and rapid use within meetings.

Pinning Key Applications within the Start Menu

The first of these is adding your manager-effectiveness software list to the upper left corner of your Start menu so you can start these applications quickly.

First let's explain the structure of the Start menu. (See Figure 4-12.)

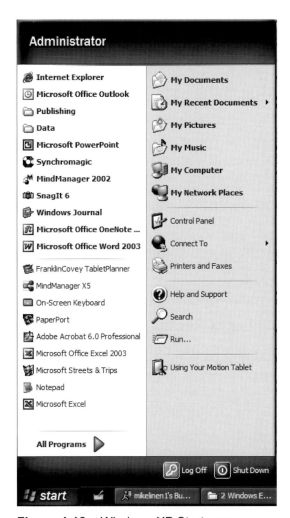

Figure 4-12. Windows XP Start menu.

When you open the Start menu, on its left side you are faced with a list of applications, a thin gray line, and below that line another list of applications. The applications at the bottom of these lists may seem to change with time. On the right side of the Start menu you'll see an unchanging list of key folders and Windows XP functionality. This right side you generally do not reconfigure, but the upper left side you can and should.

Specifically, you should decide which applications will appear in the upper left corner and in what order. Configuring applications to appear there is called "pinning" applications to the Start menu. It is a very convenient way to place key applications within reach for when you need to launch them quickly. It is my suggestion that you place your entire manager-effectiveness software list in this portion of the Start menu so that you can launch these items individually any time you need, quickly, by going to the Start menu.

To place applications in this upper left corner of the Start menu, there are two methods:

- Right-click on the application icon or shortcut wherever it may be, and choose Pin to Start Menu. This creates a shortcut within the upper left corner of the Start menu. This is by far the easiest method.

- Drag shortcuts up to that area and drop them there, following the guidelines for dragging and holding described in the next part of this chapter.

Normally you would use the first method. It's incredibly easy and I am surprised more people do not do it. Once an application appears in that list you can rearrange the order in which they are listed by merely dragging the entry up and down in the list.

Adjusting the Number of Recent Applications Shown in the Start Menu

By the way, the lower left side of the Start menu represents recently used applications (and only applications not already pinned). Its content changes over time and is automatically populated. While you cannot control which applications will appear there, you can control how many will be listed. One reason for making this count smaller is if you pin too many applications to the upper left portion of your Start menu you may run out of room there (you'll get a notice from Windows when you do). You can find and adjust the count by going to the Start menu, opening the Control Panel (right middle of Start menu), and opening the Task Bar and Start Menu icon you will see there. At the window that opens, choose the Start Menu tab, click the Customize button, and edit the count number in the middle of the resulting window.

Shortcuts Defined

You know what a shortcut is, right? A shortcut is an icon (file) that represents a copy of the original application icon but that occupies a tiny amount of disk space. You can recognize it by the small boxed arrow in the lower left corner of the icon. Look at your Windows desktop and you'll notice that many of the icons have this small boxed arrow and so are actually shortcuts to applications. If you double-click on a shortcut you will launch the application just as if you had double-clicked on the original application icon itself. To create a shortcut, simply hold down the Alt key and click and drag the original application (or a shortcut to it) to the location you want. The original will stay put and a shortcut will be created at the new location. You can create as many shortcuts to an application as you like, so this is a convenient way to place access to applications in various locations within your computer. This ensures that the software is always easy to find and launch. Note that if you delete a shortcut you will not delete the original application—no worries.

Changing the Icon Size of Listings within the Start Menu

Another thing I recommend you do while within the Task Bar and Start Menu control panel is to change the icon size of the applications listed in the Start menu so that you can pin more items there. This is important on the Tablet PC since the screen tends to be relatively small compared with other computer screens in use these days. To do this: again, go to the Start menu, Control Panel, and find the icon titled Task Bar and Start Menu. Double-click that icon, choose the Start menu tab, click the Customize button, and click on the Small Icons choice within the resulting window.

Loading Up the Startup Folder to Launch Applications

Again, having quick access to the manager-effectiveness software is critical to success in meetings with the Tablet PC. Following the steps above, you have pinned shortcuts for the key applications into your Start menu so you can find them quickly. This is a move in the right direction, but even better is to also have the entire set of standard manager-effectiveness software start automatically when you boot your computer. That way your first morning meeting will not be spent waiting for key applications to start.

To do this, I load up the Startup folder (see inset) with a shortcut to each of the key pieces of software. As a result all my key software starts when I boot the Tablet PC. All the applications will then be listed in the task bar at the bottom of your Windows screen, ready for you to click on and bring to the front instantly. This is as close to PDA speed as possible.

Do this by the way only if you have 512MB of RAM installed on your tablet, as recommended in the chapter on hardware. And also do this only if you have instituted the power-off strategy described above. Reason: loading up the Startup folder will cause your boot time to be very slow as you wait for all the applications to start. Be sure you boot at most once a day with this configuration, and preferably at a time you can go get some coffee.

Should you do both this *and* pin your applications as described in the section above? Yes, because even if you launch all your applications when you boot your computer in the morning, throughout the day you will often inadvertently close some of your open applications. So you also need the application list pinned in your Start menu so that you can reopen individual applications quickly as needed.

Startup Folder Defined

The Startup folder is a standard Windows feature that has been around since early versions of Windows. Any application or application shortcut that you place in the folder will automatically launch after Windows first boots up. I recommend that you make sure a shortcut for each of your key software packages is placed in this folder.

How to Put Shortcuts in the Startup Folder

If you place application shortcuts within the Startup folder their presence there will cause these applications to launch upon Windows boot up. You probably have some software in your Startup folder now, put there either by your Tablet PC manufacturer or during installs you've made for other software (Microsoft Office for example). Go look now. Open your Start menu, find the All Programs control, open that, and in the top half of the All Programs list you should see an entry called Startup. This represents the contents of your Startup folder. Go ahead and look inside. In Figure 4-13 you'll see an example of a tablet that has six applications that launch on startup. After examining your tablet, try to remember where this folder is, as we'll be coming back to it.

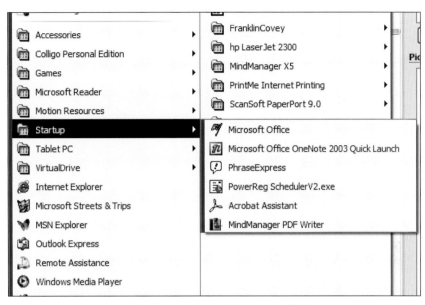

Figure 4-13. Startup folder as viewed from the All Programs portion of Start menu.

In order to place more application shortcuts there, you will need to first learn how to use the drag and drop capabilities of the Start menu, a skill which is probably new to you.

Dragging and dropping shortcuts within the Start menu

As you know, the Start menu organizes in one spot access to all the software on your computer. In reality, it represents a convenient view of the contents of various *folders* scattered about your computer. When you install new software, an entry for the software is automatically made somewhere in the Start menu (so that you can launch it). Usually it is placed in the All Programs section of the Start menu. What many people do not know is that you can copy and move applications and documents among the sections of the Start menu to make the organization of the Start menu more convenient. You do this through a simple drag and drop process. And you can even add new items there (say from the desktop) also by dragging and dropping.

Since the Startup folder is just one more item within your Start menu, you can use this technique to install shortcuts for your key software into the Startup folder.

Dragging to the Startup folder

Here is how to drag into the Startup folder, assuming the shortcut for the application you want to put there is on your desktop:

1 Click on that shortcut icon and drag the icon to the Start menu. Hold it there for a moment (without lifting the pen) and allow the Start menu to open.

2 Continue to drag the shortcut to the All Programs button. Hold it there for a moment; allow the All Programs menu to open.

3 Drag the shortcut to the Startup entry on the All Programs menu, and position it so that a black line appears just *above* the word Startup, and hold it there.

4 In a moment the contents of the Startup folder will open and you can then drag the icon into the Startup folder. Once there, lift your pen and the item will drop into that folder and the Start menu will close.

The Start menu closes too fast to confirm this worked, so after doing this, it is worthwhile to immediately navigate back to the Startup folder and confirm that the item did in fact drop there.

Repeat this for shortcuts of all of the manager-effectiveness software packages. If you cannot find shortcut icons for all these packages on your desktop then look for them in the All Programs area of the Start menu. An entry for all software is nearly always somewhere within that area of the Start menu; you may have to search for it.

However, note the following: when you drag shortcuts from the desktop this creates a *copy* of the item in the Start menu, leaving the original shortcut on the desktop. In contrast when you drag shortcuts from the All Programs menu to other places in the Start menu, this *moves* the shortcut to where you place it, *removing the original shortcut* from the place you found it in the menu. So to avoid removing these original shortcuts you need to do this: before you drag the shortcut, first hold down the control key and keep it depressed while you drag the shortcut (if using the on-screen keyboard, click once on the control key and let it remain highlighted while you complete the operation; then click it again to deselect it). Using the control key leaves the original shortcut where you found it.

Turning Off the Pen Button for Right-Clicking (Optional)

The primary purpose of the button on the side of your pen is to provide a way to emulate the right-click of a mouse. But now you know another way to right-click: hold the pen on the screen for a few seconds and then lift the pen. As mentioned in the getting started chapter, I don't like the pen button because I often inadvertently push it while using the pen. This causes a Context Menu to jump up on the screen. So I have disabled it for right-clicking.

I have been told that the reason I accidentally hit the button so often is that the pen I am using unfortunately tends to favor this accidental use, and that other Tablet PC pens are designed better. So I leave this decision to you: if you find you are often accidentally hitting the pen button, follow the instructions below; if not and all is well then skip this section.

Also note that some software packages use the pen button for purposes other than right-clicking (MindManager for example) and that disabling this button for right-clicking has no negative effect on these other uses.

To reconfigure this button, you need to use a configuration utility you may have used during the original Tablet PC setup called Tablet and Pen Settings.

As described earlier, there are two ways to open this utility. The first is to use an icon in the System Tray (these are the small icons in the lower right corner of the Windows XP taskbar). The icon looks like the one enlarged in Figure 4-14.

Figure 4-14. System Tray icon for the Tablet and Pen Settings control panel (magnified).

Or you can access this through the Windows Control Panel. Some computer manufacturers also install a shortcut to this within the All Programs menu.

Opening this utility exposes a multitab window. Select the last tab, the Pen Options tab (see Figure 4-15), and uncheck the option at the bottom of that screen: Use Pen Button to Right-Click.

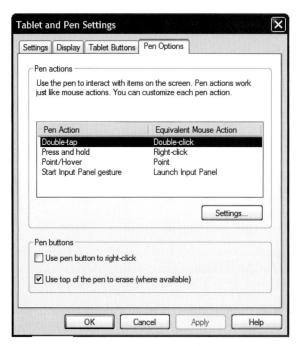

Figure 4-15.   Pen Options tab of the Tablet and Pen Settings control panel.

Also while you are at that tab, ensure that your tablet is configured to emulate a right-click of a mouse by pressing and holding the pen. To do this, choose Press and Hold from the Pen Action list in the middle of that screen, then click the Settings... button. The following screen appears. (See Figure 4-16.) At the top of that screen, make sure the box next to Enable Press and Hold for Right-Click is checked.

Then click OK to save the changes, and OK again to exit the Tablet and Pen Settings dialog.

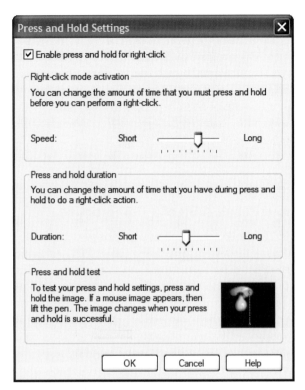

Figure 4-16. Press and Hold Settings window accessed from within the Tablet and Pen Settings control panel.

The Tablet PC Input Panel: Configuration and Use Strategies

My next recommended set of configuration changes for optimum work management use of the Tablet PC is to configure the Tablet PC Input Panel a little bit differently from how it is originally delivered. In summary, my configuration strategy is this:

■ I size the Tablet PC Input Panel as small as possible.

■ I use only the keyboard portion of the panel (for making corrections and typing symbols) and keep that open all the time when using the pen.

■ I use only the Write Anywhere tool for all handwriting input.

We'll go over the details of these below, but let's spend a little time discussing the input panel and its role on the Tablet PC.

The first important point is that the Tablet PC Input Panel is expected to undergo major redesign as of the next version of the Windows XP Tablet PC Edition, due for release in June of 2004. It will be replaced with a much improved Tablet PC Input Panel, which may or may not match the features described in this section. Since this book is being published well before that date, I will post a rewrite of this chapter to my website (www.seizetheworkday.com) as the new design is made available, so refer there for updates of this section.

The second important point is that the Write Anywhere tool is due to be retired with that June 2004 release. More on that below.

Tablet PC Input Panel: A Bit of a Compromise

Only a few fully Tablet PC–enabled applications are currently on the market. To my mind, the best examples of a fully Tablet PC–enabled application are Windows Journal, Microsoft OneNote, and FranklinCovey TabletPlanner. With these applications, you write directly within the application; you are not required to use some intermediary software like the input panel to add ink or text. There are of course other examples of well-optimized Tablet PC software, but the vast majority of applications you will be using are not optimized for the Tablet PC, and in those cases the input panel represents a bit of a compromise. I think of this as a speed-to-market solution that solves the problem: how to quickly enable all current Windows XP applications to be usable on the Tablet PC. The Tablet PC Input Panel is the current solution. But even with well-optimized software like Windows Journal you still need to occasionally use the input panel to touch up text conversions, to input symbols, and the like. So you will always need an on-screen keyboard and therefore the Tablet PC Input Panel is not going away even in the next generations of Tablet PC.

We covered in the getting started chapter the basic uses of the input panel. As you know if you're not using an attached physical keyboard, this panel is your main interface for text input into most Tablet PC applications and for all Windows XP applications that have not been optimized for the Tablet PC. The two primary modes of interest to us are handwriting recognition and an on-screen keyboard that you tap with your pen. The input panel is also the way to access the optional speech recognition software built into the Tablet PC; we will cover that later in this chapter.

Undocking and Resizing the Input Panel

I have a love-hate relationship with the Tablet PC Input Panel. It does its job well but it seems that when it's open it's always in the way. The moderately small screen on most Tablet PCs is just too small to live comfortably with the input panel because it covers too much of the open documents you are working with. That said, you need the thing, and so you should at least make an effort to size the panel as small as is practical.

Undocking

The first thing you need to be aware of is that you can unlock the size and position of the input panel by "undocking" it. When you first start using your Tablet PC, the input panel may by default be "docked." This means that it may be locked at the bottom of your screen and displayed at full width and height. (See Figure 4-17).

Figure 4-17. Docked Tablet PC Input Panel.

If yours is docked, this also means that the windows of other applications are automatically repositioned and resized to fit above the input panel. This automatic resizing feature is a nice design and possibly a good reason to stick with the docking mode of the input panel.

The two problems with this are (1) a docked input panel uses too much screen real estate and (2) a large keyboard is actually harder to pen-type on than a small one.

To regain screen real estate, there are several approaches you can take:

- You can minimize the input panel using the arrow button in the upper right corner of the input panel next to the close box (try this now and get used to using it). Note however that doing this does not re-enlarge any windows that were made smaller to make room for the docked input panel.

- Or you can completely close the input panel each time you are finished with it.

- Or you can undock and then resize the panel smaller and expose a bit more screen real estate to the side of the panel.

■ And finally, if you are using an undocked panel you can set the input panel to automatically minimize when you're done with it.

I recommend that depending upon your work pattern you try all of these. At a minimum though I recommend you resize the panel now and get used to using the smaller on-screen keyboard.

Resizing

In order to resize the input panel, you must first undock the panel using the Tools menu in the upper left corner of the panel.

Do this by selecting the Dock option so that the checkmark is removed. At this point you can resize the panel by clicking on the edges of the panel and dragging them with your pen, as you would resize any other window. I recommend you make the panel as narrow as possible. (See Figure 4-18.) You may think that this will interfere with the handwriting recognition by making the writing pad space too small. But as you'll see below, my strategy is to not use the writing pad portion of the input panel, but rather to use the Write Anywhere tool, so don't worry about this for now.

Figure 4-18. Tablet PC Input Panel, resized to smallest size.

Some other points about an undocked input panel:

- You can drag an undocked Tablet PC Input Panel around the screen like any other window.

- The input panel, once undocked, switches to an always-on-top mode, meaning that it will never be covered by any other windows.

- If you drag the input panel away from the bottom of the screen and then tap the minimize arrow, you are left with the title bar floating in the middle of the screen.

I generally do not move the input panel away from the bottom of the screen, unless there is some portion of an application window that I need to take a peek at momentarily. However some people like to drag the input panel closer to the insertion point of the document they are currently working on.

Auto-hide the input panel

If like me after using the strategies above for some time you still feel that the input panel takes up too much real estate, then I recommend you set it to auto-hide after a short delay. I discovered this feature only recently and I'm happy with it. This causes the input panel to self-minimize shortly after you pull the pen away from the input panel. Then when you pull the pen back into the title bar area of the input panel, the panel pops open again. This is almost the best of both worlds. To set this feature you have to first make sure the panel is not docked, and then from the Tools menu of the input panel choose Options, and click on the Advanced tab. (See Figure 4-19.) In the upper portion of this window check the checkbox labeled: When Input Panel Is Not Docked, Hide the Pen Input Area After.

I then recommend that you set the delay to a short delay; I use the minimum time.

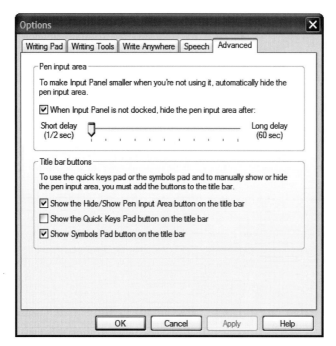

Figure 4-19. Auto-hide control panel.

One tip on using this feature: in order to unhide the input panel when you pull the pen back to it, you need to get in the habit of passing the pen over the center portion of the title bar (the portion that is to the right of the Tools menu and the left of the buttons); otherwise the panel will not unhide. With a narrow input panel that center portion is relatively small, so you may miss it a few times and wonder why the input panel has not opened.

Using the Write Anywhere Tool

When I first started with my Tablet PC, I was also unaware of the existence of the Write Anywhere tool. When I finally discovered it I was delighted; you may be too. That said, many other experienced Tablet PC users do not like using the Write Anywhere tool so be prepared to make your own judgment on this.

And one more caveat. The Write Anywhere tool is due to be discontinued as of the next version of the Windows XP Tablet PC Edition, due for release in June of 2004. It will be replaced as part of the updated Tablet PC Input Panel that I mentioned above. I am told the new input panel will have functionality better than the current Write Anywhere tool, but much different.

So it is unlikely that the contents of this section will be applicable to that new design. If you are reading this book near to that date you should consider whether you want to invest the time learning this feature now. And if you are reading this book after that date, Write Anywhere may not even be available on your Tablet PC! Check my website (www.seizetheworkday.com) for an update to this chapter around that date.

Advantages of using the Write Anywhere tool

The Write Anywhere tool is an option built into the Tablet PC Input Panel that allows you to use nearly the entire Tablet PC screen as a writing space for handwriting recognition. The advantages of this should be obvious: you are no longer restricted to a small box to place your handwriting in, so you can write longer sentences in one pass. There are other advantages:

- Because you can write anywhere, you can rest your palm more comfortably on the Tablet PC screen while you write. This leads to clearer handwriting and more accurate handwriting recognition

- Once proficient with Write Anywhere, you will presumably no longer be using the writing pad portion of the Tablet PC Input Panel. This enables you to leave the keyboard portion of the input panel constantly open, which is important because you will be constantly using the keyboard for minor corrections and symbol input.

- And if you find you rarely need the keyboard then Write Anywhere allows you to leave the input panel minimized, leaving more screen real estate available.

Some things the Write Anywhere tool does not do:

- It does not turn applications into Windows Journal–like applications so that you can write anywhere directly within the application. You still must select an insertion point where you intend the converted text to appear. All converted text appears at that insertion point, even if you write over the top of different parts of the screen.

- It uses the same handwriting conversion engine that the input panel uses. Any observed handwriting conversion improvement is the result of your ability to write more clearly given the larger writing space and better palm positioning.

Some people find the Write Anywhere tool disconcerting because it is akin to putting a thin transparent writing sheet on top of your screen. You end up writing on top of other text, other graphics, other windows, and so on. My advice is to try it out and see if you like it.

How to activate Write Anywhere

You need to activate Write Anywhere first to add its control to the input panel; you only need to do this once. To activate it, pull down the Tools menu in the upper left corner of the Tablet PC Input Panel and choose Options, and click on the Write Anywhere tab in the window that opens. (See Figure 4-20.)

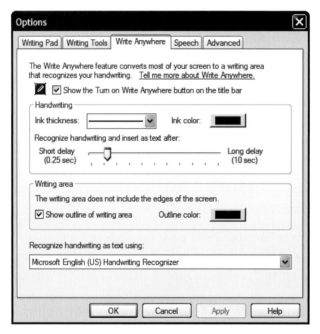

Figure 4-20. Write Anywhere controls.

Click the checkbox near the top of that screen that is labeled: Show the Turn On Write Anywhere Button on the Title Bar. Then click OK.

Now when you look at your Tablet PC Input Panel, if you look in the upper right corner, you'll see a small pen icon has been added:

Tapping this icon is how you turn Write Anywhere on and off throughout the day.

Exercise to demonstrate Write Anywhere

Let's try this out: open any application that can accept text input like Microsoft Word. Create a new blank document and click on the maximize icon in the upper right corner of the document to fill your screen with this document (we are doing this just to make your first use of Write Anywhere easier; you don't normally need to enlarge your document to use Write Anywhere). Now tap your pen in the document to activate an insertion point, and then tap on the Write Anywhere icon to open the tool. You'll see a box appear on your screen overlaying your document as in the image below. (See Figure 4-21.)

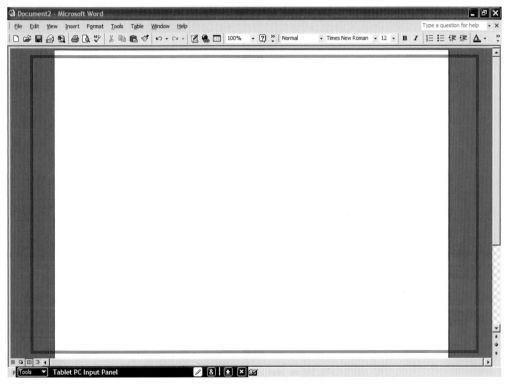

Figure 4-21.   Write Anywhere boundary box.

This box represents the writing area you are allowed to use when using the Write Anywhere tool. Why a restricted writing area? This is actually a blessing not a restriction, because it enables you, while the Write Anywhere tool is open, to tap on the edges of the screen to use menus, scroll bars, toolbars, and the like without the tablet thinking you're attempting to create handwriting; these controls tend to exist along the edges of the screen.

If you move your pen around your screen (without touching it) you'll see a thick black horizontal line follow your pen up and down your screen.

Next, with the tool open, move your pen near the upper left portion of your screen and then position it approximately above the black horizontal line. Now start writing, anything you want, taking care to keep the writing horizontal; use the thick horizontal line as a guide to do so. (See Figure 4-22.)

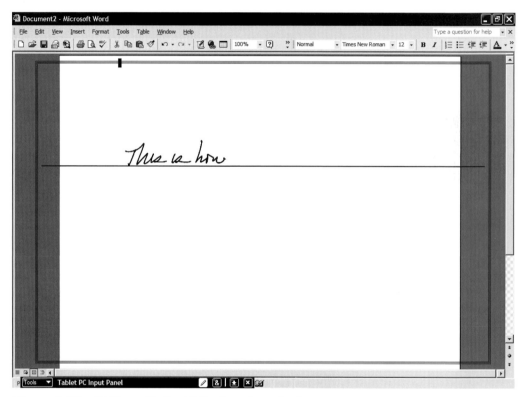

Figure 4-22.   Writing with the Write Anywhere tool.

After you pause in your writing, just like when using the Tablet PC Input Panel writing pad, the handwriting will disappear from the place you wrote it, and the converted text will appear in the document at the insertion point. (See Figure 4-23.)

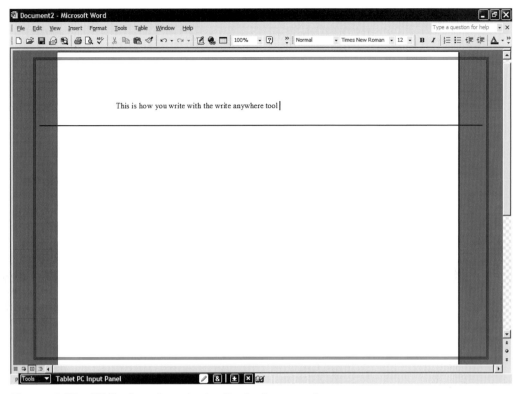

Figure 4-23. Write Anywhere tool, after text conversion.

By the way it does not matter how close to the thick black line you write, just use it as a rough guide to the horizontal. And again, ignore the objects, text, and cursor activity underneath your writing; you are writing on a transparent layer which does not care about those things.

It takes some practice to get used to this, but my experience is that users quickly get very good. Users often will like it so much that they never go back to using the writing pad on the input panel for handwriting input.

Selecting text

Text selection underneath the Write Anywhere area can be difficult. Think about it: the tablet doesn't know if you're writing or selecting when you drag your pen within the Write Anywhere area. So if you need to select text while in the middle of using the write area tool there are two ways to do this:

■ Turn off the Write Anywhere feature for a moment by tapping the pen icon as described above, and make your selection. When you are done turn the tool back on. This may be the best strategy at first, until you get good at using this tool.

- Or, hold the pen still on the surface of the screen next to the intended selection area for a second or so. After a moment the Write Anywhere tool will automatically disappear and you should immediately drag the pen and make your selection. As soon as you lift your pen again the Write Anywhere tool will return. This maneuver takes a little skill because, as you know, if you hold the pen on the screen too long then you will automatically pop up the right mouse button menu (assuming you have activated this feature). That said, the designers of the Write Anywhere tool have already considered this, and so you'll find that the length of time you need to hold the pen tip down to pop up the right mouse click menu has actually been lengthened while the pen is within the Write Anywhere area. Nicely done.

There's one frustrating side effect to the above described ability to select text while the Write Anywhere tool is active. Here's the scenario: you are merrily handwriting away using the Write Anywhere tool and as you finish writing a word you have a thought which causes you to hesitate your pen on the surface of the screen. A moment later the Write Anywhere tool disappears and the insertion point moves to where you rested your pen on the document (per the feature described in the second bullet above). At that point you are in trouble because another moment later what you were just writing is converted to text and is inserted at this new insertion point. This is clearly not what you intended to do! Quickly choose Undo from the Edit menu to reverse this. I guarantee you'll make this error a few times; don't worry, you'll get used to it. The lesson? If while handwriting with the Write Anywhere tool you need to hesitate your writing, lift your pen first!

Some Other Points Regarding Use of the Write Anywhere Tool

Changing the insertion point: to intentionally change the insertion point while the Write Anywhere tool is active you merely need to tap briefly with the pen at the new insertion point—simple. Or you can tap and hold the pen still for a moment until the Write Anywhere feature disappears momentarily, and then lift your pen.

Ignore the cursor shape: you are probably accustomed to writing with the cursor looking like a small dot. This is how it looks within the writing pad, and also how it looks within Windows Journal and Microsoft OneNote. However when you are using the Write Anywhere tool, the cursor will take on the cursor form expected by the application underlying the pen at the time you're writing. This can be a bit disconcerting and you need to learn to ignore it.

Strategies for Configuring Screen Orientation

The screen display can easily be rotated on the Tablet PC from portrait to landscape and back. Everyone develops their preferences for screen orientation. My preference for some reason is to always keep the screen in landscape mode while at work and in meetings. I think that's because I use Microsoft Outlook and Internet Explorer so much at work, and both seem best suited for a landscape mode. I also find that for handwriting recognition the longer I can continue writing without having to lift and move my hand to another line, the faster I can write, so landscape mode lends itself to this.

In contrast, if I am dictating into Microsoft Word using speech recognition, I find I like to use portrait orientation. That way I can place the input panel below the Word window and still have a relatively large unobstructed Word window open above it.

Be Sure to Learn How to Change Screen Orientation

Whichever your preference, and even if you do not change it often, make sure you know how to change this orientation.

Why? Because most Tablet PCs have this rotation capability mapped to one of the hardware buttons on the exterior of the Tablet PC. That's a curse and a blessing—a curse because you'll often find yourself accidentally pushing the button as you casually handle your tablet. Suddenly you look down and find that your screen has rotated; this is a bit embarrassing in the middle of a meeting. So even if you rarely purposely change the screen orientation, make sure you know which button controls the screen rotation. This is both so you can avoid the button and so that you can use it to reset the rotation if you accidentally push it. Study your tablet's user's manual to find these buttons.

Reconfiguring default orientation actions

All Tablet PCs have a utility that you can use to reconfigure the actions of these hardware buttons. We discussed on page 76 how to use that utility. If you find over time that you never change your screen orientation, you might consider unmapping that button so that you never accidentally press it.

If you do change screen orientation often, you will probably notice this: by default the screen orientation button is configured such that it rotates the screen 90° for each push of the button. So really you have four choices for screen orientation: 0°, 90°, 180°, and 270°. And as you push the screen orientation button, you're forced to step through all four choices. However if you're like me you only use two of these: 0° and 90° (portrait upright and landscape upright). The other two positions basically result in holding the Tablet PC upside down, something I don't need or want, and I would rather not step through those choices when I push the screen orientation button. There is enough of a pause during reorientation that the extra steps are frustrating to wait for.

So a configuration change you should make fairly early on is to turn off the other two orientation choices. Here's how you do this: bring up our familiar friend the Tablet and Pen Settings control panel. Remember, there are two ways to open this utility: by using an icon in the System Tray or accessing through the Windows Control Panel on the Start menu.

Then click on the Display tab, and about halfway down that window notice the word "Sequence" and the button next to it labeled: "Change." Click that Change button and the following window appears (see Figure 4-24):

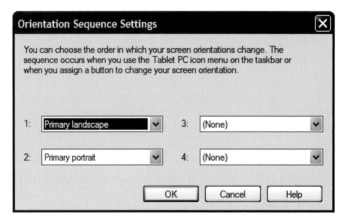

Figure 4-24. Tablet screen orientation control window.

Change the settings to match the figure above, which should mean that you need to set the selections for number 3 and number 4 to "None." Click OK, and then OK again on the main window to exit and save these changes. From now on when you click the screen orientation button, you will step through only two choices: portrait upright and landscape upright (which are officially called: Primary Portrait and Primary Landscape).

Setting a Backup Strategy

If you have followed my recommendations so far, you have transferred all your work files from your desktop computer onto your Tablet PC and are using that now as your primary workstation. This enables you to take all your work with you when you leave for meetings. It also puts your work data at a bit more risk. Consider that you will now be carrying your primary desktop computer under your arm everywhere you go, protected at best by a lightly padded leather portfolio. Now more than ever you need to design and implement a data backup strategy for your Tablet PC. Do not ignore this task.

If you are very lucky your organization has some sort of network-based backup scheme in place for desktop computers. If so, make sure your Tablet PC is added to that strategy. However my experience from years of IT management is that most IT departments do not have desktop backup systems implemented. Normally, the backup systems they do have in place are directed only toward file servers and mission critical systems.

Possible backup approaches

So after you confirm with your IT department that they in fact have *no* desktop backup system available, here's what you should do to create your own:

Ask your IT department to issue you some space on one of the networked file servers that resides on your enterprise network. This is for data-only so 50 to 100 MB should be adequate (more on that in a moment). And if access to that space requires a password, have your IT department configure a log-on script that automatically runs every time you boot your Tablet PC to grant you access to that space (if your tablet is made part of a domain that won't be necessary). Once established, here are some possible strategies for using that space:

■ At a minimum, periodically copy the contents of important work directories off your tablet onto that network drive by dragging files in Windows Explorer. My experience is that most people do not do this since the directories on your tablet may be scattered about and so hand picking the directories becomes too cumbersome to do regularly.

■ Better is to use the Windows Backup utility to automate that backup process. This comes preinstalled on your tablet. The advantage of this is it is free and easy to use and stores backed-up data compactly. The disadvantage is that the backed-up files are not in normal file format. The only way to recover the files is to run Windows Backup again and if your tablet is nonfunctional this may be difficult.

■ An even better approach (and the one I suggest) is to purchase an add-on synchronization software package which stores mirror copies of the contents of directories. This way you have access to your data on the backup drive in its native format even if your tablet is unavailable. Two shareware packages of interest are FileWare's FileSync (www.fileware.com)

and Syncromagic (www.gelosoft.com). A third choice, Iomega's Automatic Backup software, is probably the best choice. Also moderately priced (and free with their hard drives), it allows for instant mirroring as source files change, and gracefully deals with disconnections from the network (www.iomega.com).

■ You might consider using the Offline Files and Folders feature of Windows XP for backup purposes (do not confuse this with offline folders in Outlook, which is unrelated). Many books on Windows XP and even some on the Tablet PC recommend this, but use this with caution. On the surface this feature of Windows XP looks like the perfect solution for the mobile Tablet PC user: your data files are stored on a server, mirrored on your Tablet PC, and "automatically" synchronized. I do not recommend using this approach, however, because it puts the authoritative copy of your files on the server. This can cause problems for Tablet PC users because auto-synchronizing before disconnecting from the network only occurs if you actually shut down. If you instead just drop into standby or hibernation, or worse disconnect from the network and leave with your tablet still running, you may lose data. The only way to safely grab and go using Offline Files and Folders is to manually sync before departure. And since it is highly unlikely that you will remember to manually sync every time you go to a meeting, Offline Files and Folders is not good for Tablet PC users who grab and go. The Iomega software mentioned above, when configured to backup often, achieves nearly the same backup goals, but does so with an implementation that puts the authoritative copy on your local machine where it belongs, and which works well for Tablet PC use patterns.

So my recommendation is to purchase one of the inexpensive file synchronization packages on the market listed in the third bullet above, and mirror your data directories to your file server space. The Iomega software is especially easy to set up and use for automatic or scheduled backups. If you do not mind triggering your backups manually, the others work well too.

> **Back Up Your Outlook Files**
>
> If you are using Personal Folders in Outlook, don't forget to include your Outlook.pst file in your backup scripts as well; they are not stored in your My Documents directory and so will need attention to add to the backup script. That said, this is one file that tends to get very big. So you may need either to request more space from your IT department (up to 1GB) or remember to regularly archive your Outlook messages to an external drive.

More thoughts on backups

USB drive

If you have difficulty getting one of the above network backup strategies in place, then at minimum, use of a portable USB–attached hard drive is a no-brainer way to get backup in place. Look at the SimpleDrive™ hardware device that runs a backup script automatically when you plug it in. Similarly, look at the Maxtor and the Iomega line. Even using one of the keychain style USB storage devices can work if data volumes are reasonable. Look at the software called StorageSync™ for use with one of these devices. See the Appendix for source information for these products.

Image backups

But keep in mind that all the above solutions are for backing-up your data and documents only. If you are concerned about a full system loss and want to back up everything, consider an image backup solution. This will speed your time to recovery by eliminating individual reinstallation of operating system, applications, reconfigurations, and then data installation. All this is done in one step when you restore an up-to-date image.

Full image backups are a lot more work, and take a lot more time, so do this only if you absolutely must prepare for a fast recovery from a full hard drive loss. And you will probably not be doing these backups daily, so you should also still routinely do one of the daily data backups described above.

To enable an image backup you would need to set up an external USB hard drive with capacity about twice as large as your internal one, and schedule running of disk imaging backup software like Drive Image 7 (see Appendix). If you do need to use this style of recovery, it is more complicated than merely copying files. But the recovery effort and time required is reduced dramatically compared to other options. This is the next level of disaster planning, for those that really need it.

Using Speech Recognition

I wrote this entire book using the speech recognition tools built into the Tablet PC. That said, for the first six months of owning a Tablet PC, speech recognition was merely a curiosity for me. I tried it, found it interesting, but never found it practical. What goes on?

The answer is easy: before I started the book (which I wrote from my home office) my work office was a cubicle with coworkers in easy earshot of my desk. Every time I tried using speech recognition I became very self-conscious of their presence. Imagine everything that you normally type or write being broadcast to everyone around you: e-mails, Word documents, everything. In a cubicle environment I became accustomed to coworkers hearing phone conversations but somehow sharing *everything* was just too much (for both me and for my coworkers who had to listen to me all day).

My conclusion is that unless you have a private office or a very secluded cubicle, you will probably not be using speech recognition as part of your work day. And so I have not given it much attention in this book.

But once working from a private space at home, all that changed. I now cannot imagine going without speech recognition. The combination of a pen interface and speech input is tremendously effective. My wrists and arms would be a carpal tunnel mess right now if I had been forced to type this whole book using a keyboard. So if you have a private work space, read on. If not, consider this for the future when you might have such a space, or consider it for at-home work.

Speech Recognition Tips

To get you going, I now defer to the fourth of the four Tablet PC tutorials that we started at the very end of Chapter 3. These are the tutorials that come with all Tablet PCs. You should take this fourth tutorial. It's good and tells all you really need to know to get started with speech recognition. Then keep these tips in mind during and after you work through that tutorial:

- Get the good headset described in the hardware and software chapter (Chapter 2); it makes a difference.

- At the outset, take about three or four of the eight optional training sessions offered during setup.

- After training and initial usage, every time you change the physical location of where you work, run the Microphone Adjustment wizard to set your volume adjustment correctly. The acoustics of a room have a large effect on volume and resulting accuracy.

- Silence really is golden; room quietness makes a huge difference in recognition accuracy.

- Keep the on-screen keyboard open and ready for making instant corrections as you dictate words.

- I had no luck with the voice commands available with speech recognition; they just never fit into my workflow. I used dictation for text input only, and I then used the pen as a mouse on menus and on the on-screen keyboard for everything else. The one exception to this is using the Spell That voice command, which I found I used fairly often.

- If you are an instant messenger user, one very cool use of speech recognition is during your instant message sessions, but see the next point.

- You have an option to use the Text Preview capability where dictated text is displayed in a small window above the Tablet PC Input Panel, and then manually sent from there to the receiving application. I almost never use that and instead always have text go directly to the application. However some applications strip out all spaces between words (AOL Instant Messenger does this) and that's a good time to use Text Preview; it for some reason prevents this space-stripping.

Chapter 5 Strategies for Using Digital Ink

The Need for a Strategy

An occasionally heard criticism of the Tablet PC from those who have not used it very much is that handwriting recognition is still spotty. The implicit assumption is that near perfect handwriting recognition is a requirement for productive use of the Tablet PC. I could not disagree more.

First of all, let me say that I agree handwriting recognition on the Tablet PC needs improvement, and I look forward to the consistent improvement that I am sure will come over time. I still occasionally get frustrated when I have to rewrite or type out words that don't convert correctly.

Don't Convert Everything to Text

But the assumption that near flawless handwriting recognition is a precondition of productive use of the Tablet PC is wrong and is usually the result of not learning good usage strategies for the Tablet PC. These strategies include being selective about when you actually convert handwriting to text. Remember in Chapter 1 of this book I said the first time I tried the Tablet PC I gave up within 5 minutes. The reason I gave up is that I tried writing notes while converting everything I wrote to text. If you do this, you will get frustrated. Particularly if you have not practiced a bit with writing on the Tablet PC and converting writing to text.

Sources of Old Habits

One reason this conversion mode of Tablet PC usage was the first thing I tried is that I was accustomed to other pen-based devices that did not do a good job of recording and storing pen strokes as digital ink, and which relied on conversion to text instead. The Palm line of handheld devices and the Pocket PC are examples of devices that convert all handwriting to text automatically and normally do not store digital ink; you are not given a choice. It became a habit for me to always expect this conversion.

Lower powered pen-based devices such as these do not have the graphical rendering and storage capabilities needed to adequately work with ink as the target medium for your pen input. Text characters store much more compactly than graphic images do, and text is displayed on the screen with much lighter computational requirements than ink. With these earlier, less powerful devices, programmers had no choice. They were required to write software that virtually forced the user to convert everything to text; otherwise the user would find the device useless. So I along with most PC pundits arrived at the Tablet PC with the expectation that conversion to text was also the primary modality for use.

This natural bias toward text conversion and storage is also a result of long-time usage of text-based programs on personal computers. One reason we came to personal computers is to enable the creation of nice cleanly formatted typed text on our computer screens and on our printed output. To rely instead on target text that looks like handwritten paper-based scrawls appears to be a giant step backward.

What makes digital ink in fact a practical target input and storage medium for the Tablet PC is that the Tablet PC really is best used neither as a slightly more powerful Palm nor as a pen-input-based computer. It's a new category of device with new ideal use strategies.

So my hope is that you will recognize the ideal usage patterns of the Tablet PC and the mainstream opportunities these present. And my hope is that you then put aside expectations of a pen-input computer for creating long text documents and embrace the Tablet PC for the new automation opportunities it creates. The strategies presented below will hasten that discovery process.

When to Type? When to Ink? When to Convert?

After many months of using the Tablet PC eight to ten hours a day, I have some opinions and optimal approaches for deciding whether to use ink or converted text and, for that matter, whether to even use the pen at all.

First of all, if you followed the configuration advice in the earlier part of this book then you know I recommend that while you're sitting at your desk you use your tablet with a keyboard, mouse, and external monitor, just like a regular computer. There are some exceptions to this, when the pen is even easier at your desk than a keyboard and mouse (such as when drawing graphics or brainstorming). But keyboard typing is generally the best way to go when you are at your work desk and have access to an external keyboard, mouse, and monitor. The rest of the strategies below are for use when you are *away* from your desk.

Most times when using the Tablet PC away from your desk, the pen format of input is desirable. The Tablet PC form factor is nice. It's pleasant to hold the Tablet PC in your hand and use it like a pad of paper. It's comfortable to sit on the couch and work casually on it. And in meetings, it's usually the only way to go (see section in Chapter 1 about reasons to use a Tablet PC in meetings). In all these cases, the decision really is whether to use ink as your final target or convert to text. This decision should be made based on a number of factors that should be weighed together.

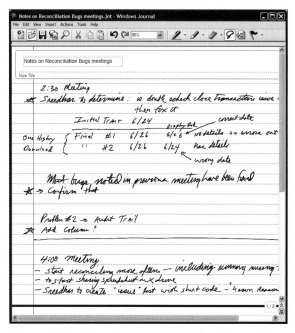

Figure 5-1. Meeting notes are often best left unconverted, to take advantage of hand-drawn tables, expressive highlights, and to show relationships among the notes.

Base Decisions on Text Volume

The first and most important strategy to decide between leaving your writing as ink or converting to text is to base the decision on the *volume* of text you are writing.

- If you are taking routine meeting notes, use ink as the final target. I find that during note taking, the ability to circle segments, create sketches or tables, sketch stars next to key points, and use pen-based highlighting tools all favor leaving the notes as ink.

- If you are recording short amounts of text, say a few words or even as much as a sentence or two, use the Tablet PC Input Panel and make converted text the final target. I use the optional "Write Anywhere" feature of the Tablet PC Input Panel if I am writing more than a few words, and this makes text conversion easier for me.

- A third strategy is to initially record your writing as digital ink and later convert it to text. For moderate-length text this is the strategy to use. Use this strategy if you later need to distribute meeting notes to colleagues and your handwriting is hard to read. It's not a great strategy because the longer you write without converting to text right away the less clean your writing will become (you get lazy). This makes it less likely to convert cleanly when you do finally get around to converting it. Plan on making lots of corrections. Also, most note-taking applications that allow this sort of conversion after the fact, like Windows Journal, present a somewhat cumbersome interface for making corrections.

- Some applications, like MindManager for the Tablet PC, have a well-thought-out delayed text conversion mode. You can read more about this in the brainstorming chapter (Chapter 11), but here is a summary of how it works. You first collect your initial thoughts in ink. When finished you are then given a chance to convert the inked text by cycling automatically through one segment at a time. The handwritten segments are clearly displayed one at a time, next to a first-guess at recognition, so that easy and quick correction if needed is possible. I use this approach quite often and it works very well.

Base Decisions on Intended Use of Target Text

Second, base your decision about text conversion on how you will use the target text later.

- For text such as routine meeting notes, which I rarely refer to again, but take just in case I need to, I use only ink and don't convert. The extra effort to convert to text just isn't worth while.

- If I know I'm going to read and refer to writing more than three or four times, I seriously consider starting out in or converting later to text. Examples of this are important reused meeting notes, brainstorming, or any handwritten documents that I know will later get used a number of times.

- Any situation where subsequent computer processing of the text is required I convert immediately to text. For example, when creating file names during a save operation, or when creating a list I know I will want to sort alphabetically later on, I usually use the Tablet PC Input Panel or convert immediately. Specific examples are task list entries in Franklin-

Covey TabletPlanner and PlanPlus, the title block at the top of Windows Journal, or the title at the top of an MS OneNote document.

- Searchable text: one might think that recorded information that needs to be searchable should be converted to text. But keep in mind that applications like Windows Journal and Microsoft OneNote do an automatic conversion of handwriting to text and save the conversion invisibly within the document. That text is automatically searched on when a text search is run. So if there's a 90 percent conversion success rate, there is a nine out of ten chance that searched text will be findable without explicit conversion. Therefore there is generally no need to convert text that you want to search on later. You may want to convert key words within such notes to ensure that they are found, such as the note title, meeting title, and the spelling of proper nouns.

- And sometimes you have no choice at all, the application does not accept digital ink directly and you have to use the Tablet PC Input Panel to enter the information. Most applications that are not Tablet PC–enabled fall into this category.

Base Decisions on Your Need for Speed

If you're taking notes or using applications in a fast-paced meeting where you are recording high volumes of text, don't even consider anything other than ink. If the meeting is slow, and/or you are only writing down an occasional sentence, sure, convert text as you go.

Another example is brainstorming: when I start brainstorming the ideas flow fast, and I need to get them down quickly. I use only ink and don't even think about text conversion until a natural pause occurs and I have time to convert.

Use a Keyboard or Speech Recognition

If you are going to use a Tablet PC for extended real-text input, such as that needed to write a memo or document, then don't even attempt pen input. Rather, use a keyboard, or use speech recognition as I did for this entire book. Obviously this is inappropriate for use in meetings, but I rarely find occasions in meetings where I need to create long text documents (other than note taking which is usually better collected as ink). So, again, for long documents that really need text as the final output, plug in a keyboard or use speech recognition.

Use Windows Journal Instead of the Input Panel for Inputting Text

For applications that are not specifically designed for the Tablet PC, the only way to get text into these applications using a pen is to use the Tablet PC Input Panel. If the text you plan to input is more than a few sentences long, however, the Tablet PC Input Panel, even using Write Anywhere, can be quite cumbersome. The main problem is that the input panel interrupts what may otherwise be a steady flow of thoughts. With the input panel, you tend to write half a sentence at a time and then stop and correct each half sentence before you move on to the next one.

In these situations try instead writing rapidly in ink using Windows Journal, converting to text and correcting text only when finished. You can then copy the converted text into your non-enabled application. This is, by the way, a practical way to write text e-mails using a pen.

In Summary

Sometimes it takes a few experiments to decide when is the appropriate time to try to convert text, when digital ink is appropriate as the final target, and when to use the Tablet PC Input Panel. After practice this decision making will be swift and accurate. At the beginning, however, I suspect you will fumble a bit. No worries, that's part of the fun of learning a new skill. The key is to not do the majority of this learning while seated in a fast-paced meeting where your fumbling and obvious distraction from the meeting could be embarrassing. Give yourself some practice at home or perhaps in more friendly, slower-paced meetings.

PART TWO: Seven Key Work Management Activities

Chapter 6 Task Management

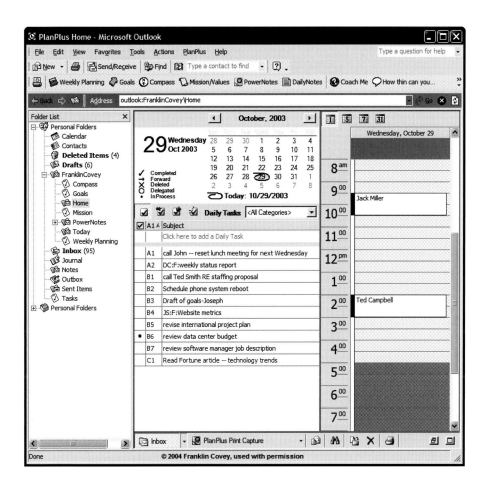

Getting Your Tasks under Control

Assuming you are in a busy management role you probably have hundreds of tasks assigned to you by others or by yourself each month. If so, of all the skills taught in this book, managing tasks effectively is probably the most important skill you can improve on as a work manager. It's a skill that can help you leave work earlier each night. It's a skill that will increase your sense of accomplishment. A skill that is key to effective use of your time, key to the perception by your superiors that you have your responsibilities under control, and if you have staff it is key to effective delegation and follow-up of work to those staff. And good task management is necessary for managing projects. The Tablet PC presents important solutions to these needs.

My productivity and effectiveness rose dramatically when I finally developed an effective and efficient personal system of task management. In the pages ahead I will describe in more detail how to use the Tablet PC and add-on software to implement task management activities. I will show you approaches that I and others have found successful in active management roles.

A Real Life Example

In Monday's operations meeting, the COO directs his attention to you and mentions an issue: the help desk is receiving sporadic reports that the internal website may be running slower than normal. After some discussion he assigns a task to you: to come to the next meeting with an explanation. In the midst of your note taking in your Windows Journal on your Tablet PC you make a note of that assignment, and place a Journal flag next to it to mark it as a to-do item. From related discussions you add other to-dos in the middle of your notes as well. As the meeting progresses and the topics move on to other managers, you sort your notes on the new to-do items, find the one about website issues, and give some thought to how you might complete this task. At that point, while the meeting is still going on, you bring up Outlook, click in the task pane within Outlook, and using pen input quickly enter a new task: "get copy of weekly web metrics report from Tom Yang." You set the due date on this task well before the next operations meeting.

During other slow parts of the meeting, you repeat these steps for any other action items that have been assigned to you or that you assigned to yourself. For any large tasks that you must spend significant time on, you examine your Outlook schedule for the days ahead and, using your Tablet PC, schedule blocks of work time to complete those tasks. During meeting events several old tasks are changed in priority; you mark those changes immediately in your system.

At the top of your Outlook task list you see an A-level task (meaning due today) that requires input from someone that happens to be in the room. As the meeting wraps up you pull that person aside and have a quick meeting that gets you the information you need.

You leave the meeting with all new tasks securely set and scheduled, with a few tasks freshly complete, and with the satisfying knowledge that you do not need to stay late that evening to clean up the loose ends from that or other meetings of that day.

This scenario is not artificial; I use this approach or one similar every day in the office, and it really works. It did not take long for me to get familiar with the technology behind this, and it did not take long to make it a habit. After starting to use this approach I quickly reached a sense of being in control of the many tasks coming my way and that sense of control has only increased with time.

Getting Tasks under Control Is Critical

Getting tasks under control is essential to becoming more productive at your job and essential to finding a way to leave work at a reasonable hour.

Having your tasks organized and under control makes you more efficient at accomplishing them; you actually spend *less* time finishing *more* activities. Why? Because when all your important tasks are clearly in front of you (and the tools you need are in your hand—that is, the Tablet PC) you can multi-task in meetings. You can take advantage of chance encounters with people and places. You can, during unexpected free slots of time, see and pounce on your most important tasks and get many of them done during "the holes in the day." And you can organize your day to attack tasks in optimum order.

But perhaps just as important is this: having your tasks under control changes your attitude. If you are like me, you probably tend to carry uncompleted tasks with you in your subconscious throughout the day (and sometimes night!). Uncontrolled tasks tend to nag at us. We carry a subtle sense of being behind the game, of being on the wrong side of the curve. A sense of something being there that should be done, something that we have been remiss about. This is often what drives us to work late nights with the thought: "If I work more hours I'll get this all done and this feeling will go away." However usually it is exhaustion that finally quenches the feeling instead, along with the thought: "I have worked far more hours than is reasonably expected; surely I can go home now." Unfortunately, without good task management we could be cursed to stay late night after night.

Once you get your tasks controlled this burden is lifted. It is such a relief to know you've identified and organized everything on your plate. It is a relief to clearly identify what is most important (and work on it first) and to know what can wait and how to defer it with appropriate follow-up. It is such a relief to be able to say to yourself: "That's all of it; I've got it all under control." Achieving this organized state enables you to know when you can leave the office guilt-free at the end of the work day. Your mind is free and clear to enjoy the evening at home or the weekend out and about.

And when your mind is free from the subconscious message "I am out of control," you can more effectively execute activities. You can plan to get at tasks before they become emergencies. When tasks are accomplished in nonemergency mode, they fall into place more cleanly and easily and with less expenditure of energy.

Using the Tablet PC to put an effective task management system into your work day is the single most effective thing you can do toward getting your work totally organized.

Automated Task Management Approaches

Our company had recently adopted Microsoft Outlook as its e-mail system so it was natural to try out Outlook's task management system. This was not the first time I'd tried to manage tasks with an automated to-do list like the one in Outlook. I've attempted this with many other automated packages including Palm handheld software synchronized with the desktop version of the Palm software. I have also tried software on the Pocket PC synchronized with Outlook.

But in the past, and again this time, I found that within a few weeks an automated to-do list quickly gets out of hand, and invariably I stop using it. What happens is that a large list of tasks builds up. These are tasks that I intend to get to but that I am vague about when I need to complete. Not wanting to lose sight of these tasks I do not delete them from the task list, and the task list grows to a size that I find either psychologically overwhelming to look at or just impossible to scan through. Of course I try assigning priorities to tasks, but then I end up with a large number of high priority tasks, most of which are important but not important for today. And so while they remain sorted high on the task list I constantly skip them as I use the list, and the list becomes weak and useless.

What changed all this and allowed me to finally implement an automated task management system that works was adopting a few simple concepts from the FranklinCovey time management system and installing the FranklinCovey PlanPlus for Outlook software to automate those principles. This, combined with some additional task management best practices I've learned, and the Tablet PC, kicked my task management capabilities into high gear. In this chapter I will share with you the lessons I learned from months of using these systems so that you can implement a similarly effective task management system for yourself.

Software Choices and Recommendation

There really are only two software choices for general task management on the Tablet PC and both are FranklinCovey products. As mentioned in the hardware and software chapter, Chapter 2, they are FranklinCovey PlanPlus 2.0 for Microsoft Outlook and FranklinCovey TabletPlanner; I'll repeat some of that discussion here.

Side Note: A third piece of software has recently come to my attention. It is an Outlook plug-in that automates the David Allen Getting Things Done approach to task management (that approach is covered briefly at the end of Chapter 7). This software is called Getting Things Done Outlook Add-In and is available at www.davidco.com. I have not yet taken a look at this software but am very impressed with David Allen's task management system. So if you are following his approach you may want to take a look.

PlanPlus 2.0 for Microsoft Outlook

Outlook, extended with PlanPlus 2.0 for Microsoft Outlook, is the centerpiece of my proposal for you as a work manager to get control of your tasks. My approach takes the task management system in Outlook and extends it to adopt the excellent FranklinCovey approach to managing tasks. I then add my own experience with managing tasks in an executive setting.

The core advantage of PlanPlus over TabletPlanner is full integration into Outlook, which gives you the ability to:

- use your enterprise Outlook system without the need for periodic synchronization, and

- take advantage of many added features of Outlook that are not available in TabletPlanner.

The downside of PlanPlus compared to TabletPlanner is that you need to use the Tablet PC Input Panel to input your tasks and appointments; more on that later in this chapter.

TabletPlanner

An alternative to PlanPlus is TabletPlanner. Designed from the ground up to be used on a Tablet PC, FranklinCovey TabletPlanner makes extensive use of ink throughout all of its functionalities. It also does an excellent job of imitating the paper versions of FranklinCovey personal organizers. It is a nicely integrated package with a consistent user interface.

The downside of TabletPlanner is that its database resides separate from Outlook. So if you're already committed to Outlook within your enterprise for calendar and task management, you'll need to constantly synchronize between these two software packages. TabletPlanner users have mixed opinions as to the effectiveness of doing this synchronization. If synchronizing with an enterprise Outlook system is acceptable to you this may be a perfect choice. I encourage you to decide for yourself by downloading a trial copy of TabletPlanner and seeing if it meets your needs; many users find it quite good. Still, as you'll see, my original recommendation remains to use the FranklinCovey PlanPlus in combination with Outlook.

Synchronize with a PDA

One other point: PlanPlus allows you to synchronize your Tablet PC Outlook-based task, contact, and schedule data with your PDA (Palm or Pocket PC). Since adopting the Tablet PC I've found I no longer use a PDA and so do not cover the steps in this book. However many Tablet PC users do still continue to use their PDAs so I recommend you consider using this feature of PlanPlus; the PlanPlus documentation covers it well.

TabletPlanner does not have the ability to synchronize directly with a PDA.

Key Principles of Task Management

Before going into the operation of the FranklinCovey PlanPlus or TabletPlanner software, let's cover the key task and time management principles from which the software was designed.

Tasks versus Appointments versus Projects versus Operations

First let's get some definitions in place. A *task* is a reasonably small unit of work that can be accomplished in one or two sittings and usually by one person. A task may or may not be assigned a particular date by which it should be done. A task is the sort of thing that you write on your to-do list. Note however, if a task is so time-specific that it actually needs to have a clock time assigned to it on a given day, it would be better to define the activity as an *appointment* and enter it on your calendar; don't put it on your *task* list.

Projects we will define here as work units that require multiple associated tasks, tasks that may individually end up on your to-do list. Projects that are large enough to warrant their own set of planning and follow-up meetings are best managed using formal project management techniques, not just a to-do list.

And similarly, operational environments that have repeated tasks and work steps are best managed by dedicated workflow systems, either manual or automated. If you process one hundred invoices a day, you would not put them on a to-do list; rather, other systems are better suited for that kind of work.

But even in the midst of a well-managed and systematic project management or operational organization, myriads of loose-end tasks arise that do not fit smoothly into the formal systems. These are the sorts of tasks that tend to fall through the cracks because they often lie outside of the daily operational flow, and they usually have less defined processes and timeframes. All organizations and staff have such tasks. Organizations that are still defining operational procedures, or that are growing or changing rapidly, have lots of them.

And regardless of project and operational excellence, at the senior management level of organizations few predefined processes exist, nor should they. Senior managers' activities are usually newly defined at the time of each new initiative or crisis.

Tasks from this wide range of ad hoc origins are best managed individually, each on its own merit and timeframe. It's these tasks that the typical out-of-control to-do list fails to rein in. And it's these tasks that the following Tablet PC–based systems get under control so well.

Two Key FranklinCovey Principles

From the FranklinCovey time management system I've adopted two key manual principles that are incredibly valuable for a busy manager. And by the way, these principles don't even require a computer to implement. Don't worry though; there are major reasons why you bought that Tablet PC, and we will get to them in a moment.

The first principle is dividing tasks into two major categories: daily tasks and master tasks. And the second is using the FranklinCovey approach to prioritize tasks within these two categories using A, B, C lettering.

Daily Tasks versus Master Tasks

Daily tasks are those tasks that need to be done today or that can be assigned to a specific date or date range in the future. So for example if time reports for the previous week are due by close of business on Monday, and you must work and complete that task some time that day, then you would assign that task to that date. Again, note that if the task must be assigned to a specific hour during the day, it is better to call this an appointment and use your calendar system.

Master tasks don't need to be done right away and have no specific due date assigned to them, but they may need to be done at some point in the future. The master task list then becomes a running task list of lower importance tasks. The idea is that periodically, at least once a week, this master task list is visually scanned to identify whether, through time and changing circumstances, any tasks have become more urgent. If so, at that point the task is assigned to a day; in other words it is converted to a daily task.

This two-list concept, a daily task list and a separate master task list, is the concept that freed me from the endlessly long single task list that I described above as becoming eventually useless for daily use. I now have two lists, one that I examine several times throughout the day for immediate action (my daily list for that day), and a longer, less urgent list that I examine much less often to search for changes in priority of previously low priority tasks (the master task list). And using the FranklinCovey software as described below, tasks assigned to work on at a future date are hidden from view until that date arrives. This approach greatly unclutters my most important to-do list: today's. But it leaves me a structured and organized way to access lower priority and future tasks as well so they are not lost.

ABC Priorities

The A, B, C prioritization system complements the daily versus master tasks approach. It is simple but effective:

- Tasks that must be completed on a given day are assigned an "A" level of importance.

- Tasks that are important but can slip without impact for several days are assigned a "B" level of importance.

- And tasks that are relatively unimportant but still at least loosely associated with a given time frame are assigned a "C" level of importance.

To these letters you then append numbers, for example A1, A2, B1. The numbers indicate the order in which you intend to do those tasks within the letter category. So the idea is that you would complete a task designated as A1 first, then the task designated A2, and onward until the entire A list was completed. At that point you would start on tasks within the B category, starting with B1. Then move on to category C.

The FranklinCovey Priority System

The A, B, C priorities system is based on the FranklinCovey four-quadrant system of identifying what activities are important in your day and life. We won't cover the four-quadrant system here, rather just the time management details you need to make a task management system viable. A full study of the FranklinCovey four-quadrant system is worthwhile when you have time later. For a complete study, I recommend two books that are referenced in the Appendix: *First Things First* and *To Do Doing Done!*

To make the system effective you should be cautious with your assignment of A category tasks. Only designate tasks within A if they absolutely must be due that day. Typically I have two or three A category tasks in any given day, often fewer or none. And over months of using this system, I've found that C category tasks are better not placed in the daily list but rather left in the master task list (more on the reason for this is discussed in the master task list paragraph below). So the bulk of your tasks on any given daily list will most likely be in the B category. And therefore the number-designations you assign to those B tasks becomes an important guide to which tasks you actually may do on a given day, and to which tasks are likely to slip to subsequent days.

This ability to slip tasks to subsequent days is an important one, and it is automated within the software. It serves two important purposes: making sure that important tasks stay on your radar from day to day until you complete them, and showing you tasks that may in fact not be important after all. This latter is shown by the fact that tasks have slipped for days and days without impact. In the latter case, you should consider moving a task back to the master task list or consider moving its due date out to a week that is less busy.

The Key Benefit of This System: Clearly Signaling When You Can Go Home

To me, the real beauty of the master versus daily tasks and especially the A, B, C priority system is that it lets me know when I can go home for the day. When I first started using the system I was amazed at the sense of relief and freedom from guilt that I would feel when I could look at my list at a reasonable hour and confidently state "all really important tasks for that day are complete, I can now go home."

This point is worthy of more discussion. Unfortunately many of us get in the habit of working late every night. If you are in this situation, I suspect your first reaction to this comment is to state proudly: "I am an important and busy person and I have just too many things to do. This is the cost of being such an important person, a cost that I must accept, now that I am making the big bucks." As many of the Covey books point out, this is usually an incorrect conclusion and one that can and should be corrected. There are chapters in Stephen Covey's books written about why this is so, but briefly the idea is that over time one loses perspective of the real importance of things, and in that blur all things at work are perceived as urgent. Without correction, every day one becomes trapped in a never-ending stream of urgent work tasks that end only when exhaustion kicks in or when higher levels of urgency call you home. Many of us are in this situation now and leaving work at a reasonable hour is difficult if not impossible.

What makes this situation hard to correct is that at the late hours of a work day one is often too tired to accurately judge which tasks really can be postponed. Or worse, because of endless meetings or poor prioritization throughout the day, the really important tasks have in fact been delayed to the end of the day and really must be done before leaving. So the Franklin-Covey system of classifying a short list of tasks that absolutely must be done on a given day (the A list) allows you to, at the end of the work day, clearly decide whether you need to stay late or not. You simply check to see if your A list is done or not. If it's not done you stay knowing you must. If it is complete and you have worked a reasonably full day you can leave without guilt. We'll talk more below about strategies to make sure you get to your A list at a reasonable point in your day. This is one of the many points where the role of the Tablet PC kicks in.

Role of Software and the Tablet PC in Task Management

As mentioned previously, none of the activities described above really depends upon the Tablet PC. In fact the system described above doesn't even require a computer at all. Note that this approach has been used in paper-based FranklinCovey systems for years. A software based system is better.

How Software Helps

There are several advantages to using a software-based task management system on any computer. Perhaps the main advantage in the area of task management is the automatic forwarding of incomplete tasks to the next business day. Without a computer you need to manually copy any uncompleted tasks to a new day's list. If you forget to do this and start on a fresh day's list with only its own originally assigned tasks, you will lose track of many important tasks. And it's just less work to let the computer do the forwarding for you. Since many if not most of your B level tasks will be forwarded from day to day, automatic forwarding which a computerized approach gives you is a big value here.

There are other advantages to a computer-based test management system:

- **Integration with e-mail and other desktop systems**: A lot of your tasks will arrive by e-mail so the ability to easily copy or convert them into a task is convenient. And your ability to copy task information into e-mails to notify others is similarly useful.

- **Sorting and searching**: You'll see in the sections ahead that the ability to search for all tasks you have assigned to a given individual is incredibly useful and easy in a software-based system. Optional techniques are also shown for classifying and sorting on classified tasks. And of course being able to sort on task priority is important as well.

- **Single point of work focus**: More and more of what you do at work is done on your computer and it only makes sense to include your tasks system there as well.

You might be wondering, "Can't I use my desktop or laptop instead of the Tablet PC?" This is a valid question. The PlanPlus software, for example, was not designed specifically for the Tablet PC. In fact I first started using it before I owned a Tablet PC. If you are reading this book as part of a decision-making process around buying a Tablet PC, I recommend you consider installing PlanPlus now on your desktop computer (assuming you are an Outlook user). Doing so will help you decide whether the overall management approach that I am advocating will work for you. You will find that most if not all the originally intended task management benefits of the PlanPlus software can be realized on a desktop. However, that said, the added benefits of the Tablet PC for task management are enormous.

How the Tablet PC Changes the Game

The portability and at-hand nature of the Tablet PC and specifically the ability to use it discreetly within meetings doubles the effectiveness of the Franklin-Covey software and any automated task management system for that matter.

Without the Tablet PC, printed copies of your system must be made to carry to meetings, or synchronization with much less powerful PDAs is required.

But the primary advantage, and a common theme of this book, is the ability to effectively leverage the "meeting hell" that many of us end up in nearly every day. Having an *up-to-date, easy-to-edit, full-powered* version of your electronic task system at hand, while sitting through hours of meetings, is a valuable way to leverage that meeting time. Here's why.

Task management within meetings

First, as described in the scenario at the beginning of this chapter, as tasks are added to your responsibility list in meetings you can add them and or delegate them within your automated system right in the meeting; this prevents you from forgetting to do this later. With urgent tasks you may even act on them electronically right in the meeting (by sending an urgent e-mail or AIM to a colleague or subordinate, for example, assuming you have wireless network access).

Second, the decisions made in a meeting will often cause many of your tasks to change in importance. Having the active list in front of you during a meeting allows you to reprioritize tasks in your list as business priorities change in the meetings (if you're lucky, maybe one of your A level tasks for that day will be eliminated in that meeting!).

Third, it is good to have updated A level tasks in front of you and to glance at them often throughout your meetings because you will find that there are many occasions where the people you need to talk to, to accomplish the A level tasks, are right in the meeting or can be found through other people in the meeting.

Task management after meetings

Fourth, having your A level task list clearly visible as the meeting concludes is a valuable way to ensure that your after-meeting activities are properly prioritized and acted upon immediately. Some of the most wasteful time during the day is immediately after meetings before you have a chance to get back to your desk and check your priority list. This is the time when low importance activities are often imposed upon you by others, who either grab you in the hall or leave seemingly urgent matters waiting for you on your desk which you may feel tempted to attend to immediately. Again, your goal is to act on your A level items first. So having them clearly in mind as you leave the meeting will allow you to accurately prioritize any new items that are handed to you after a meeting and prioritize other distractions that confront you.

Knowing when to leave a meeting

Fifth, there have been times during a mid or late day meeting when on review of my updated A list, I will realize that my opportunity for completing a specific A level task that day will be missed unless I do something immediately. In those situations, if possible I actually excuse myself from the meeting to go act accordingly. Meeting appointments may often seem important but once in the meeting it is not unusual to find that the value of the meeting to you is actually low. Having a view of your A level list in front of you allows you to easily make a judgment call to make an early exit. This is another strategy to prevent you from having to work late night after night.

Task management on the run

And of course not everything you do with the Tablet PC is done inside a meeting. Your entire up-to-date task list is available to you when huddled next to a subordinate's or colleague's desk, talking in the hall, driving between locations, having coffee in the coffee room; any time you need to glance at your current priorities they're there.

Using FranklinCovey PlanPlus Software

Enough introduction; let's get going with the software. PlanPlus 2.0 for Microsoft Outlook is an add-on software package for Microsoft Outlook. It modifies and runs on top of your already installed Outlook software. It leaves Outlook appointments, contacts, and e-mail functionality essentially unchanged, though it does integrate with them. It enhances Outlook's task management capability greatly. And it adds to Outlook these capabilities: note taking, document management, and goal setting. This chapter focuses on the task management functions; chapters ahead focus on the others.

Getting Started

Installation

If you'd like to try out the software before purchasing it, you can download it from the FranklinCovey website. This is a large download, primarily because several multimedia tutorials are downloaded at the same time, so if you have a slow Internet connection set aside some time. During installation, when asked which Outlook view to make default, choose the FranklinCovey Home screen (you can change this later if you want).

Side Note: If you run the introductory tutorial on first launch, you'll see that the FranklinCovey PlanPlus software also has extensive goal-setting tools that can be used to help identify your important tasks. We'll cover the goal-setting approach in a later chapter. In this chapter we are going to focus on using the basic task management features.

You need to have Outlook already installed before you install PlanPlus. Outlook 2000 or later is required.

When you install the PlanPlus software the installation actually modifies your copy of Microsoft Outlook. It adds a new view to Outlook that combines many of the standard elements of Outlook and, most importantly, modifies the task view within Outlook to create the master and daily task list paradigm.

Launching PlanPlus

After installing PlanPlus, every time you launch Outlook the PlanPlus modifications are launched automatically. The center point of these modifications is a new Outlook view called the PlanPlus Home screen, and it will become your new command post for just about everything you do in Outlook. This screen combines the most important elements of Outlook and PlanPlus into one unified screen. And while you still may navigate away from this screen often (say to check sent mail and the like), you will nearly always return immediately here.

Below is the default FranklinCovey PlanPlus for Outlook Home screen as first installed within Outlook 2002. (See Figure 6-1.) If you have Outlook 2003 things look a little different and we will cover that in a moment. Also note that if you already have tasks in the Outlook task section, many if not most of these tasks may seem to disappear when you first install PlanPlus. Don't worry, they are probably now in the master task view which we will cover ahead.

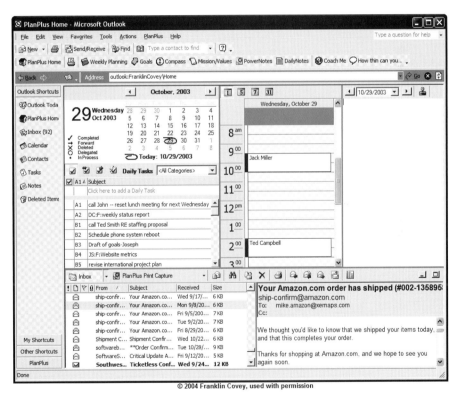

© 2004 Franklin Covey, used with permission

Figure 6-1. Default screen layout in PlanPlus for Outlook 2002.

Customizing the View for the Tablet PC

PlanPlus 2.0 for Microsoft Outlook was designed for both keyboard users and tablet users, and the busy layout of the screen is the result of a compromise to please both. I recommend you immediately make some changes to the screen above to make this work better with your Tablet PC. We're going to remove some panes that tend to clutter the small screens that Tablet PCs generally offer, and make some other changes.

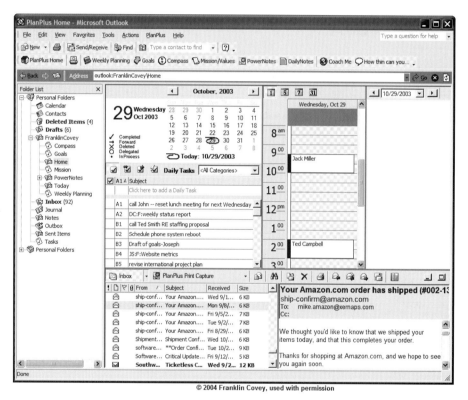

© 2004 Franklin Covey, used with permission

Figure 6-2.   Folder List view inserted on left side; Outlook Shortcuts Bar removed.

Using the Folder List View

First of all, for users of Outlook 2002, if you're still using the icon-based Shortcuts bar on the left side of Outlook, I recommend you replace that with the Folder List view that Outlook 2002 offers as an option. It provides you a much more accurate view as to what's going on within Outlook, and you're going to need this folder view for when you start using the PowerNotes and eBinder features of PlanPlus which are described in later chapters. To switch to the folder view, go to the View menu and select Folder List. At this point the Outlook Shortcuts bar is still visible so immediately go back to the View menu and click on Outlook Bar menu item to hide this pane. Your window will look like Figure 6-2.

Depending on whether you're working in a Microsoft Exchange server environment typical for large organizations or in an Internet e-mail environment, and depending on whether you've added additional Personal Folders to Outlook, your folders on the left side may look a little different from what you see in Figure 6-2. The configuration there is for an Internet e-mail environment.

Note that all your key shortcuts are still present: Calendar, Contacts, Inbox, etc., and that FranklinCovey now dominates many of the folders present.

For both Outlook 2002 and Outlook 2003 users, on the right middle part of the screen you'll notice a large blank pane. This is the PlanPlus Daily Notes section and is useful only if you use a keyboard. As a Tablet PC user I recommend that you remove this pane since much of your Tablet PC work will be done away from a keyboard. The only way to use this in meetings is using the Tablet PC Input Panel, something I do not recommend for note taking. If you are coming from the FranklinCovey paper planner world you may miss the ability to associate a notes page with each daily view. However you can still take handwritten notes and date them for each day; they are collected and displayed in a separate PlanPlus notes view which we will get to in the note-taking chapter.

To eliminate this typed notes section, you merely drag the boundary between the Schedule section and the Daily Notes section to the right until the Daily Notes section has completely disappeared. (See Figure 6-3.)

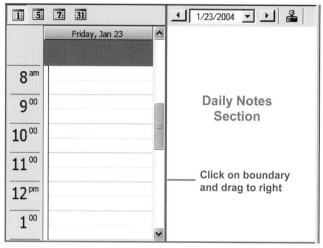

Figure 6-3.   Eliminating the Daily Notes section.

The other change I recommend is hiding the e-mail preview pane in the lower right corner. Again, with the small size of Tablet PC screens this takes up too much screen real estate and offers little value in its compressed form. Use the E-mail Preview Toggle button, located just above the e-mail section, to remove this pane. (See Figure 6-4.) Note that this e-mail preview toggle button will only be visible if the overall Outlook window has been expanded to a certain size. If you are viewing the Outlook window with your Tablet PC in portrait mode it is likely that this toggle button will be hidden. If you don't see this button, switch to landscape mode and widen your Outlook window.

Figure 6-4.   Use the E-mail Preview Toggle button to hide the e-mail preview pane.

Once you've made all these changes, your Home screen should look like the screen shown in Figure 6-5.

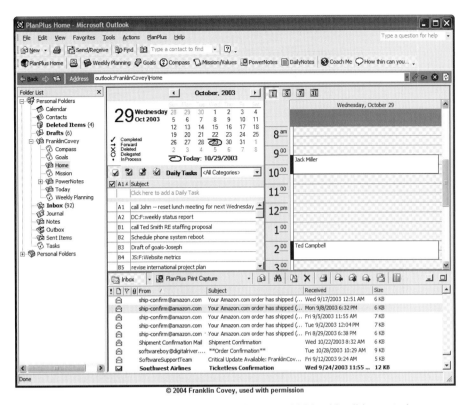

© 2004 Franklin Covey, used with permission

Figure 6-5. PlanPlus Home screen in Outlook 2002 with all layout changes made.

It's now a lot less cluttered and ready for use on the Tablet PC.

Unlike other Outlook 2002 views, this PlanPlus modified view combines the full schedule, e-mail, and task list all on the same page. I find this combination to be very useful, allowing me to scan and edit all important information at once.

Outlook 2003

With Outlook 2003 there are two folder views: one dedicated to mail alone which is shown by default, and then the complete folder view similar to Outlook 2002. The mail folder view includes just mail folders (and is called All Mail Folders; see middle left pane in Figure 6-6). This a reasonable approach since most of the folder hierarchy you need to work with is all within this area including, surprisingly, many non e-mail folders used in PlanPlus such as their PowerNotes folders (more on that in later chapters).

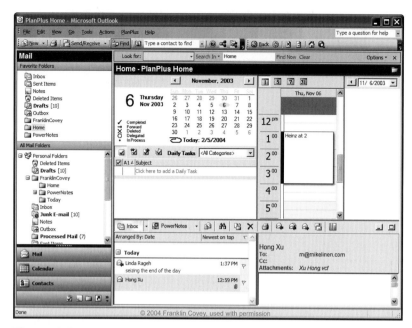

Figure 6-6. PlanPlus Home screen in Outlook 2003

Lacking from this All Mail Folders view is the Tasks folder, which I suggest later in this chapter you use during your weekly review. Because of that I still advocate displaying the full Folder List view in Outlook 2003 as well. When you select that view it replaces the Favorite Folders and All Mail Folders panes on the left side of the window. (See Figure 6-7.)

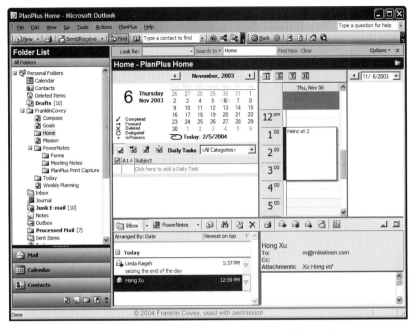

Figure 6-7. PlanPlus Home screen in Outlook 2003 with Folder List view added.

Here's how you select it: at the bottom of the left side of the Outlook window are a number of icons that represent nondisplayed Outlook features. (See Figure 6-8.) One of them represents the Folder List; clicking that icon switches to this view.

Folder List
View

Figure 6-8. How to add the Folder List view in Outlook 2003.

Get familiar with using this icon because the Folder List view tends to slip away in Outlook 2003; you'll need to know how to bring it back when you need to.

With Outlook 2003 you will still need to make the PlanPlus modifications described above. If you have made all the modifications, your Outlook 2003 window should look like Figure 6-9 below.

Throughout the rest of this chapter and this book we will be showing a mixture of Outlook 2002 and 2003 screen shots. All functionality is nearly identical across the two packages. The exception to this is in Chapters 7 and 8 where some advanced uses of Outlook 2003 are highlighted.

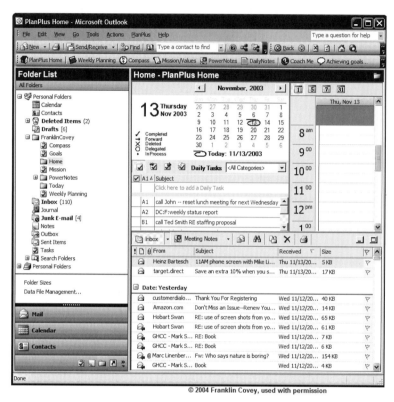

© 2004 Franklin Covey, used with permission

Figure 6-9. PlanPlus Home screen in Outlook 2003 with all layout changes made.

Expanding the Task and Schedule Panes

One more thing: you may notice that in the FranklinCovey PlanPlus Home screen the task pane, and to a lesser extent the schedule pane, are given a relatively short window within the Home screen. You can increase the size of the task and schedule pane by clicking on the boundary between the task pane and the e-mail pane and dragging it down, making the e-mail pane smaller. Or you can temporarily completely eliminate the e-mail pane by clicking the minimize button at the far right corner of the e-mail toolbar. Here's the resulting view if you do this (see Figure 6-10):

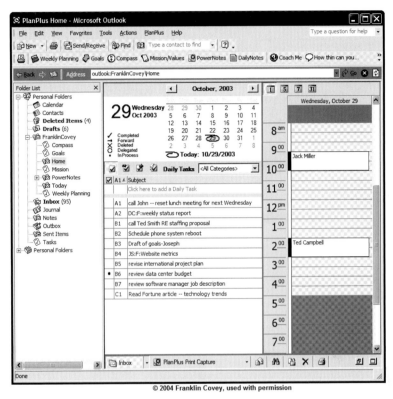

© 2004 Franklin Covey, used with permission

Figure 6-10. PlanPlus Home screen with e-mail pane hidden.

And note that using the same buttons you can also do the reverse: you can expand the e-mail pane to fill nearly the entire screen, hiding the task and appointment panes. This is virtually the same as clicking on the Inbox folder within the Folder List view on the left, except that it preserves the customized PlanPlus e-mail menu above the list of e-mails.

By the way, if you ever close this PlanPlus Home screen view, say because you navigate to the Sent Items folder, you can navigate back to the Home screen by clicking on the Home folder within the Folder List view on the left.

Removing the PlanPlus Toolbar

One more possible customization is to remove the PlanPlus toolbar. The Folder List view duplicates the functionality of this toolbar, and in fact as we work through the rest of the PlanPlus software in the chapters ahead you'll find that most of the buttons on the toolbar will lead you to nonoptimal screens. You might as well clear up some screen real estate for your small Tablet PC screen and avoid possible confusion.

To remove the PlanPlus toolbar click on the Tools menu and choose Customize. You'll be presented with the following screen. (See Figure 6-11.)

Figure 6-11. Removing the PlanPlus Toolbar.

On this screen uncheck the PlanPlus selection at the bottom. I promise you that you will not miss this toolbar.

Switching Between Master and Daily Tasks in PlanPlus

Regarding introducing the master and daily task system, note the bold label in the middle of the screen: Daily Tasks. (See Figure 6-12.) PlanPlus configures Outlook to show one task list at a time. To switch between displaying daily tasks and master tasks you use the icons to the left of the daily task label.

Figure 6-12.   Choosing between daily and master tasks.

Clicking on these icon buttons displays the respective types of tasks in the task list below the buttons.

This change that PlanPlus makes to Outlook, being able to view master tasks and daily tasks separately, is crucial. Of all the things that PlanPlus offers this simple addition is the most important. Use these buttons in order to view, edit, and enter tasks into the appropriate list (there are other ways to view your tasks which we'll get to in a moment).

New Task Headings

If you are accustomed to using Outlook's default task management capabilities, you'll probably notice that the installation of PlanPlus also modifies the headings at the top of Outlook's task pad. Instead of the sort-by column on the left and the checkbox column to its right, you now have the checkbox column on the far left and a priority column to its right with the label A1. (See Figure 6-13.)

Figure 6-13.   PlanPlus modifies the Outlook task headings.

And these two columns now behave differently than they do in the unnmodified Outlook world; we will cover these columns in a moment.

Entering and Using Tasks

Entering a New Task

Using the Tablet PC Input Panel

Storing tasks in handwriting is an option within TabletPlanner but not an option in PlanPlus. In PlanPlus you must use the Tablet PC Input Panel. As you know, the Tablet PC Input Panel immediately converts handwriting to text and inserts it wherever the insertion point is currently positioned. I prefer to have my tasks saved as text rather than ink handwriting, so using the Input Panel is my preferred input method anyway. My reasons for preferring tasks stored in text are as follows:

■ I visually scan my task list many times a day and I need them to be clearly readable.

■ The number of times I input tasks is much smaller than the number of times I read the task list, so the slight additional effort needed to use the input panel is worthwhile.

■ Each task subject entry is short in length so using the Tablet PC panel to input these few words, even in a meeting, is quite workable.

And if you feel strongly about using ink in PlanPlus, an add-on software solution called Tablet Enhancements for Outlook from Einstein Technologies (www.einsteinware.com) allows you to enter task information initially in ink, with a more friendly conversion to text than the Tablet PC Input Panel offers.

Two Methods of Task Entry

Entering a new task in PlanPlus is virtually the same as entering a task in the Outlook calendar view without the PlanPlus software added. Just below the line labeled Subject is a blank line labeled Click Here to Add a Daily Task; this is your entry point. (See Figure 6-14.)

© 2004 Franklin Covey, used with permission

Figure 6-14.   Task entry point is the blank line labeled "Click Here to Add a Daily Task."

You can use this entry point to create a new task in two ways: a quick entry method or a full entry method.

Quick entry method

To use the quick entry method just single-click anywhere on that blank line and that line will become editable. I prefer to click in the Subject field, the wide field at the right, because it then gets selected for editing and this is normally the first place you will be entering information about a new task. I then click on the Tablet PC Input Panel and I handwrite the name of my task. Conversion to text is automatic, and the text is deposited in the Subject field.

The next step is to click in the blank field below the A1 column and assign the correct priority. Note that if I do not enter a priority, the priority defaults to B when I click Enter.

Side Note: With PlanPlus 2.0, if at this point you click off that task, that task is not yet assigned. You need to click the Enter key on your on-screen keyboard while that task is selected to save it to your task list. If you forget this step and quit Outlook the task will be lost without warning, so be sure to remember to click Enter.

Full entry method of creating tasks

To use the full entry method at the tasks pane, instead of single-clicking on the blank line, you double-click on the blank line. This brings up a task entry dialog box as shown below. (See Figure 6-15.)

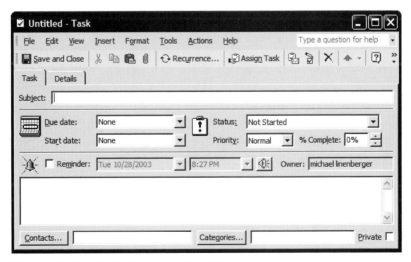

Figure 6-15. Outlook task entry dialog box.

This is the standard Outlook task entry dialog box. The most important tab is the Task tab, which opens by default and is illustrated in Figure 6-15. The most important fields are the Subject field and the two date fields. Note that there is also a Priority field which you should ignore, as this is left over from the old Outlook system and has nothing to do with the A1 field on the Home screen. And this brings up an important point: you cannot enter the FranklinCovey ABC priority using this full entry method. You enter the FranklinCovey priority only from the task list in the Home screen view, so you will need to go back to the Home screen to finish the entry.

Assigning Priorities

In assigning ABC priorities, I'm careful about creating too many A level tasks (remember to reserve these only for tasks that absolutely must be done on a given day) so I usually enter a B or a C priority. I then assign a number that generally ranks the priority of this task against other tasks for that day with the same letter level. I do not spend too much time trying to get the number portion of the assignment correct. One approach I use to simplify assigning a number rank is to use a rough high, medium, low priority, and to assume I have the numbers 1 through 10 available to assign. So if the task is high priority I give it a 1 through 3, if medium priority a 4 through 7, and if low priority an 8 through 10. It really doesn't matter if you already have a matching numbered task on your list because there's no problem repeating numbers. Later, when I review my entire daily list, I routinely reprioritize tasks anyway.

Impact of Setting the Start and Due Dates of a Task

The easiest way to set the dates in the task dialog is to click on the down arrow to the right of the Due Date field and pick a date from the popup calendar.

As you can see, setting the start and due date of the task on the Task tab display above is simple to do, but what is not immediately obvious is that setting these dates has quite a bit of influence on how the task is treated by the software. It's worth spending some time understanding this influence, and how to best make use of it.

Setting dates on the task will control what days that task will be displayed on in your task pane within Outlook. If the Due Date field is set in the future (and the Start Date field is set to the same or left blank) the task will appear on your task list on the date corresponding to the due date. The task will not appear on your task list until that day arrives. This feature keeps your daily task list uncluttered on any given day by not showing you tasks until you need to work on them.

If you set a start date earlier than the due date then the task will first appear on your daily task list the day of the start date. If you view your calendar into the future, you will see this task listed every day between the start date and due date. I have found little advantage to that behavior. And for other reasons I have found that setting a start date different from the due date is not a good practice; I will explain why later in this chapter.

Presence of an assignment date signifies a daily task

In understanding how assignment dates influence the behavior of your daily tasks within Outlook it is interesting to note that in extending Outlook, FranklinCovey PlanPlus software really has not modified its functioning dramatically. Most of the fields PlanPlus uses are standard Outlook fields. For example the Task tab you see above is just the standard Outlook task window and all the fields are standard Outlook fields; installation of PlanPlus did not add anything to this window. In fact you'll notice on the Task tab shown above that there is no master task or daily task designator field.

So how are daily tasks and master tasks differentiated? The way PlanPlus distinguishes between daily and master tasks is purely by the presence of a date entry in the Outlook date fields shown in the task tab above. Any task that has a start or due date entered is treated as a daily task. Any task without assigned dates is treated as a master task.

This is why if you already had tasks in Outlook before you installed PlanPlus your tasks seemed to have been automatically placed in either the master task view or the daily tasks view. Any tasks that you had dates assigned to were put in the daily task view, and any tasks that you had no dates assigned to were put in the master task view.

By the way you do not need to explicitly set these dates whenever you create a task. When you create a new task from the PlanPlus Home screen, if the daily tasks label is visible, PlanPlus automatically populates the Due Date (and Start Date) fields with the currently selected day's date. If the master tasks label is visible PlanPlus leaves the date fields empty when the task is created.

Converting the task from daily to master

In fact you can convert a daily task to a master task merely by removing the date entries. And you can convert a master task to a daily task by merely adding a date entry.

Assigning a daily task to a future date

When you create a new daily task from the PlanPlus Home screen, the dates that PlanPlus inserts in the task will match whatever day is selected in the monthly calendar at the time you create the task; normally that would be to-day. But if you click on a different day within the month calendar view just before you create a task that task will be assigned to the date that is displayed. For instance in the image below (see Figure 6-16) even though today (the cir-cled day) is February 11, note that the user clicked on February 20, and so February 20 is displayed to the left of the calendar. Any tasks created now will be assigned a start and due date of February 20.

© 2004 Franklin Covey. used with permission

Figure 6-16.   Day different from today selected in PlanPlus mini-month view.

Changing the assigned-to date of a daily task

If after creating a daily task you want to change the date assignment, you merely open the Task tab of the detailed task view (by double clicking on the task in the task list) and edit the assignment dates. Or you can drag the task from the list view to a date in the mini-calendar view (more on that below).

Significance of setting future assignment dates

Remember in PlanPlus a task set with a future assignment date will not ap-pear on today's daily task list until the value placed in the Start Date field arrives. At first that behavior may make you nervous; what if you are out of town on that day and you don't see the task appear that day, will you lose the task? The answer is no because once that day arrives and the task is dis-played, if you do not mark the task as complete it will then be automatically forwarded to every subsequent day as each day arrives, until you mark the task complete. This is the beauty of a computerized tasks system: automatic forwarding of uncompleted tasks. In fact Outlook, when forwarding tasks that are past their due date, changes the color of the task in the task list to red, thus highlighting the fact that they are overdue. So when you return from your trip the task will be there waiting for you on your daily task list no matter how old it is.

One exception to this being acceptable is this: what if that task was an A level task and so absolutely needed to get done the day that you were gone? Strategies to avoid this situation are discussed next.

Strategies for setting and using task dates

The first strategy to avoid the problem described above is to check your calendar for A level tasks assigned to the days you will be gone before you leave for a trip. This is not a bad strategy and it's always a good idea to examine your calendar before you travel.

A second strategy is to set a reminder to alert you some days in advance of the due date for A level tasks. While I normally do not recommend using Outlook reminders for tasks, this can be a good strategy and work well for really important tasks.

A third possible strategy you might use for A level tasks is to assign a start date that is earlier than the due date by some reasonable number of days. That way the task appears on your task list a little early. However I don't recommend this approach because this will lead to A level tasks appearing on days when they are not due, and the whole point of A level tasks is that they must be completed on the day they appear on your list. This brings up an interesting point about the use of start dates.

Using Start dates

First of all, should you even bother with populating the Start Date field? In my usage of this system I either leave the Start Date field blank or set it to be the same as the Due Date field. In other words I generally ignore the Start Date field. In fact if within the task tab you set a Start Date field first, the Due Date will automatically be set by Outlook to be the same as the Start Date field contents. And by default when you assign a task into the future from the PlanPlus Home screen PlanPlus assigns both the Start and the Due Date fields to be the same. So the default system behavior is to leave these two the same in effect ignoring the Start Date. And you'll see when we get to the Tablet-Planner section that no concept of a start date is even used in that system.

If in PlanPlus you *do* place a date in the Start Date field that is different from that in the Due Date field what will happen is this: Outlook will place an entry for this task on every day between the start and due dates, inclusively. As I said I never do this, but one reason you might want to do this is if the task is expected to take multiple days to accomplish and you'd like to see it appear on your to-do list well before its "due" date. If you must do this, here's what I recommend:

■ Start out by assigning a B level to the task, and if it really is critical to complete the task on your assigned due date, reprioritize the task to be an A level task when that day arrives. Placing the actual due date in the subject line will remind you to reprioritize when that day arrives.

■ If you think you are going to be working nearly full time on this task during those days, rather than making this activity a multiday task, consider putting it on your calendar either as an appointment that blocks out your calendar or as a nonblocking all-day event (these latter items get listed at the top of your schedule in Outlook).

Microsoft Project Start and Due dates

Note that using the Start and Due Date fields of tasks the way described above precludes integrating Outlook's tasks system directly with Microsoft Project. While Microsoft has provided a very handy integration that automatically populates those fields, I do not recommend using it. We are using the Start and Due Date fields much differently here. And tasks that go on your tasks list are usually at a different level of granularity from the majority of tasks that appear on a Microsoft Project list. Certainly you may move selected tasks from a project list to your tasks list as they become active for you. However I recommend you only make that transfer weekly and only for tasks that are due to be worked on that week (do not dump an entire project plan into your task list). And I recommend you do that transfer by hand, and rethink each task's granularity, title, and due date as you transfer it. There is a big difference in perspective between project planning and daily task assignment, so consider this as you add tasks from projects to your daily list.

Other Fields in the Task Entry Dialog Box

Reminder checkbox

I leave the Reminder checkbox on the task entry dialog box unchecked. And by the way I reconfigured Outlook to by default leave that checkbox unchecked when creating new tasks. You do that reconfiguration by going to the

Tools menu, Options, Preferences tab, click on the Task Options button, and uncheck the bottom choice: Set Reminders on Tasks with Due Dates. (See Figure 6-17.)

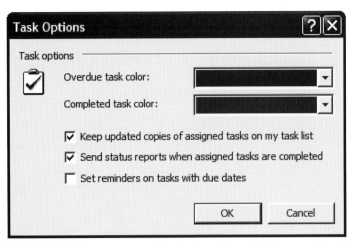

Figure 6-17. To prevent Outlook task reminders, uncheck bottom item.

I recommend you do the same. It just does not make sense if you are managing many tasks each day to have task reminder alerts popping up on your screen all day long. They are distracting and serve no purpose if they pop up in the middle of other activities. Rather you should make a habit to review your daily task list several times per day as you find available time to work on tasks. That way you'll be in the frame of mind to actually work on a task at the time that you look at a task.

Large text field

Perhaps 10 or 20 percent of the time I actually put text in the large text field at the bottom of the task tab. This is a very good place to put task details, and most commonly, is where I will paste details of a task copied from the e-mail that generated the task (automatic ways of doing this are described in Chapter 7). Or I may copy notes out of my notebook, notes that I collected when the task was assigned to me in a meeting.

Status, percent complete, priority, and owner fields

I ignore the % Complete field, and as I said earlier I ignore the Priority field. I also ignore the Owner field. All these fields are useful only when integrating

Outlook tasks with other Microsoft products such as Microsoft Project, or when using the formal Assign Task button described below.

The Status field maps to assignments made in using PlanPlus status symbols. See Chapter 7 for a discussion of this.

Assign task button

The other opportunity to use the Status and % Complete fields on the Task tab is if you take advantage of the task assignments features of Outlook. This is activated by clicking the Assign Task button at the top of the task input dialog (see image below). This feature is also available by right-clicking a task in the task list view. I recommend that you ignore this capability. However let me describe it anyway so that you know what you are missing.

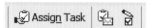

If your organization has a full Microsoft Exchange implementation, then you can use Outlook to electronically assign tasks to other staff using this button. When you do this, your copy of Outlook actually sends a special e-mail with the task attached, asking the recipient to formally accept or reject the task assignment. If it is accepted, the task is added to the recipient's own Outlook task list, and you automatically get back a message saying the task was accepted. At that point your copy of the task is modified to show that a formal assignment has been made, and your task is modified to show to whom it was assigned. Subsequently you can request special Outlook-based status reports from those recipients (sent using the button just to the right of the Assign Task button shown above) and when you receive those status reports back these fields (Status and % Complete) will be updated in your own task list to reflect the progress of work that your staff has made on the task.

This is a great concept and a great implementation. However every time I've tried to use it I've found that for various reasons, usually people-related, the team stops using this approach. The main problems are:

- It encourages the classic "dump and run" approach to delegating tasks which is largely warned against by management gurus. Rather, an important element of delegation is achieving buy-in from the staff that you have delegated to, and dropping a task assignment in someone's inbox is not consistent with this approach.

- Many staff prefer not to use Outlook's task system to manage their tasks.

I offer alternative methods of delegation in Chapter 7. However feel free to experiment with this technology, and be prepared for a large staff-acceptance curve.

Categories button

At the bottom of the task entry dialog box you'll see a Categories button. Clicking that button brings up the following dialog (see Figure 6-18):

Figure 6-18. Categories assignment dialog.

Using the dialog you can assign one or more categories to this task.

Why might you want to do this? PlanPlus allows you to filter on category types when you view tasks in the PlanPlus Home screen. You select a category to view in the PlanPlus Home screen by using the popup menu to the right of the task type label. See the field labeled <All Categories> in Figure 6-19.

Figure 6-19. Note the Categories popup at the right end of the PlanPlus tasks bar.

One use of this might be to create categories that correspond to projects. You could then view all the tasks associated with a given project using this category filter. Other uses of Outlook categories are discussed throughout Chapter 7.

Details tab

The second tab in the task input window is the Details tab. (See Figure 6-20.) I completely ignore the Details tab when working with tasks. This is another case where fields are useful only when integrating Outlook with other Microsoft applications such as Microsoft Project or perhaps with a database of some sort.

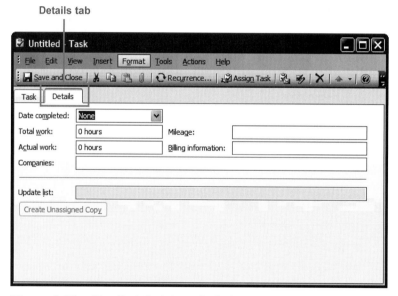

Figure 6-20.   The Details tab and window should be ignored.

Strategies for Adding and Managing Tasks

Deciding When to Add Tasks

One line of questions you may wish to ask when applying the system is: "When should I enter a task in my management system? When is a task too small to bother entering it in the system? Too big?" Here are a few thoughts on this:

■ Use the goal-setting techniques in Chapter 14 to record goals separately and use those to identify important tasks for the week.

■ If a task can take less than approximately one to three minutes to accomplish, and you have what you need at hand to do it, then do it immediately rather than writing it down for later.

■ Finally, see the section at the end of Chapter 7 that covers David Allen's approach to managing tasks and how to blend that with the Franklin-Covey system. This section focuses specifically on why and when to create tasks and takes task management to another level.

Daily Task List Management

Clearly, if you really are a very busy person, one side effect of allowing many B tasks to slip is that your B list on your current daily task list will tend to grow from day to day. If left unchecked that list can grow to the point of being unusable and you have defeated the purpose of having a task management system.

So the other manual component of this system is to periodically make a sober review of your current daily task list and manage it. Do this as follows:

■ First, rationalize your A list and move any tasks that don't really need to be done today to the B list.

■ Some slipped B level tasks, because of the delay imposed by the slip, may have now become urgent. If this has happened convert these tasks to the A level and plan to complete them immediately. Or assign them to someone who may have more time.

■ Scan through all your B level tasks and make sure the order number designation is roughly correct for each task; in other words confirm your B1 is really more important than your B5.

■ More likely you'll see that some of the B level tasks really were not that important after all. They were most likely written down when the heat of the moment gave them more importance than they were really due. Or situations may have changed and the true importance of the tasks has decreased greatly. This is the time to make sober decisions and move such tasks over to the master task list and out of daily sight.

■ If you find yourself reluctant to move tasks to the master task list and yet you are not getting them done, read the end of Chapter 7 for coverage of David Allen's approach to managing tasks and adjust your daily approach accordingly. Sometimes the language and specificity you use when writing a task influences your ability to act on it, and this section discusses that.

How often you need to do this management of your daily task list will vary greatly and I leave this up to you to discover. I try to do this every morning. Sometimes I am only able to do this every three or four days. If that fails, I certainly do a complete management job during my weekly review. It only takes a few minutes, so make a habit of doing this review.

PlanPlus offers a tool to help you to this reprioritizing more easily; it's called the Quick Prioritize window.

The Quick Prioritize Window

During your weekly planning session you may need to see all your tasks laid out in a larger view for easier reprioritizing. The Quick Prioritize window is useful for that.

You get to this window by clicking on the icon to the left of the daily or master tasks label. (See Figure 6-21.)

Quick Prioritize

Figure 6-21. Opening the Quick Prioritize window from the PlanPlus tasks bar.

Clicking this button launches the screen in Figure 6-22.

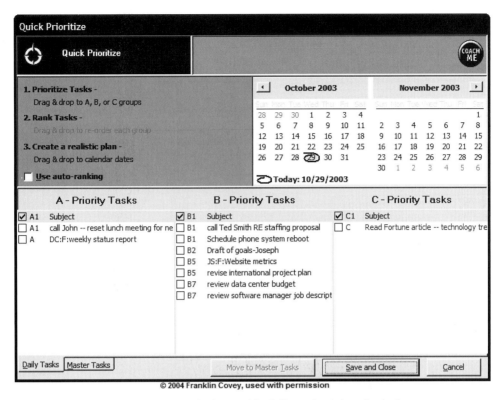

Figure 6-22. Quick Prioritize window, with daily tasks tab selected.

Here's how you might want to use the screen as you reprioritize tasks.

First of all note the daily and master tasks tabs at the bottom left of the screen; you will use this screen separately for each such set of tasks. Also note that when viewing the daily tasks tab you only see tasks assigned to a given date, a date which you choose in the upper right corner of the screen. That screen defaults to today's date when you open it.

Sole purpose of the Quick Prioritize screen

The sole purpose of this screen is to allow you to see an overview of your tasks and to reprioritize and redate them primarily using drag and drop. For instance if you felt that one of your B category tasks had now become urgent you could click and drag it from the middle pane over to the left pane, and it would automatically be reassigned as an A level task.

Similarly you can redate a daily task by dragging it to a different day on the month view in the upper right corner. As soon as you do that it disappears from view since it's no longer on today's list. When in the master task view this is a good way to convert master tasks to daily tasks; just drag them to the date you want to assign them to.

Use auto-ranking

Another nice feature of the screen is the Use Auto-Ranking checkbox in the upper left quadrant. Remember I said that I generally do not pay too much attention to how I assign numbers within a given letter category? Because of this, after a while in my list of tasks I can accumulate several at the same numeric level. For example, in Figure 6-22 you will see two B5 tasks and two B7 tasks. Generally that's not a problem. When I am finally ready to work on these tasks, however, I will need to stop and decide which one is most important, and that could delay action.

So if you check this box, PlanPlus automatically spreads these ranking numbers out so that you have only one instance of each number within a given letter category. Take a look at how the screen looks immediately after checking this box (see Figure 6-23).

Look carefully and compare this screen to the previous screen. Note how the B items have been reranked. If you use this feature you should then immediately go through the list and rank these the way you really want them ranked. That's because the software merely uses the order that the repeated items happened be listed in when it reranks, and that may not be your real priority order.

Manually reranking

Within the Quick Prioritize window you cannot type anything on the screen or open tasks by double-clicking them. So the way to change ranking numbers on tasks within a given letter category is to drag them up and down to their relative rank position in the list. If the Use Auto-Ranking checkbox is checked when you do this, the numbers will automatically be reassigned as you drag them. If it is not checked, then as soon as you are done dragging you should then check that box and the tasks will be renumbered to match the order you dragged them into.

One slight criticism of the Quick Prioritize screen I have is that the Franklin-Covey task-status symbols that we discussed earlier are not carried from the task view on the Home screen to this page. So if you are relying on the symbols to see which tasks you have assigned or to see which ones are in progress, you will not see that information here. You will see in Chapter 7 that I recommend not using those status symbols to indicate assigned tasks; I instead recommend putting the assignment information right within the title of the task.

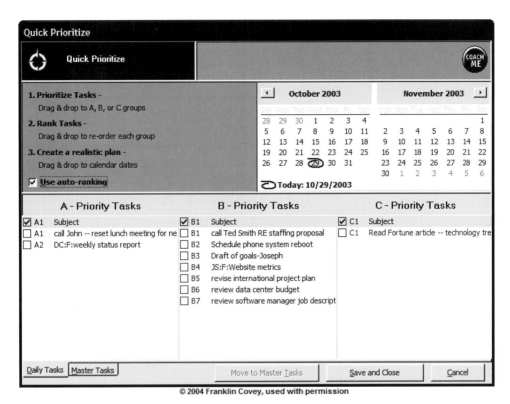

Figure 6-23. Note change in priority assignments in the B-Priority Tasks column after checking the Use Auto-Ranking checkbox (located in upper left of screen).

Caution when using Quick Prioritize

And another problem with the Quick Prioritize window is a minor glitch that will probably be fixed by the time you read this. The screen is designed to behave as a modal dialog box meaning you really shouldn't be able to do anything else on your computer until you close the window; and this is fine. The glitch is that unfortunately the software does not prevent you from doing other actions while the window is open, and those actions can leave your computer partially blocked and in an apparently unusable state. For example, if while this window is open you click on the Outlook task bar entry at the bottom of your Windows XP workspace (it will be labeled PlanPlus Home), the Outlook main screen will come to the front and likely cover the Quick

Prioritize window. The Outlook window at that point will be nonresponsive and appear frozen.

So after you open and use the Quick Prioritize window be sure to close it immediately when you're done. If you do get into the situation I just described all is not lost; just click the Outlook task bar entry again, and that should reveal the Quick Prioritize window so you can close it. If a click on the task bar does not work then right-click the Outlook task bar entry and choose Minimize from the in-context menu.

Dragging Tasks within the PlanPlus Home Screen

If you have only one or two tasks to reprioritize or redate, rather than use the Quick Prioritize window you can drag the tasks right within the PlanPlus Home screen. You can drag a task up and down within the task list and this will reset the FranklinCovey ABC priority to reflect its new position. And you can drag a task to the monthly calendar and drop it on the new date to which you want to assign the task. If you are working with the master task list view, dragging these tasks to a date on the monthly calendar converts them to daily tasks.

Master Task List: Assignment and Management

We've just covered managing your *daily* task list; now let's talk about managing your *master* task list. You can use the above Quick Prioritize screen to accomplish your periodic master task list review as we mentioned above. Or you can do it from the Home screen also as described above. Again, the point of the master list review is to identify any tasks that, due to changes over time, may have become more important and are ready to have a due date assigned to them; this effectively moves them to the daily task list. I do a quick scan of my entire master list roughly every three or four days to consider these reassignments; it only takes a minute or two. And I do a very complete review at least once a week.

The master task list helps you focus only on high priority tasks

One of my observations over time of using this system is that I find I advance a master task item to the daily list relatively rarely. In fact the reverse is usually true: I more often end up moving daily tasks I have postponed for a while to the master task list. This confirms my observation of how people often badly manage their work: people often waste time on low priority items at the expense of important ones.

You will probably see this happen once you start using a task management system: many tasks you assign yourself, either in the heat of a battle or in the euphoria of an inspiration, upon later reflection really are not that important. This highlights an important value of the task management system: without it you may tend to work on those tasks immediately as they come your way and as a result fail to leave time for higher priority tasks. Accurate use of a task management system improves that situation dramatically, leading to more efficient use of your time.

And this is the value of the master task list. Leaving tasks safely tucked away on your master task list is an effective way to acknowledge an idea without immediately spending time on it. Then time will test the task's importance, and you will either move it up in priority or lower it. You will quickly see that a good task management system is a valuable way to ensure that you go home at a reasonable hour.

Priority assignments on master tasks are less important

Another thing that you will find over time is that the priority designations within the master task list are less important to get right, and it's not worth spending much time on them. The reason for this is that you will and should rethink the priority when you move a task from the master list to a daily list; that's when to accurately assess a task priority. However you want to get the prioritization of the master list at least partly right so that when you do make a review of the master list, if your list is long, starting from the top allows you to focus on the most important tasks first. Again, you should use the A, B, C lettering system, but clearly A no longer means "must be done today." I think of A and B master tasks as "important but not yet timely." And I use the A or B distinction as relative rankings within that category. Since timeliness is the only thing that keeps these off my daily list, I review this portion of the master list relatively often.

I think of C level master tasks as "not important." These are items that are "nice to haves" and that I want to keep on my radar for occasional review. I may go weeks without reviewing the C list.

And finally, reassess this entire approach after reading the section on advanced task management at the end of Chapter 7. In that section an alternative methodology is proposed that makes much more active and specific use of the master task list.

Task Management Using FranklinCovey TabletPlanner Version 3.0

You may have opted for the FranklinCovey TabletPlanner software to manage your tasks instead of the PlanPlus for Outlook software. Compared to PlanPlus, its primary strength is that you can enter tasks, appointments, and contacts in ink and leave them in ink; PlanPlus requires you to store task information in text. Being able to enter tasks in ink allows you to enter tasks more quickly when on-the-go. The TabletPlanner's compromise is primarily for those who want to continue using Outlook: its database is separate from Outlook's database and so if you wish to continue using Outlook's task manager, appointments, or contact manager, you'll need to continually synchronize the two.

Navigating around TabletPlanner 3.0

The default TabletPlanner calendar workspace is well designed and well laid out. It inherits years of design of paper-based FranklinCovey planners. It includes five major sets of functionality: management of tasks, appointments, contacts, note taking, document management, and goal setting.

Before getting started on the application layout it is important to note this: one unusual behavior of the software compared to other Tablet PC applications is that the contents of the application window change depending on whether the Tablet PC is in landscape or portrait mode. Most other applications merely rotate the view when you change this setting on your Tablet PC. In landscape mode the TabletPlanner software displays two pages side by side (see Figure 6-24), just like viewing the facing and back pages in the paper version of the FranklinCovey planner system; in portrait mode one page is displayed.

The best way to learn the software is to place your Tablet PC in landscape mode with two pages displayed, and throughout the remainder of this chapter that's the mode we will assume.

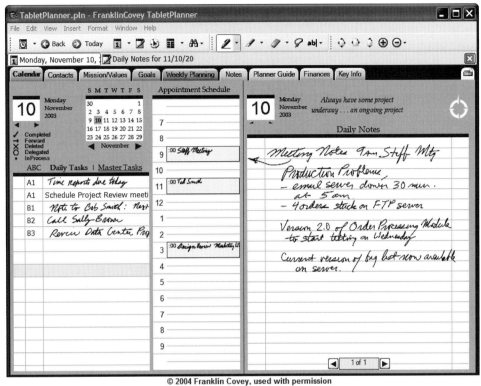

© 2004 Franklin Covey, used with permission

Figure 6-24. Two pages are displayed in TabletPlanner landscape orientation.

A Two-Page View

Another important concept is that the views that are populated in these two side-by-side pages are variable. They can be populated a number of ways. The default view is a daily appointment and task list on the left and a daily notes page on the right. Clicking on the Calendar tab in the left upper corner of the screen is what normally displays this default combination. If instead of the daily calendar view you've chosen the weekly or monthly calendar view, then that is what's displayed when you click on the Calendar tab. Those two views by default occupy both pages. We'll talk more about the two-page concept below in the section titled Switching Between Pages.

Switching Between Daily, Weekly, and Monthly Views

In order to switch between the daily, weekly, and monthly views, find the Day View button on the Standard toolbar; it should look like this:

But if you are in weekly view it will look like this:

And if in monthly view it will look like this:

There are two ways to use this button. If you click on the button itself it has the same effect as clicking on the Calendar tab. So if you have navigated away from the calendar view this is one alternative way to bring you back (though you'll probably use the Calendar tab more often for this purpose).

The more significant use of this button is to choose between daily, weekly, and monthly views within the calendar. If you click on the down arrow next to the button a menu drops down that allows you to switch these views. (See Figure 6-25.)

© 2004 Franklin Covey, used with permission

Figure 6-25.   Drop-down menu to switch between day, week, and month views.

The week view is illustrated in Figure 6-26. Note that you can enter tasks in the lower portion of this page. The month view is shown in Figure 6-27. Note that appointments are visible, but no tasks can be directly entered.

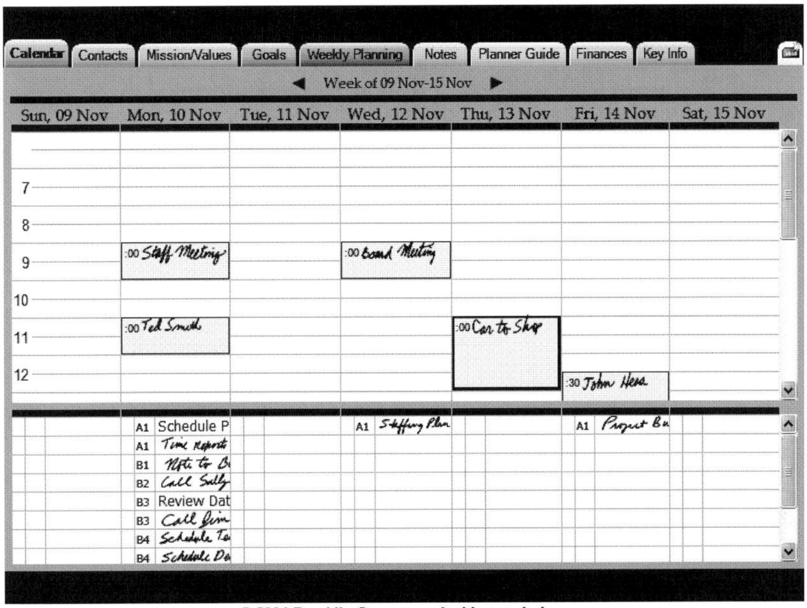

© 2004 Franklin Covey, used with permission

Figure 6-26. Week view in TabletPlanner, appointments at top, tasks at bottom.

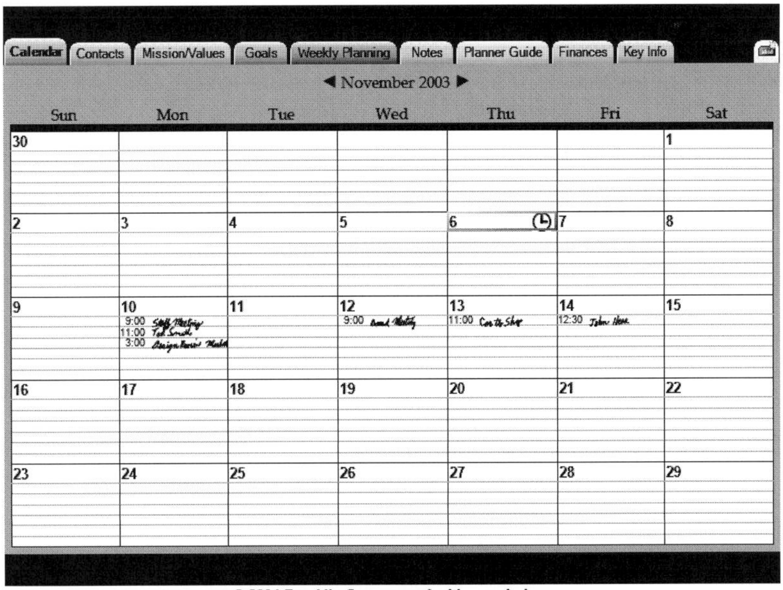

© 2004 Franklin Covey, used with permission

Figure 6-27. Month view in TabletPlanner; only appointments can be seen.

Switching Between Pages

By default the weekly and monthly views occupy two pages, but they are not *required* to behave that way. If for instance you want to show the full month in your left page and something else in the right page, do this: with a full month view as shown in Figure 6-27, go to the TabletPlanner Window menu, and choose Left Page. (See Figure 6-28.)

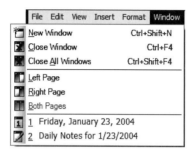

Figure 6-28.   Tablet Planner Window menu; the three choices in the middle section determine how pages are occupied.

You'll see the monthly view compress into the left side of the two-page view, and the right side will probably take on either the day view or the daily notes view. In order to get back to the full two-page view for the month calendar, select Both Pages from the Windows menu. Note that the Both Pages choice only works for the weekly and monthly calendar view.

At times when using these commands you may get a little confused as to why certain views appear when they do. In order to get a glimpse of how this works you now need to study the Navigation Bar.

Using the Navigation Bar with the Window Menu

Regarding using the Navigation Bar and the page selections within the TabletPlanner Window menu, I'm not sure whether to thank the designers of TabletPlanner for their unusually *flexible* interface or to cry over this initially *confusing* interface. This approach is unlike any other software you'll probably ever see; that's a good and bad thing.

First of all, the Navigation Bar is the narrow horizontal area just above the TabletPlanner tab bar. (See Figure 6-29.)

© 2004 Franklin Covey, used with permission

Figure 6-29. Navigation Bar.

This area lists the most recent TabletPlanner views that you've used; it holds entries for up to ten views. If you click on a view name within the Navigation Bar and your tablet is in landscape mode, the view you click will replace one of the two pages on the TabletPlanner (either the left or the right). Which of those two pages that view replaces is semideterminant: in some cases you can guide this and in others you cannot. And the rules for this I have not quite yet figured out. The good news is that you can usually achieve the combination of views that you want by combining the use of the Navigation Bar with the Left Page, Right Page selections on the TabletPlanner Window menu; it just might take a few steps of trial and error to get there. Here are some of the rules I've learned:

- The Left Page, Right Page selections on the Window menu only work if you have the tablet in landscape mode. They remain active but do nothing if the tablet is in portrait mode.

- Before clicking on an item in the Navigation Bar click once on the page where you would like it to go. This often does in fact direct the subsequent chosen view to that page; but the page often goes to the other page instead.

- If the view you click in the Navigation Bar does not end up in the page you want it, then immediately go to the Window menu and choose Left Page or Right Page as appropriate to redirect the destination. That should place that view where you originally wanted it.

- After doing this, however, you may find now that the view that replaces it when you move it is not what you expected. If so now click on the Navigation Bar again for the view you want. That should do it.

And finally, when you have a week view or a month view shown over both pages and you switch using the TabletPlanner Windows menu to the Left Page or Right Page, what fills in the other page depends on what's in the Navigation Bar at the time you do this. If the Navigation Bar is empty then the other page will be blank. If there are multiple items in the Navigation Bar, then what populates the other page will be one of those items; again, the rules for how the software decides which one are not clear to me. But a couple more clicks on the Navigation Bar should get you the combined view you want. If this sounds a bit confusing, it is. That said there is a lot of flexibility here and you can eventually get any two pages you want side by side, either for comparison purposes or for copying data between them.

And when you are using the portrait orientation of the Tablet PC all this becomes much less confusing because there's only one page that can be replaced at a time. You do lose the side-by-side advantage in portrait view.

I suspect that after a few days or weeks of using this you will get used to it, and maybe even come to love it.

Close Box

One more point about the Navigation Bar. At its far right end is a Close box. This closes the most recently opened view. When you close a view this way, it will be replaced by other items listed in the Navigation Bar, generally picking from right to left; but again, the actual choice may vary.

Also, since the Navigation Bar displays the last ten views you have used, it can start looking pretty busy. If you ever feel like cleaning out the bar so you can focus on switching between a couple of key views, just click repeatedly on the Close box; this will remove items one at a time. And you can do this to selectively remove view names from the bar; just click on the entry for the view in the Navigation Bar first before you click the Close box.

Managing Tasks in FranklinCovey TabletPlanner

Now that we've covered some basic TabletPlanner navigation we can focus on tasks again. If you are following along on your own Tablet PC, you should navigate back to the daily calendar view.

Tasks are managed in the lower left-hand corner of the calendar view space. The TabletPlanner software is designed to follow the FranklinCovey system of time management. You can ignore the system if you wish and use the task fields in your own way. However the FranklinCovey time management system is a powerful one and I encourage you to give it some study as you start to use this software. I recommend that you at least use the simplified techniques that are described at the beginning of this chapter and that are mixed in with the PlanPlus section (within the PlanPlus section, start reading at the section titled Assigning Priorities). These approaches generally work in both software packages. And again, for a complete study of the underlying FranklinCovey principles, two books I recommend are in the Appendix under FranklinCovey: *First Things First* and *To Do... Doing... Done!*

PlanPlus and TabletPlanner Task Capabilities Compared

Since both PlanPlus and TabletPlanner adopt the same FranklinCovey time management philosophy, most of the task functionality between PlanPlus and TabletPlanner are the same. You see the same ABC priority system and the same daily and master task approach. And as with PlanPlus, uncompleted daily tasks are automatically forwarded to the next day.

By far the primary advantage of the TabletPlanner is that ink input and storage are used throughout the software by default. This means that in fast-moving situations the user can rapidly make ink task entries and not hassle with text conversion issues; the inputs can remain in ink or be converted later.

The primary disadvantage compared to PlanPlus is that TabletPlanner has its own database for tasks, separate from Outlook. As a result, you may miss the PlanPlus ability to assign categories to tasks and the ability to create repeating tasks. Perhaps most importantly, in PlanPlus you can drag and drop e-mail items to automatically create tasks (discussed in Chapter 7). And you can use all of the other numerous Microsoft Office task linking capabilities of Outlook.

This integration of PlanPlus into Outlook is somewhat of a force-fit and therefore comes at a cost. Missing in PlanPlus is a checkbox on the task input dialog indicating that the task is a master task. Another symptom is that FranklinCovey task status codes do not carry throughout all of the Outlook task views. Since TabletPlanner does not need to force-fit into the Outlook system, it can more accurately follow the FranklinCovey approach. Status codes carry throughout the system well, and the concept of master tasks is more clearly displayed in the task detail view.

Entering Tasks

To enter your task within TabletPlanner, first make sure you are in the calendar workspace by clicking the Calendar tab in the upper left corner of the workspace. And for purposes of this lesson, make sure your tablet is in landscape orientation and that within TabletPlanner you pick the daily view.

Select the Pen tool and tap on an empty task line within the task space. An ink entry window pops up for you to write in and disappears automatically after you're done writing. (See Figure 6-30.) If immediately after writing the new task you find you need to edit the ink, just hover your pen over the new task entry and the ink entry window will pop up again ready for editing. Once you've selected something else hovering no longer works, so to retrieve the ink entry window just tap again on the task title once to select it again, and click again to open the editing window.

After handwriting an entry you can convert the ink to text. To do this click on the task so that it is highlighted (make sure an orange rectangle forms around the task name) and choose Convert Ink to Text from the Insert menu. Alternatively you can convert ink to text (or edit ink) from within the detailed view of the task. This we will cover in a moment.

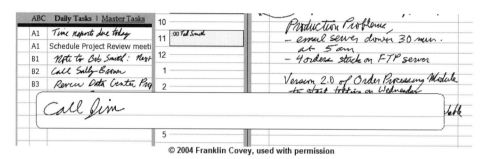

© 2004 Franklin Covey, used with permission

Figure 6-30.   Ink entry window in TabletPlanner.

If you prefer to avoid the initial ink stage of the task description, you can start out with the text tool selected (see below).

ab|

With this tool you would use the Writing Pad on the Tablet PC Input Panel and convert to text immediately. Or you would use a physical keyboard or the virtual keyboard on the Tablet PC Input Panel.

Entering ABC Task Priority in the Daily Task List View

Before we look at opening the task detail, let's continue to work in the task list view. The next step is to enter your task priority there.

The ABC priority field here is unusual for the Tablet PC in that it has a mandatory convert-to-text feature built in. What you write there is automatically converted to text whether you want to or not. And it will only accept the ABC or A1, B1, C1 style of priority system that we described at the beginning of this chapter. So if you ink something into that field, it will attempt to convert it to a designation that fits the ABC system. If your ink cannot be interpreted that way, the ink will disappear in a moment leaving the field blank again.

The ABC priority field in the task list view also has a drop-down menu choice capability. Once the task is entered into the list view, if you select it and then click on the ABC priority field for the task, a list of possible priority choices will appear that you can choose from. (See Figure 6-31.) This list is limited however, as the numbers only go up to three; but for a short task list this choice should be fine.

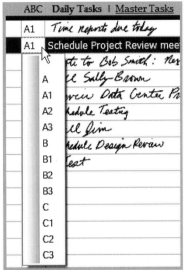

© 2004 Franklin Covey, used with permission

Figure 6-31. Drop-down priority selection for tasks in list view.

Status Field

The left-most field in the task list view is variously called the Action Code field or the Task Status field. There is no column label above that field. For a new task you would normally leave this status field blank. I generally don't use this field except for marking items complete.

Use of the FranklinCovey Status Field

For those of you interested in the Status field on the TabletPlanner Software (also called the Action Code field) in the calendar view there is a small legend above the left-most column of the task list that describes the complete status labeling approach.

For more information on how the Status field is intended to be used within FranklinCovey, the book *To Do... Doing... Done!* referenced in the Appendix describes this system well.

Also note that like the Priority field, the Status field imposes mandatory conversion of handwriting into text, in this case text symbols. By so doing the input choices to this field are limited to those accepted in the FranklinCovey system.

Sorting and Dragging Tasks

Within the task list view in the daily calendar, you can sort your uncompleted tasks by priority by clicking on the title of the priority field (labeled ABC). There is also a capability to drag a task to a new position to make various changes in its attributes. You can drag it up and down within the task list to reset its priority. You can drag it to a new date on the monthly calendar above the task list to change its assignment date. And you can drag it to the appointment schedule window to convert it into an appointment. However I had inconsistent results in getting dragging to work until I discovered a fine point of TabletPlanner use. In the daily task list there are three different selection modes for tasks, and only one of these can be used during dragging. Here's my discovery:

Three Selection Modes on the Daily Task List

One mode of selection is when there is an orange box around the task description. This selection mode is needed to convert ink to text and to edit the text of a converted entry with the text tool. This is also the mode that enables opening the ink editing window when hovering over the task. You generally reach this mode by clicking once or twice on the task. (See Figure 6-32.)

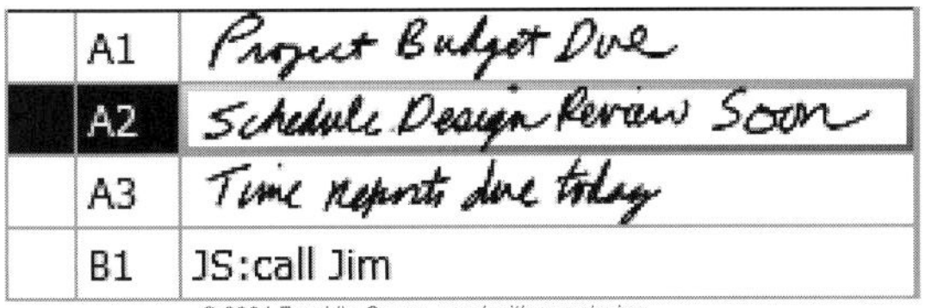

Figure 6-32. Selection mode with orange box, used for text conversion.

The next mode is the one you need for dragging. Your task is in this mode when you see a dotted line appear around the task description. (See Figure 6-33.) Once in this mode you can drag the task. This mode is usually reached after one click on a task; but once one task is in this mode, merely hovering over other tasks will put the other task into that mode.

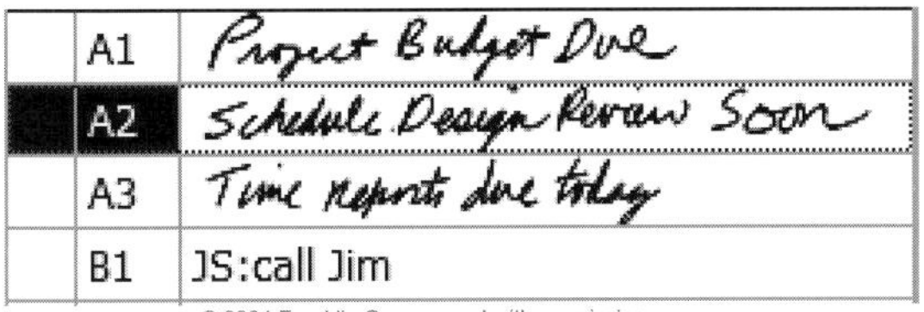

Figure 6-33. Selection mode with dotted line box, used when dragging.

The next mode as far as I can tell is useless for actions on a task. It is reached when you have a task selected and then click off the task pane and then back. The previously selected task takes on a gray color. (See Figure 6-34.) Its main purpose is, when you are working in the detail task view on the right, to show you which task is selected and being edited.

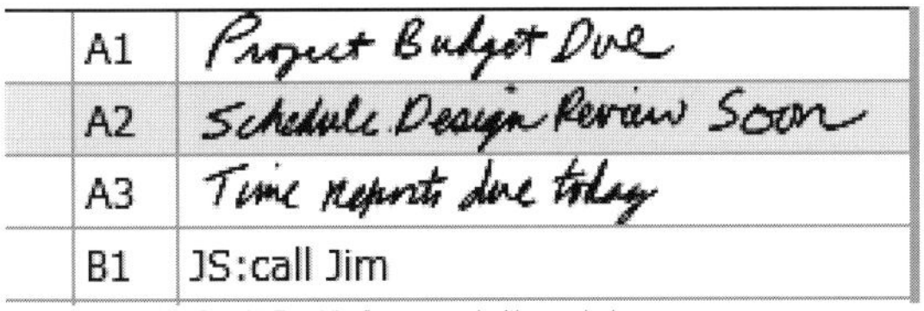

Figure 6-34. Selection mode with gray box, used to indicate which task is being edited in the detail task view.

Task Details

You may want to enter details about a new task or edit the details of an existing task. To do this, hover your pen over the right edge of the task list and you may see an orange right-facing arrow appear there. (See Figure 6-35.) You might need to click once or twice on a task list to get the arrow to appear.

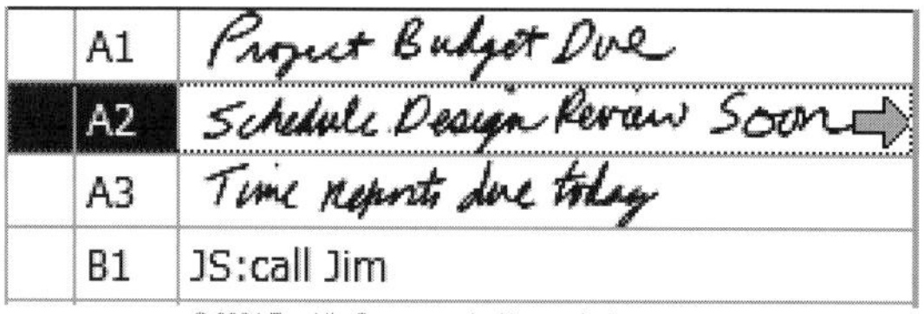

© 2004 Franklin Covey, used with permission

Figure 6-35. Note arrow at right of task; click on this arrow to open the task detail window in the right page.

When you click on this arrow, a detailed view of the task will appear in the entire right-hand side of the calendar workspace replacing whatever was in that page before. (See Figure 6-36.)

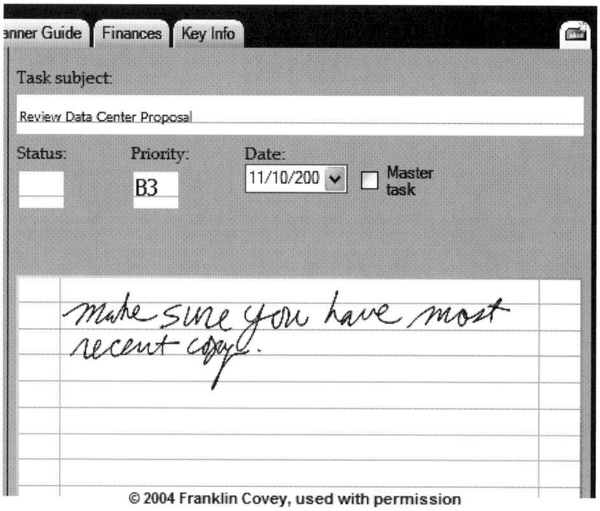

© 2004 Franklin Covey, used with permission

Figure 6-36. Task detail view.

In this task detail view, you can edit any of the fields visible in the task list, or you can convert the task subject ink to text. You can also add three additional kinds of information about the task: enter a task due date, write multiple pages of notes, and check a checkbox indicating that this is a master task. Use of this checkbox is described below.

Using the notes section of the task windows

The notes section of the detail task window is optional. You can enter notes either as ink, or type text directly into the space by selecting the text tool, or copy text into the space.

No start date

Something to note here is that there is no such thing as a start date for a task in TabletPlanner, so the discussions in the PlanPlus section above about start date strategies don't apply here.

Daily Tasks versus Master Tasks

The designation of a specific task as a master task versus a daily task is done more explicitly in TabletPlanner than in PlanPlus for Outlook. Checking or unchecking a checkbox in the task detail view as described above clearly makes this delineation (in PlanPlus, when working within the detail task view, the input of a due date is what triggers this delineation, something that is not at first obvious). When you mark the task as a master task, the date field actually disappears, which is a nice touch; this leaves little doubt as to the meaning of the term "master task."

Within the calendar view, in order to view your list of daily tasks versus master tasks, you need to click on the task list title area. Specifically, you click on the Master Tasks label to view master tasks, and you click on the Daily Tasks label to view daily tasks. When the list of daily tasks is being viewed, the Daily Tasks label is bold, and the Master Tasks label is underlined to indicate that the Master Tasks title is now an active button. (See Figure 6-37.)

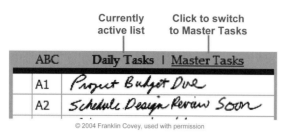

© 2004 Franklin Covey, used with permission

Figure 6-37. Clicking on the labels at the top of the task list changes the list from daily to master view and back.

Entering a Task in the Weekly View

You can also enter tasks in the weekly view as shown in Figure 6-38. Look at the bottom portion of this figure.

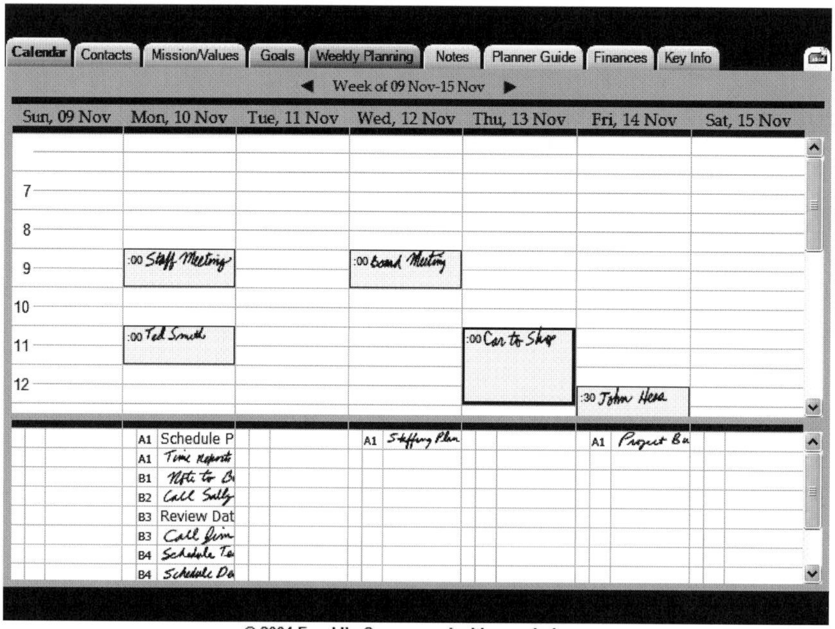

© 2004 Franklin Covey, used with permission

Figure 6-38. Weekly view in TabletPlanner, appointments at top, tasks at bottom.

Because you have much less room here to enter ink, when you click on the task line a more complete writing box pops up (compared to the popup writing box in the daily view). You use this expanded box to enter priority and status as well as the subject information. (See Figure 6-39.)

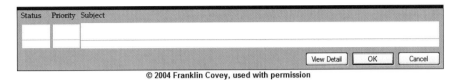

Figure 6-39. Popup input box for entering tasks in the weekly view.

And once you've entered tasks in the weekly view, the way to view the detailed task box for these tasks is different from the daily view. In the weekly view you just click on the task and that opens a detailed view in the right page (any subsequent click on the left page closes that detailed view on the right). There is no orange floating arrow as is used in the daily view. In fact there's no way to select a task item in the weekly view, so your conversion to text will need to be done within the detailed window. You delete tasks in the weekly view by right-clicking on them.

Drag and Drop in the Weekly View

And the weekly view has a nice drag and drop capability. You can drag tasks up and down to reprioritize them, or left and right to assign them to different days. Or drag a task onto the appointment portion of the page to turn it into an appointment (and visa versa). This drag and drop capability is even easier to use than on the daily calendar view because there is no confusion about how to select the task; just click and drag.

Conclusion for TabletPlanner Task Management

There are many more things to show you regarding the use of the Tablet-Planner software, but the focus of this chapter is on tasks and we have covered that sufficiently to get you started. You'll see more coverage of the TabletPlanner software in the chapters ahead, specifically in the chapters on note taking, document management, marking up documents, and setting goals.

Chapter 7 Advanced Task and E-mail Management

Augmenting Your Task Management System

After working with and digesting the material in Chapter 6, if you are ready for more ideas on how to improve your work day approach, study this chapter. Here you will find additional techniques that will further help you get your work day under control.

The steps however are somewhat detailed, so consider what follows as a graduate course on task and e-mail management using the Tablet PC. They are only appropriate to pursue if you have a very intense work day and are willing to invest the time in learning and implementing new workflows. If you are reading quickly through the book trying to get a flavor for the various dimensions of Tablet PC work use, you may want to skip this chapter and come back later. Here we cover:

- Task delegation recommendations

- E-mail processing recommendations

- David Allen's principles for task management

Delegating Tasks

Delegating tasks effectively is an essential means for clearing tasks off your list, freeing time to focus on activities that are more important and more appropriate to your role. Many new and even experienced work managers have trouble delegating effectively. As a result, too many tasks that should be delegated end up remaining self-assigned.

Failures with delegation often stem from lack of good systems to assign, track, and follow up on delegated tasks. When a due date arrives and the delegated task has not been completed, too often managers blame the delegated staff: "That person can't seem to get things done for me; if I need something done I'd better do it myself," and tasks end up back on the manager's list. It's highly likely that the delegation failure was due to the delegation methodology, not due to the staff it was delegated to.

Delegation of tasks can represent handoffs to subordinates or "requests" to colleagues. Both should be managed the same way.

With the Tablet PC, the application of good delegation techniques has just gotten much easier. The Tablet PC provides an effective platform to implement respectful and effective task delegation and follow-up techniques. You do need to learn some new workflows however.

It's amazing how much respect and attention staff will give you and the tasks you assign if you provide three things:

■ An honest and thoughtful discussion of the reasons the task is important and why this person may be the right one to work on it.

■ Plenty of lead time on the assignment of the task.

■ Consistent and reasonably spaced check-ins while waiting for the task to be completed.

It's when you fail to manage assigned tasks with these steps, using regular and timely management techniques, that tempers get short and staff feel overburdened.

It's no wonder managers are so bad at this. They have a large pile of their own tasks to manage, so how can they be expected to consistently assign and track the task list of others? The Tablet PC provides tools to solve this dilemma. It provides successful approaches to clear and organize your own task plate, and it gives you tools that allow you to manage assigned tasks as well. Most importantly, these tools are available at the moment you need them: when you first identify the task and when meeting with the staff you delegate to. The at-hand nature of the Tablet PC ensures that the delegation techniques are consistently applied. All you need is the Tablet PC configured per Chapter 4, good task management software (Chapter 6), and a good workflow (in this chapter). With these you will be able to get tasks assigned smoothly and in a timely fashion and track and follow up on tasks effectively.

A Real Life Example

In Tuesday's biweekly senior staff meeting, you are alerted to some minor issues with the corporate network that are affecting the Customer Service Department. You decide in the meeting to delegate resolution of this issue as a task to your network operations manager (Joseph). At that point, while the meeting is still going on, you bring up Outlook on your Tablet PC, and using pen input discreetly jot a quick note to Joseph mentioning that you have a minor network issue to talk about in your one-on-one meeting the next day. You then click in the task pane within Outlook and, using pen input, quickly enter a new task: "Resolve Network Performance." You use a shorthand notation to indicate that you intend to assign this task to Joseph.

In your one-on-one meeting with Joseph the next day, working with the Tablet PC in your lap, you quickly bring up the all-tasks view within Outlook and scan down to view all the open tasks you have assigned Joseph over the previous weeks or months.

After discussing issues regarding a few old tasks, you address the issue that arose yesterday. You and Joseph agree on the nature of the issue and discuss possible sources and solutions, and Joseph agrees this is in his domain and accepts this as an assignment. A due date is discussed and agreed upon. You update the task in your Outlook list to indicate it has been accepted. You set a follow-up date on this task to seven days before the next senior staff meeting. This ensures that a follow-up task, to check in on this task with Joseph, appears on your task list in Outlook well before that next meeting. At this point the task is securely assigned and follow-ups are safely scheduled. You can now, until the check-in date arrives, forget about the task and move on to other priorities.

The Task Delegation Approach

In Chapter 6 I stated that I do not use the Assign Task capability that is built into Outlook where tasks are simply sent to staff and dropped on their Outlook task list. I do use Outlook with PlanPlus on the Tablet PC to manage delegated tasks but in a slightly lower-tech, higher-touch mode. My approach to task delegation is a three-step process:

1   **Identify**: At the moment the task and need to delegate arises, enter and annotate the task in the task system as one to be delegated and indicate to whom to delegate it.

2   **Get buy-in**: Use a face-to-face or phone meeting to gain buy-in and acceptance from the staff or colleague and to set a due date for the task. Update the system to indicate acceptance, and schedule your first check-in timeframe.

3   **Follow up**: At the scheduled check-in, follow up on the assigned task, provide help if needed, and set subsequent follow-up timeframes. Escalate only after several follow-ups.

I like this approach because the staff manages their task their own way, and I use my task system to initiate regular personal follow-up activities. This avoids forcing my task management approach on other staff yet allows me a personal touch in my follow-up. Logistics for each of these steps are covered below.

Identify and Annotate a Task for Delegation

In step 1, when I identify tasks that I intend to assign to others, I annotate the subject line of tasks in my task list. This helps me plan and initiate the assignment process. My assignment annotation system is simple: I place the

initials of the staff that I intend to assign the task to in the very front of the
subject line, followed by a colon, and that followed by the subject itself. So a
task I intend to assign to Joe Smith to provide network performance resolution would appear with: "JS:Resolve Network Performance" in the subject
line. This is for my use only; I do not give the task list to Joe. I may give Joe a
head's up e-mail that something new is coming to be discussed in the next
meeting; for big tasks the more warning the better. By using this annotation
system, the next time I meet with Joe I can sort alphabetically within the all-
tasks view of Outlook, scroll down to Joe's initials, and propose the handoff
of one or more tasks in person.

FranklinCovey Status Symbols

Both PlanPlus and TabletPlanner have the option of placing a delegated symbol in front of a task. This is part of a set of status symbols that was inherited
from the paper-based FranklinCovey planner system.

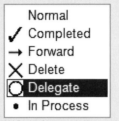

© 2004 Franklin Covey, used with permission

If you are using an assignment annotation approach like I described above
this delegated symbol is redundant and optional. I usually do not use it.
However note that in PlanPlus, these symbols map to Outlook Status field
states (they do with Outlook 2003, I have not tested this with earlier Outlook
versions). Choosing Delegate marks the Outlook Status field with a value
"Waiting on someone else." You could then display and sort on that value in
the Outlook Tasks folder view (described below) to see all delegated tasks, so
using these optional codes could be useful. The other mappings are: Completed marks the Outlook Status as "Completed," Forward moves it to a
selected future date, and In Process marks the Outlook Status as "In Progress." Of these, Completed is the only one I routinely use.

Gaining Buy-in for the Task

Assigning a task to someone, without prior discussion, is largely discouraged
by management experts. Rather, an important element of delegation is achieving buy-in from the staff that you plan to delegate to; dropping a task
assignment in someone's inbox is not consistent with this approach. Further-

more, many staff, even if they use Outlook for e-mail, may be using some system of tracking tasks other than Outlook. They may be using a paper-based system. A task management system cannot be forced on someone.

I use my one-on-one meetings to discuss and assign tasks. Or if the next one-on-one is too far off and the task urgent, I set a separate short ad hoc meeting to have the discussion. In that meeting, I use Outlook's Tasks folder view to quickly pull up tasks for that staff.

Viewing all delegated tasks in Outlook

At the one-on-one meeting, with the Tablet PC in my lap, I review all tasks in Outlook for that person that are outstanding and that I intend to assign. I sort by and visually scan the list of all tasks that have that individual's initials on them. I discuss ones that have not yet been agreed to, and if needed reprioritize and redate the outstanding ones to reflect newer priorities and meeting outcomes.

But how do you view this all-tasks list? Focusing for now on PlanPlus users, remember that some of these delegated tasks may have assigned follow-up dates in the future and so they will not appear on your task list for today. You could click, within the PlanPlus Home screen, on each day one at a time to try to find them, but that's way too cumbersome.

The easiest way to find these tasks is to use the Outlook Tasks folder view. You open this in Outlook 2002 and Outlook 2003 by clicking on the Tasks folder at the bottom of your Folder List pane. (See Figure 7-1.)

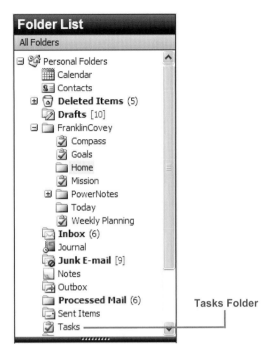

Figure 7-1. Opening the Outlook Tasks folder view from the Folder List pane in Outlook 2003.

And Outlook 2003 has a second place to open it, by clicking on the icon for the Tasks Folder at the bottom of the Navigation pane. (See Figure 7-2.)

Figure 7-2. Opening the Outlook Tasks folder view from the Navigation pane in Outlook 2003.

This opens an Outlook view showing all open tasks within the Outlook task management system, regardless of whether they are master tasks, daily tasks for today, or daily tasks assigned to the distant future. (See Figure 7-3.)

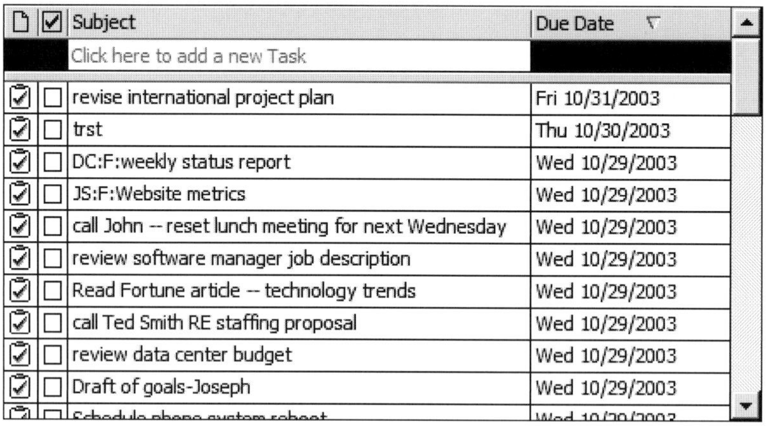

Figure 7-3.   Outlook Tasks view.

This is a standard Outlook view and has not been modified by installation of the PlanPlus software. Therefore it does not show the FranklinCovey status symbols discussed above, nor does it show the ABC priority column. The FranklinCovey status value does map to the Outlook Status field, and you can add both the ABC and Status columns to the view if you want using the Outlook Field Chooser. Doing this though is a little complicated, and beyond the scope of this book.

Custom Outlook 2003 Views

However in Outlook 2003 this is unneeded because PlanPlus ships with two custom Outlook 2003 Views that do display these fields. To get to them, go to the View menu, choose Arrange By..., and click on the Show Views in Navigation Pane choice. Then after you click on the Tasks folder, in the Navigation Pane (the Folders List view) scroll down below the folders, and you will see a list of custom task views (labeled Current View). The top two are Franklin-Covey Daily Tasks, and FranklinCovey Master Tasks. (See Figure 7-4.) Choose the radio button next to the one you want, and the task view columns and filtering changes accordingly in the task list on the right. Do not forget to switch back to the Simple List view when done, otherwise the next time you come back to the Tasks folder the previous filtered view is retained.

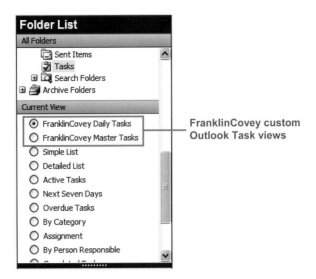

FranklinCovey custom Outlook Task views

Figure 7-4. Outlook 2003 custom view selection for the Tasks folder.

Once you have any of these all-tasks views displayed you can sort alphabetically, by task subject, by clicking on the Subject column heading. And assuming you have used the delegation annotation I discussed above you can then scroll down to the initials of the staff that you're meeting with and find all tasks you have assigned to that individual.

I have my Tablet PC with me during my one-on-one meetings and refer to this task window as I talk with my staff. This is a fantastic way to keep up with rapidly changing assigned tasks. And assuming that during your discussion about the status of each task you may have changes to make to those tasks (for example, marking the subject for follow up, extending the due date, or checking the task complete) you can edit the tasks right in this window, in the meeting. You can either do this in-line within the list view, or double click the task and edit it within the task input window. Again, this is the main reason the Tablet PC is such a useful tool for the manager; right in your meetings you can refer to and update your automated tracking systems.

TabletPlanner users will need to modify this strategy since they do not have an all-tasks view. One approach that helps is to keep tasks in the master tasks list until accepted. The other is to also list assigned tasks in a separate list document.

Following Up on Delegated Tasks

Once the task is accepted it is essential to schedule and engage regular follow-up activities. Consistent and reasonable follow-up is the key often-overlooked point. We are tempted to think that once a task is assigned, the recipient "should" do it. And even if we agree that check-ins are needed, it is easy to forget to do this well before the due date. And new managers are often afraid to disturb their staff about assigned work.

However this is an essential step of task delegation. It is good management practice to track delegated task assignment progress regularly, well before the task is due. It is bad management practice to wait until the task is due for the first check-in.

The solution is to adopt a system whereby the next "fair" date for the check-in is negotiated at the assignment and clearly scheduled as an activity for you to do in your task system. And then a very proactive follow-up is actually taken when that time arrives. To do this, you should create a dated follow-up task for each outstanding delegated item.

Creating the Follow-up Task

Creating such follow-up tasks is made very easy if you do the following: convert your task entry for the intended assignment into a follow-up task at the time the task is accepted.

Here's how this works. Recall the task that I intended to assign to Joe Smith to resolve network performance issues. Remember that at the time I decided to assign it I marked it: "JS:Resolve Network Performance." This notation indicated I intended to assign this task to Joe *but that Joe had not yet accepted it*. Once I discuss this assignment with Joe and he accepts it, I then immediately modify the annotation of the same task as follows: "JS:F:Resolve Network Performance"; the added "F" stands for follow-up. That way in my weekly one-on-one with Joe, using my Tablet PC in the meeting, I can sort separately on those tasks he's accepted already and on those that still need discussion to establish buy-in.

And at the same time I add the "F" for follow-up to my task I also change the Outlook Due Date field of the task to be the day I want to be reminded to check in with Joe. I set the priority to be either an A or at least a B1; this priority level ensures I take action on the day the task appears on my daily list. Again, I avoid the use of Outlook reminders or alarms for tasks (I only use them for appointments). Rather the appearance of a brief check-in task at the top of my daily list nearly always leads to my taking action on that check-in the same day it appears.

> ### Assign Partial Deliverables for Check-in Points
>
> You may also wish to negotiate a specific partial deliverable to be delivered at a follow-up date. If the final task includes creating something tangible, a rough draft or first pass at the final product is a good target deliverable for the check-in. This helps prevent the check-in date from merely being an agreed-to reminder date. And there is often a great deal of discovery that can occur in creating a first draft. An early required rough draft forces that discovery to occur early enough to allow time to adjust plans. And you need to convince your staff that you will be very lenient in judgment of that rough draft; otherwise they will spend too much time polishing something that may be wrong.

The agreed-to final due date of the delegated task I will put in the body of the text of the task. Or if it is a very firm or urgent due date I might even put it in the subject line to draw my attention to it. The point here is that the Outlook Due Date *field* in the task record has too many useful system functions (like the next check-in date) to be used as a place to store a really important final due date for an assigned task. This may seem a little contradictory but if you think about it the due dates on many tasks are artificial negotiated ones, not drop-dead due dates. So with those tasks that *do* have an urgent date, a distinctive way is needed to call attention to it. Placing a date reference within the subject line is one such way. If that day is close and the task is still not done, on my morning review of open tasks I convert it to an A level task.

This follow-up task system really does work. I find it is amazingly effective at clearing my subconscious of loose-end concerns about assignments and guiding me in appropriate follow-up activities. At any given time I can have twenty or more open assigned tasks that are neatly scheduled for follow-ups. They remain out of sight until exactly the right scheduled check-in point, freeing my psyche for more important activities. Without a system like this I might forget to check in, and then the task becomes an emergency. I might even check in too often, which is unnecessary and irritating to staff. The system brings order and calm to an otherwise chaotic mess.

How to Follow Up on Delegated Tasks

When the due date of the follow-up tasks arrives (in reality, my informal reminder date) and the follow-up task appears at the top of my daily task list, I then have a choice in how I follow up.

I may schedule it to coincide with the next regular one-on-one meeting. In that meeting once again I use the Outlook sort on all tasks feature to pull up the task list for an individual.

You may be tempted to make follow-ups part of a regularly scheduled departmental or team meeting. This is probably the most commonly used technique in the business world today. I recommend you avoid this. Not everybody needs to hear everyone's tasks and where they are. Such sessions lack positive energy and often lead to useless posturing.

But many tasks move too fast to wait for scheduled one-on-one meetings. Or you may need to cancel a scheduled meeting. Or you may not have regular one-on-one meetings with your staff. And you may make many assignments to staff that aren't your subordinates; you may not meet regularly with these staff. This is the beauty of having the scheduled follow-ups as individual tasks on your task list. They trigger and appear at the top of your daily task list at just the right time, whether you look for them or not, and whether meetings are scheduled or not.

How to handle follow-ups outside of meetings can vary. If I'm really busy and the actual needed delivery date is not for a good number of days more, I may just shoot off an e-mail to Joe asking: "How are things going on the network performance issue? Let me know as soon as you can, the senior staff meeting is coming up in five days." If this is to a colleague I would be much more politic: "Hi Sally, just checking in to see if all is OK on getting the product overview presentation together by Friday. Let me know if I can get you any additional information or help in any other way. Really appreciate you working on this. That report is going to make the BigCo sale a success."

With my own staff though, better yet is to call or walk over to the staff's desk. The personal touch and one-task-at-a-time nature of this check-in is usually effective at getting the task moving. And you are raising the reminder while Joe is at his desk, at his tools, where he can actually act when he sees the reminder and thinks: "Oh man, I forgot about this, I better move on it."

Setting the Next Follow-up

Whether you follow up in meetings or in between, there is one more critical step that you must do. In case you don't or can't get an immediate answer to your follow-up, or the answer indicates that the task is not yet complete, then decide and record immediately what day would be the appropriate next day to check in again. Immediately reset the due date on the follow-up task to that new date. This will cause the task to reappear on the task list on that day. If you sent an e-mail or voice message as your follow-up action, then set the new date in the task at the moment you send the message (don't wait for a reply, otherwise you will forget). If you check in in person, enter the new negotiated date into your system as soon as you finalize it at Joe's desk.

And this is the key utility of the Tablet PC that boosts your ability to get control of delegated tasks. Such tasks are too numerous and too fast moving to keep their status in your head. You need to keep the status of tasks up to date and in a system, and you need to make those updates immediately. Loose notes or memorized actions that you intend to update later "at your desk" will not suffice; otherwise those tasks will fall through cracks. You can do such a status reset in your Tablet PC system right in your meeting with your staff. Whether that meeting is in the hall, in a conference room, or at his desk, this will get updated because the Tablet PC is with you and that system is open, all the time. Keeping tasks updated ensures a steady follow-up approach. It avoids forgotten agreements and sends a consistent management message to your staff. If staff learn from experience that you *always* follow up, they are less likely to relax on deadlines or take chances that you might not notice slipped deliverables.

Escalation

If the above reminder scenario repeats itself a number of times on the same task, however, you need to escalate management of this task beyond a simple reminder system. The weekly one-on-one meeting with your staff can be a good forum for this escalation because it allows time to brainstorm solutions to whatever is holding the task up. Or if the deadline is too close, call an urgent ad hoc meeting to review impact of the problem and together plan out a course of action. The latter at least only happens after a few check-in points, so all involved will feel the escalation is fair. The beauty of this approach is that you can stay ahead of assigned tasks and manage them in a timely and fair fashion.

Processing Your Outlook 2003 E-mail Inbox

Your Outlook Inbox is probably out of control. This is true for most e-mail users; it's usually only the *degree* of disarray that varies. Outlook 2003 brings solutions to this problem, solutions that when combined with PlanPlus and the Tablet PC may finally get your Inbox under control. If you have upgraded to Outlook 2003, read on. And even if not, read on, and see if this motivates you to make the upgrade. And if you are a TabletPlanner user using Outlook 2003 for your e-mail only, most of this will be useful.

Letting mail sit in your Inbox will leave you with a nagging feeling of unprocessed to-do items. It will probably lead to dropped tasks. And it will complicate your search for important saved e-mails.

Not acting promptly on e-mails frustrates the goals of team collaboration. It lowers the impact of your interactions with outside business associates. And if sloppy e-mail handling becomes common behavior in an organization, it hinders the effectiveness of the organization.

And while e-mail processing is not a task management topic per se, it will greatly impact your ability to get tasks done. Setting up an effective e-mail processing workflow is essential toward increasing your effectiveness as a work manager. Making an empty Inbox one goal of this processing goes a long way toward helping you know that you can finally focus on important but not urgent activities (like strategic thinking or going home on time).

Problems with Filing in Outlook Folders

The commonly recommended approach to processing and emptying your Inbox is to create a series of custom Outlook folders and to file your e-mails in those classified folders as you process the Inbox. I have never, until recently, been able to achieve this goal of consistently keeping my Inbox relatively clear.

The reasons I'd never succeeded before is that every time I attempted to clean up the Inbox by filing into multiple custom Outlook folders I experienced several negative outcomes:

- In the old days (before PlanPlus) I would often use my Inbox as one of my task lists, and so would leave mail there as reminders.

- Even after establishing a useful task system, I was never really sure when I was "done" enough with an e-mail to file it away. Often I had a vague sense of uncompleted tasks associated with an e-mail that made me want to let it sit in my Inbox until I was sure it was ready to be out of my line of sight.

■ Sometimes it seemed like the item belonged in several different folders. In my indecision I'd leave the item unfiled.

■ Once filed, I would forget which folder I stored items in and get frustrated with having to hunt through multiple folders to find them.

■ And finally, whenever I instituted the filing system, I regretted no longer having one chronological view of *all* my e-mail. I often locate an e-mail by approximately how far in the past it arrived and by proximity with other events. And so in those cases I missed the ability to scan through my Inbox backward, through all my e-mail, newest to oldest, to accomplish that search. Scanning historical e-mails helped me recall the order of events and build context for solving complex issues. Having my saved mail split among multiple folders precluded that.

For these reasons, I have always given up on filing e-mail into a collection of various category-driven Outlook folders. Yet there remained many times that I wished I did have a good filing system for my Inbox.

Outlook 2003 Changes All This

Outlook 2003 has two new features that accomplish a folderlike role but overcome these shortcomings. They are called Search Folders and Show in Groups. When used in combination with Outlook Categories and a good e-mail processing workflow, they are a godsend toward keeping your Inbox clear and enabling you to find important e-mails.

Search Folders allows you to view virtual folders that are created on the basis of search criteria. This allows you to store all your processed mail in one chronological spot but view virtual folders that meet criteria like "Web Project," or "Personal," that are assigned through Outlook Categories. You get the best of both worlds. And individual mail messages can be viewed in multiple Search Folders, freeing you from the angst of choosing a correct category assignment at processing time.

Show in Groups is an alternative that plays a similar role, but groups like mail together right in the main mail folder.

Initial Setup

Before we cover using Search Folders, here are some initial setup steps you should do to prepare your system for the e-mail processing work flow.

First, you need to create one destination for all processed e-mails. This will be a single Outlook folder that all your e-mail, once processed, gets moved to. This allows you to keep a single chronological list view of all e-mail but still process and clear your Inbox. If you do not know how to create Outlook folders, follow the instructions starting on page 271: Creating Additional Outlook Folders for Your Notes. Follow those steps, but do not store this folder in the PowerNotes section as suggested there, rather place it at the highest folder level. Name this folder "Processed Mail" or "Saved Mail."

Side Note: *For those of you in a Microsoft Exchange environment, I recommend this folder be created as one of your Personal Folders. It could even be your Inbox within your Personal Folders section. Personal folders are partially discussed on page 83: Using Outlook in Offline Mode. There is a good chance you are already using Personal Folders; however determining this, and the full steps for creating Personal Folders, are beyond the scope of this book. I recommend you gain assistance from your IT department or use the online help in Outlook 2003 and search on the topic. Internet POP mail users have a clearer path: all Outlook folders are already Personal Folders and there is no extra effort required to ensure that.*

You should also confirm that your copy of Outlook is configured to automatically create an entry in the Sent Items folder for all mail you send (this is the default setting, so just be sure you did not turn this off). To confirm this go to the Outlook Tools menu, choose Options, Preferences tab, click the E-mail Options button, and ensure the Save Copies of Messages in the Sent Items Folder option is selected.

My Recommended E-mail Processing Workflow

The Outlook Inbox processing workflow I recommend, that includes steps necessary to use Search Folders and Show in Groups, is this:

Read each mail, and one at a time:

1   Decide if the mail has no action and no later value and should be deleted (junk mail, useless banter, and so forth). If so delete immediately. Don't spend much time on this. If you are uncertain, plan on keeping it and move on to the next step.

For all mail you do not delete:

2 Assign Outlook categories to all mail that you do not delete. We'll cover categories more below, but in general they represent your filing system. The beauty of categories is that you can assign more than one to a message; it does not hurt to assign too many. Use project names, general categories, anything that will help you find the e-mail later. We will use Search Folders to create virtual folders around these categories later.

3 Next, decide if the e-mail generates the need for an immediate action and if that action can be done quickly (completed in 1 to 3 minutes); if so just do it now. That action might be to reply to the e-mail, forward it, make a quick call, send a new e-mail to someone else, and so on.

4 If the action needed is to reply to the e-mail and you do not have time now, flag it with an Outlook follow-up flag (right-click on the message and choose Follow Up), and leave it in your Inbox until you can reply. These should be the only items left in your Inbox. If the reason you cannot reply immediately is because there is some other action that has to happen first, follow the next step.

5 If an action is needed but cannot be done now, create an Outlook task and copy/convert the mail to that task using the steps described below called Converting E-mails to Tasks. Note that the Outlook task will automatically take on the Outlook category of the mail it was created from, which is why you always assign categories first.

6 In all cases except mail flagged for pending replies, the next step is to move the processed mail item out of the Inbox and into the Processed Mail folder.

7 Go to the next mail item in your Inbox and repeat.

Try to empty your Inbox. Again, the only read-mail left in the Inbox should be mail that requires a reply and only if that reply would take longer than what you currently have time for. If you see read-messages in there without follow-up flags, you are slipping. And commit yourself to processing those replies within a day.

Some would say that nothing should be left in your Inbox, but I feel strongly about replying relatively promptly to all request mail sent to me, even if that reply is to say I cannot help, or to say that I cannot get back to them for a few days. By leaving such pending reply mail in my Inbox, this ensures I'll see it often. This keeps the reply task a high priority for me. It's either that or convert it to an A level task, which takes a few more steps.

If your immediate reply to an e-mail is "I will get back to you in a week" then also create a task from it now to do so and process the mail out of the Inbox. Any mail that requires a later action other than a simple ASAP reply should be converted to a task.

For mail that you send or reply to, the workflow is this:

1 For all mail that you send, decide if a follow-up task needs to be set to remind yourself to follow up on the e-mail (see section below titled Converting E-mails to Tasks for more discussion of this). If so:

2 Send the mail, immediately go to the Sent Items folder, set a category on the sent item, and convert the sent item to a follow-up task.

3 If no follow-up task is needed, do nothing other than send the mail. Optionally you can set categories on outgoing mail before you send them, but this is probably overkill. This does make it easier to find items in your Sent Items folder later.

Converting E-mails to Tasks

There are easy methods in Outlook 2003 (and earlier versions) to convert e-mail messages directly into tasks. You should take advantage of these methods. Since they are so simple, they will encourage you to actually create tasks when needed. TabletPlanner users will need to adjust the details of the steps here to make this work for them, using copy and paste as appropriate.

Create a Task by Dragging an E-mail within the PlanPlus Home Screen

In the PlanPlus Home screen you can instantly turn an e-mail into a task by dragging the e-mail (from the list view) onto the task list. When you do this, the task is automatically created there with the e-mail text already copied into the body of the task. Once the task is created, you'll want to edit the subject line to actually state the task action. When dragging within the PlanPlus Home screen, the position where you drop the task in the task list sets its priority automatically. And when you drag, the original e-mail remains behind as well, so don't forget to then drag it to the processed folder.

You need to decide whether to drag this e-mail/task to the daily or master task list. Certainly if this is very low priority, go directly to the master task list and mark it as a C item. But even if it requires action, you also need to determine if the task generated by this e-mail represents one discrete action or a miniproject with several required steps. If the former, drag the task to the daily task list. If the latter, drag and create two tasks: a next action task in your daily list and a miniproject in your master task list. Doing the latter allows you to then clear the e-mail out of your Inbox knowing both current actions and attention to future steps have both been set in place. This is a new approach we have not yet covered and so it may be confusing. Use the section at the end of this chapter on David Allen's task management system (page 226) as a guide to this approach and then come back to this paragraph.

Create Tasks for Important E-mail Responses You are Waiting for

When I send an important "request" e-mail I often set for myself a corresponding follow-up task to look for a reply. Reason: I am sometimes frustrated by colleagues and staff who fail to respond to simple requests I send them; I suspect you are too. Often their one-minute effort to respond will advance my miniproject immeasurably. The trouble is that to be polite I usually give them a few days to respond, and by then I have forgotten that I am waiting. I often only realize I received no response on the day my miniproject is due. It's too late by that time, and then with many in this situation the blame game starts ("Bill never got back to me; I would have completed this if he hadn't dropped the ball").

If you are on the hook for completing a multistep task, and if a key step of that activity requires you to receive information from someone by e-mail, do the following. At the moment you send the e-mail request, set a follow-up task for yourself to remind that person later, in case they don't reply. Set your task to appear on your daily list at some reasonable number of days into the future but well before the due date of your multistep task. That way if they drop the ball on getting back to you, you are reminded to escalate this while you still have time to get your task done.

To do this easily in Outlook: after you send the e-mail open the Sent Items folder and find the item, *right-click* and drag the item to the Tasks folder (or to the Tasks icon in Outlook 2003). When you drop the item there a popup menu appears from which you should take the second choice: Copy Here as Task with Attachment. (See Figure 7-5.)

Side Note: *If you drag the item without right-clicking, no menu appears, and the e-mail item is deleted from the Sent Items list. This outcome is undesirable as it complicates later tracking, so always right-click before dragging.*

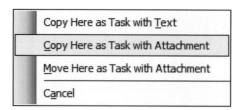

Figure 7-5. Context menu when dragging an e-mail to the task folder.

Making this choice ensures that when you are acting on that follow-up task later you can open the message from within the task and even resend it as part of your escalation with the recipient.

Assigning Categories to E-mail

In order to use Search Folders and Show in Groups in Outlook 2003 for our purposes you need to first know how to assign categories to e-mail.

When deciding what categories to create, keep in mind that you can do this as you go. Unless you are synchronizing with a Palm, there is nothing wrong with creating too many categories. I recommend you let your list grow organically. Discover which categories are most useful. You can always assign multiple categories to an e-mail, the more the better. Create whatever categories best help you search and find your e-mail.

Note however that PlanPlus users may want to share these Outlook categories with their tasks, PowerNotes, PlanPlus eBinder documents, and so on, so some thought about their intended use is worthwhile.

Also note that you can assign multiple categories to a single message, and if you do, the message will show up in multiple Search Folders. This is a fantastic behavior because it eliminates difficult decisions on where to file mail. If two categories apply, just assign it to both.

The section at the end of this chapter regarding David Allen's task management system has additional discussion about choosing categories.

Assigning Categories in E-mail List View

Right-click on any e-mail item in your mail list. From the context menu choose Categories. The following Categories window opens, displaying whatever category list is currently populated in your system (see Figure 7-6). Yours will probably look different from the list below. In the list, place a checkmark next to every category that applies to the message.

Figure 7-6. Outlook Categories window.

Prior to right-clicking an item in the e-mail list to assign a category, note that you can shift or control-select multiple e-mails at once in an e-mail list before you open the above window. Whatever assignments you make in the above window are then assigned to all the selected e-mail items. This is useful to speed category assignment.

If none of the categories in your category list fits your needs and you want to add another category, click the Master Category List... button at the bottom of the window. This opens the following window where additional categories can be added or existing ones deleted (see Figure 7-7). There is no way to re-name a category.

Assigning Categories to an Open E-mail

If you are reading an e-mail and ready to make the assignment, or if you have just written a new e-mail, here's how to assign categories from the e-mail editing window. With the e-mail open, choose Options from the View menu. In the middle of the mail options window you will see a Categories button. Click that and the same Categories window as in Figure 7-6 opens, ready for category assignment.

Figure 7-7.   Editing the Master Category list.

Assigning categories to outgoing mail has two benefits. The category stays with the mail in the Sent Items folder, making finding mail there easier. And if the mail is sent to an Exchange user, any replies to that mail that you receive back retain the original category; no need to assign the category later when you process that mail.

One more point about assigning categories: you can easily write an Outlook rule that will automatically assign a category to all incoming mail from a particular sender. For example I have done this to assign the Personal category to mail from family members. This saves a few steps later.

Search Folders

Here's the reason for assigning all these categories: Search Folders. This is your filing system, your folder replacement system. This is the solution that allows you to keep all processed mail together in one list but still view your mail as if filed in multiple folders. The feature is only available in Outlook 2003.

Search Folders appear within and under the Search Folder master folder, right in the Folder List view of Outlook (see Figure 7-8). In this sample, six search folders are shown.

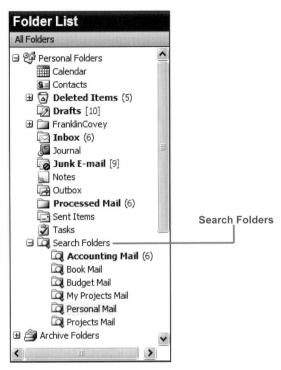

Figure 7-8. Search Folders are virtual Outlook 2003 folders that appear and act like "normal" Outlook folders.

Search Folders are virtual folders that are populated with an entry for every mail item that matches a certain search criteria, criteria that is defined at the time the particular search folder is created. One folder is created for each set of search criteria. The best criterion to use for our purposes is collecting mail that has a given category assigned; however many other search approaches are possible. Once created, clicking on the folder opens a view of all matching mail in a folder view, as if it were a real Outlook folder.

Creating Search Folders

Creating search folders around categories is a moderately complex process, with four levels of nested dialog boxes to open and set criteria in. This is not difficult, though, and the full steps are shown below. Once created, they are very easy to use:

1   From the File menu in Outlook 2003, choose New, and then Search Folder. The following window is presented (see Figure 7-9).

Figure 7-9.   First step of creating a new Search Folder. Scroll to bottom of this window.

2   Scroll to the bottom of the scrolling list and click once on the very last choice, called Create a Custom Search Folder, so that it is highlighted.

3   Then click the Choose... button that appears in the lower right corner (note that double-clicking the Create a Custom Search Folder item has the same effect as clicking the Choose... button).

4.   A small Custom Search Folder dialog box is presented (see Figure 7-10). Enter the name of your Search Folder within the Name field at the top of that dialog box. This is the name that will display on the folder, so choose a name that reflects the category you will be accumulating.

Figure 7-10. Naming your new Search Folder.

5 Next set the scope of where the Search Folder draws from. In the lower portion of this window, you will see a field named Mail from These Folders Will Be Included in This Search Folder. Next to that is a Browse... button. You use this field and button to indicate the scope of mail that you want this folder to collect from. Do you want to include mail from all folders? Or include only mail from inside your Processed Mail folder? To set choices like this, click the Browse... button. If you are in an Internet e-mail environment you'll see a mail folder selection window with the Personal Folders folder at the top of your folder hierarchy, selected by default (see Figure 7-11).

Think about this carefully. If you leave this default set as it is, your search folder will collect items from *all* your Outlook folders, including Sent Items, Deleted Items, and even nonmail folders. This is not a good choice for our intentions. I recommend instead checking just Inbox and Processed Mail (see Figure 7-12). Be sure to *uncheck* the Personal Folders checkbox at the top of the list. Then click OK.

If you are in an Exchange environment, this list will look different. You may see both the Exchange Server folders and your Personal Folders. However Search Folders have a limitation in an Exchange environment: you will only be able to choose from one mail store, either the Exchange Server or your Personal Folders. I recommend choosing from the Personal Folders mail store. Choose the equivalent of your Processed Mail folder; uncheck everything else and click OK.

Figure 7-11.   Default setting of the Outlook folders that will be searched during population of a Search Folder.

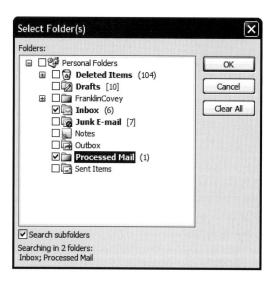

Figure 7-12.   Recommended Outlook folders to include during population of the new Search Folder.

6 After you click OK you'll return to the Custom Search Folder dialog. Now we need to define which category to look for. This is what really defines this particular Search Folder. Click the Criteria... button and you'll see Search Folder Criteria window open. Immediately select the second tab called More Choices (see Figure 7-13).

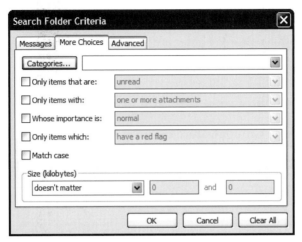

Figure 7-13. More Choices tab, where the Categories button can be found to finally indicate which category this Search Folder will collect.

7 Click the Categories... button, and you will see the by now familiar Categories selection window. Choose the category of interest (Projects for this example) and click OK. Then click OK in the Search Folder Criteria window, click OK in the Custom Search Folder window, and finally click OK in the Custom Search Folder window.

You should now see the My Projects Mail search folder added to the Search Folder hierarchy within your Outlook Folders List view. If you open that search folder, you will see all mail that you have assigned to the Projects category.

These folders self-update, so if you assign the Projects category to more mail later, that new mail will also appear in the previously created Search Folder. Once a Search Folder is created, there is nothing you need do to maintain it.

Deleting Search Folders and Mail Inside Search Folders

Search Folders are a virtual view of your mail. The actual mail sits in real Outlook folder(s) such as the ones you defined above as the source of your search (Processed Mail most likely). So if you are done using a Search Folder, you can delete the folder, and the mail itself is not deleted but is retained in the Processed Mail folder.

However, while viewing individual mail inside a Search Folder the opposite is true. If you delete an individual e-mail item from within the Search Folder, the actual mail item is deleted from its source folder. Any operations (delete, change category, edit item, for example) you perform on *individual* e-mail items within a Search Folder are made on the actual item wherever it is located.

Show in Groups

The Show in Groups feature of Outlook 2003 is another gem. When you first opened Outlook 2003, Show in Groups was probably already turned on in your Inbox for the Received field. If you are seeing your mail grouped in groups like Today, Yesterday, Last Week, then this is it (see Figure 7-14).

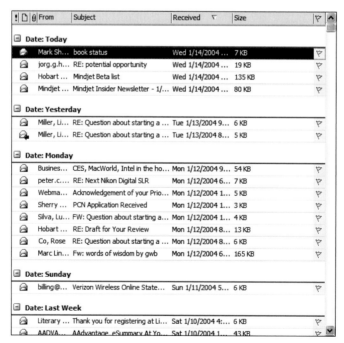

Figure 7-14.   Typical use of the Show in Groups feature is to group your mail by day. Your copy of Outlook 2003 may open by default in this configuration.

What Show in Groups also enables (among other things) is using your Processed Mail view as a category grouping view. If you open your Processed

Mail folder and activate the Show in Groups view based on the Category field, your processed mail list is now grouped by category and each category group is clearly labeled. The list-view contents of each category can be collapsed or expanded like an outline view. In Figure 7-15, I show such a view with all category headings collapsed.

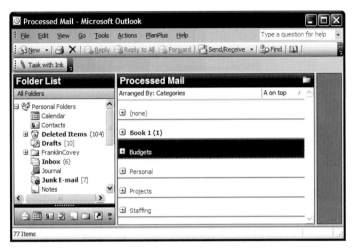

Figure 7-15. The Show in Groups feature can be used to group your mail in category groups, which can be expanded and collapsed like an outline view.

Clicking on the plus sign next to any category expands that category list underneath the heading, showing the mail that match the category. For example if I click on the plus sign next to the Personal category, the mail within expands below that category label (see Figure 7-16).

If a message has more than one category assigned to it, the message will show up multiple times in this list, once under each category group.

The Show in Groups by Category view is an alternative to using Search Folders, and it could be used if you are merely viewing all the messages by individual category. It does not require the multistep setup that Search Folders require. It is a little slower to use than Search Folders because *all* categories will be shown, and so you will need to scroll down the category/mail list to find the category group of interest to you. Plus, you will not be able to sort within a category by various criteria; you can do that with Search Folders. One approach is this: create Search Folders for your main categories, and use Show in Groups when occasionally viewing less-used categories.

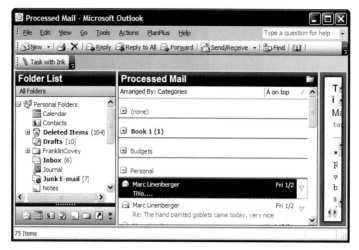

Figure 7-16. Show in Groups view with the Personal group expanded to see the items inside.

Configuring Show in Groups

If you want to use Show in Groups to view e-mail grouped by categories, do this:

1 Open the folder you want to view. This will probably be your Processed Mail folder.

2 From the View menu, choose Arrange By, and place a checkmark next to Show in Groups, near the bottom of the choice list (see Figure 7-17).

3 Immediately go back to the View menu, choose Arrange By again, and now place another checkmark next to Categories. That's it.

4 To start the view with all categories collapsed (so you can find a specific category quickly) from the View menu, choose Expand/Collapse Groups and then choose Collapse All Groups. The view will open fully collapsed as in Figure 7.15. You can then scroll through the group list and expand the group of interest by clicking on the plus sign next to it.

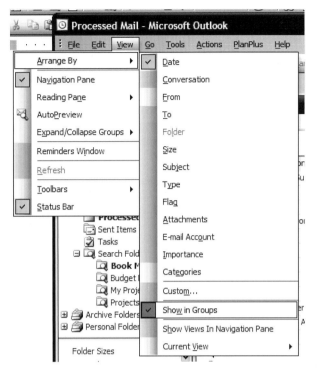

Figure 7-17. Configure Show in Groups from the View menu, clicking on the Arrange By command.

These steps constitute just one of many ways to get to and use Show in Groups within mail views. You can also get to these commands by right-clicking the title area above the e-mail list columns. Some approaches produce slightly different views. And using this right-click approach there are other ways to group without actually checking the Show in Groups box. I'll leave experimenting with this to you.

Creating this view destroys the purely chronological view in the Processed Mail folder, so be sure you know how to reverse the above steps.

David Allen's Methods for Getting Things Done

We are now going to attack a very different need: we will take an advanced look at identifying and working on your own tasks. If you've found that the task management approaches presented in Chapter 6 and thus far in this chapter still leave you with questions about how best to manage your tasks, this section should help.

I recently studied a book by management consultant David Allen called *Getting Things Done*. I found that many of the nagging questions that I was left with after months of managing my tasks using PlanPlus for Outlook were answered by David's book; I encourage you to read it.

For instance, I was bothered by the way my daily tasks B list grew large as I forwarded them on each day. Sure, I followed my own advice and moved some to A and some back to the master task list. But I often felt that some items seemed important even though they continued to sit on the B list, never really presenting themselves as "doable." I was left wondering if something about the way I was approaching these tasks prevented me from acting effectively on them.

David's book answered this question by using a couple of simple but profound concepts that can be integrated into the usage of the PlanPlus or TabletPlanner software described in Chapter 6. Again, to do this topic justice I encourage you to read David's book and then follow the recommendations below. In the meantime, give the ideas below some study now, and see if they help in your task management.

Next Action List

David feels that the concept of a daily to-do list is overemphasized in most time management systems. Instead what should be focused on is the concept of a *next action list*. This is a list of next actions for projects and priorities that you have on your plate that need to be done as soon as possible but that aren't actually assigned to any given day. So they don't appropriately sit on your master task list because they *do* need to be done as soon as possible, but they aren't urgently assigned to any given date either. This accurately describes many items on our long list of B level daily tasks that automatically advance from day to day. And it explains why letting them move on day after day is not such a bad thing.

Action Language

But this perspective also provides significant opportunities for improvement to our earlier approach. One reason many important tasks may hang around on your B level list is not because the priority is in fact low, but rather because the task may not be described in an *action language*. David recommends that all tasks be written in a language that describes a discrete physical action such as "Call Fred and ask for new meeting date," "e-mail James about proposal," or "review Ted's summary notes." They should not be generally stated tasks such as "James's proposal," or "Ted's notes," because these descriptions leave you, on cursory review, uncertain of what to actually do. It may take a minute or two of thought to decide what the action really is, and in the heat of the busy business day that delay will prevent you from acting. A better approach is at the time you write them down on the list you clearly state them as actions.

Very Next Action

And more importantly they should be written as the *very next* discrete physical action that you need to do to progress a task forward. David spends chapters on this point in his book and it is worthy of further discussion here. Most stuck-tasks get stuck because you really haven't thought through and identified the *very next* action needed on the task. It is essential that you clearly think through what this very next action is, and write *that* down on your to-do-next list. This thought process often leads to the creation of what I am calling miniprojects.

Identify Miniprojects

In identifying a next action for a particular task, you will probably find that more than one action-step is required to accomplish the goal of that task. So when multiple actions are needed, David recommends you reclassify the task as a *project* (I like to call these *miniprojects* when they are not separately managed). For instance let's say after further analysis we determine that the task called "Acme sales proposal" will take at least three discrete physical actions to complete. David Allen suggests that you identify this as a project, put it on a list of projects, and then ask yourself "what is the very next action I need to take to move this project forward?" Place only the very next action item for the project on your next action list: "call Jim and get Acme sales notes." This keeps your tasks list action-oriented and focused on the immediate. Then David suggests that in your weekly reviews you review each of these projects, you identify any new next action items that should be placed on your next action list, and put them there.

Combining Systems

All of these recommendations are good. They helped me tremendously to move past many of my stuck tasks, and they can be effectively combined with the PlanPlus or TabletPlanner system described in Chapter 6. Note however that when combining these, you will probably find the PlanPlus software easier to integrate than TabletPlanner since it gives you access to Outlook categories.

In *Getting Things Done*, David teaches his system in a general way, so he does not spend much time telling you how to apply it to a specific automated system like Outlook, and certainly he spends no time on PlanPlus or TabletPlanner. So below I offer recommendations on how to adopt key principles from David's system and implement them in the FranklinCovey software. These are very much just my suggestions; you may find other ways to merge these two systems.

Side Note: David does sell a separate 37-page booklet on how to apply his principles to Outlook, available on his website: www.davidco.com, or you can buy his Outlook plug-in, available at the same site. I suspect however that the plug-in may not be compatible with PlanPlus; this may be an either-or choice.

New Approach to Daily Tasks List

Adopting my recommended combination of these approaches, your daily tasks list will now become the equivalent of David Allen's next action list. The auto-forwarding feature of Outlook or TabletPlanner is what makes this possible. Use your daily list as follows:

■ Continue to assign yourself A level daily tasks that must be completed on a given day. Assign them either to today or to a day in the future as appropriate. This treatment of "must do today" tasks is generally consistent across both systems.

■ Next, take a look at your current list of B level daily task items and identify what the next physical action is for each of these. If this simply means rewriting the task in action-oriented language, then do that.

■ If however you discover that this is a larger task requiring multiple actions, identify what the first of those actions is, write that as a new B level task on your daily list for today, and then make an entry in your master task list for this new miniproject. Put a "P-" in front of the task name so that you can find all your projects easily later. Or for PlanPlus users, consider assigning it a Projects category in Outlook. Give this project in your master list a B priority; we are going to use the B level for all these miniprojects and reserve the A level within the master task list for listing your large, separately managed projects.

■ As before, the "due date" of B tasks on your daily list should represent when they should first appear on your daily list, not when they are actually due.

■ Don't enter any C level tasks in the daily task list; they don't belong there.

New Approach to the Master Task List

C Level Master Tasks

Continue to reserve C level master task items for tasks or projects that you have no intention of doing right away but for which you want to leave a placeholder. David Allen would probably call our C level master task list his "someday maybe" list; the definitions seem equivalent.

B Level Master Tasks

Again at the B level of the master task list: I recommend you make this B level master task list into your miniproject list as described above under Daily Tasks. These are tasks that are too small to be treated as separately delegated projects but too big to accomplish in one physical action. For example "Landscape front yard"; the next action on this is probably "Call Smith's landscaping service for quote." That's what goes on my B level daily task list, and "P-Landscape Front Yard" goes on my B level master task list so that I can refer back to it week after week to see if there are other next actions required. For this B level master task list, if you're uncertain whether the item is really a miniproject or just a B level master task, don't worry, define it either way, we will treat it the same in our weekly review.

Use the Notes Field

All Outlook and TabletPlanner tasks have a notes field. Within the notes field of the master task entry for projects write any other upcoming steps that you may brainstorm at the moment but that can't be acted upon now. You will look at this notes list weekly to move these steps out to your daily task list as needed. This notes field may be a good place to create a project planning sheet that lists the intended outcome of the miniproject, the stakeholders, intermediate steps, and whatever else is needed. After you get good at this you might create a template that you copy into the notes section of all miniprojects in your B level master tasks list. You study this planning sheet every week, during your personal weekly review meeting.

Also, as you complete daily next action tasks for these miniprojects, immediately go back and examine that notes section in the master list. The completion of that task may have freed up a dependent next action to move out to the daily list.

A Level Master Tasks

The A level of the master task list I suggest be reserved for those big projects that you have actually started or intend to start separate management activities for. These are your projects that require separate project meetings, separate formal project plans and so on. You may have delegated these projects to other staff. You want these projects to sort to the top of the master list because they deserve your highest discretionary attention; that's why we're marking them with an A. Rather than using the notes section of this A level item for a planning sheet (that should be done in separate documents and applications for big projects), use it to enter any quick brainstorming ideas you may have during the week on those projects but that you do not have time to integrate into your formal plans when you think of them. Then you use your weekly review or your formal project meetings to apply those brainstorming ideas appropriately to detailed plans.

Weekly Review

Within David's system the weekly review is extremely important. This is when you review your project list and discover additional next actions for your projects. In your weekly review, step through the projects on your B level master task list and ask yourself: "What is the next action needed to move this forward?" If you identify something, write it on your daily task list. If it is something that is moderately urgent but could be done any time, write it on today's list, set it at a B level, and let it forward along until you can get to it. And if it won't become important or doable for week or so, perhaps assign it to a date a week or so out so that it does not start appearing on your daily task list until then. If it needs to be done today or tomorrow, give it an A level priority and assign it to that day.

Open the notes view of each project and see if you have any items listed there that need to be moved to the daily task list. For A level separately managed projects, pull your project folders and update the formal project plan based on the notes fields of these items in your projects list. Or use this time to plan and create agenda items for the next formal meeting on that large project.

And with your daily tasks list, this is the time to do the review described in Chapter 6 in the section called Daily Task List Management. You may need to convert some B items to A, to finally get them done. Or you may move some B items back to the master list, recognizing that their importance has waned over time.

The weekly review is also when to review your C level list in the master task view to determine if the needs for any of those ideas have matured enough to warrant moving them to the daily list or project level of the master list.

Why This Works So Well, and What's the Cost?

The beauty of this approach is that in your short moments of available time throughout a day, you will find that it is much easier to act on a task that is described in physical action steps. Only next actions are put in front of you during those "what can I do next" moments during holes in the day. I suspect you will find that you are able to work through your daily list much more quickly when your tasks are selected and specified this way. The approach helps avoid those hand-wringing moments when you stare at your task list and just can't move on important tasks. Usually the inertia is due to no actual next action jumping out at you from your list.

This efficiency does not come for free, though. To make this really work you need to transfer your "hand-wringing" time to what may be an extended weekly review period. With this approach you now more than ever need a time where you can sit quietly and calmly figure out what the next action is for all the things on your plate. The advantage is that if you can really pull away to do this planning, you can during that period keep yourself in the proper frame of mind to creatively and clearly identify all project next actions all at once. Trying to do this on and off during sporadic moments of free time throughout a hectic business week doesn't work.

Just Scratched the Surface

I've only scratched the surface of the good ideas that can be found in David Allen's book that can help you with your task management efforts, ideas that can easily be applied to the PlanPlus or TabletPlanner systems. For example, he recommends that all next action tasks should be categorized into context categories such as "calls," "at home," "read/review." By doing that, for example when you have a gap in time and are at a phone, you can sort on your calls list and make them all at once. Or if you are about to jump on a plane, pull up your read/review list and bring some high-priority reading material along. To make this happen, something that works well with the PlanPlus for Outlook system is to use the Outlook categories capability to make such assignments.

And David also has excellent strategies for organizing physical filing systems, which you may need to augment your task management approach.

Force Fit?

Note that in some ways I have force-fit David's system into the Franklin-Covey software. I've done this because FranklinCovey has embraced the Tablet PC across multiple dimensions of use and deserves to be considered as a whole. You may find, however, after studying David's book that you want to adopt his approach directly within Outlook or in his Outlook Plug-in software, exclusively, and leave the FranklinCovey software behind. This is a reasonable decision as there are alternatives described in the chapters ahead to nearly every function the FranklinCovey software provides. You would lose and possibly miss the all-in-one packaging in the FranklinCovey approach.

Reconfigure Outlook

Overdue Items Are Not Overdue

Here's a next action for you: if you do decide to adopt this approach, I recommend that you reconfigure Outlook to make one minor change: change the color of tasks that are not completed on their due date. By default that is set to red. I dislike seeing a long list of red tasks occupying most of my Outlook tasks list. According to the ideas we've been discussing, that red color is inappropriate. The due date is really just the first day the item appears on my "next action list," so forwarding it on each day should not be thought of as "overdue."

When making this change, you could change "overdue" items so they look identical to new items (black), but I changed mine to dark blue so at least I can still see a minor distinction between those and tasks that first appear there (new tasks remain black).

Make this change by going to the Tools menu, Options, Preferences tab, click on the Task Options button, and change the color shown next to Overdue Task Color. (See Figure 7-18.)

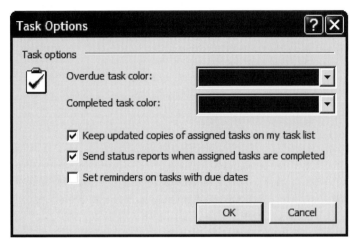

Figure 7-18. Changing the color of overdue tasks in Outlook.

The exception to this adjustment is that A level daily tasks really are overdue when they slip. Unfortunately there is no way to differentiate how Outlook treats these. But since I treat all A level tasks with extra attention, even a blue A task catches my eye.

Also note that this change only works on the Outlook tasks view. In case you were thinking of doing this with PlanPlus, the PlanPlus task view still retains red as the color for overdue items, even after making the above setting change.

Move Tasks to Current Date

But all is not lost for PlanPlus. If you want to eliminate the red color of all daily tasks this is possible, but you will need to do this once each day, since the change does not stick. Luckily, doing this only takes a half second. Click a button that advances the due date for all tasks in your daily list to today. Just click on the Move Tasks to Current Date button in the bar just above the PlanPlus task list, and the red will go away. (See Figure 7-19.) You do not have to select any tasks first; it operates on all daily tasks.

Move Tasks to Current Date

Figure 7-19. In PlanPlus the Move Tasks to Current Date button will advance the due date of all daily tasks to the current date.

Chapter 8 Note Taking with the Tablet PC

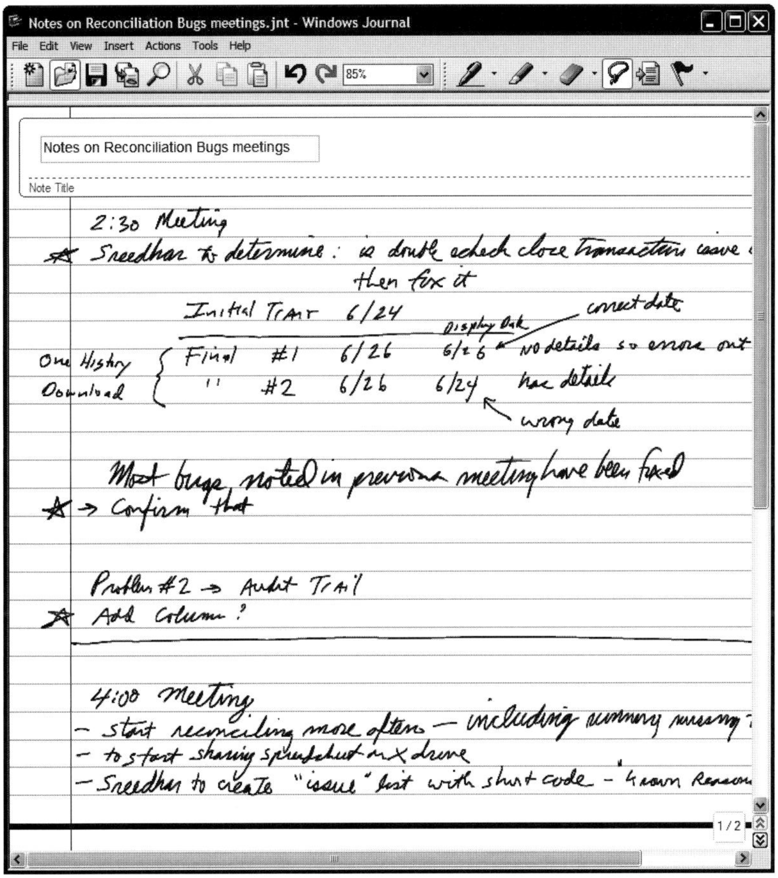

The Business Case

T aking notes on my Tablet PC is fantastic. It is so incredibly convenient to have all my notes in one place, even a year or more worth of notes. Being able to search and find old notes, nearly instantly, has saved my neck many times in business situations.

Studies have shown that approximately 25 percent of workers who take handwritten notes cannot find information they need from those notes later. That same study pointed out that 77 percent of workers who take handwritten notes type at least a portion of those notes into their PC later. The Tablet PC solves both these problems.

Other studies have shown that transcribers using a Tablet PC can increase their productivity 39 percent, and those searching notes save 62 percent of their time.

But most importantly, beyond the cumulative benefit of time savings, the ability to get to and view important saved notes quickly can make or break the success of a meeting.

Real Life Scenario

I am in a budget meeting with my boss and CFO in attendance. In this meeting we're formalizing budget allocations for my department, basing the discussion on informal agreements made two months earlier among the three of us. A series of line-by-line amounts is proposed to me in this new meeting, and a few of them seem small in comparison to what I thought we had agreed to in the initial meeting. Within seconds on my Tablet PC, I find and pull up my handwritten notes of the original meeting. In those notes, in my handwriting, I had a sketch of the budget information matching the table my boss had written on the whiteboard two months earlier. He instantly recognizes his table in my note, and instructs the CFO to use my numbers. I just avoided losing $20,000 of budget from my department.

Ink Is Your Friend

Perhaps the single most discussed feature of the Tablet PC, and for that matter of pen computing in the past, is the ability to take handwritten notes and have those notes stored in an easily accessible and searchable way on a portable computer. That's exactly what the note-taking tools on the Table PC give you: easy input and fast retrieval of handwritten notes.

For the majority of Tablet PC owners, this is their most-used feature. The pros and cons of various note-taking tools are discussed endlessly on the Tablet PC forums. And, in general, this is the feature Tablet PC owners love the most about their machines.

Surprisingly, though, one of the great disappointments expressed by a number of industry reviewers upon superficial review of Tablet PCs is that representation of notes as digital ink is still the primary practical way for storing notes on the Tablet PC. As discussed in the ink strategies chapter (Chapter 5) many reviewers still expect all notes to be converted to text and express a sense of loss when that is not practical.

If you share this expectation, to convert all your notes to text, I encourage you to read Chapter 5 on ink versus text conversion and to get mentally past this surface-level expectation of the Tablet PC. Note taking in ink is effective and workable. In fact, I find it generally preferable to conversion of notes to text. Taking notes in ink:

- facilitates creativity in your note taking

- communicates more about the meaning of your notes

- integrates better with sketches and expressive marks on the note-taking page

- is a better way to represent information copied from whiteboards and presentations

- is a faster way to record notes, faster than even the most speedy and accurate handwriting recognition

I can virtually guarantee that after a few days or weeks of taking notes primarily in ink, you too will be convinced that this is a highly effective and preferable method of note taking on the Tablet PC. The ability to later convert those handwritten notes to text, with some editing efforts, will then be viewed as an added benefit, not a show-stopping requirement.

Tablet PC: Best for Taking Meeting Notes

In keeping with my theme that the Tablet PC is most valuable when used within meetings, it follows that note taking on the Tablet PC is most valuable when done for meeting notes. If I were sitting at a desk browsing the web on my own, or reading through physical books or magazines, and I needed to take notes on what I was reading, I would probably use the mouse to copy and paste sentences and use the keyboard to type additional notes. However within the context of a meeting, the dynamics change dramatically. As discussed in Chapter 1, typing on a laptop computer within a meeting is usually inappropriate: it's noisy and distracting. Typing notes in a meeting usually leads to lack of eye contact between you and others, which can be perceived as rude or inattentive. The placement of a laptop with the screen flipped open on a conference room table in front of you creates a physical barrier between you and the others in the room. And perhaps most importantly, two-handed typing during a meeting will lead to a lack of your attention to the activities in the meeting. This is because the use of both hands tends to engage a larger percentage of the brain in the typing activity, leaving reduced mental processing available for the dynamics of the meeting.

In contrast, one-handed note taking with a pen onto a padlike device in your lap or on the table in front of you imitates a universally acceptable activity within meetings. It is virtually silent; it does not present a physical barrier between you and others; it generally allows regular eye contact between you and others in the room. And because it requires only one hand it distracts a smaller portion of your brain, leaving you attentive and participatory in the meeting.

So the point here is if you are going to take notes in a meeting using a computer, make sure that computer is a Tablet PC using its pen interface. This is true whether you are meeting in a large group or one-on-one. In either case your positive engagement in the meeting when note taking with a Tablet PC will be equivalent to note taking with a pen and pad of paper.

Reasons Why Taking Notes with a Tablet PC Is Better than Taking Notes on Paper

There seem to be three approaches that executives commonly use when taking notes in business settings.

- The first is to write on a pad of tear-off paper. Notes are taken on the top sheet and, when that sheet is full, it is torn off and placed into a file folder corresponding to the topic of the meeting. Presumably if information is needed later the user knows which file folders to look in. I've never liked this approach because meetings often cover a mixture of topics, and so the file folder never correctly indicates what the notes are about. And finding documents in those file folders later is cumbersome.

- The second is to use a personal organizer calendar system in a physical notebook in which notes are taken for each day and filed in the calendar's loose-leaf notebook for that day. Searches for notes then take a chronological approach.

■ Third is the use of a bound notebook or journal. Starting at the beginning of the notebook, notes are taken in chronological fashion until the notebook is full. Again searching is done chronologically.

The last two are probably the best of the physical approaches, since the value of notes tends to age quickly, and so searching backward through chronological note pages is usually the most fruitful. Regardless of which physical method you use, there are shared fundamental reasons why the Tablet PC methods are always better.

Search Capability

The number one vision most people have when thinking of storing their notes in a computer is that notes converted to text are easy to search for. This is the primary reason most people new to the Tablet PC think all notes should be converted to text. However when I take notes on the Tablet PC I rarely convert my handwriting to text. As I will describe below I generally convert only the title of the notes, or key spellings that I need to capture such as names and addresses.

What most people may not realize is that behind the scenes, all the major note-taking applications that we're discussing here are actually converting your handwriting to text and storing that text information in the background with your file, whether you explicitly convert it or not. Later, when you do a text search on your handwritten notes, that search will search through these background conversions. So if, say, the Tablet PC is 95 percent correct on text conversion, whether you explicitly convert your text or not, you have a 95 percent chance of finding text within your handwritten notes; not bad odds for an automated search. And if your automated search was unsuccessful, you can flip through the pages visually just like you can in a paper notebook. Sometimes graphic sketches and highlighting offer the visual clues you need to find a section of notes you're looking for, and a visual scan is the only way to find these clues.

Distribution of Notes

The second most important reason for using the Tablet PC is the ability to easily distribute notes from a meeting. Whether you distribute the notes as handwriting or take the effort to edit the text that results from a conversion to text, the process is much easier and quicker with the Tablet PC than with the paper-based system. There are several reasons for this:

- You can distribute the handwritten notes as files attached to an e-mail, without the need to scan or fax.

- If you do decide to convert to text, it is likely that at least 95 percent of the text is converted accurately, leaving a fairly minor editing effort to finish the job.

- Hand sketches are often a bit sloppy at first; Windows Journal allows you to convert roughly sketched shapes to their geometric equivalent; your notes with sketches will go out looking much more readable if they are in a Tablet PC and able to be cleaned up.

Storing a Year's Worth or More of Your Notes in One Place, for Easy Review and Searching

Prior to the Tablet PC, my method of taking meeting notes was to put a college spiralbound notepad in a fancy looking executive notepad cover, and write day after day notes about each meeting and phone call. I did this until the notebook was full, which was generally in two to three months. At that time I would put the filled notebook on my shelf, insert a new spiralbound notepad, and start afresh. This was fairly effective because when I needed to search for information recorded from previous meetings, I would commonly be looking for recent meetings, and a three-month limit on information was rarely significant. The problem came when I was doing my search within a meeting and had recently switched notebooks. My leather cover would not hold two notebooks at the same time, so if I had switched recently my information searches could be limited to just a few days or just a few weeks worth of notes.

And it was not unheard of to need to search for information from a meeting six months or more earlier. Although it was no problem pulling the old notebooks off the shelf for such an extended search, flipping visually through the pages of six months worth of paper notes is not a very fun task. The result was that I rarely did long-term searches through old notes.

The Tablet PC frees you from these limitations. Furthermore, all the notes are stored in a single place, your Tablet PC, and so you can carry these notes everywhere you go.

Rapid Search for Key Items

Both Windows Journal and Microsoft OneNote allow you to "flag" specific parts of your notes for easy retrieval later. We'll describe how these features work in more detail, but for an example of the value of this, consider if you marked to-do items in your notes with an easily locatable flag. Think how valuable the ability to rapidly find those flags is with the Tablet PC. In fact with Microsoft OneNote, you can actually extract and consolidate all flagged items into a list document, leading to the instant creation of a to-do list.

Your Note-Taking Software Choices

Of all the activities I do with my Tablet PC, note taking probably involves the most pen-on-screen time. I predict this will be your major activity as well. So it pays to pick a note-taking software package that meets your needs and that you can use easily and comfortably. And if you're anywhere as busy as I am, you don't want to learn three different packages with the hope that one will meet your needs. Rather you'd like to pick the right one upfront and spend the learning time just once. In the remainder of this chapter and the entire next one I will review these note-taking software choices, hopefully providing enough observations and details for you to both make a selection and learn software use.

You Have Four Choices for Note-Taking Software:

- Windows Journal

- FranklinCovey PlanPlus for Outlook

- FranklinCovey TabletPlanner

- Microsoft OneNote

The first three software packages we will review in this chapter, and I've reserved the entire next chapter for Microsoft OneNote.

Recommendations

How do these software choices fare? Until I tried out the new versions of FranklinCovey PlanPlus and TabletPlanner, my recommendation for the busy manager with simple note-taking needs was easy: use Windows Journal. However version two of PlanPlus and version three of TabletPlanner both include a new note-taking tool nearly equivalent in power and simplicity to Windows Journal. And the fact that they are both integrated with other key software makes these both compelling alternatives. So these three packages may now be neck and neck for simple note taking. And OneNote fills a special need for more complex note taking capabilities. The decision between these four comes down to this.

- Do you prefer a separate note-taking application that uses the Windows file system to store and launch notes? And do you have moderate needs for searchable note flags? If so use Windows Journal.

- Do you prefer using a fully integrated package that stores notes merged in with Outlook? If so choose PlanPlus.

- Do you prefer a fully integrated package that replaces Outlook's non-e-mail functionality and favors digital ink storage for most activities? If so choose TabletPlanner.

- And do you find yourself cleaning up and reorganizing handwritten notes a lot, either because you refer back to them consistently or because you plan to distribute them? And do you need a powerful note flag capability? If so choose Microsoft OneNote (which is reviewed in the next chapter).

Windows Journal

By far the most popular, most referenced, and most beloved application on the Tablet PC, in any category, is Windows Journal. And note taking is the primary purpose of Windows Journal. Note taking with Windows Journal is a pleasure in simplicity. While you'll find disadvantages when compared to the more advanced and just released Microsoft OneNote application, the simplicity and versatility of Windows Journal continues to impress, keeping it the note-taking tool of choice among many in the Tablet PC user community.

Windows Journal will probably remain the centerpiece of your Tablet PC activities, even beyond note taking. Its many uses include (each of these are detailed in their corresponding chapters in this book):

■ Note taking (of course)

■ Document markup and annotation

■ Brainstorming and sketching

■ Presentations

■ Simple forms tool

But the focus of this chapter is on note taking, so read on.

There are two reasons I greatly appreciate Windows Journal for simple note taking compared to other note-taking tools on the Tablet PC. First is the simple and intuitive writing interface, and second is a feature which helps me find and open specific note files quickly using an excellent intuitive method of listing and grouping notes chronologically. Let's start with the intuitive writing interface now, and I'll cover the chronological list features a little later.

Strategies for Taking Simple Notes with Windows Journal

I'd like to spend a little time describing how I take notes with Windows Journal; often it's the fine points of software usage that make or break its effectiveness. I hope that sharing these points will get you on the road toward regular usage of the Tablet PC for note taking. And even if you think you may decide to use another note-taking tool, I recommend at least reading about how Windows Journal is used and taking at least *some* notes in Windows Journal. It will serve as the basis for your future note-taking adventures.

Below is the default note-taking page that appears when you launch Windows Journal. (See Figure 8-1.)

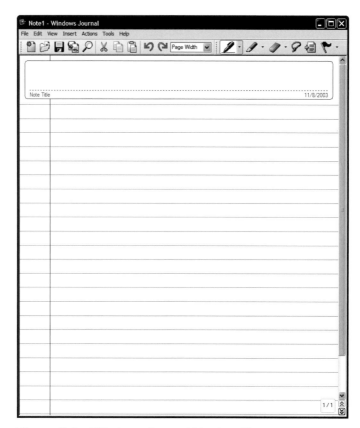

Figure 8-1.   Windows Journal blank writing page.

What you see is basically what you get: nothing fancy, just a simple blank lined piece of paper, ready to write on.

Usually I come marching into a meeting just as it starts or maybe even a little late, and have to quickly start taking notes because our meetings usually start getting serious quite quickly. As mentioned in the beginning part of this book Windows Journal is one of the applications that I keep running all the time. Because of this, and because I use the configuration recommended in Chapter 4, within about 5 or 10 seconds I can get from late arrival mode into ready for note-taking mode. This is a key advantage of the Tablet PC and something that makes it practical to use day after day; it is as ready for action as your paper notebook.

Journal usually opens to the most recent page of notes that I have taken, per-haps notes from the meeting I just came from or a meeting earlier that day. So this is just like flipping to the open page on your paper-based notebook where you're ready to add more notes to the page that you were recently writing on or to start a new page.

Creating a New Note Page

Normally, since this is a new meeting, I want a new page that I can give a new note title to. So to pull up a new page I simply click the New Note icon which is the left-most icon on the upper toolbar within Windows Journal.

This creates a new blank page. As I said I am usually moving pretty fast as I arrive at meetings, so my first action is probably to start writing notes on the first blank line, below the notes title section. I do not start with trying to populate the title section.

Normally Windows Journal opens with the Pen tool selected, so I am able to start writing immediately; if the Pen tool is for some reason not selected just click on the pen icon and start writing.

The default pen is usually the best one, a match for a fine-tipped ballpoint pen.

We covered basic writing in Windows Journal in the getting started section so I won't repeat that information here; read that section now if you have not yet done so.

Getting back to my meeting that just started, since I am usually in a rush, I might immediately start recording points from the meeting, or I might make the first sentence a long description of what the meeting is for, or I might write down the name of some attendees in the meeting in case they just intro-duced themselves and that information is fresh in my mind. I do not need to write the date of the meeting at the top of my notes because that data is automatically stamped within the title bar.

Entering a Note Title

Within a few minutes, after the meeting startup activities have eased, and after I may have taken a flurry of initial notes, the meeting settles down enough for me to decide how I want to title this note. Only then do I actually write a title in the Note Title box at the top of the page. The reason for waiting a few minutes is that whatever gets placed in this Note Title box is the default name of the Windows file that gets saved for these notes, and thus becomes the title that you'll see if you start searching for this note later by title. So you want to give at least a little thought to how this title should read. And you'll want to keep the title relatively short so that you can understand it when you see it in a scrolling list later.

Once I decide on the title name I write it into the Note Title box, and I then usually immediately convert that title to text. Or if the meeting is moving fast I do that as soon as I have time within the meeting to pause again from note taking. We covered conversion of handwriting to text earlier, but let's repeat it here since it's been awhile.

Converting handwriting to text is easy; simply select the Lasso tool,

and draw a circle around the text you want to convert. (See Figure 8-2.)

Figure 8-2.   Selecting text in Windows Journal.

You then choose from the Actions menu Convert Handwriting to Text.

You'll than see a text correction dialog box which allows you to fix any particular words prior to inserting the converted text. In that box, words that the software suspects may be wrong are highlighted in green, and alternative choices are displayed in a scrolling list at the right of the box. Instead of selecting suggested alternative conversions, you can select the incorrect text, and then correct the text using the Tablet PC Input Panel.

Once you fix any words here, and click OK, you'll be presented with a dialog box asking you to decide whether you want to have Windows Journal copy the text to the clipboard or insert the text into the Journal note; select the second choice.

A Couple of Points about Converting the Note Title to Text

After you convert the note title to text, you'll be presented with an oversized text box and the converted text will be in the upper left corner of that text box. I recommend that you immediately resize this text box to fit inside the title area of the Windows Journal page.

And here's another important point: make sure that none of your actual notes from the writing area below stray into the title box area. This is very important because otherwise these notes will interfere with the Recent Notes listing option that I discuss below. Even stray marks like the top of a letter or the dot on an "i" will cause a problem. If you see any such stray marks in the Note Title area, use the Windows Journal Eraser tool (in one of the nonstroke modes described below) to remove them before you save your notes. (See Figure 8-3.)

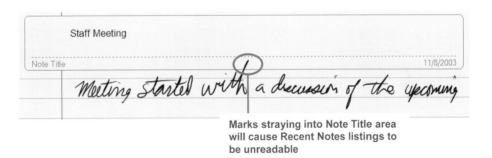

Figure 8-3. Marks straying into the Note Title area should be avoided.

The next housekeeping job I do as I find a pause in the intensity of the meeting is to save the note by clicking on the disk icon in the upper toolbar of Windows Journal.

At this point the standard Windows Save As dialog box appears. Assuming you converted the title to text and corrected any spelling or recognition errors, the text in the Note Title area of the note will now appear as the default filename for this note document. (See Figure 8-4.)

Figure 8-4.   Default filename is picked up from note title.

Clicking OK saves the note as a separate file that you can easily open later and leaves the note document open for additional notes.

Again, choosing a good title is important because searching for notes by looking for the title of the notes will probably become your most common way of retrieving notes. Usually my notes are for meetings, and so I usually make the notes title the same as a meeting title.

The other search guide is how recently the meeting occurred, and that's where the Recent Notes feature of Journal comes into play.

Viewing Recent Notes

Windows Journal has a highly intuitive way to view recent notes chronologically that seems to always help me find my notes quickly. The way to use this is to choose the View menu, click on the Recent Notes selection, and from the submenu choose By Creation Date. This opens a split pane window above your note-taking area, within the Windows Journal application, that lists all notes by name. (See Figure 8-5.)

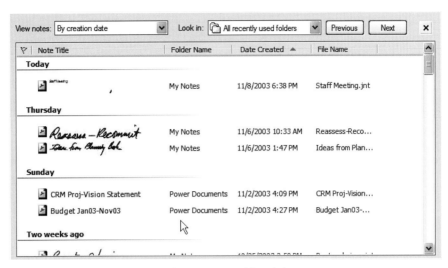

Figure 8-5. Recent notes view, grouped by date.

The very useful design element here is the way that the notes are listed as groups with subheadings. These subheadings very descriptively show when the notes were taken. Groups of notes listed under headings such as "Today," "Yesterday," "Last week," "Two weeks ago," "Earlier this month," or even "Earlier this year," make a visual search for notes by recentness and name very intuitive. This is similar to the Show in Groups command available in Windows Explorer and in Outlook 2003. Also Microsoft OneNote has a similar view available.

Take a careful look at the above recent notes window; a couple points on this.

I've purposely left a few note titles without conversion to text. Notice that Windows Journal displays under the Note Title column of the Recent Notes window the handwriting that is in the Note Title area of the corresponding note. Sometimes this is a good approach, but sometimes it's unreadable. That's why I generally recommend converting the title to text. Luckily if you do forget to convert to text and the note title is unreadable, the note is not lost: the actual filename is displayed in the far right column of the Recent Notes window.

Side Note: Also note that even if you do convert to text, as mentioned above a stray mark in the text block can still make this unreadable. See the entry under Today in Figure 8-5 above? That title entry has been converted to text; however notice how it's almost unreadable. This is the result of the stray mark that we left in the title area. If when viewing the recent notes section you see your title is very small, it's probably due to a stray mark in the title block area. You can always go back to the original note later and clean this up.

There are other ways to view lists of notes and other ways to search for specific notes (such as using the full text search capability), but using Recent Notes is nearly always the way I list and find my notes. In fact I keep this Recent Notes list window open at all times while in Journal. I am often referring to notes made earlier in the day or the day before; this is my way of jumping around within my recently taken notes. If you do decide to keep this open, you may want to resize this panel by dragging its lower edge; this way you can balance the list view and your writing area appropriately.

Printed Notes

Another thing I really like about Windows Journal is how nicely it prints notes on a laser or ink jet printer, if for example you need to distribute printed copies of your handwritten notes. I don't know why this is, but the printed notes look even better than they do on screen. The notes look just as though they were taken in your handwriting with a ballpoint pen on paper and then run through a high quality copy machine. They are very sharp and very clear. And the underlying template prints perfectly as well. This is one reason why I feel Journal is such a great way to fill out forms: blank forms that are input as templates, filled in by hand, and later printed.

Adding Additional Pages to Your Notes

As you get to the bottom of your first page of the notes by writing and scrolling, you'll notice that Journal does not act like a word processor; it does not create additional space for you automatically. With Windows Journal when you reach the bottom of the page you come to a hard stop; the page just stops and you can scroll no farther. This may seem odd, but this is Windows Journal's way of reminding you that you need to explicitly create each page that you take notes on. This allows you to preserve the visual integrity of sketches or groups of words that need to display together. When you print these notes you don't want to split the pages across the middle of a sketch or the middle of an important group of words.

The way you explicitly tell Windows Journal to insert a new page is by clicking on the downward-facing chevron in the lower right corner of the page. A new blank page will be displayed. Notice it will display without a new title bar.

Once you have created a number of pages, these same chevrons are then used to navigate amongst those pages.

Next Steps

With the information covered so far, you can be successfully taking notes for weeks. You may want to stop here and do just that. It important to get in the habit of using this new tool regularly, and if you make it too complicated at this point, you may not actually use it in the heat of a fast-moving meeting.

In my first days of using the Tablet PC I continued to bring a paper notebook to all meetings. This was because there were times when I felt I just didn't yet trust this new method of taking notes. And the meetings were moving too fast and were too important to take the chance of my not recording some information. Within a week however I completely stopped bringing my paper notebooks to meetings.

After a few weeks I felt I was nimble enough with the Tablet PC and Windows Journal to start using some of Journal's more advanced features within the combat of a fast business meeting. These are covered next.

Taking Advantage of Added Features of Windows Journal

Highlighter Tool

One of the first additional features that I started to use in Windows Journal was the ability to use digital highlighting to emphasize portions of my notes. I found it very useful to be able to drag the wide-tipped felt yellow marker tool across sections of notes, just like I would with a physical yellow highlight ink pen. The Highlighter tool appears as follows on the main toolbar:

One thing to keep in mind is that any time you add color to a note document, you may lose the ability to print out a clear representation of your notes.

Eraser Settings

Next, I recommend that you learn the differences of the various eraser settings. The stroke setting is the one I always use and the one you'll probably like the most. It erases in chunks, where each chunk represent all the ink laid down in any given stroke of the pen. When drawing graphics however you may actually want to shorten some lines without erasing the entire line. In that case you should use one of the nonstroke settings that act more like a normal eraser. With the nonstroke settings your choices are based on the size of the erased area: small, medium, or large. (See Figure 8-6.)

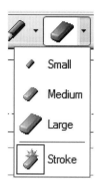

Figure 8-6. Eraser choices in Windows Journal.

Changing the Pen Tool Size and Color

The next slightly advanced thing I did was to use different pen choices. Perhaps the default fine point pen just doesn't feel right to you given the nature and size of your strokes when writing.

And you can also change pen color. Imagine being able to come back through your notes and make edits in red ink. You can also change the thickness or style of the pen.

To start using these different pen settings just click the down arrow next to the Pen tool on the Standard toolbar. You'll see five pen choices in the upper portion of this menu; they may not match those in Figure 8-7 below so ignore those for now and immediately select the Pen Settings menu choice at the bottom.

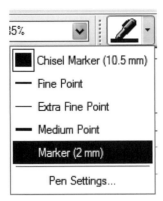

Figure 8-7. Pen choices menu.

The following dialog box (see Figure 8-8) presents itself; make sure the Pen Settings tab is selected.

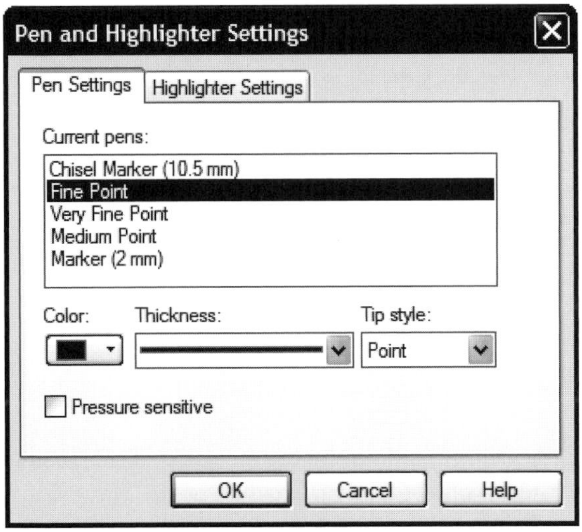

Figure 8-8. Pen and Highlighter Settings.

This window is actually a little confusing so let me explain how it works. The upper portion marked Current Pens represents the five pen setting combinations your copy of Journal currently has configured for fast selection. These were the pens that were presented to you at the top of the pen arrow menu when you first pulled it down a moment ago. The idea is that the average note taker will probably need no more than five pen types throughout the day, but he or she may want to custom configure which five pen types are presented. This window allows you to configure those five fast-pen choices from a nearly unlimited number of combinations of color, thickness, tip styles, and pressure sensitivity.

The place to make your full custom settings is at the bottom of this window. Here you can choose color, thickness, and tip styles. So the way to use this is this. First check to see if the pen type that you need is already in the list of five pens in the Current Pens list. If so no change is needed. If not you need to edit one of the existing five choices. To do this, highlight one item in that list that you do not mind losing, and then edit it using the color, thickness, and tip style selections in the bottom portion of the window. As you edit, you will notice that the name of the highlighted selection in the list changes to match your new settings. Once done, click OK to close this window. That new pen setting will now appear in the list of five pens that you can choose from when you first click the arrow next to the pen icon on the main toolbar.

Pressure Sensitivity

If you have a pressure sensitive screen built into your Tablet PC, clicking the pressure sensitive checkbox on the above window for a given selected pen will allow that pen to draw thicker lines when you push harder and thinner lines when you push softer. When you click that box, the setting only applies to the one pen you are currently configuring. If you want this to apply to all pens, select each one and click the box, one at a time.

Inserting Text Blocks

We showed you how to convert handwriting to text, but what if you want to type directly into your Windows Journal note window, with no intermediate handwriting stage?

You do this by choosing from the Insert menu the Text Box command. The cursor beneath the tip of your pen then changes to a crosshair cursor. Use this cursor to draw a box on your document and when you release your pen that box is now ready for you to type into. Once you complete typing and you click out of the box, in order to edit it some more you will need to choose the Lasso tool.

Formatting Handwritten Text

Here's an interesting formatting capability, although I've never needed to use it in business notes. You can actually select handwritten ink and apply text formatting to it. Try this:

1 Write a sentence of text.

2 Select one or two words within that sentence, using the Lasso tool.

3 Go to the Edit menu and choose the Format Ink... selection.

Note that you can actually make your current ink bold, italic, or a different color.

Using Different Background Templates

All the notes we have taken so far have been on a college-rule-style notebook paper template. This is probably all you'll need for your standard note taking, but you do have some options. For instance if you're doing more drawing then note taking, why not use a graph paper–like grid as your underlying background. If you want to do this, you need to make this change when you start the new document. Choose from the File menu: New Note from Template... and you will see the following window (see Figure 8-9):

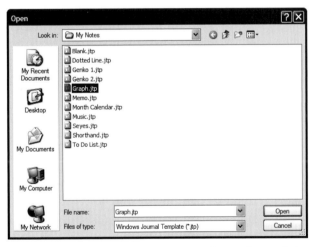

Figure 8-9. Choosing a Windows Journal template.

Choose Graph.jtp, and the new document that opens (see Figure 8-10) will look like a piece of engineering graph paper. In your spare time, I suggest you try creating new documents from each of the templates in this list just to see what is offered.

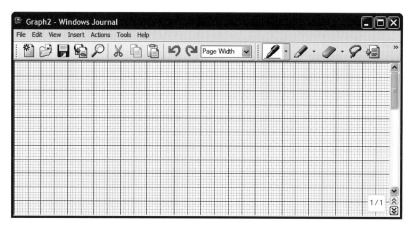

Figure 8-10. Graph paper template.

Importing Documents into Windows Journal

You can import documents into Windows Journal and use them as background images. This is a very powerful and useful capability that leads to three distinct uses.

- The first of these uses is to create additional templates like those above. If you want to make an imported document available as a background for multiple note-taking sessions, once imported you would use the Save As... command and choose the Template file type. That document would then be added to the above list of templates. For instance when I interview potential staff for hiring, I take notes on a template that has all my standard interview questions on it. This capability can also be used to create electronic forms in which needed information is jotted into blank boxes.

- The second and most common use of Journal's import capability is to import documents you want to mark up for editing or emphasis. This capability is the topic of Chapter 12.

- The third use of Journal's import capability is as the basis of a document management tool. This is described in Chapter 10.

For all three of these purposes, you would use the identical import commands. See Chapter 10 for instructions on importing documents into Windows Journal.

Searching Notes in Windows Journal

The search function in Windows Journal is simple to use and effective. From the Standard toolbar click the Find tool, which looks like a magnifying glass, or choose Find... from the Edit menu.

This opens a search tool area between the Standard toolbar and your note-page. (See Figure 8-11.)

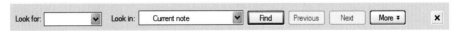

Figure 8-11. Search tool

Type your search word in the Look For field, and adjust the scope of the search by choosing from the Look In popup menu. Then click the Find button. The results are displayed as a list of matching documents in a search results window that appears between this search bar and your notes window. Clicking on any of these documents opens the document and selects the first occurrence of the word. (See Figure 8-12.) If you get too many returns, click the More button at the right end of the search tool to expose additional advanced search fields allowing you to refine your search further.

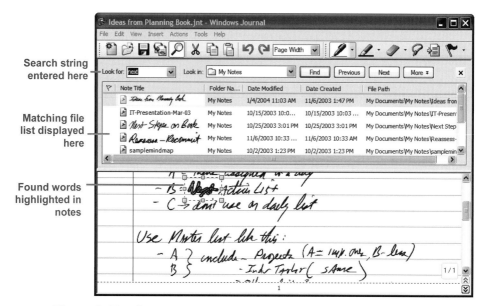

Search string entered here

Matching file list displayed here

Found words highlighted in notes

Figure 8-12. Search results in Windows Journal.

Sharing Windows Journal Note Documents

Once done creating a note, if your colleague has a Tablet PC, you can now e-mail this document to the colleague. The colleague can then simply open the document in Windows Journal to view or print. Using the Send To... command from the File menu makes this a one step process.

If the colleague does not have a Tablet PC, there are two approaches you can take. You can send a copy of the Microsoft Windows Journal Viewer application to your colleague, which is a free application that opens Windows Journal documents on any Windows computer. This application can be downloaded from the Microsoft.com/downloads web site (see Appendix).

Or you can use the Export As... command under the Windows Journal File menu to save the document as a Web Archive file (.mht). Once saved and sent in that format the document can be opened by your colleague as a graphic image within Internet Explorer (version 5.0 or later required, for both Macintosh and PC).

In that same Export As... command you can instead choose the .tif file format, which gives your colleague more viewing application choices. For some reason color information is lost in the .tif conversion in Windows Journal, so this method is not generally recommended.

Note Taking with FranklinCovey PlanPlus for Outlook

With the October 2003 release of version 2 of FranklinCovey PlanPlus for Outlook, and of version 3 of TabletPlanner, FranklinCovey added a note-taking tool that rivals the note-taking capabilities of Windows Journal. And the fact that in PlanPlus this tool is integrated with Outlook, along with a number of other PlanPlus integrated capabilities we will be using, makes this choice very compelling. It does not however have the Recent Notes view that Windows Journal has (unless you are using Outlook 2003). Instead notes documents are stored and located right in the Outlook folder structure, which has its own advantages.

By the way, if you are a TabletPlanner user, I encourage you to read this section on PlanPlus anyway. This is where I cover most of the features of PowerNotes. I then cover additional perspectives on how PowerNotes are implemented in TabletPlanner in the sections at the end of this chapter.

PlanPlus users: before we get started reviewing the note-taking capabilities of PlanPlus for Outlook, do this. If you are going to follow along on your own Tablet PC (which I recommend) make sure that you have studied the first portion of Chapter 6 on task management. I also recommend that you first implement the PlanPlus Home screen customizations that I recommended at the beginning of Chapter 6. Chapter 6 is where I first introduced the FranklinCovey PlanPlus software and specific Tablet PC customization recommendations.

PowerNotes

The note-taking capabilities that we will be using within PlanPlus are called "PowerNotes." This term actually refers to two capabilities: making handwritten (or typed) notes and importing documents into PlanPlus. This latter capability is also referred to as eBinder. We'll cover eBinder in Chapter 10 and focus purely on note-taking here. Also, in the spirit of using the Tablet PC, we will focus on *handwritten* notes, leaving the keyboard behind for now. This is why we won't be examining the Daily Notes feature of PlanPlus; a keyboard is required to use that feature effectively.

There are a couple of different ways to access the PowerNotes tool that PlanPlus installs within Outlook. One method is advertised in the help screens for PlanPlus, and then there is another, less-documented method, which I actually prefer.

In the first and more advertised method, PowerNotes is launched from the PlanPlus Home screen e-mail toolbar; doing so replaces the small e-mail pane of the Home screen with a PowerNotes view.

In the second method, the one that I prefer, PowerNotes is launched from the Outlook Folder List view; doing so replaces the entire PlanPlus Home screen with a PowerNotes view. Given the small size of the Tablet PC screen I think this second approach is better because it provides a larger view of your notes list and note preview. And it uses Outlook's primary folder view to navigate through the note document tree, something I think is clearer. But we'll go over both approaches so you can decide for yourself which you prefer.

Accessing PowerNotes from the PlanPlus E-mail Toolbar

As mentioned, the first method replaces the lower e-mail pane of the Home screen with a PowerNotes pane. In this approach, you launch PowerNotes from the e-mail toolbar located just above that e-mail viewing pane. On this e-mail menu, you should notice a PowerNotes button to the right of the Inbox label. (See Figure 8-13.) If you do not see the PowerNotes button there don't panic; read the callout box below titled Selecting Folders to View in the Plan-Plus Lower Pane.

Click here to start using PowerNotes

© 2004 Franklin Covey, used with permission

Figure 8-13. Starting PowerNotes from the e-mail tool bar.

Selecting Folders to View in the PlanPlus Lower Pane

If you do not see the PowerNotes button in the e-mail toolbar, but see what appears to be the name of some other folder, do this: click on the small triangle to the right of whatever is in the place of the PowerNotes button shown in Figure 8-13 and the following window will pop up. In that window, click on the plus sign next to the FranklinCovey folder so that you expand its contents:

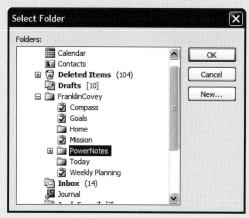

Then click once on the PowerNotes folder itself so that the words PowerNotes are highlighted as above. Then click OK. The PowerNotes button should now appear on the toolbar, as in Figure 8-13, and you can continue with the tutorial.

Note that this Select Folder capability can be used to pick *any* Outlook folder and view its contents in that lower pane. And the similar small triangle next to the word Inbox on that toolbar gives you that same capability from there; these two controls are identical. This enables you to access all components of Outlook without ever leaving the Home screen, for instance, Sent Items, Drafts, Contacts, and Outlook Note—anything that fits the Outlook lists/preview view approach. This offers a tremendous level of flexibility. The only drawback is that when used on a small Tablet PC screen, this lower pane can be a bit small to work with. A better approach for the Tablet PC is to use the Folder List view on the left side of the Outlook window. More on that in the section titled The Other (Preferred) Method of Launching PowerNotes.

Clicking the PowerNotes button changes the screen significantly; the e-mail pane disappears and is replaced by a notes list pane on the left and a notes preview pane on the right. Assuming you have no notes to start with, your screen will probably look something like Figure 8-14.

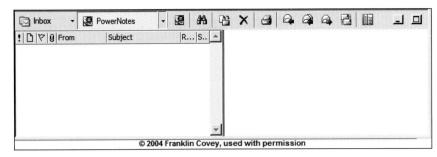

© 2004 Franklin Covey, used with permission

Figure 8-14. PowerNotes view that opens when opened from the e-mail toolbar.

Another change made when you click the PowerNotes title is that the e-mail toolbar changes slightly and a new icon appears just to the right of the PowerNotes label. (See Figure 8-15.) Use that icon to create a new handwritten PowerNote.

Click here to create a new PowerNote ———

© 2004 Franklin Covey, used with permission

Figure 8-15. New PowerNotes button.

When you click that new note button the following window appears, giving you a chance to choose the notes template. (See Figure 8-16.)

Figure 8-16. Selecting the notebook paper template.

And then after choosing a template the following notes application is launched in a separate window. This note page should appear familiar; it should remind you greatly of Windows Journal. (See Figure 8-17.)

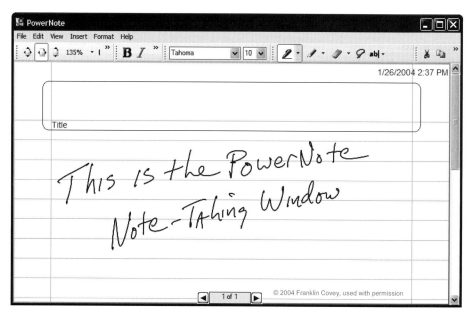

Figure 8-17. PowerNote writing page.

The PlanPlus Notes Window and Windows Journal Notes Windows Are Similar

Just to make this comparison more clear, let's display a Windows Journal page. (See Figure 8-18.)

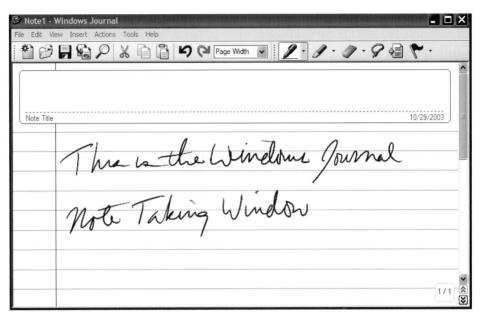

Figure 8-18. Windows Journal Writing Page, for comparison.

Compare the two; they look nearly identical, don't they? So if these two screens look so similar what are the differences? And are the differences significant?

First of all, the note-taking experience is nearly identical. Just like in Windows Journal, in PowerNotes you can write anywhere on the page, you can select and use pens, highlighters, erasers, all in almost exactly the same way as Windows Journal. You select handwriting and drawings using the Lasso tool, just like in Windows Journal. And like Journal, once handwriting is selected, it is converted to text using a menu command (in this case, go to Insert menu, Convert Ink to Text). One difference is in selecting converted or typed text. In Windows Journal you use the Lasso tool. In PowerNotes you use the Text Selection tool.

ab|

There is a minor difference in how you create added pages and flip between pages: rather than using the chevron arrows in the lower right corner of the screen as in Windows Journal, the PowerNotes screen puts a set of navigation buttons in the bottom middle of the screen:

© 2004 Franklin Covey, used with permission

Clicking the right arrow creates a new page of notes, and these pages are of fixed length like Windows Journal pages.

There are other more significant differences, mostly in the area of output from handwriting conversion and in text formatting tools; but before we get to that, let's finish the topic on other ways to launch PowerNotes.

The Other (Preferred) Method of Launching PowerNotes

Here's one area about which I have a strong opinion; you should use the Outlook folder structure to launch PowerNotes; in fact, you should get used to using this means of folder navigation for most other Outlook navigation needs. It will serve you well.

To get started with this, remember that within Chapter 6 where we first introduced PlanPlus, I had you replace the Outlook Shortcut Bar with the Outlook Folder List view. This replacement is important for PowerNotes too; it makes launching and storing your PowerNotes handwritten notes much easier. And you'll see soon that using this approach is essential for when we start using the print capture capability of PlanPlus in the document management chapter (Chapter 10). So if you have not made this change do it now.

With the Folder List view open in Outlook you'll see the following (see Figure 8-19):

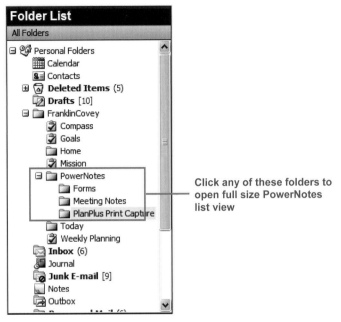

Click any of these folders to
open full size PowerNotes
list view

Figure 8-19. Outlook Folder List view method of launching PowerNotes.

To launch PowerNotes from this view, click either on the PowerNotes folder
or on any of its current subfolders (such as Forms or Meeting Notes). You will
see the following view (see Figure 8-20):

Figure 8-20. PowerNotes view, when launched from the Folder List view.

This view (see also Figure 8-21) is similar to what we saw in the e-mail toolbar method: a list view on the left and a preview view on the right. But the views are much larger than on the e-mail toolbar. This larger size is much more suitable for the small screens Tablet PC users are accustomed to.

To create a new PowerNotes document, just click on the button labeled New PowerNote in the middle of the screen (visible just below the large Power-Notes label). Once clicked, the resulting template and editing windows are the same as those seen in the e-mail toolbar method.

After you are done writing the note and close it, its title will appear in the list in this window, and a preview will appear in the pane on the right. We'll walk through another note creation example to demonstrate this.

Side Note: You can navigate back to the PlanPlus Home screen at any time by clicking on the Home folder, under the FranklinCovey folder, within the Folder List view on the left.

The other advantage of reaching PowerNotes this way (using the Folder List view) is that in Outlook 2003, notes that are listed by date are displayed using the new Show in Groups feature. This is similar to the Windows Journal Recent Views feature that I like so much (see left side of Figure 8-21). This feature is much more useful in a larger list view like this.

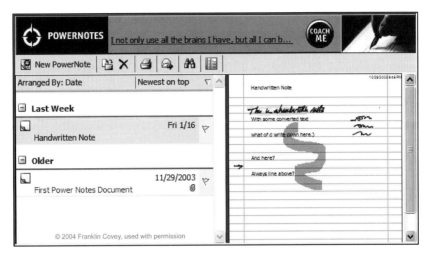

Figure 8-21. PowerNotes view in Outlook 2003 uses the new group-by-date feature, similar to Windows Journal Recent Views.

Saving Notes into Folders

One reason I recommend launching PowerNotes from the Folder List view is that PowerNotes automatically saves documents within whatever folder they were launched from, so you need an easy way to launch from any folder; the Folder List view gives you that.

Stating this another way, with PowerNotes you do not explicitly save documents after they are created like you do in Windows Journal, which means you do not have an easy way to indicate where the notes should go after you've written them. So before you actually launch PowerNotes it's important that you identify the folder the documents are going to be stored in. While FranklinCovey has provided a way to do that using both launch methods, the Outlook Folder List view is by far the easiest way to choose folders and launch at the same time.

Let's work through another PowerNotes example to show how this works and to give a little more detail on note creation and saving.

Creating and Saving a PowerNote from a Specific Folder

Referring to the Folder List view above, you'll notice that PlanPlus comes with three subfolders installed by default under the PowerNotes folder: Forms, Meeting Notes, and PlanPlus Print Capture. Assuming you'll be taking notes mostly in meetings, the natural place for you to store your notes is in the Meeting Notes subfolder. And to ensure they are stored there you would click on the Meeting Notes subfolder to launch PowerNotes. Let's try that now:

1   Click on the Meeting Notes subfolder; the window displayed in Figure 8-22 will appear.

2   Click on the New PowerNote button in the middle of the screen; the note-taking window will appear.

3   Write some practice notes.

4   Put a title in the title block (you may have to scroll the notes window up to see the title block).

5   Select the title with the Lasso tool and convert it to text. The command to do this (Convert Ink to Text) is under the Insert menu. Or you can use the button at the far right end of the PowerNote editing window toolbar.

6   Now close the window; your document is automatically saved; there is no Save command under the File menu.

7   You should now see your document title appear in the list on the Power-Notes window as in Figure 8-22 and a preview of the document will appear to the right of that list.

8   This note has now been saved in your Meeting Notes folder. How do you know it's in that particular folder? Looking again at Figure 8-22 the fact that the Meeting Notes folder is still highlighted on the left confirms that. Also in Outlook 2003 the large folder name label above the PowerNotes pane shows which folder is active. In Outlook 2002 the Address field shows the folder name in its path.

Should you ever need to view this note again, just click on the Meeting Notes folder within the Outlook Folder List view, on the left side of the Outlook window.

Folder location labeled at
top in Outlook 2003

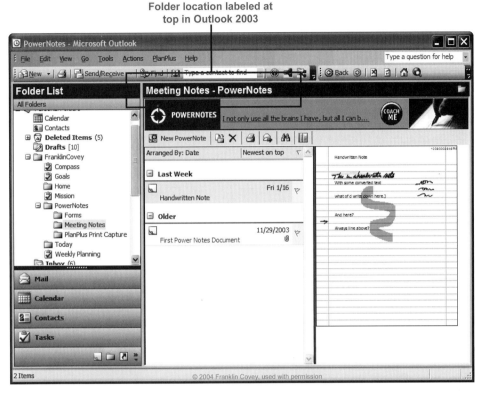

Figure 8-22. In Outlook 2003, the folder location of the currently open PowerNotes list window is labeled at the top. In Outlook 2002, the path in the address bar shows the same.

Side Note: Be sure to always convert your note titles to text before you close the note; unlike Windows Journal where this is optional, with PowerNotes it is required to ensure that the note title shows up in your scrolling list of saved notes.

Creating Additional Outlook Folders for Your Notes

But what if you want to have additional folders? Say you want separate folders for each project. Or perhaps you like the FranklinCovey paper planner approach of having a note page for each day, so you want a daily notes folder for handwritten daily notes. Outlook and PlanPlus let you create additional Outlook folders and you can store your notes in these.

Technical Note: Outlook Folders

Outlook folders are not the same as Windows file system folders. They are virtual folders within the Outlook data storage system, and so you cannot create or view these folders using My Computer or Windows Explorer.

First, you need to create a new Outlook folder within Outlook and configure it a certain way:

1   Go to the File menu of Outlook; choose Folder, and then New Folder from the submenu. The window in Figure 8-23 will appear.

2   Type the name of the new folder in the top field; in this case I've used "My Projects Folder."

3   And then from the Folder Contains popup, leave the current choice: Mail and Post Items (an early version of the PlanPlus documentation incorrectly tells you to choose Notes as the folder type in this step; ignore that instruction).

4   Click once on the PowerNotes folder in the scrolling list at the bottom of this window, so that PowerNotes is selected; this tells Outlook this new folder will be stored within the PowerNotes folder.

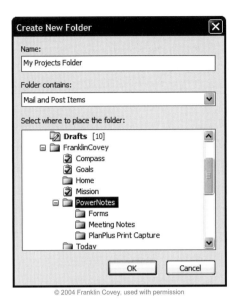

© 2004 Franklin Covey, used with permission

Figure 8-23. Creating a new PowerNotes folder in Outlook.

And now for a trick: with Outlook 2002 you may need to quit and restart Outlook to get this folder registered as a PowerNotes folder. Note also that the help files that come with PlanPlus describe an additional registration step for new folders which involves going to the PlanPlus tab under the Outlook Options window; I have found that this step is not needed.

You can now start using this folder in the Folder List view within Outlook to launch PowerNotes; and any notes created as such will be stored in that new folder.

A Third (and Fourth) Way to Launch PowerNotes

There are two more ways to launch PowerNotes into the large notes list like the one we were using above, but I do not recommend using either of them:

■ You could use the main FranklinCovey PlanPlus toolbar at the top of the Home screen view (I hope you've removed this entire toolbar, as recommended in Chapter 6).

■ Or you could use the PowerNotes entry on the PlanPlus menu. This menu was added to the main Outlook menu bar when you installed PlanPlus.

The reason I don't recommend using either of these methods is because they only display notes that happen to be stored within the PowerNotes folder itself and not any of its subfolders; and they give you no way to navigate to other folders. And finally if you launch from there, by default any created notes are stored only within the upper level PowerNotes folder. As discussed earlier you should probably be storing your written notes within subfolders of that folder.

Moving PowerNotes Documents to Other Outlook Folders

So if you decide you want to change your filing system and move documents around, how do you get individual PowerNotes into different Outlook folders? Remember these are not Windows file system files and folders so you cannot use My Computer or Windows Explorer to move these documents around. You have to do this within the PlanPlus application. There are two ways.

Using the Move PowerNotes button

Here's the first way to move documents among Outlook folders:

1 Navigate to the source PowerNotes folder or subfolder using the Outlooks Folder List.

2 Once you are there click once on the document you want to move to select it.

3 Then click on the Move PowerNotes button in the PowerNotes toolbar just above the scrolling list of documents. (See Figure 8-24.)

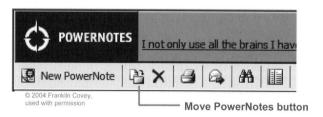

Figure 8-24. The Move PowerNotes button

4 Clicking that button brings up the following navigation window (see Figure 8-25):

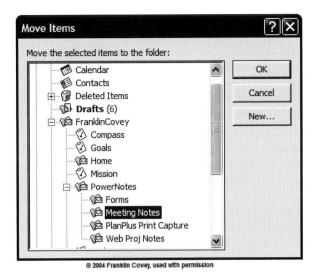

Figure 8-25. Choosing the move-to destination.

5 In that window you simply choose the destination folder and click OK.
Your note will move. If desired, at the first step above you can use the
shift key to select more than one document to move at a time.

Second and better method of moving PowerNote documents

I have had some problems using the method above in Outlook 2003. And
there is a faster method. My preferred method of moving PowerNote documents to other Outlook folders is to simply drag the documents to the folder
of choice within the Outlook Folder List view. To do this, first make sure the
destination folder is visible in the Outlook Folders List view on the left. Now
open the PowerNotes folder listing the document you want to move, click
once on that document in the list view, and then simply drag the document to
the left until you reach the folder you want to copy it to, inside the Outlook
Folder List view (see Figure 8-26), and release the pen; your document will
move there.

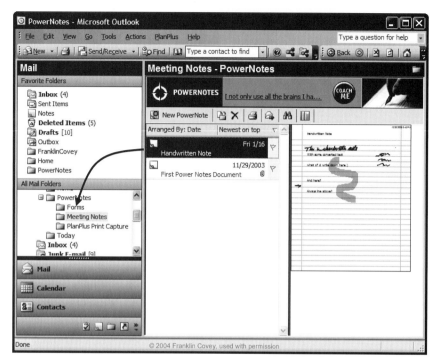

Figure 8-26. Moving PowerNotes by dragging into a folder.

As when using the Move PowerNotes button, you can depress the shift key to select more than one document to move at a time. As an added feature (something not available using the Move PowerNotes button), with this method you can also use the control key to *copy* documents to the new location, leaving the original documents in their original folder.

Using Categories Instead of Folders to Organize Your Notes with Outlook 2003

One downside of storing your notes within hierarchical folders is that as you search multiple folders visually for a particular note you are forced to open each folder, then close it, open another, and so on. This can make a visual search rather painful. If you have upgraded to Outlook 2003 you have a very significant added capability that may eliminate your need to use hierarchical folders altogether. See the paragraph in the advanced section below titled Assigning and Searching Outlook Categories in PowerNotes for description of this very powerful capability.

Some Quirks of PlanPlus for Outlook

FranklinCovey programmers have done a great job of implementing add-on functionality into Outlook, although they were limited by some of its constraints. For example if you look at the list of notes in the PowerNotes view, the one that you see when you click on the Meeting Notes folder, notice that the labels above the list of notes refer to e-mail message fields, not note fields. This is no big deal, but in case you're wondering whether your installation was defective, it's not; this is what the engineers had to work with when cracking into Outlook. The other place these limitations become apparent is in the search window that you used to look for notes by content. Read the next section to see what I mean.

How to Search

First bring up the folder you want to search in by clicking on that folder in the Folder List view of Outlook. If you want to search within all your PowerNote folders then click on the PowerNotes folder name.

On the now familiar PowerNotes view that comes up notice that there is a binocular icon within the toolbar below the large PowerNotes label.

Clicking that button starts the search function. You'll see the Outlook Advanced Find dialog box. (See Figure 8-27.)

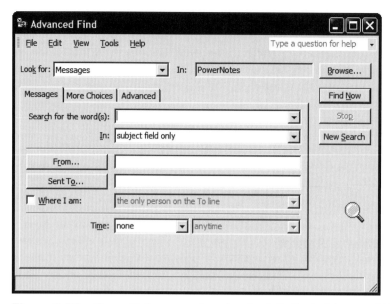

Figure 8-27. PowerNotes uses the standard Outlook Advanced Find search window.

This is not a PlanPlus dialog. Instead the software is repurposing an Outlook e-mail search dialog box; note the references to "Messages," "From," and "Sent To." These fields mean nothing in a PowerNote and so normally the only fields to use are the Search for the Word(s) field and the In field. You need to translate a bit as you use this search dialog. For instance within the In field you would most likely choose the second choice: Subject Field and Message Body to ensure your search is within both the title and the note contents. The choice: Subject Field Only refers to the note title only.

When you click Find Now, a list of matching documents appears. See the next section for advanced search capabilities.

By the way, early versions of the PlanPlus Handbook that shipped with PlanPlus describe a very different method of searching. That has been confirmed as a documentation error.

Advanced Features of PowerNotes in PlanPlus

Here is a short selection of advanced features that you may find useful. You will discover more as you use the software.

Importing Documents for Mark Up

As in Windows Journal, you can import documents into PowerNotes and use them as background documents on top of which you can take notes. You could also create forms this way. See Chapters 10 and 12 for descriptions of how to use this capability.

Using Outlook Follow-Up Flags with PowerNotes

There is an interesting set of undocumented features that results from having these notes stored in an Outlook message store: you can apply several Outlook message store functionalities to your PowerNotes. In particular, with Outlook 2003 (this may also be possible with Outlook 2002, I have not tested it) you can set the Outlook Follow Up flag on one or more PowerNotes. Do this in your list view of PowerNotes by clicking in the Follow Up field at the right of the PowerNote subject. Or right-click on the PowerNote in the list, and choose Follow Up; this latter approach allows you to set various kinds of Follow Up flags in Outlook 2003. This undocumented feature leads to some other interesting capabilities for searching for your notes as discussed next.

Advanced Searches

In Outlook 2003, if you flag the notes as described above, you can search on them two different ways.

First, display the Outlook's Favorite Folders pane (click on the Mail button at the bottom left portion of the Outlook window to display this). Then scroll and open the For Follow Up folder in that pane. Note that your flagged PowerNotes show up in that list. This is an excellent way to find important notes that may be buried in your folder hierarchy. This somewhat offsets the lack of the flag tool in PowerNotes, when compared to Windows Journal and OneNote.

Second, when you use the binocular icon search method and open the Advanced Find dialog, if you click on the second tab called More Choices, you can search for flagged PowerNotes. It's the fourth choice down on that tab. You can also search for Outlook Categories using this tab.

Assigning and Searching Outlook Categories in PowerNotes

Yet another useful undocumented feature that results from using the Outlook data system to store PowerNotes is that you can assign Outlook Categories to your notes, and search on them. Here's how to do this (again, I have only tested this with Outlook 2003; I leave it to you to try these steps on Outlook 2002): after the PowerNote is created and closed, right-click on the note name in the PowerNotes list and choose Categories; then check off the categories you want. To search later for these notes, use the More Choices tab on the Advanced Find dialog box, and click on the Categories button to select which categories to search for. When you click the Find Now button, only notes with these categories assigned, and any other matching criteria you enter, will be displayed.

Organizing Your PowerNotes Using Categories in Outlook 2003

This brings up a very important point: if you are using Outlook 2003 (this does not work in earlier versions of Outlook) you can sort your PowerNotes based on assigned categories. Just navigate to the PowerNotes folder of choice using the Folder List view, and then right-click on the column heading in your PowerNotes list and choose Categories. Right-click again and make sure Show in Groups at the bottom is selected. Your sorted list is now grouped by category and has each category group clearly labeled. Furthermore the list-view contents of each category can be collapsed or expanded like an outline view.

The reason this is so important is that this may eliminate the need to create a folder hierarchy for storing notes. Folder hierarchies can become quite painful when doing visual searches for notes; having to open and close folders one at a time is slow. So just store all notes within the single top level PowerNotes folder, and assign categories to your notes to classify them. Then use the Category grouping described in the paragraph above.

As you probably know, you can create new Outlook categories, and you can assign as many categories as you wish to a given note. If you assign multiple categories to a single note it will show up repeatedly in each of the category groups (when you sort and use Show in Groups as described above). This is a very nice feature and something not possible using folders. This ability to display your notes list by category is a significant and important advantage that Outlook 2003 gives to PowerNote users and a reason to avoid subfolders altogether.

Furthermore, these same Outlook categories can be applied to PlanPlus eBinder documents (described in Chapter 10) and even e-mails (see Chapter 7). And the Search Folders approach described in Chapter 7 could be applied simultaneously to all these document types. This leads to the possibility of collecting a list of all document types for one project, including e-mails,

PowerNotes, Outlook notes, and power documents (but not tasks), together within one Outlook Search Folder view. I leave this to you to explore.

Sharing and Exporting Your PowerNotes

E-mailing PowerNotes

You can e-mail PowerNotes from either the list view or the editing window. From the list view, click on the item in the list, and click the icon that looks like an envelope with an arrow on it.

Or with the document open in the editing window choose File, Send To, E-mail Recipient...

Sending from the list view causes the notes to be copied into the body of the Outlook mail message (not as an attachment) and your recipient will see the full page of notes within the e-mail when they open it in Outlook or Outlook Express. This is the simplest way to send notes given that you know your recipient uses Outlook; however results could be unpredictable with non-Outlook users.

Using the File menu approach from the editor sends the note as an attachment only. This is good if your recipient is also using PowerNotes or if they may not be using Outlook. You will be asked to choose a file format to send the notes in. (See Figure 8-28.)

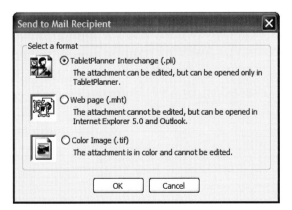

Figure 8-28.   Choosing a file format to send your PowerNotes in.

As with Windows Journal you need to be alert as to what file format you send this as. If you're sending it to another PlanPlus user or a TabletPlanner user, you can save it in the TabletPlanner Interchange format and recipients can import it directly into their notes collection. Otherwise save it either in the Web Archive format (.mht, described as Web Page in the figure above) so that your recipient can open it within Microsoft Internet Explorer, or as a .tif file to enable a wider variety of file viewers. Interestingly, unlike Windows Journal, the .tif option *does* retain color information when exporting from PowerNotes, which makes this a more viable option.

Exporting PowerNotes

If you want to save your PowerNotes locally for use in other applications, you can invoke the equivalent of an export command. To do this, from the PowerNotes editing window open the File menu and choose the Send To, File... command. This allows you to save the file to your hard drive, outside of the PowerNotes Outlook folder system. A Save as... style dialog box is presented and the same three file format choices are given as eligible file types.

Choosing Between Windows Journal and PlanPlus PowerNotes

How does one decide between the two applications? As you can see the method of navigating to PowerNotes is much different from Windows Journal. PowerNotes embeds its notes within the Outlook folder system. Windows Journal uses the Windows XP file system to hold and organize notes. This difference alone may guide your decision if you have a preference on how you find and manipulate note files.

Beyond that, there are many differences in the editing environments and editing approaches, which I describe below.

PowerNotes Is Geared to Both Handwriting and Typed Text Input

The Windows Journal editing window focuses mostly on taking handwritten notes. PowerNotes in contrast is intended to be used both by keyboard users and by pen users. This is consistent with the fact that PlanPlus is directed to both desktop and Tablet PC markets. With Windows Journal, direct entry of typed text is more of an afterthought. Text in Windows Journal must be typed into a separately defined text block; with PowerNotes, you just click on the screen with the text tool and start typing and the text appears on the screen, with no need to create a text box.

PowerNotes Has Easier Access to Text-Formatting Tools, and More of Them

Because of this dual-use philosophy, the tools in the PowerNotes toolbar are more equally oriented toward both text and handwriting needs.

In Windows Journal, formatting tools for converted or typed text are buried under menus and not available at the toolbar. With PlanPlus PowerNotes, most of the formatting tools are on the toolbar and many can be applied to both handwriting and text. For example PowerNotes has text-indenting tools that can be applied to both text and handwriting; indenting is a tool not present in Windows Journal. Some of the formatting tools in PlanPlus can be applied only to text, for example font selection and bulleting. Bulleting is another formatting choice not present in Windows Journal.

PowerNote's pen definition method is similar, but easier to use than Windows Journal. Like Windows Journal five pens at a time can be defined, but PowerNotes uses a much more straightforward definition window. The application of each attribute to each pen, including pressure sensitivity, is shown in a clear table. (See Figure 8-29.)

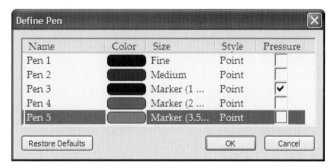

Figure 8-29. PowerNotes uses a much clearer pen definition window than Windows Journal.

In summary, if you are in a keyboard environment during part of your note-taking experience, or if you convert a lot of your handwriting to text and then format that text within your note-taking tool, PowerNotes does it better.

Output from Converted Handwriting Is the Major Differentiator

The biggest difference between the two packages is in the output from converted handwriting. Windows Journal seems weaker in comparison, when text is sent back to the note page:

- Windows Journal loses the positioning of the original text lines.

- Vertical spaces between lines are eliminated so all converted text is compressed into one collapsed text block.

- The font size of the converted text is much smaller than the size of normal handwriting.

- The text box that contains the converted text is created too large and always requires manual resizing.

The net result of these issues is that in Windows Journal, when you send converted notes back to the page, the page of notes *looks* much different after text conversion. You lose any spatial intentions you had when you placed the text where you did on the page.

PowerNotes takes a different approach. First of all the only option with PowerNotes is to send the converted text back to the page; there is no clipboard option. You can copy that text off the page later.

And when PowerNotes converts text, each line of text is inserted into its own text block on the page at approximately the same location and approximately the same font size as normal written text.

So for example say you handwrite a line and then skip down four lines and handwrite another line. When you convert this to text there will likely be four blank lines in between the converted text lines. You are left feeling that the spatial notes layout is maintained by the conversion process.

Here's a demonstration of that difference: I've written similar text within Windows Journal and within PowerNotes, and then converted them in place leaving the results on the page (see Figures 8-30 and 8-31).

The difference between the spatial integrity of these two conversions is obvious. Keep in mind that both software packages use the same text conversion routines which are built in to Windows XP Tablet Edition, so the accuracy of the converted text should be identical.

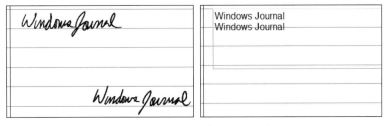

Figure 8-30. Windows Journal before and after conversion to text.

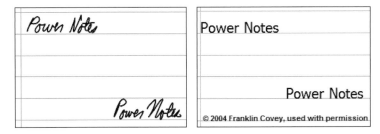

Figure 8-31. PowerNotes before and after conversion to text.

One other nice feature of PowerNotes is that the individual text blocks that are the output from each line of notes can be moved separately from the rest. There is a nice little hand-shaped handle placed to the left of each of these blocks that allows you to grab and move them about easily (see Figure 8-32). And the boundaries of the individual blocks are well defined by a slight shaded color that surrounds the text when you click it with the text selection tool. This is similar to how Microsoft OneNote manages text lines, and it allows reorganization of converted text (importantly, though, OneNote also offers the same reorganization ability with *unconverted handwriting*, while PowerNotes does not).

Paragraph Handle

Figure 8-32. A segment of typed or converted notes can be dragged around the page using the Paragraph Handle.

Problems

All is not perfect with PowerNotes text conversion, however, and here are some problems:

- Since PowerNotes treats each line of handwritten text separately, the converted blocks sometimes interfere with each other. For instance let's say during conversion the first line of text needs to wrap to a second line; in doing so it may overlap the second converted line, making both of them unreadable. The good news is you can drag each line and separate them, easily cleaning up what at first appears to be a major mess.

- PowerNotes often inexplicably creates a separate text block for components within the same sentence, such as punctuation. These text blocks then need to be dragged and positioned separately if you intend to rearrange your page.

- While PowerNotes, unlike Windows Journal, at least *tries* to put the converted text close to where it was originally handwritten, it often misses the location by a full line or so. You can see this in the sample above where there are only two blank lines between the converted text and three in the original. So don't think that converted text will be precisely positioned, say next to adjacent sketches

- And if your intention in converting handwritten notes is not to maintain spatial integrity but rather to just output a large contiguous block of text for export and further editing, then all the extra spaces that PowerNotes inserts is a bit disconcerting.

So which text conversion engine do I prefer? I think if I were converting a lot of text rapidly for the purpose of creating a Word document of neatly typed text notes, I would choose Windows Journal. If I wanted to preserve the original layout of the notes and leave the converted notes within the notes document I would use PowerNotes.

Other differences between PlanPlus and Windows Journal

- In PowerNotes you cannot place flags in the text.

- The note-saving experience is different; Journal asks you where to save the note after you create it, with PowerNotes you need to indicate where to save it when you start *creating* the notes (or it will go to a default location).

■ PowerNotes does not ship with as many templates as Windows Journal has.

■ PowerNotes does not have the presentation capabilities of Windows Journal (see Chapter 13).

■ Unlike Windows Journal, upon text conversion PowerNotes does not display the dialog box that gives a first estimation of conversion. In Windows Journal you are given useful tools to clean up errors. The converted text in PowerNotes goes directly to the page (same behavior as OneNote by the way).

■ As discussed in the Advanced section above, PowerNotes when used with Outlook 2003 provides a very useful capability of assigning, grouping, and searching by note category.

■ The page-width tool in PowerNotes is on an optional toolbar and uses icons.

■ You need to quickly get a title converted to text within PowerNotes, or your notes title will be blank in the Outlook folders and you may lose an easy way to find the notes. At least with Journal you are forced to define a text title during save, and the ink version of the title is also saved and displayed in the recent notes view.

Note Taking with FranklinCovey TabletPlanner 3.0

We introduced navigating within the TabletPlanner software in Chapter 6. If you are skipping around in this book and skipped that chapter, you should refer back now and read the TabletPlanner navigation section, and then come back here. You should also read the section above in this chapter on Power-Notes as used within FranklinCovey PlanPlus. Much of that coverage is applicable to TabletPlanner and an understanding of it is assumed in the discussion that follows.

Differences in TabletPlanner PowerNotes from PlanPlus

The primary note-taking engine within TabletPlanner is nearly identical to that used within PlanPlus; this is not a surprise, since they were created by the same company and share the same code base. This note-taking capability is named PowerNotes within both applications. The main difference between the two packages is in the user interface. You will notice this in both the menu interface at the top of the note-taking window and the interface used to launch, store, and retrieve notes.

Regarding the note-taking window, you will recall that PlanPlus launches a separate note-taking window when you click a control to open or create a note document. Windows Journal does this too. In contrast, TabletPlanner merges the note-taking window in with the rest of the application window. As a result, TabletPlanner needs to share its toolbar space with other application functionality, and thus TabletPlanner has less toolbar space to devote just to note taking. So compared with PlanPlus, you will see fewer note-taking tools on the TabletPlanner toolbar (they occupy only the right half of the toolbar). The "missing" toolbar functionality is still accessible; it has just been relegated to pull-down menus, primarily the Format menu.

Another difference compared to PlanPlus is that the Daily Notes page on TabletPlanner is functional for ink. Within PlanPlus the Daily Notes page only accepts text and so is not really practical for Tablet PC users.

And regarding the differences in navigation among note files: PlanPlus leverages the Outlook folder system while TabletPlanner uses its own tab and folder interface. More on the TabletPlanner navigation approach will follow.

Other than these differences, taking notes using PowerNotes within Tablet-Planner is nearly identical to taking notes using PowerNotes within PlanPlus.

Daily Notes

With TabletPlanner you have two ways to write notes: you can write Daily Notes or you can write notes from the Notes tab view. The Daily Notes portion of TabletPlanner is the first note page you are likely to see. It appears as the default right-hand page view when you click on the Calendar tab and have your Tablet PC set in landscape orientation. (See Figure 8-33.)

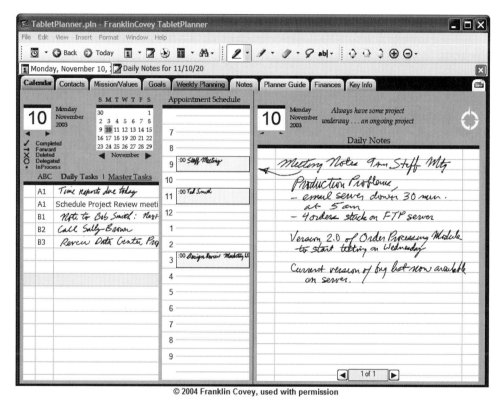

© 2004 Franklin Covey, used with permission

Figure 8-33. Daily Notes page in TabletPlanner occupies the right side of the screen when your tablet is in landscape orientation.

Why use Daily Notes? The concept of Daily Notes comes from the paper version of the FranklinCovey system, where notes can be associated with any given day. The idea is that while you might take and file project notes in a separate project file, there are many notes that are somewhat miscellaneous and are best referred to by referencing that day in your planner. In the TabletPlanner implementation of Daily Notes, making this association with a given day causes the Daily Notes page to act slightly differently from the Notes tab version of PowerNotes.

The first difference is that there is no New Note tool on the Daily Notes page or toolbar. This is because with Daily Notes you only get one daily note per day. You can of course add as many pages as you wish to this note, using the tool at the bottom of the note page.

You'll also notice that there's no editable title section in the Daily Notes. This is because the implied note title is "Daily Notes" for that day. So navigation back to a given Daily Note is not done by note title, but rather is done by navigating back to the appointment section for a given day.

If you ever lose this Daily Notes view you can get it back by clicking on the Daily Notes icon within the TabletPlanner toolbar.

There's also a good chance that a link to the Daily Notes page is floating on the navigation bar at any given time (use of the navigation bar was covered in Chapter 6).

I just mentioned that TabletPlanner does not launch a separate note-taking window; rather notes are taken directly in the TabletPlanner window. This forces all the note-taking tools described in the PlanPlus section into the right side of the Standard toolbar, or under the Format menu. This also puts Daily Notes users at a slight disadvantage. If you prefer to use the landscape orientation of your Tablet PC this approach forces the daily notes page to occupy at most only half your Tablet PC screen, making it for some users a little small for handwriting. The only solution is to put your Tablet PC into portrait mode. As you'll see in a moment, notes created under the Note tab of Tablet-Planner don't have this limitation.

Notes Tab

The other way to create and access notes is to use the Notes tab. Clicking that tab takes you to the following view (see Figure 8-34):

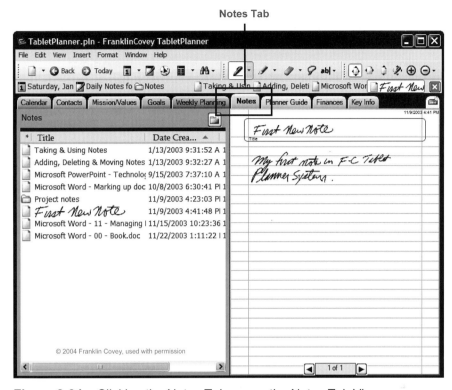

Figure 8-34. Clicking the Notes Tab opens the Notes Tab View.

On the left is your list of notes currently stored under the Notes tab, and on the right is the actual note-taking area. Notice that, compared with Daily Notes, this note-taking area has a title area to write into. The same note-taking tools on the Standard toolbar are used. And once you open the Notes tab, a new icon is added to the far left of the Standard toolbar.

This is the New Note tool, and any new notes created with that tool are stored within the currently open tab.

You can sort the note list by name or date by clicking on the Title or Date Created column title respectively. You can delete and rename notes in this list by right-clicking on the individual note item in the list. You can move notes from the list of notes to other note tabs simply by clicking and dragging the note name and dropping it on top of another note tab (more on adding additional note tabs below).

Enlarging the Notes Page

To handwrite with your tablet in landscape mode, you will probably want to enlarge the note-taking window. Recall that, with the Daily Notes page, the only way to have the note-taking page fill the screen is to switch the display orientation of your Tablet PC to portrait mode. In contrast, with notes under the Notes tab you can accomplish this in landscape mode as well. To do this: from the TabletPlanner Window menu, choose Both Pages; this expands the notes document to the full width of the landscape window. By the way, the Both Pages menu choice is dimmed out when viewing Daily Notes.

Using the Tabs and Folders System for Storing Notes

While the Notes tab may initially seem the more logical place to put notes, you can create more tabs with any titles, and place notes in any of them. In fact you will learn in Chapter 10 that this Notes tab is where your eBinder documents are dropped by default, so you probably will want to create a different set of tabs to store your handwritten notes. And this ability to create tabs allows you to organize your notes by project, category, anything really. You create new tabs by clicking the new tab icon at the far right edge of the tab area.

Once within a given tab view, any new notes you create are automatically stored within that tab. You can create hierarchical subfolders within a tab view by simply clicking on the New Folder icon to the right, just above the list of notes (see upper right corner of Figure 8-35); when you do that a box pops up giving you an opportunity to give the folder a name.

Once the folder is created within the tab, you can navigate inside the folder simply by clicking once on the folder within the tab notes list. And once inside the folder the hierarchical path is displayed at the top of the notes list for that folder (Figure 8-35). Clicking on underlined portions of the hierarchical path allows you to navigate to different levels within the folder hierarchy. For instance, clicking on the underlined Notes word in Figure 8-35 takes you back to the top-level Notes tab view of your notes. This approach works no matter how deeply you create your folder hierarchy.

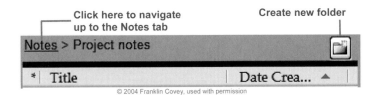

Figure 8-35. Click the <u>Notes</u> portion of the folder name (upper left corner) to navigate back to the top-level Notes View. Click the folder icon at right to create a new folder within the current tab.

Forms

Just as in Windows Journal, you can import documents into PowerNotes and use them as background documents on top of which you can take notes. You can create forms using this approach. TabletPlanner, out of the box, comes packed full of helpful, ready-to-use forms. These are found under the last three tabs: Planner Guide, Finances, and Key Info. Some example forms are listed here.

- Travel Itinerary
- Meeting Planner
- Car Mileage Log
- Budget Worksheet
- Check Register
- Expense Sheet

The last document in the Planner Guide tab discusses how to copy these forms to preserve the originals.

Searching Notes

Searching in TabletPlanner for text in notes and other documents is accomplished by choosing Search from the View menu, or by clicking the Binocular icon on the main toolbar. Doing so brings up the following search dialog box. (See Figure 8-36.) After clicking the Search button, the documents containing the searched string are listed below the search box.

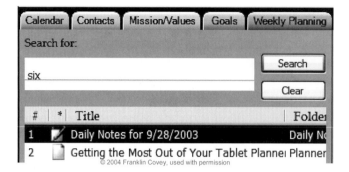

Figure 8-36. TabletPlanner search window

Sharing TabletPlanner Notes

Just as in PlanPlus you use the File, Send To command to export the document, and you have the same three file format choices. TabletPlanner has the same limitations (see the PlanPlus section above for details). Unlike with PlanPlus, however, with TabletPlanner you cannot send directly from the notes list view.

Chapter 9 Note Taking 2: Using Microsoft Office OneNote 2003

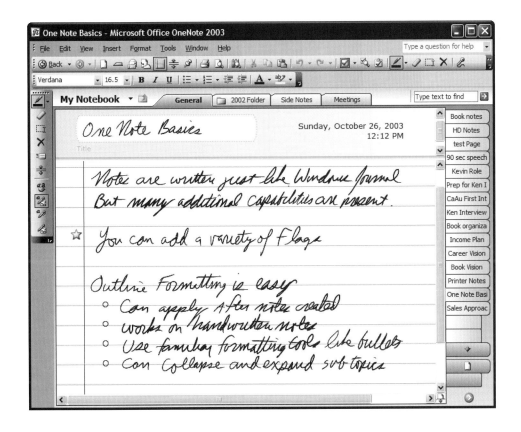

Introduction

Microsoft Office OneNote 2003 is a superior note-taking tool that in nearly all ways goes well beyond Windows Journal, PowerNotes, and all other note-taking software choices. It has a clear and logical note organization approach, an extensive set of note-formatting tools, a nicely integrated sticky notes feature, and a host of other tools that just may fit your note-taking needs perfectly. This recently released software from Microsoft represents the latest results of research on note-taking patterns among businessmen and students, and it is being positioned as a significant add-on package to Microsoft Office 2003 for use by both Tablet PC and traditional keyboard users alike.

Don't throw away Windows Journal yet, though, as Windows Journal provides a few key functions that are not duplicated in OneNote. Plus, you may decide that the extra features (and cost) of OneNote are not of advantage to you compared with the simplicity of Windows Journal. And if you have adopted one of the FranklinCovey packages and are happy with the Power-Notes note-taking capability within each, you may not need OneNote. Read this chapter and you decide if the features of OneNote warrant purchasing, learning, and adding this tool to your toolbox. And even if you do decide to take the plunge, remember that you will continue to use Windows Journal for other tasks that OneNote is not suitable for. I will go into a detailed comparison between Windows Journal and OneNote later in this chapter, but first here are the major reasons to consider OneNote.

Business Value to the Busy Manager

OneNote has four key features that I feel make it valuable to the busy manager who handwrites notes on the Tablet PC. And it has a fifth "bonus" feature that, if you have an application for it in your work day, will yield significant rewards. Let's go over these.

Notebook Metaphor

First, it has an excellent visual note document organization metaphor that will help you find your notes quickly. Using a combination of section and page tabs, like the tab-based dividers in three-ring notebooks, you can easily organize and find notes. This is in my opinion OneNote's most important feature and alone is worth the cost of the software. FranklinCovey TabletPlanner 3.0

software also uses tabs for organizing its notes, but they are not used as extensively as in OneNote.

Easy Ink and Text Reorganization

Second, for those of you who tend to clean up or reorganize notes after they are written, OneNote has a word grouping approach that makes reorganization of notes easy and effective. One example of this is the ability to quickly restructure unstructured notes into an outline format, after the notes are written. And you can add automatic bulleting or numbering to your note lists. Interestingly, this restructuring capability works whether you convert notes to text or leave them as ink (see Figure 9-1). This is especially useful for students, or for staff who need to refer to their notes again and again, or for anyone who needs to clean up their notes before distribution.

Other users who will find this ability to manipulate blocks of ink text useful are those who put a lot of drawings in their notes and use ink text to annotate those drawings with callout notes. OneNote's ink manipulation capability is perfect for arranging mixtures of text and graphics. More on this feature when we address some advanced implications of OneNote.

By the way the PowerNote function within FranklinCovey PlanPlus 2.0 and FranklinCovey TabletPlanner 3.0 also provides the ability to add bullets to your notes. However your notes must be converted to text first to do this; with OneNote you can do this formatting on raw handwritten ink.

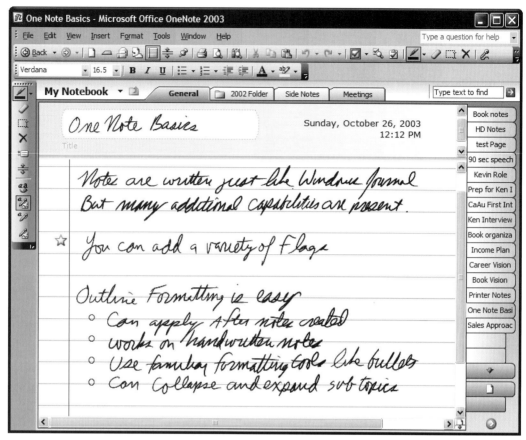

Figure 9-1.   Microsoft Office OneNote application window with handwritten notes.

Expanded Flags Capability

Third, OneNote allows the user to mark sentences with various types of flags (for example see star flag in Figure 9-1 above) and then to extract those flagged entries later, creating a single merged collection of items that are flagged. Included in these flag types are to-do boxes that take a checkmark when you click on them, and this checked status can be searched on. This goes well beyond the simple flagging that Windows Journal offers. One obvious use for this is the ability to periodically extract open to-do items into one single to-do document. OneNote comes with five types of flags predefined and the ability to add four more, all of which can be searched and extracted separately.

Side Notes

Fourth, OneNote has a built in sticky note–like feature called Side Notes, with nearly all the advantages of the standard Tablet PC sticky notes program (that comes free with all Tablet PCs) plus the extra advantage of being integrated in with the master OneNote software (see Figure 9-2).

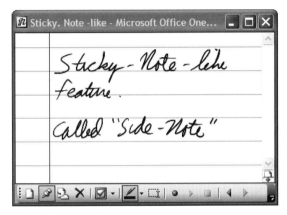

Figure 9-2.   Side Notes window.

"Bonus Feature": Synchronized Audio and Written Notes

One other very interesting feature of OneNote is worth mentioning, because for those of you who can use this, it really is a killer capability. This is the ability to within OneNote make an audio recording of a meeting, make notes while the recording is underway, and synchronize the two for playback.

The use of OneNote, including these five features and much more, will be examined ahead in this chapter.

OneNote Is Not Just for Tablet PCs

You'll see a lot of comparisons in this chapter between OneNote and the two Tablet PC–only applications Windows Journal and FranklinCovey Power-Notes. OneNote, however, can also be used with a laptop or desktop. The software has been designed to be useful to those who are typing their notes as they receive them, and Microsoft is positioning the software perhaps even more toward those without Tablet PCs. One minor restriction with non Tablet PCs: if you write with the Pen tools using a mouse, you cannot convert that handwriting to text; only the Tablet PC has the text conversion software built in.

In keeping with the goals of this book, the focus of this chapter will be on the pen-based note-taking capability of OneNote. For a good book on the full capabilities of the software, see *Complete Guide to OneNote* by W. Frederick Zimmerman.

The Name

You may be wondering why the program is called OneNote. That's because it is being marketed as "One place for all your notes." It can store all your notes in an organized way in one easy to retrieve location. Again, this is largely a feature of the user interface, where a collection of notes can be organized into tab-based folders, sections, pages, and subpages, all visible at a glance. And again, this is one of OneNote's most useful features for the manager.

Also factored into this name is the ease of import into OneNote of text and graphics from a variety of sources. This includes using the Research feature of OneNote. And, finally, it refers to the ease of inserting audio notes.

Purchase and Installation Strategy

OneNote 2003 is a Microsoft Office 2003 module that is purchased and installed separately from the rest of Office 2003. If your work environment has remained standardized on an older version of Office and has no intention of upgrading to 2003 soon, the best strategy is to install OneNote by itself. It does not require the presence of any particular version of Office, nor does it require that Office be present at all. The disadvantage of doing this is that some features of Office integration will only work with Office 2003 installed, but this represents a small subset of OneNote functionality.

At the time of this writing a free trial download of OneNote was available from the Microsoft website.

Using OneNote 2003

Note Organization Structure: The Notebook Metaphor

At the start of this chapter I mentioned that a key value of OneNote is the note organization approach that OneNote uses and how this will help you find notes later. OneNote uses a three-ring binder metaphor, like those binders you may have carried to school or that perhaps you use at the office. However OneNote has a few twists on your standard physical three-ring binder. Let's go over the application of this metaphor; understanding it is very important to gaining value from OneNote.

My Notebook

Here's how the notebook organization works. At the highest level of documents is the concept of a notebook; with OneNote you get one of these and one only. If you look at the OneNote application, note the large bold title My Notebook in the upper left corner of the OneNote work area (see Figure 9-3).

Figure 9-3. Section tabs at top of OneNote page.

Sections

Within this notebook you can create Sections, just like the paper divider sections you used to use in your physical school or office three-ring binder. These are displayed as tabs at the top of the OneNote work area and are created by using the File menu. By default, OneNote comes with three such sections: General, Side Notes, and Meetings. The Side Notes section may not appear until you have used the sticky notes feature of OneNote (called Side Notes) at least once. These all function essentially the same way and you can use them as you like. Note however that Side Notes by default stores its notes in the Side Notes section, so it is probably best to leave that section for that purpose.

Pages

Within the default sections, or within new sections you may create, you enter pages of notes. Page titles are displayed as tabs at the right side of the One-Note work area, and once a page is created you navigate to a page by clicking on the corresponding tab (note the labeled tabs on the right edge of the screen in Figure 9-1). Page titles are assigned by writing the title into the header area of the page, similarly to how you do this in Windows Journal. See the title area in Figure 9-4 where the words "Sales Approaches" are written.

Figure 9-4.   Page title entry area in header at top of OneNote page.

Whatever title you write in the title section will be displayed within the corresponding page tab on the right side of the work area. If you handwrite the title and do not convert it to text, OneNote will still do the conversion behind the scenes and display that conversion within the tab corresponding to the page.

You can also move these tabs to the left side of the screen by going to Tools, Options, Other, and then choosing Page Tabs Appear on Left.

The word "page" is a bit deceiving here because, like common computer documents, in the OneNote world pages are not limited by the length of the paper. Rather they can run on forever with the user adding more space at the bottom of the page as needed. So think of a page really as one document, or the results of a single note-taking session. The fact that a OneNote page does not correspond to a physical printed page will cause a bit of confusion when printing; more on that later.

When starting new notes, new pages are created by clicking on a special page tab near the bottom right of the screen. That tab has an image of a page on it as shown on Figure 9-5 (there are several other ways to create new pages as well). The newly created pages are automatically stored in whatever section is open at the time that you create the page; they can easily be moved to other sections if needed.

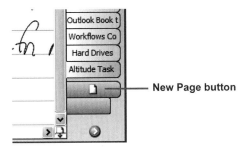

New Page button

Figure 9-5. Add pages by clicking on the tab marked with the page graphic.

Subpages

There's one more notebook element to cover and that's subpages. There may be times when you need to call out separate subsegments within the context of one meeting or note-taking session. You may want to do this because of a major topic change or as an attempt to organize note segments within the notes for one meeting, or for print-formatting purposes. So OneNote allows the creation of untitled subpages. These subpages once created represent a fresh blank page of notes for you to write in, and they are logically grouped with (or attached to) the main page "above" it. You create a subpage by clicking on the shorter blank tab just underneath the Create Page tab. Once created, subpages are visually represented on the tab list as shorter tabs, underneath the page tab to which they are attached (see Figure 9-6).

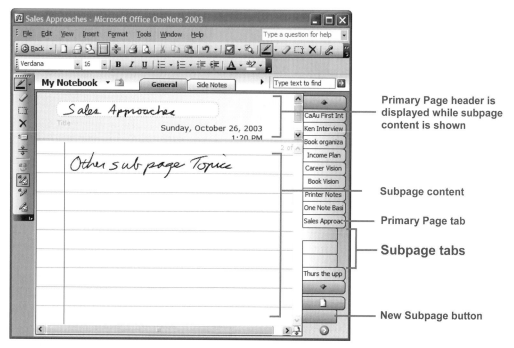

Figure 9-6. Subpages are shown as shorter tabs beneath the primary page to which they are attached. They inherit the header area from the primary page.

No title information is put on these subpage tabs; they remain blank. While writing on or viewing the content of these subpages, the header (title) information for the main or primary page which the subpage is attached to is displayed at the top of the notes area. In other words subpages inherit the header area for the primary page they are attached to. A primary page together with all its subpages is called a page group.

One of the main reasons to use subpages is if you prefer to preserve a fixed page length for your notes. You might want to use fixed page lengths so that you can view pages without scrolling, or to enable later printing of notes with more predictable page breaks. Subpages in that case are the way to create additional note space after you have written to the bottom of the first note page. More on that later.

Working with the Notebook Metaphor

Figure 9-1 provides a summary of these graphic elements. Again, the section tabs are placed along the top of the OneNote work area, and the page tabs are placed along the right edge. This placement works well given that sections are going to be less numerous and therefore their horizontal aspect is acceptable. Pages are going to be more numerous and their vertical placement of the page tabs facilitates a large number of labeled pages.

My only complaint with the system is that I can see no way to enlarge the width of the page tabs so that they can display longer page titles. That said a tab's full name and note dates can be displayed temporarily on the screen by positioning the pen (or mouse) over the tabs without clicking. And there are other ways to view a list of notes (discussed later in this chapter) which do show the complete titles. My other complaint is that if lots of subpages are used, say to take advantage of the fixed-page-length feature, the subpage tabs take up quite a lot of tab real estate. Other than these two minor complaints, the notebook metaphor works very well.

Primary Note-Taking Tools

Representations of the five primary note-taking tools on the OneNote toolbar are very similar to those tools on Windows Journal's toolbar (see Figure 9-7 below). The pen operates essentially the same. The New Page button on the toolbar is similar and has the same action as the New Page button on the right-hand tab space in OneNote. Notice that compared to Windows Journal, the eraser functions in the stroke mode only.

The only tool icon that looks very different from Windows Journal is the Selection tool, which, rather than looking like a lasso, looks like a dotted-line square and text cursor (see Figure 9-7, right side). This graphic representation is actually more appropriate for OneNote since to select text you do not circle the text the way you do in Windows Journal. Rather the Selection tool works very much like a cursor within a traditional word processing program where you click to one side of the text and drag over it. The same tool is also used to select graphic objects. You'll use this tool quite a bit throughout this chapter, so become familiar with its name, its appearance, and its location on the toolbar.

Figure 9-7. Standard toolbar showing primary note-taking tools.

By the way, when you have this Selection tool selected and move your pen over your notes you'll see gray boxes appear around sections of your notes. These are called *containers* and are used primarily for moving and reorganizing your text. We're going to cover moving and reorganizing text in later parts of this chapter so it is best to ignore those for now. Do not attempt to move text until we cover how to do it, otherwise it can get confusing.

Saving Notes

Unlike Windows Journal, all notes for a given section are saved in one file, so you do not need to name your notes files as you create them, nor do you need to explicitly save them. OneNote automatically saves all notes as you take them. You'll notice there's no Save command on the File menu; there is a Save As command, but this is for saving the entire section notes as a new section and should be used rarely.

Side Note: OneNote saves notes within the Windows XP file system as one file per OneNote section tab. This structure has implications for printing and notes export, as you will see in the pages ahead.

Time for You to Practice

At this point you have all the tools you need to write some notes in OneNote, and if you have a copy of OneNote at hand I suggest you put the book down, launch OneNote, and create some actual notes. Try creating new pages, new subpages, entering titles, and converting text. On first examination you'll probably conclude that with respect to recording simple notes OneNote acts very much like Windows Journal for note taking. That's true; however regarding those notes there's a lot more going on just beneath the surface than you realize, and the value of that extra power comes into play when you need to rearrange or reformat your notes. Hold that thought; I am going to cover it fully in the advanced part of this chapter labeled Reorganizing and Moving Ink Text within a OneNote Page. First we need to cover a few more of the basics.

More OneNote Basics

Adding Additional Page Space

You can expand the space at the bottom of the page by clicking the icon below the scroll down arrow in the lower right corner of the work area:

 ——— **Expand Page**

Unlike Windows Journal where a distinct new page is added using a button in a similar location, OneNote merely adds additional space at the bottom of the given page. Keep in mind that this may have some interesting side effects when you print these pages. If you need distinct presized pages for printing purposes, use the New Subpage button instead. See the section on printing below for more discussion of this.

And similar to Windows Journal, you can also add space between existing text lines by using the Insert Extra Writing Space tool on the toolbar shown above, or the same command under the Insert menu.

Converting Handwriting to Text

To convert handwriting to text you select it with the Selection tool, and choose Convert Handwriting to Text from the Tools menu. OneNote does a generally better job than Windows Journal in this department, mainly because once converted, the resulting text box is not supersized like in Journal, and the font size is more appropriate. Spatial placement of the converted text on the page more closely matches the location of the original handwriting.

A Minor Twist Regarding Drawing and Sketching within OneNote

Adding drawings and sketches is as easy and intuitive in OneNote as it is in Windows Journal. There's one added twist, however: OneNote needs to distinguish between ink you enter as handwriting (whether you intend to convert it or not) and ink you intend to enter as drawings. This is to enable the handwriting manipulation capabilities which are described in the next section. Normally if your handwriting is relatively well formed, OneNote will recognize your intentions and distinguish these easily. If you find that One-Note seems to act odd with your handwritten text, it is probably because OneNote thinks your handwriting represents a sketch rather than handwritten text. If you are having this problem and you do not intend to enter sketches, then you can and should tell OneNote that you are entering text-only using the Tools, Pen Mode menu command: Create Handwriting Only (see Figure 9-8). If you use this command OneNote will not accept sketches, lines, arrows, and so on, so use this command with care. Study the other related choices in Figure 9-8.

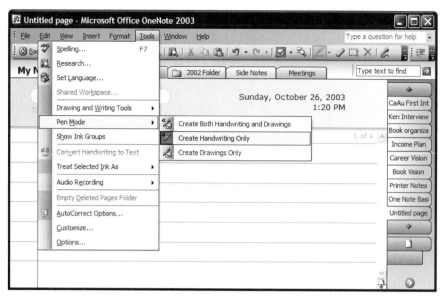

Figure 9-8.   OneNote allows you to indicate your note-taking intentions, which optimizes its processing of your entries.

About the Page Header

Just like in Windows Journal, OneNote pages have a page header into which you can write a title. Like Windows Journal, the title put in the Title field becomes the title of the "saved" note. Similar to Windows Journal, the header contains a date and timestamp for the note. There are also significant differences. Of the differences listed below, the second bullet is the most important:

■   Unlike Windows Journal, when you scroll the page of notes, the OneNote header does not scroll off the page but rather remains visible. This is helpful to ensure you are on the correct page of notes and even more useful when applied to the next point.

■   You can write notes anywhere on the header region; you are not restricted to writing within the Title field portion of the header. This is important because the header remains visible when you scroll the body of notes. It is valuable because you can place important notes there that need to be visible no matter where you have scrolled to within the body of your notes. A good use of this is to place there the names of new people you have just met during a client meeting and continue to refer to those names as you converse with them during your note taking (see Figure 9-

9). You can resize the header to fit more such nonscrolling notes; do this by dragging the bottom edge of the header.

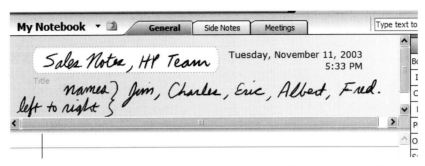

Figure 9-9.   The page header is expandable and multipurpose. You can write outside the title area of the header.

■   You can custom set the color of the header region for each section; this color becomes the theme for all notes within that section. To do this, right-click on the section title and choose Section Color.

Switching Between Displaying Page Names and Page Numbers

Page tabs within a section, behind the scenes, get assigned a page number starting from one for the topmost tab; by default these numbers are not displayed. If you like, you can show page numbers instead of page titles within the tabs on the right (see Figure 9-10).

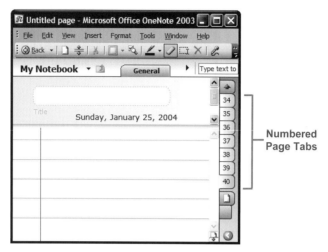

Figure 9-10. Page tabs can display page numbers instead of names.

You can switch between these two by clicking the small arrow (see Figure 9-11) in the lower right corner of the OneNote window (there is also a menu option in the View menu to do the same thing). You will see one use for displaying page numbers when you get to the section ahead on printing OneNote pages.

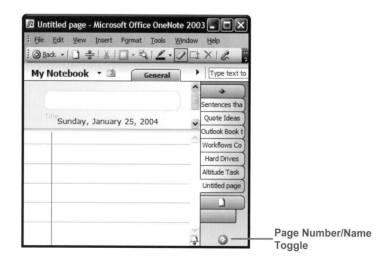

Figure 9-11. Switch to showing page numbers in tabs by clicking the right-facing arrow icon in the lower right portion of the OneNote window.

Flipping Pages by Dragging over Tabs

One very nifty feature of OneNote is that if you take your pen and click and hold on the top page tab and then drag the pen down over the page tabs (and subpage tabs), OneNote displays instantly the image of the page for each tab as it is reached, just like flipping through the pages of a paper notebook. Try this, you will like it. This is a useful way to search by overall visual context, and it extends the notebook metaphor even further.

Another Way to View Page Titles

If you're unhappy with the width of the page titles within the tabs, and/or if you run out of vertical space to view all the page tabs, there is another way to view the page titles for a given section. And I'm gratified to say that this view can be used to nearly reproduce the View Recent Notes feature of Windows Journal. Go to the View menu and choose Page List. This displays a new task pane (see Figure 9-12).

Side Note: By default, this pane opens to the right if your tablet is in landscape mode and to the bottom if your tablet is in portrait mode. But once it opens, you can drag it to either location and/or resize it.

In the middle of this pane is a list of all the pages within the currently open section. On this list there is room to show the full title and note date. Clicking on any of these titles takes you to that page of notes.

The way to use this window to imitate the View Recent Notes feature of Windows Journal is to open the Sort List By menu on the left and choose Date. Figure 9-13 shows how that view looks once invoked.

You can if you wish resize this pane and keep it open as you take notes. Doing this enables you to quickly locate other recent notes, based on when they were taken. This is particularly useful if you have saved notes in various sections throughout the week. All notes above are displayed in the one list no matter what section they are in.

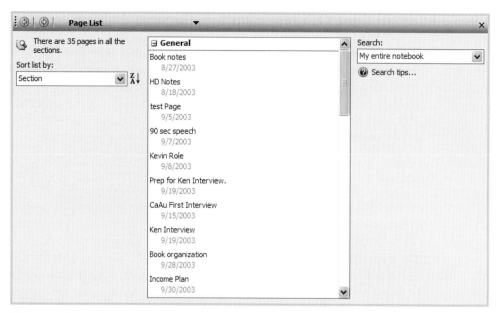

Figure 9-12.   The Page List pane is an alternative to using page tabs to look for notes by title. Open this from the View menu; choose Page List.

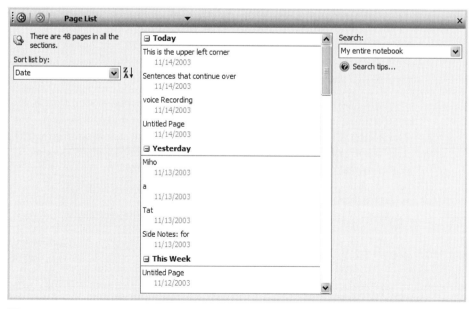

Figure 9-13.   Sorting by date invokes a recent notes view, similar to Windows Journal.

Fixed Pages, Subpages, and Printing Notes

Fixed page sizes

I mentioned above that page sizes will grow indefinitely as you add space at the bottom of your notes. The problem is that if you intend to print your notes, you could get a page break in an unexpected place on the notes; page breaks are not shown on the screen as they are in Microsoft Word. If the printed appearance of your notes is important and you'd like to know exactly where the page breaks are, then it is better to use fixed page lengths. You would then add subpages as needed to continue your note taking. The problem with using subpages for every printed page of notes is that they consume an enormous amount of tab space along the right edge. So choose the lesser of two evils.

By default page sizes are not fixed. You change this setting by using the File, Page Setup... command. The controls there for setting fixed page sizes are self-explanatory.

Printing pages versus OneNote pages

Unfortunately when you start dealing with printing, you run into the distinction between physical printed pages and what OneNote calls pages (which are the contents of one tab). If you do not use fixed page sizes, then these two things can be very different. If you take five "pages" of notes by extending the page (in other words they would print out as five pages), these five printed pages in fact all count only as one page to OneNote since they occupy one page tab.

For the purposes of printing, the fact that extended pages all count as one page can limit you somewhat. For example with five pages of extended notes on one tab, you cannot ask OneNote to print selected "pages" within those five. As far as I can tell, there is no way to tell OneNote to print fewer than the full number of "pages" that represent one OneNote page tab or subpage tab. Again you would need to use subpages and fixed page lengths of printer paper size to gain this control.

The practical reason for this limitation is that when you open the Print dialog box and use the page range entry there, this page range number refers to OneNote page tabs, not physical printed pages. So the smallest printable unit is one page tab (or subpage tab).

A OneNote "document" is a section

And to further complicate things, OneNote counts the whole section as one document when printing. So if instead of an entire section (unlikely for business notes) you want to print a few OneNote pages within a section (more likely) you need to figure out what the section page numbers are that correspond to your notes, and enter them in the page range box on the Print dialog. OneNote counts page tabs from the section top, the first tab being page 1. Luckily, if the page or page range you want to print is currently selected, the dialog box opens with the page number corresponding to that page already populated, ready to print.

As an example, let's say you have taken a page of notes in a meeting, notes that you now want to print, and this page of notes is represented by the twenty-second tab in your current section. When you use the Print dialog box to print those recent notes the Print dialog will display the number 22 in the page range field.

Combining this information with the information above about page sizes, this tells us if these notes occupy five "pages" created by expanding the page size, then to print those notes you instruct OneNote to print page 22; this automatically prints all five "pages." If rather the five pages of notes are each represented by a subpage, you will need to indicate pages 22–27 within the page range field in the Print dialog.

This may sound confusing at first, but you will find that you quickly get the hang of it. Perhaps the easiest way to approach this is to select the page tabs you want to print before you open the print dialog box. If you want to select multiple tabs for printing, you can use the shift key or control key as you click them. From there OneNote will figure out what pages you intend to print and everything will proceed smoothly.

Moving Pages

You can reorder the pages in a section by simply dragging the page tab in the tab list to the new location. To do this, click twice on a page tab and it turns orange. At that point you can drag the tab to a new location.

To move a page to another section, right-click the tab and choose the command Move Page To..., and then choose Another Section... from the submenu.

More on Note Organization: Folders

Folders are a solution to a space problem. They answer what to do if you run out of tab space. They also provide another hierarchy level within which to organize your notes. Here the why and how of folders.

Folders Defined

First of all, I like the tab metaphor that OneNote offers; I like to be able to quickly visually scan my list of notes by viewing the tabs down the right edge of my notebook, just like a physical notebook with note tabs. However, given the available vertical space on the right edge, it would be easy to fill up that space within a few weeks of meetings. And if you use fixed page lengths and subpages for each page you could fill the right edge of a section in even a few days of note taking. Once the right side is filled, a tab with an arrow appears indicating that there are more tabs out of view. Click on that tab and the hidden tabs scroll into view. At some point though there are going to be too many tabs to work with easily.

At that point you can always add more section tabs along the top of the One-Note page. Since page tabs are always associated with a given section, every time you add a new section you start with a new blank tab space along the right edge. But this will also be only a temporary solution because the horizontal space for section tabs will fill up as well.

Therefore a fourth hierarchy structure is available called folders. In the One-Note hierarchy, folders sit between the My Notebook level and the section level. Folders are used to collect groups of sections. So My Notebook can have multiple folders, and each folder can have multiple sections. And each section can have multiple pages. The use of folders is purely optional. Out of the box, OneNote skips that hierarchy level; unlike sections there are no folders pre-created for you. And it is suggested that you add folders only later as you run out of section space; you can easily reorganize your pages and sections at that time.

Using Folders

Creating new folders

Folders are created using the File, New... command. Newly created folders appear at the top of the work area as tabs mixed in with any section tabs that are currently part of My Notebook. They are clearly designated by a folder icon embedded within the tab graphic. In Figure 9-14 you'll see a folder named 2002 Folder that I created to store old notes from a previous calendar year.

Figure 9-14. Newly created folder tabs are listed among section tabs.

You can use folders to group your sections any way you want. Since folders are optional you can put some sections in folders and leave other sections directly under My Notebook. For example observe that in the hierarchy in Figure 9-14 the sections General, Side Notes, and Meetings are not part of any folder but sit directly within My Notebook. This can get confusing though, so a better approach might be to also create a 2003 Folder tab, and put these sections in there. This would clarify the hierarchy and would avoid mixing free section tabs with folder tabs.

Folders are populated by moving preexisting sections into them or creating new sections while the folder is open. To move a section into a different folder, right-click on the section tab, choose Move..., and use the resulting dialog box to indicate which folder to move the section to.

Choosing open folders

After you create a folder you click on the folder tab to make it the currently open folder. When you do that, that folder replaces the My Notebook label in the upper left corner, and you now only see sections that are stored within that folder. All the previous sections are now hidden.

So for example referring to Figure 9-15, within my sample notes organization using the 2002 Folder, once I click on that folder it is now in the far left position at the top of the OneNote workspace, replacing My Notebook. To the right of it are sections that are stored in that folder. In my 2002 Folder you will see that I've created and stored two sections: a 2002 Meetings section and a 2002 General section.

The 2002 Folder name replaces My Notebook

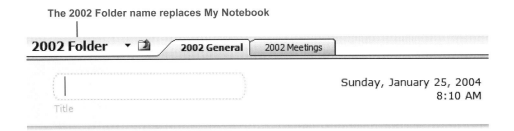

Figure 9-15.   When a folder is open, its name replaces the My Notebook title at the left of the section tabs, and sections within are displayed.

In order to navigate back to the My Notebook level view you can click on the small folder graphic with the return-arrow on it, which is just to the right of the 2002 folder label in Figure 9-15 above and enlarged below:

Or you can click on the black down-facing triangle (also to the right of the 2002 Folder label) which then displays a hierarchical drop-down menu that allows instant navigation to various levels. This latter approach is shown in Figure 9-16.

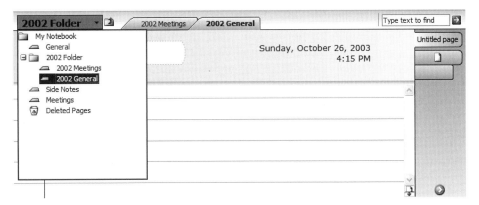

Figure 9-16.   Navigation throughout the entire notes hierarchy is possible using the drop-down arrow next to the currently open folder name.

Folders work well and are an effective way to group sections. But are you confused about how the concept of folders fits into the notebook metaphor? I

Folders work well and are an effective way to group sections. But are you confused about how the concept of folders fits into the notebook metaphor? I was too. Clearly, folders do not fit the three-ring notebook metaphor very well. However if you instead think of the entire notebook as a filing cabinet drawer with the title tabs of hanging folders corresponding to folders, and the nonhanging file folders placed inside these corresponding to sections, then the folder concept starts to work. You need to mix your metaphors a bit to fit this all together.

Side Note: OneNote folders actually correspond to Windows XP file folders. They are stored within the My Notebook folder, which is within the My Documents area of your hard disk. Sections are represented by individual files within those folders. OneNote pages and subpages are stored within the section files and are not visible within the Windows XP file hierarchy. This file structure explains why, as discussed above, for printing purposes sections rather than pages are considered to be the OneNote document.

Using Side Notes

OneNote's Side Notes is a built-in sticky note–like feature with nearly all the advantages of the standard Tablet PC Sticky Notes program (Sticky Notes comes free with all Tablet PCs) plus the extra advantage of being integrated in with the OneNote software. In case you've never used the Sticky Notes program on the Tablet PC, this is a small application that imitates the yellow sticky notes we have all used at the office.

The key beneficial features of a Sticky Notes–like application is it is easy to get to, it launches quickly, it takes up a small amount of screen real estate, and it can be configured to float on top of all your other application windows. Sticky Notes are commonly used to make spur-of-the-moment notes from hallway conversations or midwork inspirations. These notes, like a sticky note stuck to the monitor of your desktop computer, stay "in-your-face" until you have time to do something about their contents.

The advantage that Side Notes brings over the standard Tablet PC Sticky Notes application is its integration into the main OneNote application. Why is this so important? First, your OneNote text searches will search over both sets of notes at the same time; why have notes stored in two places? Second, many times what starts out as a short note on a Side Note quickly expands into a full-blown page of notes. Any Side Note you create in OneNote can instantly be expanded to a full OneNote page of notes just by enlarging the window. And when you do enlarge the window, the full OneNote application automatically opens, ready for your more ample note taking.

Starting Side Notes

On installation, OneNote puts a small icon in the system tray (the collection of icons in the lower right corner of your Windows XP desktop) so that you can open a new Side Note instantly (see Figure 9-17).

Figure 9-17. System tray icon for launching Side Notes.

Clicking this instantly pops up a small blank OneNote window ready for inking and configured with a small subset of OneNote's functionality on its small toolbar as in Figure 9-18.

Saving and Retrieving Side Notes

Like any other OneNote page, Side Notes are automatically saved as you write them. Side Notes are by default saved in the Side Notes section of One-Note (unless you consciously move them) and a new page tab is created on the right edge of that section for each Side Note you create. So to view a complete history of your side notes all you need to do is launch OneNote and click on the Side Notes section tab at the top; your most recent Side Notes note will be the tab at the bottom of the right edge of the page. Unlike other OneNote pages, the title to a Side Notes note is taken from the first contents of the note; this is logical since there is no header or title field on a Side Notes note.

The Toolbar

The Side Note toolbar includes a reduced set of OneNote tools such as the Pen tool, the Selection tool, and a New Note button (see Figure 9-18). There is also a Move to Folder button in case you don't want to store the note in the default Side Notes section. One other important set of tools is included at the right end of the tool bar: the recording tools (shown in Figure 9-19).

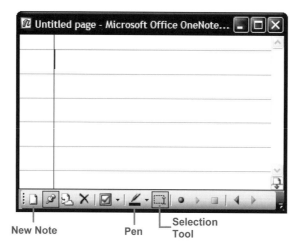

Figure 9-18. The Side Note toolbar is a reduced toolset from the OneNote toolbar.

Recordings in Side Notes

Here's one very useful way to use Side Notes: as a voice note collection and labeling tool. The Sticky Notes application included with all Tablet PCs has this capability too; OneNote's capability is very similar.

We've already mentioned that the full OneNote program has a very powerful voice recorder built in that synchronizes recorded audio with corresponding notes. This feature is covered in the next section, but you may go years before you need to use this powerful feature. However, you might use Side Notes to make quick voice notes daily. It's like using one of those handheld voice recorders to record quick thoughts, but better.

If during the work day you are inspired with the sudden need to record a voice notation, then simply launch a Side Note, click the record button, record your voice note (the microphone built-into all Tablet PCs is adequate for this), click stop, and then do this: write a very short description of what the voice recording contains on the side note. Suddenly you have an easy way to find your voice note recordings without having to listen to each of them. See Figure 9-19 for an example.

Record ⎦ Play   ⎣Stop

Figure 9-19. The recording tools on the Side Note tool bar can be used to take audio notes.

As you would expect these side notes are saved in your Side Note section within the main OneNote screen, so you have a convenient way of finding your voice note recordings later. One subtlety I discovered about using this is that if you want a title to be displayed on the tabs for these voice recordings be sure to write the short title in the space *above* the "Audio recording started..." annotation on the Side Note, otherwise the note is stored as "untitled." If you write the title before you take the audio note the order is correct. If not, you'll need to slip the title into the small space above the audio timestamp, as I have done above.

Synchronized Notes with Audio

The "bonus" feature built into OneNote I mentioned at the start of this chapter is the ability to synchronize recorded audio with corresponding notes. In OneNote, as you audio record a meeting, your written notes are linked with the audio recording. What this means is:

■ If you play back the entire audio recording, as you progress through the playback, the corresponding notes are progressively highlighted on the OneNote page.

■ If you are reading your written notes, you can choose to selectively play back the audio that corresponds to specific portions of those notes.

While I've never had a use for this feature in my business setting, it has gotten tremendous reviews from those who do use it. This would be useful for note taking during any presentation or interaction that you think may be moving too fast for complete notes. Some examples follow.

- You are attending a fast-paced class, training session, or meeting.

- You are interviewing someone.

- You are receiving a detailed briefing.

Taking Audio Synchronized Notes

Using this feature is simple.

1   Have your document open and any introductory notes already in place. When you are ready to start recording simply click the recording button at the right end of the Standard toolbar (see Figure 9-20).

Figure 9-20.   The Start/Stop recording tool on the Standard toolbar.

This starts the recording process and immediately inserts an annotation time/date stamp in your notes indicating when the recording started (see Figure 9-21).

Audio recording started: 3:17 PM Wednesday, December 17, 2003

Figure 9-21.   The time/date stamp inserted within notes when an audio recording is begun.

This also causes OneNote to place a floating recording control panel on the screen (see Figure 9-22).

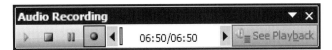

Figure 9-22. The floating recording control panel.

2 You then start taking notes below the inserted annotation.

3 When you are done with the recording session, click the stop button on the floating recording control panel (the blue square).

No other intervention is needed. In fact appearances are deceiving as it appears that nothing special has happened. The value suddenly becomes apparent when you start to use your notes.

Using the Recorded Audio with Your Notes

There are two ways to use the audio. You can listen to the whole recording and watch which notes you took as the original event was unfolding. To do this simply hover your mouse/pen cursor to the left of the audio annotation time/date stamp at the very beginning of your notes. A small speaker icon appears; click on that icon and the playback starts from the beginning.

As the audio progresses, the corresponding line of text written during the original event is highlighted. So as you listen to the audio you will witness a highlight rectangle march down the corresponding portions of your notes page selecting one line at a time (see Figure 9-23). This progresses until the end of the recording.

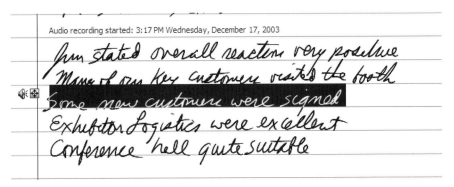

Figure 9-23. When listening to a synchronized audio recording, the corresponding written notes are progressively highlighted one line at a time.

The second way to use your recording is to listen is to small segments of the recordings that correspond to individual portions of your notes. Let's say you are reading your notes without playing the audio and you suddenly see a line of notes that you want more details on; you decide that you would like to hear the actual audio for that written line. To do this hover your cursor at the left edge of the written line in question. The small speaker icon will appear there. Click on that icon and the recording corresponding with that line of notes will play. In OneNote audio recordings are always linked to written notes one line at a time. Once you play the audio for one line, the recording will continue to play beyond that. The highlighted notes will then march down from line to line until you click the stop button on the floating recording control panel.

If you think you are going to be using this second approach here's a tip: the more notes you take the easier it will be to find sections of audio later. Don't pause your note taking very long while making a recording without at least placing some reference notes on your note page. Even if all you write is "talked about sales strategy here," this will give you a way when viewing notes later to jump to that section of audio notes.

One other point about using the OneNote recording capability: if you think you are going to be doing a lot of note recordings in meetings or classrooms, I recommend you purchase and use an external microphone rather than rely on the built-in tablet microphone. Because it's built in to the body of the tablet, the tablet microphone picks up the tapping noise of your pen on the screen surface as you take notes. The external microphone I am referring to here is different from the headset microphone you may have purchased for speech recognition. Don't try to use that as it is designed to cancel out noise from external sources.

And if you are going to be recording both sides of a phone conversation I am told you can simply plug a phone extension line into the modem jack on your tablet. You will still need a handset plugged into another extension, or split line, to dial and speak. Don't try this with an office phone system without proper adapters though; the voltages are different and you could ruin your tablet modem. Once hooked up but before you start recording, you will need to tell OneNote to use the phone line as you input source. To do this go to Tools menu, Options, Linked Audio, and from the Input popup choose Phone Line.

Side Note: When I briefly tested this capability on my Tablet PC, I was not able to get this working as advertised; additional configuration changes may be required to fully enable this.

Simple Text Formatting

OneNote has some interesting twists on the ability to format notes, the most significant of which we will cover in the advanced section. But even at the intermediate level there are some useful capabilities.

Changing the Pen Tool

You could go for months of writing notes without ever changing the Pen tool. I know I have. But there are times when you want to add comments to existing notes and you want those comments to stand out as a different color or line thickness. Or if you are sketching on the page you may find the standard fine-tip felt pen is just too narrow to make the sketch clear. At times like these you will want to choose another pen.

Compared to Windows Journal, OneNote has a much smaller selection of pens and pen colors. I find the selection adequate, but some users have complained. The good news is the smaller selection makes choosing pens much easier than with Journal. You choose pens from the Standard toolbar by clicking on the arrow next to the Pen tool (see Figure 9-24). The upper two-thirds of that menu represents the writing pens.

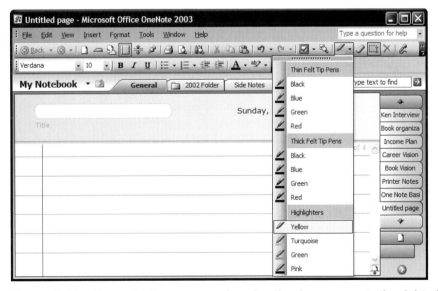

Figure 9-24. Pen selections are made using the down arrow to the right of the Pen tool on the Standard toolbar.

Pressure sensitivity

You'll notice there is no place to change the settings for each pen, as there is in Windows Journal and PowerNotes; what you see on that menu is what you get. You may wonder then about pressure sensitivity. Unlike Windows Journal and PowerNotes (where you can turn pressure sensitivity on and off individually for each pen), with OneNote the setting is made globally for all pens at once. It is controlled from the Tools menu, under Options, Handwriting.

Highlighter Tool

The formatting tool that I use most often is the Highlighter tool which acts like the yellow highlighter which I am sure you have used in the paper world. Whether in Windows Journal or OneNote, using the highlighter is a great way to quickly emphasize notes that you are taking. The Highlighter tool within OneNote is a little confusing in comparison to Windows Journal primarily because OneNote has two "Highlighter" tools, and the tool with the icon that looks like the Journal Highlighter tool does not work the same way. You need to learn the difference between the two or you may get a bit confused. But first let's show you the Formatting toolbar (see Figure 9-25).

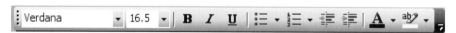

Figure 9-25.   Formatting toolbar.

If this toolbar is not visible at the top of your window screen, select the View menu, then Toolbars, and select the Formatting choice from the submenu. You may need to drag the left edge of the toolbar to expand its size. To see the entire toolbar and the Standard toolbar at once, you may want to drop the Formatting toolbar down one level beneath the Standard toolbar so that they both can coexist fully open (click and drag the left end of the toolbar to do this).

At the far right of this toolbar you'll see what looks like a highlighter tool with the letters "ab" within the symbol:

If you mouse-over this tool it will describe itself as a Highlight tool. It is, but it is not what you may expect; it does not turn your pen into a yellow highlighter pen. Rather, this tool and all the tools on this toolbar expect you to select the text first with the Selection tool from the Standard toolbar (described earlier in this chapter) and then apply the formatting with the formatting tools. These tools are more like the formatting tools you find in text editor rather than a drawing program. The resulting highlighting using this technique colors a perfect rectangle which represents the computed object space for each line of your handwritten text (see Figure 9-26). Again, this is much like the Highlight tool used in Word or even Excel.

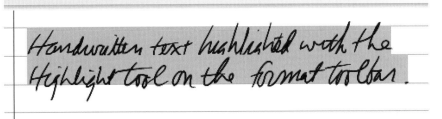

Figure 9-26. Result of using the Highlighting tool from the Formatting toolbar.

In contrast the Highlighter tool that acts like the Windows Journal Highlighter tool, which you can essentially paint with (and so use much more like an actual physical highlighter pen) is in a very different place. It's at the bottom of the pen choices list and is to be found on the Standard toolbar by clicking on the arrow next to the Pen tool (see Figure 9-24, lower portion of the displayed menu).

Using this Highlighter tool, you do not need to select the text to be highlighted first, and the results are much more free-form in nature. I prefer using this Highlighter tool. You might also want to use this tool if you intend to highlight a mixture of text and odd-shaped graphics. Here are the results of using the Pen menu Highlighter tool (see Figure 9-27):

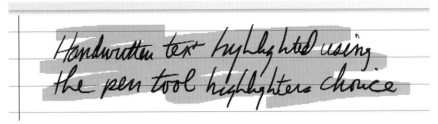

Figure 9-27. Result of using the Highlighter tool from the Pen menu on the Standard toolbar.

So the lesson here is that tools on the Formatting toolbar require text to be selected first, and in general they are more appropriate for formatting text. In contrast the Highlighter tool at the bottom of the Pen menu is more like a physical highlighter, and it can paint highlighting anywhere on the note-taking screen.

Resizing Handwritten Text

Here's something else very interesting that you can do with the Formatting toolbar: resizing handwritten text. I will demonstrate using an exercise.

1 Handwrite some text anywhere on a OneNote page.

2 Select the text using the Selection tool.

3 Now click on the Font Size tool on the Formatting toolbar and set the size to something very big, say 72 points.

You just resized handwritten text! There's nothing like this built into Windows Journal, and this is just part of the extended functionality that OneNote brings you. By the way, this formatting of handwritten text using the Formatting toolbar in OneNote 2003 apparently represents a work-in-progress on the development of the OneNote software; there are many things you cannot do to handwritten text with the Formatting toolbar that, given the resizing capability, you might also expect you could do. For example you cannot bold, you cannot italicize (you can do both of these in Window Journal), and you can't change the font style (not really expected though!). But you *can* underline, although the underline is misaligned and looks more like a strike-through than an underline. This is one of the few places OneNote's formatting capability actually falls short of Journal, but in an insignificant way.

Bulleting, Numbering, and Outlining Handwritten Text

And probably the most useful formatting feature is the ability to apply bullets, numbering, and especially outlining structures to common handwritten text. Let's do an exercise:

Write the following text or something like it on a OneNote page, where the top line of text is a title, and the lines below it represent items described by that title; make sure each item occupies only one line (see Figure 9-28):

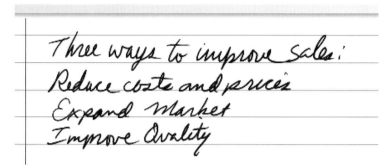

Figure 9-28. Sample writing for bulleting exercise.

Now, select the bottom three items using the Selection tool, and click on the Increase Indent tool on the Formatting toolbar (that tool is shown in Figure 9-29).

Figure 9-29. The Increase Indent tool on the Formatting toolbar behaves the same as similar tools within other Microsoft applications.

And without changing the selection, then click on the Bullet tool on the Formatting toolbar (that tool is shown in Figure 9-30).

Figure 9-30. The Bullet tool on the Formatting toolbar.

The results should look as below (see Figure 9-31):

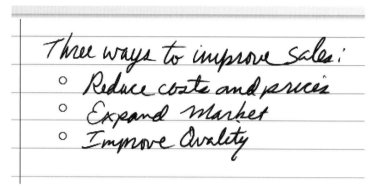

Figure 9-31.   Results of applying indents and bulleting to handwritten text.

When you consider that you are applying these formatting rules to handwritten text, you may feel some awe as to the programming accomplishments here. And in practical terms this provides the note taker with many ways to clean up written notes without being forced to convert to text first, a very useful capability.

And how do you apply outlining? Well actually you've already done it; by applying the indents you've defined an outline structure. You can now collapse and expand this outline; here's how:

1   Select the Selection tool.

2   Hover your pen over the text without actually touching the screen so that the bar at the top of this text area becomes visible.

3   Move your hand to the upper left portion of your text so that the four-sided arrow becomes visible in the upper left corner of the text group; see Figure 9-32.

4   Now double-click on the four-sided arrow in the upper left corner.

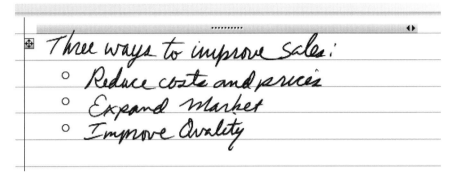

Figure 9-32. Indenting creates an outline relationship; use the four-sided arrow icon to the left of the top line to collapse the outline.

You should see the three items below the title disappear (see Figure 9-33); they are not deleted, but rather they are actually collapsed just like an outline.

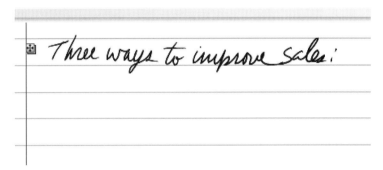

Figure 9-33. Outline after it is collapsed; the appearance of the four-sided arrow changes slightly, and it remains visible until text is expanded again.

After an item is collapsed the four-arrow icon changes slightly in appearance, and if you double-click that icon again the item will fully expand. While in the collapsed state the four-sided arrow icon remains visible even after you move your mouse or pen to other portions of the notes; this way you can easily see what notes are collapsed as you read.

If you tend to review notes a lot, outlining notes is a useful way to make your notes easier to read. By collapsing sections as you review notes, you can skip quickly through your notes to more pertinent sections.

Side Note: *You do not need to use the indent tool or bullets to create an outline. If you write a title line and then write list items underneath it starting those lines to the right a bit (inserting an indent manually, so to speak), the resulting list will automatically take on an outline relationship. And as expected double-clicking next to the top line will collapse and expand this outline. You can also drag lines to the right to create the indent relationship; just click and drag using the four-sided Paragraph Handle to the left of the line. More coverage of moving individual lines like this can be found in the advanced section of this chapter, and I recommend you read that section before doing extensive moving of lines within your notes.*

Formatting Multiline Sentences

Now we're ready for one slightly more challenging exercise.

Not all individual topics in a list occupy only one line; sometimes a single bulleted sentence needs to continue to a second or third line. When adding bullets or outlining to lists with handwritten multiline sentences, OneNote needs help. By default it tends to treat each line of the multiline sentence as a separate list item rather than recognizing the subsequent lines as continuations of a single thought. So instead of one bullet in front of the top of three lines you get three separate bulleted lines. Let's demonstrate the wrong behavior, and then show you how to fix it and even avoid it.

Side Note: This behavior is limited to handwritten notes. With typed text notes word wrap is much more accurate in OneNote.

Below (Figure 9-34) are two sentences that each requires three lines to fully express. How is OneNote going to handle this? Why don't you do the same: handwrite the following text or something like it and be sure that your sentences require multiple lines; in other words your sentences are continued on a second or third line.

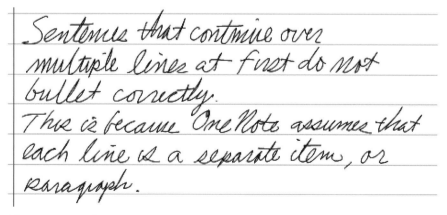

Figure 9-34. Sample text to demonstrate default paragraph behavior of OneNote.

Now, select this group of words with the Selection tool, apply bullets, and note that a predictable mistake seems to have been made: the software interpreted this as six separate items in a list (see Figure 9-35).

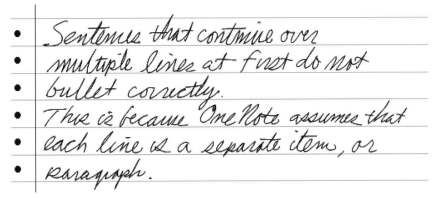

Figure 9-35. OneNote normally assumes every handwritten line is a separate paragraph.

This is understandable, since there's no way that OneNote can determine whether two or more lines represent a continuation of one thought or multiple items in a list. You might think that you could insert an explicit paragraph mark somehow, something equivalent to hitting the return or enter key at the end of a sentence or paragraph on a keyboard, such as when typing in Microsoft Word. The reason this solution does not exist is that under normal settings, OneNote assumes *every* line is a separate paragraph, and in fact there is already a paragraph mark hidden at the end of every line.

So to fix this we need to use a tool within OneNote that allows us to *remove* hidden paragraphs marks between lines. This effectively merges two lines together into one paragraph.

To get to that tool we need to add another toolbar to OneNote. From the View menu choose Toolbars and then select Drawing and Writing Tools. This adds a new toolbar to the left edge of the OneNote window, and the middle of these tools is the one of interest to us, called the Continue Previous Paragraph tool (see Figure 9-36).

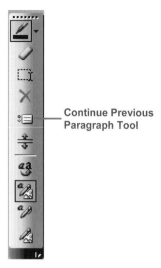

Continue Previous
Paragraph Tool

Figure 9-36. Drawing and Writing toolbar, with the Continue Previous Paragraph tool shown.

This is actually not the official name for this tool. The real name is the "Make current paragraph a continuation of previous paragraph" tool, but that's way too long to repeat over and over again so we'll use the shorter name. Now here's how you fix the problem described above using this tool:

1   First, using the Selection tool, click anywhere in the bottom-most line.

2   Click on the Continue Previous Paragraph tool.

Bingo, OneNote now knows that the bottom line is a continuation line, and it removes the last bullet. Continue these steps working up the lines; you need to start at the bottom and work up, applying the tool one line at a time. Remember to skip any lines that truly do represent new paragraphs. See Figure 9-37 for the result of this exercise.

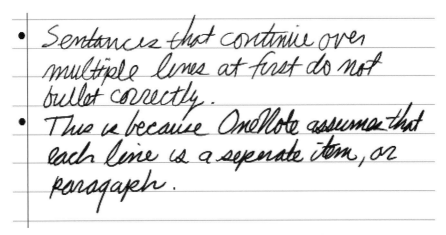

*   Sentances that continue over multiple lines at first do not bullet correctly.
*   This is because OneNote assumes that each line is a seperate item, or paragaph.

Figure 9-37.   Result of using the Continue Previous Paragraph tool: bulleting works correctly on multiline sentences.

If you make a lot of bulleted lists and find yourself making the corrections above often, there is a way to prevent this in the first place and force OneNote to recognize your continuation lines. We'll cover that solution in the advanced section of this chapter, under the heading Show Ink Groups. We'll also have more discussion there about merging OneNote paragraphs. There are still some subtle points to learn about this topic to make the merging of handwritten paragraphs work correctly with respect to word wrap.

Some Features Lacking in OneNote

Before moving on to the advanced action, let's list how OneNote is different from Windows Journal and PowerNotes (PlanPlus and TabletPlanner). Specifically let's list what OneNote is missing compared with these other programs.

A number of the key features that we covered in the last chapter, available in Windows Journal and PowerNotes, are not (yet) available within OneNote. These include:

*   Ability to import documents from other programs and use them as background templates such as forms (you *can* create new templates from documents created *within* OneNote).

*   Ability to import documents as background images for marking them up with annotations (you *can* import text and graphics from text-oriented programs like Word and mark them up with the pen).

- Ability to send tasks to Microsoft Outlook within Office XP (you *can* send to Office 2003).

- Ability to configure a wide range of pen types.

- Ability to export to .tif files

- Ability to convert rough graphic shapes into perfect shapes.

- Ability to, as in PowerNotes, format ink handwriting using bold or italic.

Some of these features are relatively unimportant; others, like importing documents as images for markup, are pretty useful. The best strategy is to use both products. My current approach is to use OneNote for all note taking and Windows Journal for the import documents capabilities when needed.

End of Basic Skills Section for OneNote

The skills you have learned up to this point in OneNote are sufficient to satisfy your basic note-taking needs as a work manager. Move on to the next chapter if you would like to more quickly maximize your value from the Tablet PC, coming back to the rest of this chapter later. Proceed with this chapter now only if you have time and are willing to do the extra study required to master the added skills. Don't let the concepts and exercises distract you; you can in fact start using OneNote with the skills you have so far.

Advanced Note-Taking Features of Microsoft OneNote

I have delayed the advanced and lower priority features of Microsoft One-Note until now, so you could get up and running in OneNote. The rest of this chapter contains:

- Features that are slightly harder to take advantage of, and/or that take a little more thought to understand.

- Other low priority features that you may never use.

Reorganizing and Moving Ink Text within a OneNote page

Reorganizing handwritten notes on the page falls under the category of "slightly harder to take advantage of"; but I recommend you take the time to learn this skill because it is useful and may in fact keep you out of trouble in your day-to-day use of OneNote.

One of the key design elements of OneNote that distinguishes it from the other note-taking tools is the powerful ability to move and reorganize text, especially unconverted ink text, on the page after the notes are taken. And even if you think you will not be doing this, learning these concepts will help you understand why OneNote acts the odd way it does sometimes.

I'm going to assume that you will leave most of your handwritten notes un-converted and so will focus on the ability to manipulate ink text. This is consistent with my experience and the experience of others; most Tablet PC meeting notes remain in ink format. It is this ability to reorganize ink text that is the most amazing and useful advanced feature of OneNote.

In Windows Journal you have the ability to do limited text reorganization of ink text; you can select some ink text with the Lasso tool and then move it about. PowerNotes has more capability to move ink text. In contrast OneNote has extensive ink text reorganization capabilities that go far beyond these two programs. We've already had a peek at this when we went over outlining and bulleting of ink text. But there's a lot more you can do with ink beyond that.

But first, let's list a few reasons you may want to reorganize ink text:

- You've written some notes and you need to insert a few words in the middle of your handwritten sentence.

- You're mixing text with graphics and you want to reposition the text around a graphic for labeling purposes.

- You want to change the order of your sentences to make your notes clearer.

- You want to create a simple table on your note page and move already written note elements into the table.

All of these things you could not easily do within Windows Journal and you can within OneNote. The capability to manipulate ink text in these ways is the result of a fairly elaborate ink and text container approach built into the design of OneNote.

OneNote Recognizes Individual Ink Words and Lines

First of all, OneNote recognizes the gaps between ink words and identifies individual words as individual units. Similarly, OneNote recognizes the gaps between lines and between groups of lines. As a result of the way OneNote does this, lines can be moved about and reshaped in ways that are much more flexible than in Windows Journal.

Reordering handwritten lines

For example, you can reorder the lines in a list merely by clicking and dragging them.

Try this now:

1 Create a list of four or five items on a OneNote page, each immediately one line below the other.

2 Hover over the left margin of one of the middle items; a four-sided arrow (called a "Paragraph Handle" in OneNote speak) appears to the left of any line that you hover to the left of.

3 Now click and drag that Paragraph Handle vertically up or down, and you'll find that the list will be reordered.

You can drag lines completely out of a list if needed and into other lists. You can also indent the individual items in a list by dragging them left or right using the Paragraph Handle; be careful though, because this creates an outline relationship, so be sure that's what you want.

Text Groups or Containers

The most important object within OneNote is the text group, also called a *container*. You've probably been wondering about the light gray shaded box and the darker gray bar at the top of those boxes, which appear over blocks of text when you have the Selection tool selected. This identifies a text group, or container. Containers are created automatically as you begin to write, and they are delimited when you leave at least one inch of space between your adjacent writing areas. Containers can be moved and resized in various ways.

Containers have two components that you'll be using to manipulate them as a whole: the Container Handle which is the darker blue line at the top of the container, and the container Resize tool which is the double arrow at the right end of the Container Handle (see Figure 9-38). Associated with containers are a number of Paragraph Handles that sit next to each of the paragraphs within the container.

Figure 9-38. Container manipulation components: Container Handle and Container Resize tool affect the container as a whole. The Paragraph Handle manipulates individual paragraphs within the container.

Note also that containers are not paragraphs as a whole, even though they sort of look like paragraphs. In fact by default every line within a handwritten container is a separate paragraph; that is unless you apply the Continue Previous Paragraph tool that we discussed earlier or use the Writing Guides described ahead. So if you hover your pen over the left edge of a container you'll see multiple Paragraph Handles form one at a time to the left of each line in the container.

Simple Container Exercise

Let's try the following to get a clear understanding of containers:

1   Using the Pen tool write a few sentences within OneNote, making sure to keep words and sentences relatively close to each other so that they form one container.

2   Now move your hand down the page at least an inch or more (two or three lines) and write some more text.

3   Now click on the Selection tool in the Standard toolbar so that your pen pointer takes on the shape of the Selection cursor. With the Selection tool, hover your pen anywhere in the top text group. You'll see a light blue box appear around that container, and a darker blue gray bar at the top of the text group. This represents a text container and now delineates one distinct group of text.

4   If you hover over your second text area, you'll notice that a separate box and handle forms.

5   Either of these containers can now be moved about the page by grabbing the Container Handle with your pen and dragging it; read the moving tips below and then try it.

Important Tips for Moving Text Containers

If you have more than one container on a page and you move a container by grabbing the Container Handle with the Selection tool, you need to note the following:

- OneNote assumes that you are going to insert the container where you are moving it to, and so it will try to make room for the container by moving other text containers out of the way. You'll see other containers jumping about the screen as you drag the first, and it may look a bit confusing.

- If you drag a container over the top of another container and let go while on top, the two containers may attempt to merge into one and an unpredicted formatting change may result. Or the two will not actually merge but rather overlap, and you will have a jumble of text as both sets of handwriting will be visible. So avoid dropping a container on top of another one.

- If you drag a container up close to the bottom of the container above it (but not on top), the two containers will merge cleanly into one.

Go ahead now and finish this exercise; experiment with moving the two containers about the writing page.

Container Woes

I describe below why containers are valuable for reorganizing text on pages and therefore a great blessing. Before getting to that, though, I need to point out that containers are also somewhat of a curse. This is because if your note-taking needs are very simple, and you do not need to reorganize notes, the overhead of learning and understanding containers may seem out of proportion to their usefulness. Yet learning them may be needed to prevent some craziness from occurring in your notes.

The problem with containers is that they can greatly complicate some simple actions. Moving containers even slightly (perhaps accidentally) can cause them to jump and merge in odd ways. And when moving on purpose, words you may think are part of one container may in fact be separate, and sentences you thought were separate containers may be part of one container. So the move does not appear correct. Simple graphics, like lines and arrows, are sometimes separate from the text containers they may be drawn on top of and so need to be selected and moved separately. Start to move one container, and your whole notes page can become a mess as the separated containers get left behind.

All this said, once you learn how containers work, you *can* keep them relatively well behaved. And more importantly, using containers allows you to do great things with reorganizing your note page.

Here are some tips to make your introduction to containers more successful:

- To better understand containers I suggest you, at least for a while, turn on the Show Ink Groups setting described in the section with that name below. Then you can track where containers are and how they are behaving as you take notes. This will make your page appear a bit unattractive, so use this approach only as long as needed to get a feel for containers.

- Get in the habit of holding down the Alt key when dragging containers. This prevents containers from attempting to resize or merge with adjacent containers and makes their movement and repositioning much smoother and more intuitive. It is fairly rare that you will *want* to merge containers, so leaving the Alt key engaged when moving containers usually invokes the expected behavior. Be sure to disengage the Alt key however if you are rearranging lines within a container; otherwise the moved line may separate from the container and will not merge back in when you reposition it.

- If you need to move a container that has drawings in it (like circled words, and arrows between words), don't attempt to move it by dragging the Container Handle. There is a good chance some of those graphics are not part of the container. Instead, using the Selection tool, click well outside the container and "draw" a rectangle that selects the container and drawings. Then drag the selected area.

Resizing and Reshaping Containers

The width of the container can be resized horizontally by clicking on the container Resize tool (the double arrow in the right-hand corner of the Container Handle) and dragging left and right. If by doing this you make the container narrower, this will probably make your container taller as the container reshapes to contain all the text. Note the way ink words are wrapped along word boundaries as you do this resizing; this clearly shows that OneNote is able to distinguish between individual ink words, and it is in effect treating the ink words as if they were text.

The value of resizable containers

The value of this ability to resize ink paragraphs and intelligently wrap at word boundaries may not be readily apparent to you until you start doing moderately creative manipulation of text notes. For example let's say you are annotating a sketch by writing small blocks of text and drawing arrows from those blocks of text to different parts of the sketch. The ability to reset the shape of those ink text boxes as you drag them around the sketched area is useful.

Container resizing exercise

Let's try an exercise that demonstrates container resizing:

1 Start a new blank OneNote page and write on the top line the sentence "This is the upper left corner."

2 Skip down two lines (so that you create a new container) and write the line "This is the lower left corner."

3 Repeat this twice more creating sentences corresponding to the upper right and lower right corners, making sure that each occupies a separate container, and each occupies only one line.

4 Now, select the Selection tool, and on the bottom sentence, drag the Re-size tool on the container holding that sentence to the left, to reshape the sentence into a more compact shape (see Figure 9-39).

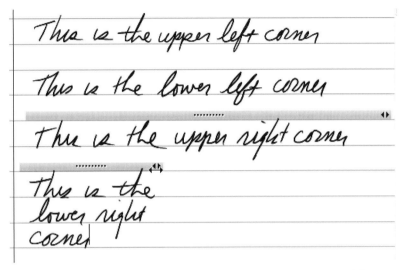

Figure 9-39. Exercise to demonstrate word wrap when resizing containers.

5 Move this reshaped container down into the lower right corner of your screen, out of the way, and do the same reshaping for the other three lines. Then move these individual containers into the respective corners of the screen.

6 And now in the middle of the screen, sketch a rectangle and draw arrows from the text labels to the respective corners of the rectangle (see Figure 9-40).

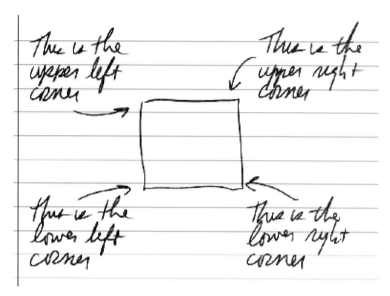

Figure 9-40. Word wrapping within resized containers is a useful way to rearrange text around graphics.

Being able to reshape text containers suddenly looks interesting, doesn't it? Chances are in the not-too-distant future you will need to do something like this.

Side Note: Resizing handwritten text that has drawings mixed in with the text container can produce some odd results, so be ready to undo your resize if the results don't meet your expectations.

Note also that the only reason the exercise above worked so smoothly is that the sentences were each only one line in height. Read on to see issues with re-sizing multiline sentences and to discover approaches to prevent the issues.

Paragraphs versus Lines

Refer back within the bulleting and outlining section of this chapter to the ex-ercise where we needed to combine multiple lines into one continuous sentence in order to bullet a list correctly. Recall we needed to use a special tool to merge lines together into one bullet. The fact that we needed to do this pointed out a default behavior of OneNote that we highlighted then: all handwritten lines are by default formatted as individual paragraphs. One-Note inserts an invisible line return or carriage return at the end of each ink line even if your intention is for the multiple lines to represent one long sen-tence. In other words, OneNote always assumes you're making the equivalent of a list of items, each line being an item on the list.

This default behavior works well if you never need to apply formatting or resize the text container. This default behavior also works well if in fact that's what you're doing: creating a list with each list item occupying no more than one line of text. However if your intention is to write one long paragraph or sentence that extends over multiple lines, and you want to invoke bullets or outline formatting or container resizing, the automatic insertion of paragraph or line breaks can lead to problems. Luckily, these problems are correctable and preventable.

Using Show Ink Groups and Writing Guides

Getting control of paragraphs

To change the "every line is a paragraph" default behavior, OneNote has a partial solution. Under the Tools menu choose Show Ink Groups. This has two results. First, unrelated to paragraphs, it reveals the gray background of *all* containers, even those that are not selected or that you are not hovering over. This is useful to engage as you make notes because it clearly shows the boundaries of containers, and it makes your container manipulation decisions easier.

But more significantly, invoking Show Ink Groups turns on the Writing Guide feature of OneNote, and this feature changes the "every line is a paragraph" behavior. It fixes almost all the problems I've described.

A Writing Guide is a container-like gray shape that defines where the logical next writing space for handwriting is as you write. If you stay within that guide space, OneNote will keep everything written as one paragraph, even if your writing continues on multiple lines.

The guide progresses about half an inch to the right of your pen tip as you write. The key here is that as your writing reaches the right margin, the guide will jump to the beginning of the next line. If you wait until that happens before progressing writing to the next line, and if you then keep your writing within the guide on the next line, no paragraph break will be inserted between these lines.

The result of using the Writing Guide is that if you then apply bullets, bingo, there will be only one bullet applied—correct behavior. And if you instead want lists, all you need to do is move the pen down to the next line before the guide jumps to the next line. The paragraph break is inserted and the list will bullet correctly.

Other reasons to use Show Ink Groups

And even if you are not concerned about paragraph and bullet behavior, enabling Show Ink Groups can help you understand OneNote as you take notes. It helps you understand and predict how OneNote will structure your notes, and this may prevent getting trapped by unexpected container behavior.

There are also some other side benefits of working with Show Ink Groups invoked. One is this: you do not need to switch to the Selection tool to select or move a container. With Show Ink Groups invoked your Pen tool acts like a Selection tool when you click on the Container Handle. This saves some trips to the toolbar.

The only cost of working with Show Ink Groups enabled may be that you feel a bit manipulated during your writing and you have to live with gray rectangles appearing throughout your on-screen notes. You can adjust the darkness of those rectangles so that they are nearly invisible. Do this by using the Tools menu, choose Options and then Display on the category list at the left.

Some subtleties of using Show Ink Groups

Unfortunately, even beyond living with gray rectangles, using Writing Guides as a solution to bullets and paragraphs is not perfectly simple. First of all, sometimes it may appear to work *too* well. What if your bulleted list of single line items happens to include lines that extend to the right margin? When you reach the right margin, as soon as the writing guide jumps to the next line and you start writing, you lose your hidden paragraph mark and lose the bullet for that next line.

Luckily an easy operation takes control of this: after the Writing Guide jumps to the next line, but before actually writing the next line, tap your pen on the screen once, to the left of the new line, outside the container. This single tap tells OneNote that this is a new list item (effectively inserting the hidden paragraph mark at the end of the line above). If you have bullets turned on as you write, you will see the bullet appear at the new line after you tap. Then start writing. This is a very nice touch from the creators of OneNote.

If you forget to tap in the margin before you start writing on the new line, no problem, there is another fix.

1 Go ahead and finish your writing on that next line.

2 Select the Selection tool.

3 Click once at the end of the line above, and using the Tablet PC Input Panel keyboard hit the Enter key.

This reinserts the missing hidden paragraph mark and your bullet will appear.

A bug in paragraph behavior in OneNote

Another problem is a bit more subtle and I have confirmed it is actually a known bug in OneNote. It may be fixed by the time you read this.

Whether you use the Show Ink Groups command to prevent paragraphs or use the Continue Previous Paragraph tool to remove them, OneNote does not completely prevent or remove the hidden line breaks. This issue becomes apparent when you try to resize text containers and expect resulting word wrap to be accurate. The incorrect behavior mostly affects handwritten notes, but the problem is partially present even in typed text. I'll demonstrate the issue with an exercise:

1   Turn on Show Ink Groups.

2   Handwrite a long sentence that continues down at least three wide lines; be sure to follow the Writing Guide all the way to the right margin and onto the next line, so that the writing forms one paragraph.

3   Now choose the Selection tool and select the entire multiline sentence, and then apply bullets to the sentence. If you used the Writing Guide correctly, you should see only one bullet next to the top line.

4   Presumably you now have one large paragraph. This conclusion is correct; you do have one paragraph with regard to bullets but not with regard to word wrap; this is the bug.

5   To demonstrate the bug, drag the Resize tool in the upper right corner of the container to the left about one quarter of the way across the screen — or about one inch. Assuming Microsoft has not fixed this by the time you read this book, you will observe that the lines do not wrap correctly; some form of line breaks still remain which causes a jagged edge to the block of text (see Figure 9-41).

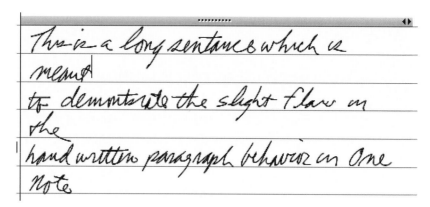

Figure 9-41. Example of incorrect word wrap when resizing containers.

So what's going on here? There is a bug in the paragraph behavior of One-Note; some form of hidden line break object still remains even when lines are all part of one paragraph. The act of "rounding the corner" from line to line when handwriting on the OneNote screen seems to insert some subtle form of a line return, even with Writing Guide turned on. And because of this, resizing multiline handwritten text containers containing a single flowing paragraph will not produce the intended word wrap results.

A couple of points: merging lines into one paragraph using the Continue Previous Paragraph tool does not solve this problem. And the problem is less apparent with typed text, but it still presents itself when you use the Continue Previous Paragraph tool to turn typed lists into merged paragraphs (although this is probably desirable behavior for text).

There is some good news: this behavior can be corrected after the fact by a (simple but somewhat painful) workaround.

1   First, if your sentence still looks like the one in Figure 9-41, drag the Resize tool back to the right so that you reshape your container back to its original shape.

2   Now here's the workaround: with the Selection tool selected, tap in front of the first word in the bottom line so that you place a blinking cursor just in front of the first letter of the bottom line.

3   Now tap the backspace key on your on-screen keyboard once; most likely nothing will appear to happen. Or what might happen is that the first word on that line will wrap up and around to the end of the line above it. Either outcome is fine.

4   Repeat steps two and three for each line except the top one. By doing this you have just deleted the remaining invisible paragraph return for all lines.

5   Now try dragging the Resize tool to the left to resize the container; you'll see that the text wraps correctly this time (see Figure 9-42).

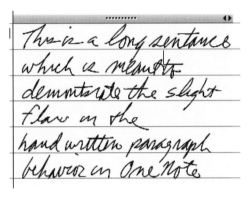

Figure 9-42.   Results of correct word wrap in a resized container.

Clearly if you had tens or hundreds of such lines to correct, this workaround would be painful. If you need to resize often, we can hope this behavior will be fixed by the time you read this book or shortly thereafter. In general, though, for an initial release of a brand new software concept OneNote is surprisingly bug-free. And this bug is pretty minor.

Other Ways to Manipulate Text Containers

Adding text at the end

If you want to add text to the end of one container, click at the end of the existing text (within the container) and just start writing more text; it will automatically merge with the container.

Adding ink text in the middle of a sentence

This often happens: you create some notes and then you realize you need to add some words in the middle of a sentence; you normally cannot do that with handwritten text. Instead you end up squeezing the additional text in between lines or above lines with arrows; very messy. With OneNote you can add handwritten text in the middle of a handwritten sentence. Here's how:

1   Write the new text at the end of the text container or in its own new container.

2   Switch to the Selection tool and select the added text.

3   Drag the added text to where you want it inserted in the original text; the existing text will automatically expand to make room for the new.

If you are at a keyboard when editing your handwritten notes this is even easier; just click where you want the words to go and start typing. It's not the prettiest thing to look at (mixed handwriting and typed text), but it gets the job done.

Note that entering words in the middle of a handwritten sentence is something you could never do with ink in Windows Journal or PowerNotes.

Merging text containers

Sometimes, after creating separate text containers, you may realize that there's no need to have these containers separate from each other; for example, perhaps you do not need to move the containers around the page separately. You may as well combine the text groups together into one large group. To do this simply drag a lower text group up to and touching the bottom of an upper text group, and the two containers will automatically merge cleanly into one large container.

You can also drag a container from above down to the container below, and they will merge cleanly from above. What you cannot do is merge containers from the sides.

If you ever *accidentally* merge containers, no worries, simply select all the text that accidentally merged and drag it out of the container. Or use the undo command.

Note Flags: Using and Defining

OneNote has a note flag capability which is much different from, and much more powerful than, Windows Journal's note flag capability. And you may have noticed that there is no note flag capability built in to FranklinCovey PowerNotes.

However, out of the box, OneNote is configured with fewer "normal" flag choices than Windows Journal. Other than the To Do flag, a flag which has a special behavior, there are really only two "normal" flag symbols available in OneNote: the Important (gold star) flag and the Question flag. Interestingly no flags are configured that have an actual flag symbol. So if you've grown accustomed to the flag symbol in Window Journal, you'll need to learn how to define flags in OneNote to create one.

Using Note Flags

First let's learn how to find and use the Flag tool on the toolbar. On the Standard toolbar you'll most likely see a star symbol and that's the entry point for flags. However if you or someone else has been using the flag capability, then whatever flag was last used is what will be displayed on the Standard toolbar. So if you don't see the star symbol on your toolbar look for something there that matches one of the four top flag symbols in the menu below (see Figure 9-43).

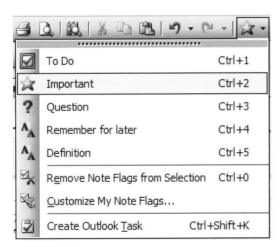

Figure 9-43. Flag menu displayed by clicking on the arrow to the right of the Flag tool on the Standard toolbar.

Assuming you have found the Flag tool, click on the arrow next to the tool to open the menu displayed above. In the upper portion of this menu are the actual flag choices; there you will see three kinds of flags:

- The To Do flag, which is a special action flag. This flag you can check and uncheck and search based on its checked state; no other flag acts this way.

- Symbol flags like the star-shaped Important flag and the Question flag.

- Style flags such as those labeled Remember for Later and Definition.

Below these on the menu you will see some flag-related commands.

The To Do flag is useful; place one next to to-do items in your notes, and check them off as completed by merely clicking on the square symbol; the square symbol image changes to include a checkmark when you click on it.

The Symbol flags are the flags that correspond to the flag capability that Windows Journal has: a simple and customizable symbol is placed in the margin of your notes. It has no special action, other than being searchable.

Both of these types of flags are placed in the left edge of your notes by first clicking anywhere on a sentence with the Selection tool and then choosing the flag from the menu above.

The Style flags are unusual. Using them doesn't drop a flag in the margin but rather changes the formatting style of the sentence. For example, using the Remember for Later flag causes the sentence to take on a yellow highlight. Why not just use the highlighter tool instead? Because you can search on application of these style flags. More on the search capability later.

Examples of these three flags in a OneNote document are shown in Figure 9-44. The style flag is represented by the shading on the "Decrease Cost" text (this looks gray here, but when viewed in color it is yellow).

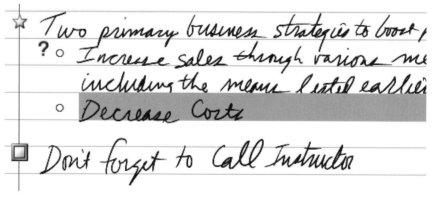

Figure 9-44.   Examples of flags applied to OneNote notes.

Defining Flags

So if you want to define a new flag, in particular a flag with an actual flag symbol, how do you do this?

In the menu displayed in Figure 9-43 above, you'll see a choice near the bottom called Customize my Note Flag... Selecting this splits your OneNote screen and displays the following task pane (see Figure 9-45):

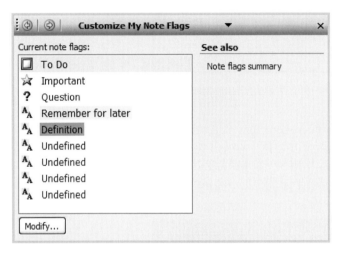

Figure 9-45.   Flag customization window.

The way to use this to add a new flag type is to select the first flag labeled Undefined, and click the Modify... button at the bottom. This opens the following window (see Figure 9-46):

Figure 9-46.   Modify Note Flag window.

Now type in your new flag title (I chose "Red Flag" as the title in this case) and choose the flag symbol from the popup symbol list (see Figure 9-47). Ignore the Font Color and Highlight Color selectors to the right; those are just used for Style flags.

Figure 9-47.   Inputs to the Modify Note Flag window that are needed to add a Windows Journal–like Red Flag type of note flag.

When you click OK you'll see that the Undefined flag you'd selected earlier has been replaced with your newly defined Red Flag (see Figure 9-48). This flag will now appear in the Flag menu on the Standard tool bar.

Figure 9-48.   Results of creating the Red Flag note flag.

Here's the entire list of note flag symbols you have available (see Figure 9-49):

Figure 9-49.   Available note flag symbols.

In this list note two things. First, there's only one actual flag symbol, which is much different from Windows Journal that has five flags with a flag symbol (each a different color). Second, notice the large number of different To Do symbols, twelve in all. I suspect Microsoft's research showed that note flags are usually used to mark action items, and the To Do approach (flags that you can actually check off as you complete the associated action) was found most suitable for this. You can use these various To Do symbols to represent different priorities or types of to-dos. Keep in mind however that you only have a total of nine flag types that you can define as being available at once, and five are consumed out of the box; so you'll have to pick a subset of the available To Do flag types to actually use.

Finding Flagged Notes

Once you have flagged some notes, how do you find them? You can visually scroll through your notes, but a better way is by displaying the Note Flags Summary pane. You display this by clicking the icon just to the right of the Flag tool on the Standard toolbar. (See Figure 9-50.)

Figure 9-50.   Tool icon on Standard toolbar to open the Note Flags Summary pane.

This splits the OneNote window and displays the following Note Flags Summary pane (see Figure 9-51).

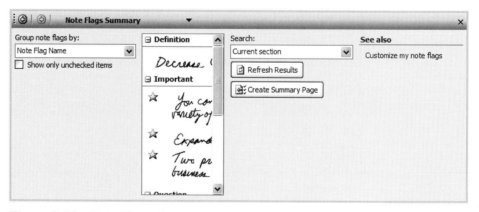

Figure 9-51.   Note Flags Summary pane.

This is a moderately complex but very powerful window that collects and summarizes all note flags in your notes. Here's how you use it.

Starting from the left, you will see a Group Note Flags By selection box. Use this to indicate what attribute you want to summarize by, selecting the appropriate choice from the choice list. Most likely you will want to group together all note flags of a certain type, so leave the default choice which is Note Flag Name.

Then in the middle right, under the label Search, indicate the range of note documents that you want a search across. The choices are as shown in Figure 9-52).

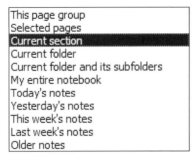

Figure 9-52. Search range choices.

The upper half of this list focuses on various levels within your note collection hierarchy, and the bottom half focuses on the time dimension. You can only select one from this list. There's no obvious or default choice here, it really depends on why you are searching. If you are collecting to-dos from the last week, choose "This week's notes." If you know what you need is in the current section, use that choice. Choosing "My entire notebook" will probably return too many hits, but that's the most inclusive choice.

After you've made these two choices, click the Refresh Results button, and view the narrow scrolling list in the middle left portion of the pane. This is a list of all notes that meet the criteria. Note that you cannot filter on what flag type you want to see, rather you'll see all flag types, grouped by type.

This scrolling list really is too narrow to be of much use other than to see if you need to tighten your search any based on the volume of notes returned. The real result is seen when you then click the button labeled Create Summary Page. This copies all the notes within the scrolling list to a new OneNote page and displays them fully. They will be grouped per your specifications. It's likely that you're looking for one particular kind of flag, so your natural next step is to scan the document for the group that matches that flag, and then examine that portion of the list.

You can use this approach to, for example, create a document that lists all your open to-do items; that's where the checkbox in the left side of the Note Flags Summary pane comes in: Show Only Unchecked Items (see Figure 9-51). Checking this will return only open to-do items.

One recommendation: after you are done examining or using this summary document, immediately delete it. Otherwise the next time you search, the contents of the summary document will be included in the search results, and you will appear to get twice as many hits.

Using Stationery

Just like with Windows Journal, you can use existing stationery that simplifies the creation of certain kinds of notes. To see the list of available stationery, use the File menu and choose New. That will open an additional task pane (to the right if your tablet is in landscape mode and below if your tablet is in portrait mode) and in the lower (or right) portion of the pane you'll see selections of various predesigned stationery under the Change Stationery heading. In Figure 9-53, that stationery pane is displayed on the right, and one of the stationery choices, the Simple To Do List stationery, is displayed within the notes section of OneNote on the left.

You can turn any existing note into a stationery form using the Save Current Page as Stationery command at the bottom of the pane.

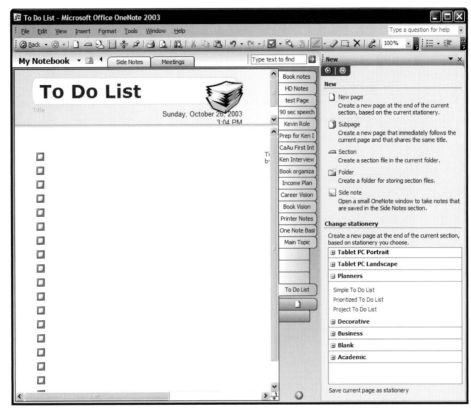

Figure 9-53. An example of available preexisting stationery.

Do not get stationery confused with the Rule Lines command under the View menu. In Windows Journal and PowerNotes there is no distinction. In One-Note they are different. In OneNote you use the Rule Lines command to control simple background lines, and you use stationery to invoke or create more complex templates.

Full Text Search

What if you want to search on a given text string, not on flags? As you would expect, OneNote also has a full text search capability. Like Windows Journal and FranklinCovey PowerNotes, the search will be done even against unconverted handwritten text (all handwriting is converted in the background), assuming OneNote can reasonably translate your handwriting.

You access this search by choosing Find from the Edit menu. This adds a search box on the right of the section folder tabs, just above the page tab area.

In the sample below (see Figure 9-54) I've typed in the search term "decrease costs."

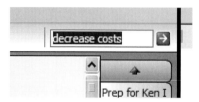

Figure 9-54.   The Find input window appears just above the page tab area.

Click the green arrow to the right of the search field and you'll see a results selection tool take the place of the search box, showing that two instances of "decreased costs" were found (see Figure 9-55).

Figure 9-55.   After a search, the Find input field is replaced by a results selection tool.

The full note page containing one of those two instances is then displayed in your OneNote screen, with the search text instance highlighted. Clicking the arrows on either side of the instance count allows you to pull up the other note page instances that match the search.

If you click the View List button to the right of the instance count, your One-Note screen splits and the following Page List pane appears, allowing you to see the list of instances and to refine your search even more (see Figure 9-56).

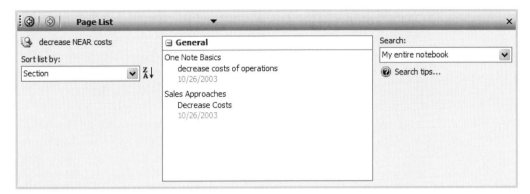

Figure 9-56. More details of the search results can be shown by clicking the View List button shown in the previous figure; this displays the Page List pane.

Sharing OneNote Files

If you have Outlook 2003, you can e-mail the current OneNote page or page group using the E-mail... command from the File menu. Or use the equivalent button on the Standard toolbar.

Invoking this command adds an e-mail header pane to the top of the current OneNote page; you use this to address the e-mail and send it. OneNote sends the note page as an HTML image pasted into the body of the text. If the current page is part of a page group (a page with subpages), the primary page and all subpages are appended together in the mail message.

Side Note: If you invoke the E-mail... command and then change your mind about sending the note, you need to invoke the command again to get rid of the addressing pane; it's a modal command.

Sending a note via the E-mail... command also attaches a file copy of the note page to the message (in the OneNote .one file format), enabling recipients who own OneNote to import the file into their note collection. Keep in mind that many recipients may have trouble receiving HTML e-mails, and many spam filters will reject a message with the .one file attached since it is such a new format.

If you do not own Outlook 2003 or you suspect your recipients may have problems receiving the mail as described above, don't use the above approach. Rather, export the OneNote page first and then attach it to an e-mail. Exporting is done via the Save As... command from the File menu. You can save the section as another OneNote .one file, or as an .mht file (viewable in Internet Explorer version 5 and later, Macintosh or Windows PCs). Use the latter if your recipient does not own OneNote. Unlike Windows Journal and PowerNotes, OneNote strips out the notebook rule lines when it does the conversion to .mht. And unlike Windows Journal and PowerNotes, no .tif export format is available.

Also, recall that OneNote saves files an entire section at a time and the Save As... command is no exception. So if you need to export and send only one page or page group (a likely scenario), then you'll need to create a new section and move the pages to that section before invoking the Save As... command.

In Conclusion

We've covered nearly everything you need to know to use OneNote effectively as a meeting note-taking tool on the Tablet PC. Use it for a while and see if it brings you added value compared to Windows Journal or Power-Notes.

One area I did not touch on is using OneNote as a research collection tool. This is not a typical use case for the goals of this book, but it is something that may be applicable to you in your work. Should you wish to learn more about this topic, and others, I refer you once again to the book *Complete Guide to OneNote* by W. Frederick Zimmerman. There you will find coverage of Microsoft Office OneNote that extends well beyond Tablet PC note taking.

Chapter 10 Manage Your Power Documents

The Business Case

S tudies have shown that up to 60 percent of white collar work time is spent managing documents. Not being able to find key documents quickly is a common complaint of many work managers. This is particularly important when in meetings, where you do not have the opportunity to retrieve filed documents but where your access to key summary documents is particularly important.

A Real Life Scenario

As project manager for a number of projects, you are attending a budget meeting with senior management. You've come prepared with copies of your budget and project documents. In the middle of the meeting, your the head of finance suddenly asks "what's your staffing plan for next quarter, and when are your new staff scheduled to arrive?" Unfortunately, the staffing plan is one document you didn't bring to the meeting, and the information just is not at the tip of your tongue. Having it handy could have changed the outcome of the meeting.

Keeping Key Documents at Hand

How many times have you been in a meeting and been asked questions about a project or task that you've been working on and not been able to produce the answer rapidly? In many such cases, you knew if you had in front of you a key document (the one pinned on your bulletin board back at your cubicle, or sitting in an often used file folder on your desk) that you could answer the question effectively. Your effectiveness as a manager is measured among other things by your ability to appear on top of your areas of responsibility. While an answer such as "I don't have that information at hand" in a meeting is certainly understandable, having key information retrievable when needed goes a long way toward conveying an impression of being in control of your domain. If you consistently have the information needed in meetings at hand, your performance will stand out from others. And for those meetings that you are actually running, having key information at hand can make the difference between a productive, effective meeting and a meeting where only weak outcomes are achieved.

Having access to key information when needed is extremely important. In my view, once you get to the point where you are attending meetings a significant portion of your day, your role in your organization has expanded from being a key "doer" to include what I call an "information funnel": you collect information to filter and then distribute to your peers or the staff below you and, more importantly, you provide filtered summary information to your colleagues or superiors about the activities of your projects or staff. This is a key manager role. Meetings are often where this summary information is received, digested, and processed by the thought leaders in your organization, so that the organization can successfully and efficiently meet its goals. So having your key information well summarized and at hand during meetings is absolutely your responsibility for making your meeting contribution effective. And unless you have an incredible memory, you need to develop a system whereby key summary documents can be kept at hand during meetings.

Document Management

If you are like most knowledge workers, you are constantly searching for your most important documents. This is not a new problem, and elaborate physical and computerized systems have been created to try to solve it. At the high end on the scale of solutions are expensive network-based enterprise document management or knowledge management systems. With these systems, nearly every document entering or created in an organization is classified and placed in the computer system for search and retrieval over the enterprise network or intranet. At the low end of the scale are personal filing or software approaches that staff can use to try gain control of the documents that litter their desk. The goals of using the large and small software-based systems are simple: become as paperless as possible and find your documents quickly, usually based on keywords searches.

For Maximum Return Focus on Your Power Documents

Documents managed in these systems can be anything from a critical corporate report down to a flier advertising latest prices at the local office supply store. And in spite of the automation successes the large systems have achieved, these systems still require an enormous amount of energy to enter documents, classify them, and deploy retrieval systems to staff.

However there's a key subselection of these documents that I call your "power documents." These are key summary documents that if managed for easy access will offer the maximum return for the management effort. What is a power document? It's any document that you refer to over and over again because it summarizes key work information so well. It's your departmental budget that was set in quarter one and that you refer to all year. It's the summary list of all your projects. It's your one-page project plan overview for each of your most important projects showing key start dates and deadlines for that project. It's your staffing plan. It's the org chart for your organization. Or it's your one-page cheat sheet that you use when you are struggling to learn a new computer application. Or it's the e-mail from your boss that you refer to over and over again because it lists his view of your key tasks or goals for the quarter. It's the handout that you received at the last staff meeting that summarizes the new corporate policy on travel expenses. It's a map of your corporate campus.

Power documents are your high-use documents that you refer to throughout your work day to find key information. These are documents that you pin to your cubicle wall, or slip inside your notebook cover, or keep a shortcut for on your computer desktop. These are not your read-once-and-file documents; rather these are your gems that you find yourself looking for over and over again because they're not at hand when you need them. Getting control of these documents and keeping them at hand will save you enormous time and increase your work effectiveness. And, most of all, having the most important of these documents instantly available to you in meetings (or at spur of the moment times throughout the day) can make or break your effectiveness in those meetings. And the Tablet PC can dramatically help you get these documents organized and instantly available to you.

How You Might Keep Power Documents at Hand

Let's first focus on several ways of having your power documents available to you in meetings:

- Print out key documents related to the meeting just before, either for distribution or for your own reference.

- Keep at your desk a set of physical file folders mapped to possible meeting topics with your related power documents in them and bring that folder with you to the appropriate meetings.

- Create a three-ring binder with copies of all your power documents for all projects, organized with tabbed section dividers for each project, and bring that to all your meetings.

- Bring your laptop or Tablet PC with you to the meeting, and access the original computer files of all your power documents, or even an intranet over a wireless network.

- Create an electronic binder with images of all your power documents stored in one central place and format (this is my recommended approach).

This is a good list of approaches commonly used by knowledge workers around the world both for in meetings and for general ad hoc power document access. Let's look at each of these individually.

Printing Key Documents before the Meeting

A common strategy is just before a meeting to rush-print copies of key documents. I've done this, you've done this; it's not elegant but it often works. If you have time, that is, and if you can get to the document quickly enough and still make it to the meeting on time. It's at those times that the printer seems to jam, or be in the middle of a 200-page print job from one of your colleagues, or out of toner, right? And because you usually think of the document list just before the meeting, how do you know for sure that those are the only documents you'll need? Not a great approach, but still, the most common.

File Folder Approach

What many managers do is bring a file folder that is applicable to the scheduled meeting at hand. This often works, but is your folder up to date? And often the topics that come up in the meeting go well beyond the contents of the specific folder you predicted that you would need. You could attend all meetings with a full set of file folders in your arms, but this would be impractical, and even if you could do this, the time it would take for you to find documents in that set of folders would be too long to be useful within the context of a meeting. Even searching for documents in only one folder is often cumbersome and slow.

Furthermore, many meetings are not scheduled, and so your ability to prepare by collecting the appropriate file folder before the meeting is not an option. Often meetings take place spontaneously in the hallway, or at the end of a meeting based on another topic, over lunch or coffee, or even during a phone call to you while you are away from the office.

Three-Ring Binder

So if file folders do not work well, you could do as I have done in the past and create a three-ring binder, and spend an afternoon printing or Xeroxing all your key power documents and inserting them into that binder with convenient divider tabs indicating key areas of responsibility; and then bring the binder with you everywhere you go. I have created one of these a number of times, and each time it has worked quite well for me; for about a month at a time that is. The problem is that the material starts to get old and incomplete, and I always find that the moments that I think about updating the binder are not the moments when I am near a Xerox machine, or a printer, or a three-hole punch. And so, inevitably, the binder becomes out of date and less useful; at that point I find I stop carrying it with me to meetings, and then it becomes useless.

Bringing Your Laptop and Accessing Computer Files

The other approach is to just use the file system of your tablet or laptop, launching the power documents into the program that created it. Launching documents during meetings occasionally is actually a recommended approach within my management-effectiveness Tablet PC system and one reason I recommend that you make your tablet your primary desktop as well. It's just that you cannot rely on this as your primary access to power documents during meetings, and so you should augment it with my recommended approach, the electronic binder approach (covered next); here's why this approach falls short:

■ If you really are doing this on a laptop rather than on a Tablet PC, it is likely that the laptop is not even booted at the time you are requested to discuss the information, and a long boot up precludes efficient access to the information. But even if you are doing this on a Tablet PC that is likely turned on and accessible during the meeting, or perhaps a laptop that is already turned on, the following other problems usually arise if you try launching the document from its application.

■ You forget which computer folder you've filed the document in, and it takes too long or is too distracting to sort through the file system to find it.

■ You find the file folder but cannot remember which version of the document is the one that is important to view; often a key document of interest is not the latest edited version but rather a distributed and approved earlier version.

■ The document file is easy to find, but it takes just too long to launch the application that created the document. As a result the moment passes and the meeting moves on to other topics.

■ The document launches but it's not in a view that is easy to read or has the information that you need; Excel spreadsheets often have this problem.

■ If it is a Microsoft Word document it may be very long and the portion that you need is buried somewhere; again, by the time you find the key page, the moment has passed in the meeting.

■ Often you will find that you have trouble launching the application either because you have too many other applications open or because once launched the application asks for attention to too many general house-keeping tasks before you are allowed to actually view the document.

■ You're looking for that key e-mail that was sent two months ago, that you refer to almost every week; however, these days it's so far down your e-mail list that it takes too long to find within Outlook.

■ And by the way, most of the above statements also apply to attempting to use network or intranet based document management systems within meetings, should you be thinking about one of those to solve your problem.

This is a question of appropriate technology and of finding productivity aids that actually work, aids that can become a habit and are repeatable over time. Launching applications to view documents within a meeting has never been a consistently successful technique for me. Nor have paper-based binders.

Your Power Document Electronic Binder

However I'm happy to say that another approach, used in conjunction with the Tablet PC, solves this problem in a usable and repeatable way. It's similar to the three-ring binder, but it overcomes the physical limitations of the binder system. It's best called an electronic binder and it's essentially an electronic version of our three-ring binder. The key to making this work effectively is not having to launch every document in its native application when you want to view it, but rather converting your power documents into a common document format. This approach is best suited to documents that you need to view often and quickly. There is a small to moderate amount of effort to convert and enter the document into the system, and an almost zero effort to view the document. Perfect for what we are calling power documents.

Common Document Format

Back in the days when most documents were made of paper, a number of software vendors created software solutions to allow scanning of paper documents and storage as images. The same software was then used to index those documents, and then used again to search on the documents to locate them. One reason these systems were effective is that every scanned document was treated the same within the system and launched with the same software.

These days most power documents are already available in a computer format, but usually a different computer format each. So the challenge is not so much getting them into the computer but rather finding them and getting them visible on your screen in a timely fashion, timely enough to match the rapid pace of today's business meeting. The key now to getting at a variety of computer documents quickly is to *convert* those documents into a common computer format and store them in an easily retrievable structure. So then only one program and possibly one file running is needed to view the variety of documents. Fast on-screen retrieval is the key.

And presumably the solution would have an intuitive document location method that allows you to locate your power documents quickly. The good news about the search approach needed for power documents is that it's likely your power document list is fairly short, say fifty to five hundred documents, so powerful database driven classification engines are not necessary. Rather a simple document filing and text search engine will suffice.

Finally, the solution would need to have a very easy way to get your power documents converted into this format, easy enough that you can do it on a moment's notice when you see a document that you know is important.

Side Note: One might think that HTML would be a candidate for this common document format. However the difficulties and inaccuracies with HTML conversion preclude this.

FranklinCovey Software Approach for Managing Power Documents

One of the features of the FranklinCovey TabletPlanner 3.0 and the Franklin-Covey PlanPlus 2.0 software that attracted me was the eBinder feature built into both of these software packages. The purpose of the eBinder is exactly what I've defined above: a place to store your key power documents and have them easily at hand for instant viewing. The idea is that you can convert key documents to application-independent PDF-like images and store them all within easy reach inside the TabletPlanner or PlanPlus Home screen. And you can view them nearly instantly just by navigating through a simple folder structure and then clicking on the title of the document; the document will appear instantly. There is no need to launch the creating application, because the software displays them as a native document, no matter which program they originated from—Microsoft Word, Excel, PowerPoint, Outlook, Visio, even web pages off the Internet.

The key to making this work in the FranklinCovey software is a very rapid way to get at and view the documents and an easy way to get the documents into the format. The TabletPlanner software stores its eBinder documents under its planner software tabs; you can add additional tabs to further organize your documents. The PlanPlus software uses Outlook's Folder List system to store and view its eBinder documents; you can build as extensive a document hierarchy as you need within this folder system to store and find your documents. Both applications use the same document-imaging technique, which uses a PDF-like format to store and display the documents. And in both applications documents are added to the system by merely "printing" them from their original application. A virtual print driver is available to all of your applications and this driver allows you to convert documents to the FranklinCovey viewing format by simply using your application's native print command.

And perhaps the most important feature of this and the other electronic binder applications discussed below is that you can add documents to your Tablet PC based binder while sitting in meetings, right at the time the importance of a document is identified. It's this capability which enables maintaining a current and useful binder.

Three Other Software Approaches

There are a few disadvantages to the FranklinCovey approaches, which we will cover in a moment, so to expand your choices here are three other software approaches that also work.

Windows Journal

The venerable Windows Journal saves the day again here. You can use it to create a binderlike system, and if it has become your note-taking tool of choice why not use it for this?

Adobe Acrobat

The Adobe Acrobat Distiller module is the original convert-to-PDF software. Due to its extra strong set of specialized tools, it and Adobe's more recent incarnations, are arguably still the best way to create a collection of application-neutral documents for quick viewing and distribution.

ScanSoft PaperPort

A company that built its business around a personal document management system, ScanSoft, has expanded into the PDF electronic binder world with its latest release of PaperPort Pro 9 Office.

One advantage of both Adobe Acrobat and the ScanSoft PaperPort products is that if you have an attached scanner, they both also allow you to scan paper documents into your electronic binder.

All These Systems Really Work, Especially on a Tablet PC

The important thing is that no matter which of these approaches you choose this concept of an electronic binder really does work. It really does simplify your ability to store, find, and view your key power documents, to the point where this approach becomes quite usable even for the technology-challenged manager. And all of these approaches work so well that within a short time you will start using and relying on the system for accessing power documents within meetings and throughout your day. Mix a system like this with the universally at-hand nature of your Tablet PC hardware and you have an awesome combination.

Recommended Software Choice

As stated there are five software packages to choose from to create your electronic binder:

- Windows Journal

- FranklinCovey PlanPlus for Outlook

- FranklinCovey TabletPlanner

- Adobe Acrobat

- ScanSoft PaperPort Pro 9 Office

Which to use? Once again it depends.

If you find Windows Journal meets your note-taking needs and you are handy with the product, using it to create a power document binder is a natural next step.

Regarding the FranklinCovey products, first of all the eBinder approach in the two FranklinCovey packages is nearly identical so your decision between those two will be based on other factors. If you have already selected one of the two FranklinCovey products for your task management and especially for your note-taking needs, you should strongly consider using the same package for your power document binder.

That said even if you are already using one of the FranklinCovey packages, a few potential disadvantages of the eBinder feature may drive you to choose one of the other solutions for document management. Read this list and decide if any of these points are an issue for you. Otherwise, stick with one of these packages.

- The resulting documents are stored within a proprietary file system which is good and bad. Good because this puts everything in one place, but bad because this complicates easy distribution of your whole note set to nonFranklinCovey users. And it potentially complicates backups. Also, I have not tested this approach for managing large quantities of documents.

- While the fact that the eBinder approach is integrated into one piece of multifunction software is an advantage, there are also advantages to having separate software packages for your different key functionalities. There can be some benefits to using Windows for switching between running applications compared to switching between views within an integrated software package. Windows often switches faster for example.

- The eBinder feature does not have an easy workflow for scanning paper documents should you need this; Adobe Acrobat and ScanSoft PaperPort Pro 9 Office both do.

- Both FranklinCovey products force your document lists into alphabetical or date order within a folder (as do all the other approaches other than Adobe Acrobat). You can work around this by appending some sort of numbering system to the front of file names. Also note that PlanPlus when used with Outlook 2003 allows category ordering as well.

- You cannot merge or add to documents within the FranklinCovey applications; you can with all the other solutions.

Which did I choose? I started with and still use Adobe Acrobat. But I hesitate to recommend it for the average user because Adobe Acrobat requires more skill to get documents into the collection. Unlike these other products it was not designed with a document binder approach in mind, and that shows whenever documents are added.

In addition you cannot add notes and annotations on top of your stored documents as easily. And Adobe Acrobat is a fairly expensive piece of software, by itself costing more than either PlanPlus or TabletPlanner (you cannot use just the Adobe Acrobat Reader, you need to buy the Standard version at a minimum). So the better approach is to choose one of the FranklinCovey products. And with the release of Outlook 2003, the ability to use Outlook categories to organize PlanPlus eBinder documents is a real plus.

That said, I continue to use Adobe Acrobat because:

- I prefer the more flexible hierarchical approach that Adobe Acrobat uses to find and view documents. Because it uses an outlinelike display of my document list, I can get to documents more quickly and more intuitively than having to navigate through a folder system. Key here again is that Adobe does not force my document lists into alphabetical or date order. I can place items in the expandable outline view in any order I wish, and I can easily drag them around to a new order as some documents become more important than others.

- I like that it runs as a separate application so I don't need to lose my current PlanPlus view to go look at documents; rather I just use the Windows task bar to switch between the applications.

- I like that the documents are stored in an industry standard file format (PDF). I also like the ability to easily distribute my entire collection of power documents when I leave for vacation and need to hand off my responsibilities to a subordinate. The subordinate only needs to have a free copy of Adobe Acrobat Reader.

Let's look at each of these packages individually. After you do and after you settle on the approach you would like to take, I suggest you read the final section of this chapter, called Binder Application Best Practices, to gain additional tips on how to organize and use your binder.

Using Windows Journal to Create a Power Documents Binder

Let's start with Windows Journal, since it's one of the simplest approaches, it's free, and it demonstrates some of the key concepts that we are going to want to use with power documents.

Windows Journal is such a simple program, my feeling is that until you find key features that are lacking enough to drive you to more advanced software, it's always the best place to start for nearly any category of functionality. As a power document binder approach it works moderately well. The key differentiator from the other approaches in this chapter is that you'll be using the Windows XP file system to create your document folder hierarchy, so you need to be handy with creating and using folders within Windows XP. This is a pretty basic skill and essentially unchanged since Windows 95, so I will assume you are proficient at this. But just in case we will walk you through all the steps.

If being able to use the Windows folder hierarchy is an advantage, it is also the primary disadvantage of using Windows Journal as your binder approach because:

- The Windows XP file system does not offer a preview view of Windows Journal documents; you have to rely on the document names when visually searching for documents.

- The folder approach does not offer much flexibility in the way you list your documents (though suggestions are made in this chapter on ways to increase that flexibility).

- Windows Journal opens a separate document window every time you open one of these power documents; if you forget to close these windows as you go, your Tablet PC desktop and taskbar can get pretty cluttered with all the open documents.

None of these issues are showstoppers but just make the approach less than ideal.

The Windows Journal Power Document Workflow

Previously we mentioned the ability to import documents into Windows Journal and use them as background templates to write and take notes on top of. For instance you may want to import a new graph paper–like grid document to use as a guide for drawing on. You will use this same import capability to create your binder documents.

The workflow that incorporates this approach is summarized here and detailed below:

1 As a very first step, create a Windows XP folder where you will store your binder documents; call it Power Documents, and configure it for easy use.

2 As you add power documents you will want to create Windows subfolders within this Power Documents folder, subfolders that represent your hierarchy of power documents.

3 To add a power document, launch the original document within its original software.

4 From within that software, use the Windows Journal virtual printer to convert the document into a Windows Journal document (described below).

5 Save the document into the appropriate Power Documents folder.

6 Repeat steps two through five for each of your power documents.

Create and Configure Your Power Documents Folder

You only need to do this once. This is basic Windows XP stuff but it's worth walking through the process so that you don't skip over it.

Key to making the system work is having quick access to your Power Documents folder. I suggest you create your Power Documents folder on your desktop so that it is easy to get to. Here's how you do that.

Create the Main Power Document Folder

Right-click on any blank spot on your Windows desktop; from the context menu choose New and then Folder (see Figure 10-1).

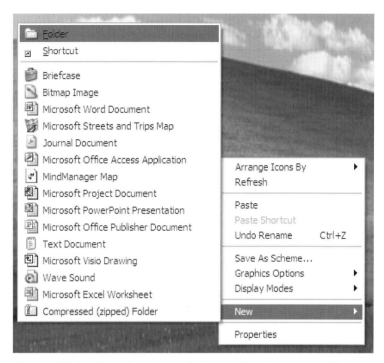

Figure 10-1. Creating a new folder on the desktop in Windows XP.

Right-click the resulting New Folder and choose Rename. This highlights the name and allows you to type a new name (see Figure 10-2).

Figure 10-2. Naming a new folder in Windows XP.

Call this folder Power Documents (see Figure 10-3).

Figure 10-3. The new Power Documents folder.

If you already have some power document categories in mind, you may want to open your new Power Documents folder now and add some folders using the same right-click technique we used to create the new folder; title them to match your category list.

Side Note: See the section below called Advanced Windows Folder Configuration for an alternative approach to setting up your Power Documents folder that avoids creating subfolders but instead uses the Windows XP Show in Groups feature.

Configuring Your Power Documents Folder

We are now going to configure your Power Documents Windows XP folder into a format more usable for our purposes. Basically we're setting the folder view back to the more traditional Windows Explorer view from previous versions of Windows. Doing this configuration is easy and I'll show you how now.

First open the Power Documents folder created above. See Figure 10-4 for one example with some subfolders and documents already created.

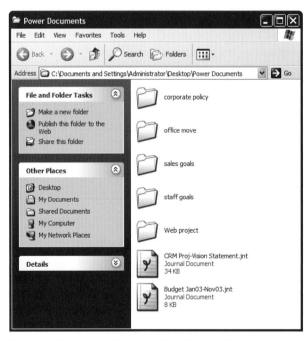

Figure 10-4. Configuring the Power Documents folder.

We're going to change this view to display a more traditional folder list view on the left and a detailed list view on the right.

Next, click on the Folders button at the top of the folder window (see Figure 10-5).

Folders button

Figure 10-5. Choosing the folders view within Windows XP.

This switches the task pane in the left panel of the folder configuration to show the Folders bar, which contains the more convenient hierarchical folder view. This view is much easier to use when searching for key power documents (see Figure 10-6).

Side Note: Unfortunately this particular setting will not stick permanently; you need to click the Folders button each time you open the folder window (unless you covert all your folders to Windows Classic View; study the Windows XP book listed in the Appendix to learn more about that).

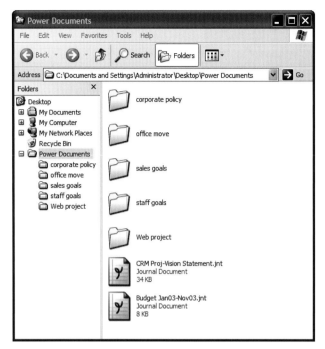

Figure 10-6.   Appearance of window with Folders bar displayed on left.

And now we will change the view of the right pane to show what's called the Details view of your files and folders so that you can see more at once. Do this by using the View menu at the top of the folder window and choosing Details from the selection (see Figure 10-7).

Figure 10-7. Choosing the Details selection from the View menu will create a detailed list view of your documents.

Now let's get rid of some of the columns shown in this Details view to simplify the list. To do this: right-click on the word Name above the list of folders and documents on the right; you'll see the following list menu appear (see Figure 10-8). Now, as shown in that figure, remove the checkmarks from all but Name and Date Modified.

Figure 10-8.   Choosing which columns to show in the Details view.

When you're done your folder will look as in Figure 10-9; this is a clean and useful way to view your power documents. Your power documents and document folders are organized in a way that will allow you to navigate quickly.

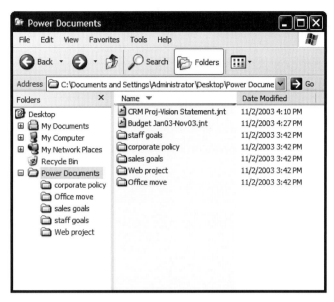

Figure 10-9. Final appearance of your Power Documents folder.

Side Note: You now will want to create a shortcut to the Power Documents folder and pin it to your Start menu; then add a similar shortcut to your Startup folder. Follow the instructions in Chapter 4 to do this.

Importing Documents into Your Windows Journal Power Document System

The easiest way to import a document into Windows Journal is to open the document in its originating program, and then "print" the document into Windows Journal. This may seem odd at first, but the technique really is incredibly easy and is a fantastic "free" feature that Windows Journal automatically adds to all Windows applications.

Here's how you do it. Once the document is opened on your Tablet PC in the application that created it (or at least in an application that can open it), all you need to do is go to the File menu and choose the Print command. When the Print dialog box opens, in the drop-down list of available printers you will see one called Journal Note Writer; select this printer. Take a look at Figure 10-10 for an example of selecting this printer from within a Microsoft Word document.

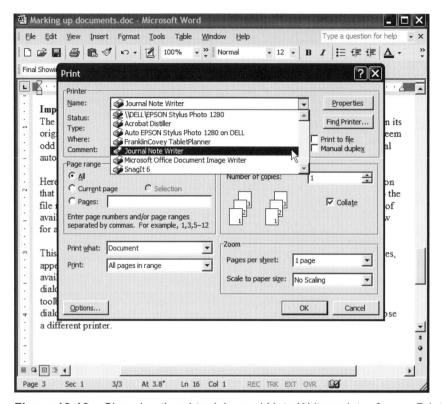

Figure 10-10. Choosing the virtual Journal Note Writer printer from a Print dialog box.

While this appears to be a printer in your printer list, this is not really a printer but rather a printer emulator. But for all intents and purposes it appears as a printer to all Windows applications running on your Tablet PC. This means virtually any application can send documents into Windows Journal for converting to a power document; you can even send web pages that you may see online to Windows Journal for this purpose.

Side Note: You should not use the printer icon in the toolbar of many Windows applications, because this icon normally bypasses the Print dialog box and uses the current default printer. This does not give you a chance to choose the Journal Note Writer printer.

At this point if the original document is multipage you should choose the page range that you want for your power document representation of this. It's likely that you only need a page or two within your power document; the fewer pages the better.

Once you click the OK button on the print command, you will be asked where to save the new Windows Journal document you're creating, so pick a filename and location within your Power Documents folder or subfolders that will help you find this document quickly later. Once the document is saved, in some cases Windows Journal will launch and display the document. You may want to examine the document within Windows Journal to make sure that it includes the pages you intended. After that you're done; you now have added another document to your collection of power documents.

Side Note: Chapter 11 discusses how to use the Windows Journal Import command as an alternative method of importing into Windows Journal.

Using Your Windows Journal Power Document Binder

If you've placed a shortcut to the Power Documents folder in your Startup folder, and you've also pinned it to your Start menu, then this folder should be open and on the taskbar at all times. So in the middle of a meeting, if you need access to a key document, all you need do is click on the taskbar for this folder to bring it to the front, and eyeball search for the document in your hierarchical folder and document list. Double-click, and you're there.

One nice feature of having this in Windows Journal is that you can now mark up the document with your pen if you decide changes are needed as you use the document. This is how you might indicate changes that you may want to add later to the original document, the next time you update your collection.

Advanced Windows Folder Configuration: Show in Groups Using Categories

While the approach above is adequate, I do not like filing power documents in multiple subfolders. Too often documents end up not fitting a particular classification, and so on retrieval I am forced to open two or three folders to find the document I am interested in. Fast retrieval is a key to success for using power documents, so having to hunt through several folders defeats that purpose.

Luckily, Windows XP has a feature that can help. It's called the Show in Groups command. This is similar to the Outlook 2003 Show in Groups command, but not quite as capable. My implementation of it takes advantage of the Categories field in the file properties of most Windows files (not to be confused with the Categories field in Outlook).

Using Windows XP Show in Groups and categories, I can avoid the use of subfolders. Instead, all my files are within my one Power Documents window but grouped under major category groups. This way I can quickly see all my documents at once by scrolling the contents of one folder.

You should consider doing this as well. Scan the steps below, especially the last step that shows how the Power Documents window will look, and decide if this works for you.

Place All Files at the Base Power Documents Folder

Since we will not be using folders any more, you should pull all your Windows Journal files out of the subfolders and leave them at the Power Documents folder level. Then delete your empty folders.

Add the Category Field to Your Folder View

The Category field, associated with all Windows XP files, is rarely used. We are going to use it to classify documents. Again, do not confuse this field with Outlook's Categories; they are unrelated.

To do this, we need to add the Category column to your Power Documents folder window. As in the step above where we limited the Details view to two columns, Name and Date Modified, we are going to add a third column called Category. To add this column we use a similar method as above but with a slight change:

1 Right-click on the word Name above the list of documents on the right; then click on the More… button at the bottom of the list.

2 Now, as shown in the figure below, add a checkmark next to Category and click OK (see Figure 10-11).

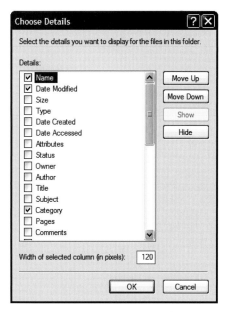

Figure 10-11. Adding the Category column to a Power Documents window.

Assign Category Information to Your Files

Next we need to add Category information to each of your Journal files. Do this now for all current Journal files within your Power Documents folder and in the future as you add new files.

1 Right-click any file and choose Properties at the bottom of the context menu that appears.

2 In the Properties window click the Summary tab, and then click the Advanced button at the bottom of the screen. Click once to the right of the Category entry (see Figure 10-12).

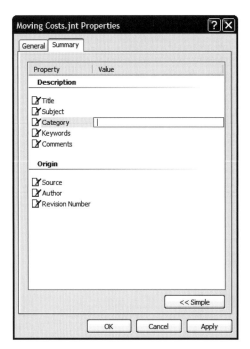

Figure 10-12.   Entering Category information for each document.

3   Enter a Category name that correspond to the subfolder names you may have considered before.

Keep the Category names short and easy to spell. These will not appear in a popup but rather must be retyped each time you enter them. For projects, I put a "P-" in front of the Category name—this is just one possible approach. I also created a Category called *Hot which will sort to the top of the Category list; this is for documents you absolutely want immediate access to.

Repeat setting the Category property for all your files in the Power Documents folder. You can set an identical Category name for multiple files at once by using the Control key when you select them above in step 1, just before you right-click. Then when you edit the Category value in the Properties dialog box (steps 2 and 3), the entry will apply to all the selected files.

Here's how your Windows folder window might look (see Figure 10-13). Note the Category column at the right. Since we are not using subfolders there is no need to display the folders list view on the left.

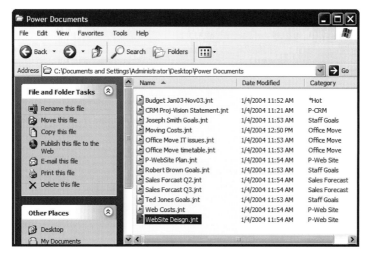

Figure 10-13. The Power Documents folder with the new Category column added.

Use the Show in Groups Command

And now for the final step, we are going to apply the Show in Groups command to enable you to group like categories together.

1 From the View menu of the Power Documents folder, choose Arrange Icons By, and then choose Show in Groups (see Figure 10-14).

Figure 10-14.   Engaging the Show in Groups view in Windows XP.

2   Then in the resulting Power Documents window, click on the Category column. This causes the files to be grouped by Category (see Figure 10-15).

Figure 10-15. The Show in Groups view fully implemented in a Power Documents folder.

This view of documents is in my opinion the best way to organize your Windows Journal Power Documents in Windows XP. You can visually scan your entire document list, and you can easily see given category groups. And given the relatively modest number of Power Documents you will normally work with, the single folder approach works well.

Three things present in the Outlook 2003 version of Show in Groups would make this capability better if present here in Window's XP:

■ If each group list could be expanded and contracted like an outline.

■ If multiple categories could be assigned to an individual document.

■ If categories once entered appeared on a checkbox list.

Unfortunately, none of these are possible at the file window level of Windows XP.

Using PlanPlus 2.0 to Create Your Power Documents Binder

If you are using one of the FranklinCovey products, you should try out their corresponding power document capability, called eBinder.

As you'll see, the eBinder approach within PlanPlus for Outlook is essentially the same as the eBinder within TabletPlanner which is covered in the next section. The main difference is in the navigation approach and in storing and retrieving those documents.

Both the TabletPlanner and the PlanPlus software, like Windows Journal, create a common document format collection of documents. They both use a virtual print driver like Windows Journal. The main difference from the Journal approach is that they use a document access system integrated in with their software suite, rather than using Windows XP files and folders to navigate to documents.

The eBinder Document Is the Same as a Note-taking Document

If you've read any of the FranklinCovey documentation, or experimented with the software, you have probably realized by now that PowerNotes and eBinder are virtually equivalent. The underlying PowerNote functionality that FranklinCovey software developers created is the basis of both PowerNote note taking (covered in Chapter 8) and their eBinder; they use the same document engine. A PowerNotes note-taking document is exactly the same as an eBinder document. They both display in the same window with the same tools at the top, and any eBinder document can be used to take notes on, just like a blank notes document. The only difference during use is that the imported eBinder document is stored in a different layer from the writing layer used during note taking, and so cannot be modified, only written on top of. The other difference is how the documents are originated.

And storage and retrieval of eBinder documents in PlanPlus is identical to how PowerNote *note* documents are stored and retrieved within PlanPlus. Both kinds of documents are stored within the Outlook folder system, and if desired, within the same folders. So the same navigation principles apply as were covered in the PlanPlus section of Chapter 8 on note taking. I recommend you reread that section now if needed to regain familiarity with this navigation approach.

> **Annotating PowerNotes**
>
> The fact that the same document engine is used for both PowerNotes and the eBinder documents is one reason why you have such extensive annotation capabilities within the FranklinCovey eBinder approach; an eBinder document is merely a PowerNote with an underlying imported document image, and you can mark it up, write on it, highlight it and so on, all as though you were writing on a blank PowerNote.

eBinder Documents and PowerNote Documents Are Originated Differently

The difference between an eBinder and PowerNote document is in how you originate the document. With PowerNotes notes you create a blank document from within the PlanPlus application. In contrast PowerNotes eBinder documents are originated from the virtual print mechanism within your document source application. Most importantly, this changes the way you direct documents into storage folders.

As you may recall, to determine where PowerNote note documents are stored (following recommendations in Chapter 8) you first launch PowerNotes from the Outlook storage folder of choice within the Outlook Folders List view, and the PowerNote note document is automatically stored there when you close it later.

Creating a PlanPlus eBinder Document

In contrast PlanPlus eBinder documents originate from other applications by printing from those applications just like you did with Windows Journal on page 383, but this time using the print driver labeled FranklinCovey PlanPlus. However unlike Windows Journal, there's no chance to pick the saved location. Rather all such eBinder documents get initially stored in the same destination location: the default PlanPlus Outlook PowerNotes folder. And so if you do not like this location you must then move just-created eBinder documents from their default landing point to your Outlook folder of choice. You can however change where that default landing point is.

The Dual Use of the Default eBinder PowerNotes Folder in PlanPlus

By default, all created eBinder documents in PlanPlus are stored in the Outlook PowerNotes folder. You may notice that there is a subfolder within the PowerNotes folder called PlanPlus Print Capture. You might think that that would be the default location of documents created using the special print driver but it's not; the reason it is not is because PlanPlus has only one default PowerNotes folder designation method and it applies to both PowerNotes note documents and PowerNote eBinder documents. As mentioned, out of the box, this default location is set to the PowerNotes folder. If you change it then the default Outlook folder for PowerNotes note documents changes as well. So you cannot have different default folders for these two functionalities; rather you need to decide which of the two functionalities is most important and set the default for that.

There's good news here: if you use the PowerNotes launching method that I described in Chapter 8 where you launch directly from the Outlook Folder List view, then this dual use of the default folder is not a problem. Here's why: the only way the default folder is used in PowerNotes is to control what folder you navigate to when you click the PowerNotes button either on the e-mail toolbar or on the main PlanPlus toolbar. But as you recall I recommended that you use neither of these ways to launch PowerNotes; rather I recommended you launch only from the Outlook Folder List view. So if you're following my recommendation you can feel free to change the default eBinder folder to point to the PlanPlus Print Capture Outlook folder, and get the best of both worlds.

How to Set the Default eBinder Folder in PlanPlus

Here's how you set this default folder: go to the Tools menu and choose Options, click on the PlanPlus tab at the far upper right, click on the button at the bottom labeled Default PowerNotes Folder... and you will see the following window appear (see Figure 10-16).

Note the text at the bottom of this window above the OK button; this text is consistent with the discussion above about the dual use of this default Outlook folder.

Now click once on the PlanPlus Print Capture choice and click OK. From now on, all created eBinder documents will be initially stored in this folder.

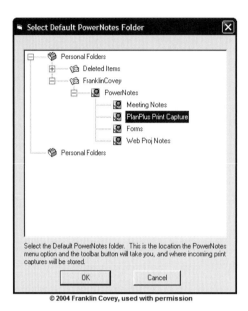

Figure 10-16.   Setting the default eBinder and PowerNotes folder.

Organize Your PlanPlus eBinder Documents

You could leave all created eBinder documents in this default location, but after you've created a few you will want to set up an organization approach.

You can set up a hierarchical Outlook folder system as discussed in the PlanPlus section of Chapter 8, and move the documents to the appropriate folders as you create them. You could create this hierarchy of folders within the print-capture folder if you like, or at a higher level within the Outlook folder structure so that it's easier to get to. You create such folders and move documents between these folders using exactly the same techniques that were taught in the PlanPlus section of Chapter 8.

And if you are using Outlook 2003, consider using categories instead of multiple folders, and use the Show in Groups by categories approach also discussed in the PlanPlus portion of Chapter 8. This is the best solution.

Which hierarchy or categories to create I leave to you; you may want to use a project orientation, a document-type approach, or anything else. If you have an existing paper-filing system you may want to match that hierarchy. It is best to keep the folder structure shallow, perhaps just one level of folders or categories, so you can find documents quickly.

Using TabletPlanner 2.0 to Create Your Power Documents Binder

As stated before, the eBinder facility within PlanPlus for Outlook is essentially the same as the eBinder within FranklinCovey TabletPlanner, which is covered in the previous section. The main difference is in the navigation approach to storing and retrieving those documents.

Both the TabletPlanner and the PlanPlus software create a common document format collection of power documents. They both use a virtual print driver like Windows Journal. And they both use a document access system integrated in with their software suite.

Below is displayed the FranklinCovey TabletPlanner 3.0 eBinder view with the default Notes tab selected and the top document under the tab within view; this document happens to be a help page that comes with the planner software (see Figure 10-17).

The user interface works well. It's integrated nicely into the overall TabletPlanner user interface, and the method of organizing binder documents is simple and intuitive.

From this point on, the entire interface for viewing and organizing already inserted eBinder documents in TabletPlanner is identical to that for viewing and organizing PowerNote *notes* in TabletPlanner; this is fully described in Chapter 8 on note taking. You only need to learn how to add documents to your eBinder, which is discussed next.

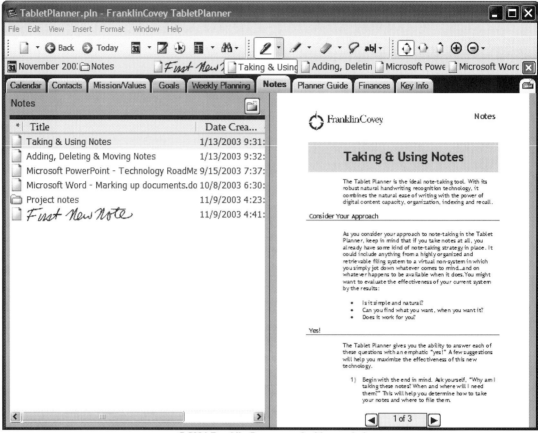

© 2004 Franklin Covey, used with permission

Figure 10-17.   The FranklinCovey TabletPlanner Notes tab.

How to Add Documents to the FranklinCovey TabletPlanner eBinder

The difference between eBinder documents and PowerNote notes lies in how you create the documents. Just like with PlanPlus, when you install the TabletPlanner software a virtual printer is installed in your computer's standard printer list, and this printer is available to all of your Windows applications. So to create an eBinder document, you merely launch the originating application, and print to the FranklinCovey TabletPlanner virtual printer. The resulting electronic image file of your document by default drops into the Notes tab of the TabletPlanner software. This new document appears at the bottom of the scrolling list of documents under that tab; you can either leave it there or move it to other more appropriate tabs or subfolders.

Organizing Your eBinder Documents

The tab and folder organization metaphor of TabletPlanner is what makes this solution especially attractive. Prior to automating my power document approach, I used a three-ring binder with section tabs and inserted documents. With TabletPlanner you can imitate this paper method. You can create one tab for all your power documents and use folders under that level, or create separate tabs for projects, or document types, or whatever; you choose a tab and folder hierarchy that suits your needs.

Since all newly created eBinder documents drop into the Notes tab, it may make sense to build your eBinder document hierarchy within this one tab. The name of the tab is a bit unfortunate because it seems more suitable for storing your handwritten notes. The good news is that you can rename the Notes tab and TabletPlanner will still find it when you create a new eBinder document. So I recommend this: rename the Notes tab to, say eBinder, or PowerDocs, or some such thing, and then create a new separate tab collection for all your handwritten notes.

You could mix your notes and eBinder docs in the same tabs. This may make sense for a project organization, where you have one tab per project. All new tabs you create in TabletPlanner are eligible to hold both handwritten notes and eBinder documents, so you have a lot of flexibility here.

Using Adobe Acrobat to Create Your Power Documents Binder

Overview

What is an Adobe Acrobat–based document binder? It's similar to the other power document approaches reviewed in this chapter, where images of your documents are stored for easy viewing on your computer in a common document format without needing to launch the original applications for each document. But rather than using proprietary file formats to store your documents, the major advantage of using Adobe Acrobat is that you can store your images in an industry standard document format: PDF.

Advantages of Using Adobe Acrobat

One reason an open standard document format is so useful is that you can easily hand your entire document collection to a colleague, subordinate, or supervisor, and they can view it without an intermediate document export process. It also means you could share your collection on a central file server for access by others without regard for whether they have the correct software to view it. Being able to hand off an entire power document set can be very useful. Should you leave for vacation and/or transfer responsibilities to another worker, this allows a remarkably easy transfer process.

Another advantage of Adobe Acrobat is that it has a scanner input capability so that if some parts of your power document collection need to originate from paper documents you have an easy way to do it.

You have two choices when using Adobe Acrobat: you can create one document for each of your power documents and then use the Windows XP file system to find these documents when you need them. This approach is the same as what we did with Windows Journal at the beginning of this chapter. Or you can insert all of the documents as separate pages within one single PDF file and use Adobe bookmarks to build your document map. The latter is the technique I used. I found the resulting bookmark navigation approach within the single file to be more usable than the Windows folder system.

Advantages of Using Adobe Bookmarks

And this may be the single most important advantage of the Adobe Acrobat approach; if you use the single file approach you can, using bookmarks, do a much better job of building a map to your power documents than you can if you rely on a folder system. This is true whether that folder system is part of Windows XP as for Windows Journal, or an internal folder structure like the FranklinCovey software uses. The weakness of these folder structures is that you are forced to list the folders and documents in an alphabetical or chronological order; it could be that the optimal list order is much different from that. The Adobe Acrobat single file approach gives you much more control over building this table of contents and does not suffer the same limitations.

Furthermore, when using the bookmark-based document hierarchy that Acrobat allows you to build, you can open multiple sublists at once. This helps you more quickly find documents. The problem with folders is that when scanning for documents, you need to open one, close it, open another, and on and on, which can get slow.

Side Note: If you apply the same advanced approach I described for Windows Journal in this chapter (using the category field and one folder), this problem is mitigated. The same holds true for PlanPlus if you are using Outlook 2003; using categories and one folder makes that more usable as well.

The other advantage to bookmarks is that you can save the zoom factor of the document so that it opens at just the scale you like when viewing that document. This increases quick usability of documents. For example, I like to open high-level plans zoomed-out showing the entire document. Word documents I want to open zoomed-in at a readable scale, focused at the top of the document.

And finally, if you sometimes wonder which category to file a document under, the bookmarks approach solves the problem by letting you place a link to a single document in more than one place.

The Acrobat Binder Document

Again, the Adobe Acrobat power document approach I use is simply to create a single PDF document which contains as inserted pages PDF versions of all my power documents, and then build a bookmark list that matches my ideal organization. To manage this insertion process, you will need to use the Acrobat software in a simple but specific way that I describe below. And you will have to use either the Adobe Acrobat Standard or Professional versions of the software to do this; the free Acrobat Reader software that you can download does not allow you to create PDFs.

Most of us have used Adobe Acrobat to read the PDF documents created by others, but only a small number of us have actually used Adobe Acrobat to create PDF documents. This is unfortunate, because it is easy and powerful. Adobe Acrobat software offers a wide range of features; to make the document binder we will use a small subset of those.

Figure 10-18 displays what my binder document looks like with the bookmark-based table of contents displayed on the left, showing the hierarchical list of documents.

You can expand and collapse the categories within the bookmark list, and when you find the document you are looking for in the list, clicking once on it displays it in the right panel. If you need to see the document in full screen view, you can close the bookmark pane on the left and the document expands to fill the screen.

The document displayed on the right side of Figure 10-18 was converted from an Excel document into a PDF and inserted into the binder. It happens to be a competitor feature matrix for the category of software that my company was creating.

Once created, I recommend you keep this file open on your Tablet PC at all times with the bookmarks pane displayed. I refer to my binder file ten or twenty times a day. I even put it in my Windows Startup folder so that every time I start my Tablet PC this document is launched and ready for use. Next to Outlook, it is by far the single most important file I have on my Tablet PC.

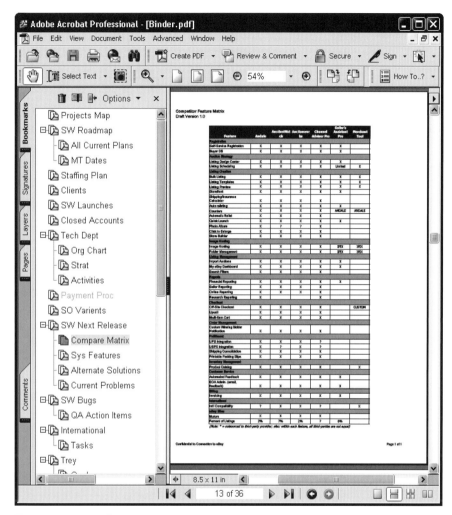

Figure 10-18.   Sample Adobe Acrobat binder.

Creating the Binder Document

Software Needed

The free Acrobat Reader software all of us have probably downloaded at one time or another is not sufficient to create PDF documents; you will need to purchase a copy of Adobe Acrobat Standard or Professional. The less expensive Standard version will give you all the features you need to create the binder document. Once installed, both versions of the software place a virtual printer within your printer list (just like Windows Journal and FranklinCovey software) that allows you to create PDF documents from the print command of the creating application. As you add additional documents to your binder document, you will use the Acrobat application itself to arrange pages and edit bookmarks.

You can download a free 30-day trial of the Adobe Acrobat Professional from the Adobe site should you want to try this binder approach before committing to the purchase.

Workflow for Creation and Maintenance of Adobe Acrobat Binder Documents

There is no difference between what I am calling a binder file and any other PDF document. Your binder document represents a single PDF file with multiple pages. Each new document you add to the binder adds one or more pages to this growing PDF document. You will use the Adobe Acrobat bookmark capability to label these pages in your binder document. You then build a hierarchical outline view of your binder documents in this bookmark list, so that whenever you need to view the document, you can click on its name in the bookmark list. And as you add documents to the binder file you will use Adobe Acrobat to arrange those documents logically and to rearrange your bookmarks as your document hierarchy develops.

So the high level steps for creating and maintaining your binder document are these (details for each of the steps are provided below):

1 Convert your first key document, and name that file "Binder.pdf."

2 Convert one or more additional key documents, and insert them into the original binder file.

3 As you add documents to the binder file, create the bookmark entry for each document and organize the bookmark list into a logical hierarchy for easy later viewing.

Step One: Converting Your First Document to a PDF

Refer to the list of candidate document types at the end of this chapter, and use that to select one of your own most-referenced work documents. To make this first exercise easier, choose a one-page document.

There are a few ways to create PDF documents using Adobe Acrobat tools:

■ Use the printer approach from within the document's own application.

■ Use Acrobat toolbar icons that are installed into most of Microsoft's applications when you install Acrobat.

■ Or from within Acrobat itself use the File menu, or in version 6, the Create PDF button on the Adobe Acrobat toolbar.

I routinely use the first two of these, and primarily only the first one, the printer approach.

Using the Printer Approach

At the time you install Adobe Acrobat, a virtual printer is installed in your printer list, like that for Windows Journal, PlanPlus and TabletPlanner. Like those other virtual printers, it is available to any application that can print within Windows, using the standard Print dialog box that virtually all applications use. In Adobe Acrobat version 5 and earlier, this printer appears in the printer list labeled Acrobat Distiller; in Adobe Acrobat version 6 the printer is labeled Adobe PDF.

For instance, assuming the first document you want to add to your binder is an Excel document, choosing Print from within Microsoft Excel, you then select Adobe PDF from the drop-down list of printers, select any particular page numbers you want to convert, and then click OK (see Figure 10-19).

Once you click OK, the PDF creator application runs in the background and presents a Save File dialog box asking you where to save your newly created PDF file. I've created a subfolder in my My Documents folder called PDFs into which I temporarily save all my converted documents. In the workflow discussion below you'll see why. Click save, and you'll see a dialog box displaying the progress of the PDF creation, and once complete the PDF file is then saved in your PDF folder; Adobe Acrobat then launches with your new document open.

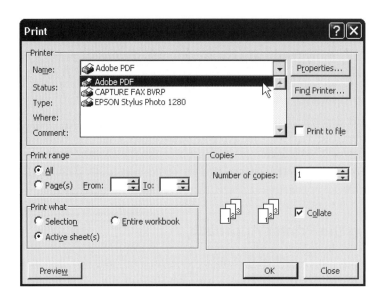

Figure 10-19. The virtual printer in Adobe Acrobat.

Using the PDFMaker Approach

Before we go on to step two, let's talk about the other method of creating a PDF document in Adobe Acrobat: using the optimized PDFMaker approach for Microsoft office documents.

I mentioned that when you install Adobe Acrobat, it installs a Convert to Adobe PDF icon set into nearly all Microsoft applications. This appears as an additional toolbar with, depending on the version of Acrobat, two or three icons.

Side Note: These icons are actually custom buttons that launch Microsoft office macros created by Adobe. If after installing Adobe Acrobat you start to get warning messages when you launch your Microsoft applications, messages referring to a macro that is not approved, you may need to change the security levels of your Office installation in order to activate these buttons. Until you change the security level, you will not see these buttons on your toolbar.

By clicking on the left-most of these icons, you run a small program that acts just like the print method we described above to create a PDF document.

Note the icons within the bottom toolbar in the Excel application below (see Figure 10-20).

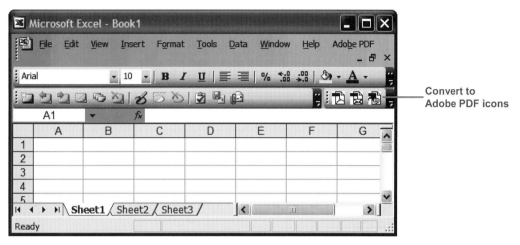

Figure 10-20. Adobe Acrobat PDFMaker icons in Excel.

In Adobe Acrobat version 5, there are only two icons and they look like this:

Why use these icons rather than the printer approach? First of all, only the left-most icon is of interest, as it roughly emulates the printer approach we described above; the other one or two icons are for e-mailing and document review purposes and should be ignored for our binder usage. But even using the left-most icon is in fact not exactly the same as using the printer approach. The icon represents a small application called PDFMaker that has been customized for the particular application it was installed into. Creating PDF documents is a quite complicated achievement for a piece of software and different approaches can have varying degrees of success in the conversion. My experience is that if I use the icon instead of the print approach, for some applications the converted document looks more like the original document. Excel is the case where I found this to be true; Excel PDF documents created using the PDFMaker icon retain formatting and original document appearance much better than if created using the printer approach.

The other thing the icon-based PDF creation tool does is attempt to create bookmarks automatically based on the structure of the document it is importing. This is something you do not want take advantage of because you will be creating your own bookmarks. So if you use the icon-based tool, turn off the bookmark creation feature.

In general I like the workflow of using the printer approach better than using the PDFMaker icon within the Microsoft application. I also find that using the printer approach allows me to select page ranges to convert right in the Print dialog box, which is very convenient. So, unless I am converting an Excel document, I use the printer approach for creating all my binder documents.

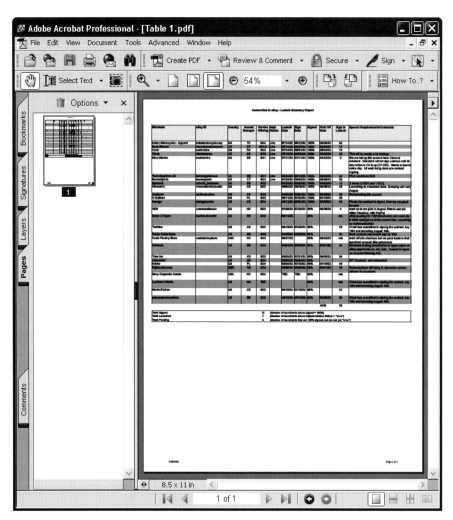

Figure 10-21.   Thumbnail or Pages view is on the left side of the Adobe Acrobat window.

Step Two: Inserting Additional Documents

Assuming you completed the steps above using either the printer approach or the PDFMaker icon, you now have a document called binder.pdf open.

In that document, you'll notice four or more tabs on the left border. Click on the tab titled Pages (it's called Thumbnails in Acrobat version 5 and earlier). This opens a split screen that shows a thumbnail view of your page (see Figure 10-21). As you add more pages to this document, each of those pages will show in the Thumbnails pane.

Now pick another one-page document that you want to insert into your binder, launch the application it was created in, and use the print approach to create another PDF document. This time when you're asked to save the document, allow the title of the document to remain the same as the default title presented to you. We don't want to reuse the name "Binder" because that file already exists. In fact from now on it is better to keep the name of the original document. This is so that in the next step, when you add this document to your binder file, you can recall what its original purpose was. Again, save the document in the PDF folder I described above, and when the new document opens in Adobe Acrobat, immediately close that document window.

So now you have two files: your original binder file and this new converted file. The next step is to insert or merge the new file into your binder file. Here's how.

1 To make this easy for now, arrange only two things on your screen: on the left your binder document, open in Adobe Acrobat Standard or Professional, and on the right your open PDFs folder as shown in Figure 10-22. My new document happens to be called Table 2.

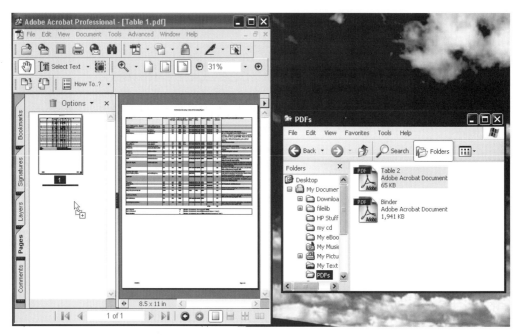

Figure 10-22. Dragging newly created PDF documents into the Binder document.

2 Within the PDFs folder on the right, select the icon of the newly created PDF file, and drag it over to the Pages view (or Thumbnails view) within the open binder document; the cursor will take on a plus sign appearance (note in Figure 10-22, the cursor's appearance and location on the left side of the screen).

3 When the cursor is positioned below the thumbnail of the first page in the open binder document (as in Figure 10-22) release the document (lift your pen from the screen surface). Your new document will now be inserted into your binder file, as shown below (see Figure 10-23).

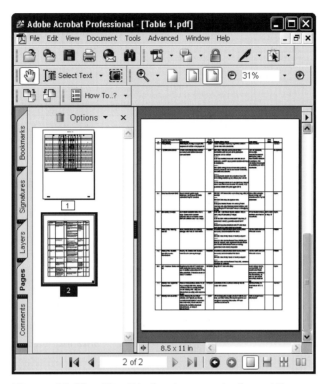

Figure 10-23. The Binder document after adding a second item.

If the document you're copying was printed in landscape mode you'll notice that it now appears sideways within your binder document; we'll show you how to rotate the document in a moment.

Step Three: Add and Organize Bookmarks

When you add documents to the Binder file, you next create the bookmark entry for each document. You may also organize the bookmark list into a logical hierarchy of documents, for later ease of use.

For the two documents we just added, here is what you do.

1 In your Pages or Thumbnail view on the left, click on the first thumbnail representing the first document in your binder document. We are doing this to select the first page of the binder document, which you'll notice now comes into view in the right pane.

2   Next click on the Bookmarks tab on the left edge of the Adobe Acrobat window. It should create an empty view on the left.

3   In Acrobat version 6, you'll notice an Options drop-down menu at the top of that empty view on the left (the drop-down menu is called Bookmark in version 5). Select that menu and then select the first choice called New Bookmark (see Figure 10-24).

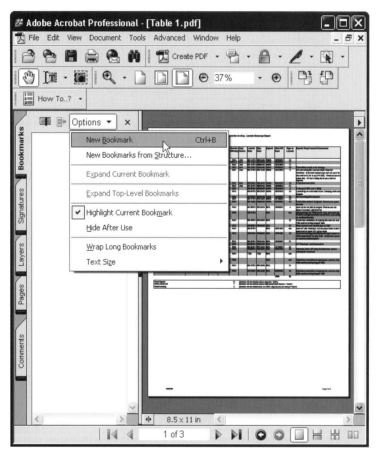

Figure 10-24.   Use the Options menu to add new bookmarks.

4   This creates a new bookmark entry on the left pane, ready for you to edit. Give this a name that is meaningful for the document that you have stored. In my sample in Figure 10-25 I called it "Staff Table."

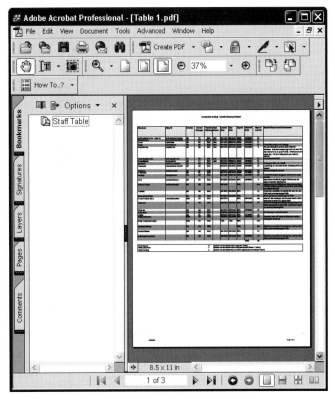

Figure 10-25. A new bookmark added to the Binder document.

5 Now navigate down to your second document; you can do this using either the Pages or Thumbnails tabs as we did above, or you can just use the scroll bar on the right pane. What's important is that your second document is clearly selected by filling the right document view pane. At the time a bookmark is created, whatever document is currently in the view pane on the right is what gets associated with the bookmark that you create on the left. Repeat the steps above to create a bookmark for this second document.

Create a Hierarchy of Bookmarks

Let's pretend both of your documents belong to a category called Staffing. We are now going to create a category bookmark entry called Staffing and place these two documents' bookmarks as indented entries under this category name.

1   Select again your first document.

2   And again, create a new bookmark and call it "Staffing."

3   This new bookmark will probably appear between or below your two previous bookmarks, so now we need to move it to the top of the two bookmarks. To do this click and drag the icon associated with the new bookmark upward until a thick black line appears above the top of the current first bookmark; once that happens release your pen and the bookmarks will rearrange their order placing the Staffing bookmark at the top.

4   Now to indent the two bookmarks below Staffing, we need to do this one bookmark at a time. Click on the second bookmark (the first bookmark to be indented) and drag it upward but slightly to the right of the icon associated with the Staffing bookmark. You should see a small black arrow appear in the lower right corner of the icon associated with the staffing bookmark (see Figure 10-26); once you see this, release the pen and the second bookmark should now be indented underneath the word Staffing. Repeat this with the third bookmark; you may need to rearrange their order after this operation.

Figure 10-26.   The small black arrow shown when you drag a bookmark indicates creation of a hierarchical relationship.

5   Below is how the bookmarks should look when you are done. Try clicking on the small minus sign to the left of the word Staffing in order to collapse and expand that category (see Figure 10-27).

Figure 10-27. Bookmarks after creation of hierarchical relationship.

If you add multipage documents, create a bookmark only for the first page. If you add a category bookmark, link it to the first document in that category; this means that first document will have two bookmarks pointing at it, which is fine.

This routine of adding and ordering a bookmark must be done every time you add a document. This complexity makes Acrobat slightly more difficult to use for creating your Binder.

Rotating Pages

If the document that you are importing was virtually printed in a landscape format then you'll need to rotate the page after you import it into your binder document. If you don't make this setting, you'll need to physically rotate your Tablet PC every time you view this page. To rotate an inserted page:

1 Within the Pages or Thumbnails view select the page you want to rotate.

2 Right-click on the thumbnail of that page; from the menu that pops up choose Rotate Pages...

3 You'll then see the following dialog box (see Figure 10-28). Normally, you would use the settings shown below.

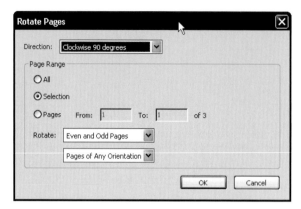

Figure 10-28.   Rotate Pages dialog box.

Reordering Pages within the Binder Document

You already know how to rearrange the order of bookmarks in the bookmark list. You'll soon learn that the order of bookmark entries does not need to match the order of page entries within your binder document. This is useful in case you want to have more than one bookmark for a given document; a document that may logically sit in more than one category can be scattered amongst your table of contents entries without regard for the actual position of the document. However you may find that it is more convenient and less confusing if documents do generally match their bookmark order. To rearrange the order of pages within the binder document, you need to do this from the Pages or Thumbnail tab. With that tab open, drag the corresponding thumbnail icons to the position within the document you prefer. The bookmark linkage remains, even after dragging the documents.

Acrobat Workflow Tips

Once you start inserting lots of these binder documents, you'll discover that you want to create them quickly. You'll want to get good at this so that there is no hesitation to create binder documents whenever you see a document that you want to include in your binder. Here are some tips to keep in mind when inserting new documents into the binder:

- Be sure to follow the recommendations at the end of this chapter regarding which documents are most appropriate to put in to your binder; there is no sense wasting time on documents of low value.

■ Also recall that you can use the page range fields within the Print dialog box to limit the pages that you save in your binder document to only the most important pages within the source document.

■ When inserting multipage documents into your binder, create a bookmark entry for only the first page.

■ If you are inserting a number of documents at once do the various steps in batches. Create the individual documents and drop them all into the PDF folder fist. Then after they are all created, insert them all at once into the binder document and add bookmarks.

■ Once you have inserted any document into the binder document, delete the individual file for that inserted document from the PDF folder; you no longer need the original converted PDF file once it is merged into the binder document.

■ When using your binder to find documents, don't forget that you can use the pages or thumbnails tab to visually scan for your documents.

Marking Up Pages in the Binder Document

Once a document is inserted into the binder document, it can be marked up and highlighted using your Tablet PC pen and the markup tools included in both the standard and professional versions of Adobe Acrobat. There are two Acrobat tools you can use with a Tablet PC: the Pencil tool and the Highlighter. These tools can be found on Acrobat Tools menu, under the Commenting and Advanced Commenting submenus. Or the contents of these submenus can be added as toolbars at the top of the application window using View, Toolbars. See the section in Chapter 12 called Marking up Documents Using Adobe Acrobat for more details.

One previous disadvantage of using Adobe Acrobat as a binder tool was that Adobe had not optimized the pencil tool within Acrobat to be used with the Tablet PC pen; the resulting handwriting was not as smooth as other note-taking tools. Updated releases of version 6.0 have improved this considerably and one can now make relatively legible notes.

For extensive comments, you might consider using the elaborate review and commenting tools built into Adobe Acrobat. Similar to the review tracking capabilities of Microsoft Word, the latest versions of Adobe Acrobat allow you to add and track typed comments throughout the document. You'll need to use a keyboard or the Tablet PC Input Panel to enter this text, as there's no pen interface.

Other Uses of Adobe Acrobat

Scanning In Paper Documents

It is not always possible to find the file original copy of all key summary documents you need in your binder document; consider the handouts you may receive in meetings from others. Adobe Acrobat has a TWAIN interface built in that allows support for most popular scanners, so if your document import needs range into the printed paper realm and you're willing to spend the effort needed to do this, the solution awaits you. My complaint with scanning has been that the flatbed scanners occupy a huge amount of desk space that seems out of proportion to the few times that they are used. Hewlett Packard has just released a very nice upright flatbed scanner that takes little desk space, looks attractive, and works well (HP Scanjet 4670). Still, scanning with all but the most expensive scanners is slow and cumbersome and probably not appropriate for most work managers.

Electronic Forms

One application of Acrobat that I have not taken advantage of has great potential for certain business cases. That's the use of the Adobe Acrobat to create and collect information from online forms. If you have the need to fill in paper-based forms in your management tasks and need a simple way to automate that, Adobe may have a solution for you here.

Even TabletPlanner or Windows Journal can be used to create formlike templates which you can enter information into, but Adobe Acrobat goes beyond this in its ability to collect the data inserted into the form fields and link them either to databases or to separate spreadsheet files.

As with Windows Journal and TabletPlanner, you can create the form by simply printing an electronic copy of a form into Acrobat. You then can write or type into the fields.

Note that you'll need the professional version of Adobe Acrobat to make use of this capability.

Using PaperPort Pro 9 Office to Create Your Power Documents Binder

ScanSoft's PaperPort Pro 9 Office is the most recent version of PaperPort, a longstanding leader in the field of personal document management software. This most recent version has the ability to convert documents directly from Microsoft Office software into PDFs for storage in the PaperPort documents environment. This capability is generally what we're looking for in a binder solution. Plus PaperPort also has the ability to scan paper documents into your binder collection. Making use of PaperPort to create a power document binder solution is a natural use for the software.

It is comparable to Adobe Acrobat in its advantages:

- It can store documents in a standard PDF format.

- It has an effective scanning interface in case you have paper documents you want to add to your power document collection.

- It collects thumbnail sketches of the documents for easy visual location.

- It's a separate application from your other tools.

The main reasons to use PaperPort instead of Adobe Acrobat are that:

- It is roughly one-half to one-third the cost of Adobe Acrobat.

- PaperPort was designed from the ground up for personal document management and so is a much simpler piece of software to use for this purpose; the design of Adobe Acrobat as a document management tool is somewhat of an afterthought.

- PaperPort's scanning capability also includes an OCR engine to convert scanned documents to text if needed.

- If you are not wed to PDF, PaperPort can store documents in a variety of file formats including some that are still fully editable, great if you need to make changes to documents when you see them.

- If you've toyed with the idea of going paperless and trying to replace your paper-based file cabinets by scanning all stored paper documents into your Tablet PC, then PaperPort may be your solution. This goes well beyond the intentions of a power documents binder system and the recommendations of this book, but it's something to consider.

Between PaperPort and Adobe Acrobat, for a simple power document binder solution, Adobe Acrobat still has an edge in the way it displays your document list. Remember viewing your document list to quickly find a key document is the most common use of your binder solution, something you'll be doing many times a day. I like to use a list view of my documents and put the most important documents at the top of the list. Adobe Acrobat allows you to organize your documents list in any order, which means you can in fact place your most-often-used documents at the very top of the list; PaperPort, if you use a list view, does not allow you to do that. And if you use subfolders, which I recommend, these are forced into an alphabetical list as well. Note that if you use the Thumbnail view within PaperPort, you can arrange documents in any order.

Adobe also allows you to expand your hierarchical view of documents, even subordinate documents, into one long list, either of document names or of thumbnails; with PaperPort you need to open one folder at a time to visually search for documents stored within subfolders (you can of course use a search command to find documents instead).

The Main Window

The PaperPort application is all about personal document management; it is simple and direct in its interface. On the left is your folder structure for storing the documents, and on your right are the thumbnails of the documents themselves. This is called the PaperPort desktop (see Figure 10-29).

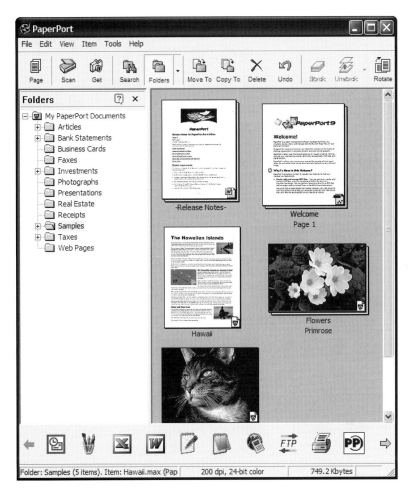

Figure 10-29. The PaperPort 9 desktop.

When you are ready to view a document simply double-click the thumbnail and the document is brought up nearly instantly in the PaperPort viewing window, which replaces the desktop view (see Figure 10-30). When you're finished viewing the document simply click on the Desktop button in the upper left corner of the viewing window and you are returned to the Desktop view. A minor inconvenience is that you cannot view both the documents list and the document at the same time.

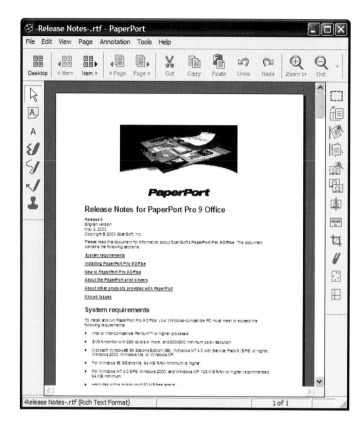

Figure 10-30.   PaperPort 9 has a separate viewing/editing window that replaces the desktop while viewing documents.

Getting Documents into PaperPort

There are many ways to get documents into PaperPort largely because it accepts so many different kinds of documents. Unless you are scanning in documents, the kind of documents I recommend you focus on are those already existing on your computer that you will convert to PDF for display within PaperPort. This leaves you two methods of acquiring documents and both are done from within the original document itself: using a virtual printer like the many other applications we've reviewed in this chapter; or using the Print to PaperPort (PDF) command which was added to many of the Microsoft office programs when you installed PaperPort. My vote is for the virtual printer because:

- It allows you to choose a page range when you print; the Print to Paper-Port (PDF) command forces you to convert the entire document.

- It's similar to the other virtual printers that you will be using on the Tablet PC.

- It's available to all applications.

You are pretty familiar by now with using virtual printers; the only thing to learn is what name to look for now in your printer list. In this case the name is not immediately obvious because it doesn't have the word PaperPort in it; the name is DocuCom PDF Driver. Other drivers are also installed upon installation of PaperPort, including one that does have a logical name (called PaperPort PDF), but ironically the DocuCom driver creates the best quality PDF document and is the one the PaperPort software manual recommends.

Printing with this virtual printer leads next to the software asking you where you want to save the resulting PDF. You need to name a folder somewhere on your computer. This brings us to the topic of creating your PaperPort folder system.

PaperPort Folder System

The PaperPort folder system viewed within the PaperPort main window desktop is really just another view of folders stored on your computer file system. Out of the box, PaperPort comes with a collection of folders that you'll probably want to delete immediately and replace with a system of folders more suitable for your work. These folders are stored within your My Documents folder under the main folder called My PaperPort Documents. You can manipulate these folders either using Windows Explorer or from within the PaperPort desktop environment; in either case the changes are reflected in both places. Once you have your folder hierarchy set up the way you like, simply point to an appropriate folder as you print your documents. You can move documents between folders by dragging them either within Windows Explorer or within the PaperPort desktop.

Changing the Thumbnail View

Finally, what you will be using every day is the Thumbnail view to visually find documents you need to refer to. The Thumbnail view shows the contents of whatever folder is currently open in the left pane of the PaperPort desktop. You can leave this view in the Thumbnail format, or you can change it to a variety of filename list views which are comparable to the filename list viewing selections you have within Windows Explorer. To make these changes, click on the down arrow next to the View button which is located in the upper right corner of the PaperPort desktop.

Beyond the Binder Approach for PaperPort

We've only scratched the surface of all the capabilities PaperPort has because we've focused on only one way of using it: to create a power document binder solution.

As mentioned you can use the software for scanning in documents. This is useful for getting the occasional paper-only document into your binder system. It's also useful if you want to attempt to make your office totally paperless. This would mean using PaperPort to scan all your infrequently used reference documents into your Tablet PC as well as the often used ones. This is probably where PaperPort's capabilities really shine, because this is what the software was originally designed for. Mobile workers may want to study this aspect of PaperPort in some detail. It's a lot of work and well beyond the scope and intention of this book but certainly something to consider.

Binder Application Best Practices

No matter which application you choose for creating an electronic binder, let's discuss more about why we do this and how best to manage the process.

Advantages of Using an Electronic Binder

First of all, here are the primary advantages of creating an electronic binder in a common document format:

- All key documents are at hand and retrievable within a second or two.

- They have been pretrimmed to only important pages.

- Depending on the approach, you have a hierarchical and collapsible outline view of all your documents that facilitates visual searching.

- All documents are full-text searchable across the whole binder.

- There is unlimited capacity.

- Documents can be easily printed.

- Documents can be more easily distributed as soft copy.

- Documents are easy to mark up to record changes.

- Additional documents are easy to add while in meetings.

This last is actually one of the key advantages of using an electronic binder on a Tablet PC compared to paper-based binders. During slow or dead times within a meeting you can easily add to your binder; you can bring new or updated documents into your binder with a few pen strokes. Everything you need to create documents is on your Tablet PC and easily accessible. From my experience, this results in having an up-to-date binder, which is much more difficult with paper-based binders.

Types of Documents Appropriate for Your Collection

There are some rules of thumb that you should use when choosing which documents to put in this power documents collection.

- First, this binder should be for key, stable, often-used documents. This is not intended to be a catchall filing system for every document you have ever created or received. The emphasis is on the word "key." Appropriate documents are ones that you refer to often enough that in a physical environment you may have printed and pinned them to your cubicle wall. They are the documents you have brought to or distributed at a meeting several times. Documents you have sent to colleagues for reference a number of times, or referred to verbally a number of times. In other words, include only documents you access multiple times. Often I will purposely not insert a document into my binder until I have referred to the physical or file version of that document a number of times, and it has thereby passed the test of time.

- Second, this should be for relatively short documents, or short sections of larger key documents. For example, include only a key table within a larger Word document or a page with a key paragraph on it; don't attempt to include the whole document. My rule of thumb is one or two pages max for any given document; any longer than that and you've missed the point of power documents.

- It should be for documents that will "live" for at least several weeks or more. Otherwise it is not worth the effort to insert the document.

- This should be for documents that you are likely to refer to in meetings, where this system really shines.

- Note also that to make this work, you need to have access to the electronic source of the document; I am not a fan of scanning in physical documents. While that can be done, the actions and associated hardware necessary are a bit cumbersome and may preclude your acceptance of this system. That said the Adobe software and the PaperPort software both have a scanning interface.

Document Categories That I Put in My Binder

So what kind of documents am I talking about? Below is a typical list of the kinds of documents that I, as a department and project manager, put into my binder (your list may vary depending on your role).

- **Budget summary**: How many times have you wished you had key budget figures readily at hand in a meeting?

- **Staffing plan**: Particularly valuable if you hire a lot of contractors and consultants, the plan shows arrival and planned roll-off dates and possibly incurred costs.

- **Key e-mails**: E-mails that you refer to over and over. An example would be that e-mail from your boss that in effect becomes policy; don't try to search through your Outlook saved mail over and over again, but instead insert the key e-mail in your binder.

- **Key handwritten notes**: notes that turn out to be significant summaries of an important business topic and therefore are referred to over and over again. Consider converting these to text before placing in the binder.

- **Organization charts**: It's amazing how important organization charts are in meetings.

- **Program high-level plan**: As a program manager this is probably my most referred-to document, a one-page summary showing all the projects with their key schedule milestones.

- **Project high-level plan**: This is the same as above but focused on one project. A useful strategy for organizing documents is to create a section for each project, and place key project documents hierarchically underneath those projects sections.

- **Project vision or scope statement**: It's ironic how often stakeholders lose track of the agreed-to vision of a project; keeping the project vision statement and project scope document at hand is a lifesaver in meetings.

- **Key summary pages from contract documents**: There were one to two key pages from my data center contract clearly stating pricing and services that I referred to over and over again in planning meetings.

- **Organization Mission statements**.

- **Staff goals statement**: Keeping these on hand is incredibly useful during your frequent one-on-one meetings with your staff. Being able to instantly produce these at the start of each meeting enables you to start with the big picture. This provides a consistent picture of your expectations, before drilling down into reviewing progress on individual task assignments. And your staff will appreciate this, because this is what they're being measured on. They expect consistent and frequent feedback on these goals prior to the periodic evaluation event. You'll see in my sample binder in the Adobe Acrobat section an entry for each of my staff.

- **My goal statement from my boss**: Having this on hand for my one-on-one meeting with my boss achieves the same goals for me as the bullet above, in case the topics are not raised by him.

Binder Creation Timing

As you add pages to the document, you may be tempted to sit down and convert all your key documents at once. My recommendation is rather that you let this binder evolve over time. Start with a few important documents, get used to using the binder to refer to those documents, and then slowly over time as you identify documents that you use over and over again, in paper or computer form, insert them into your electronic binder. This is the ideal way for you to determine which kinds of documents work well in the binder and which do not.

Chapter 11 Brainstorming on the Tablet PC

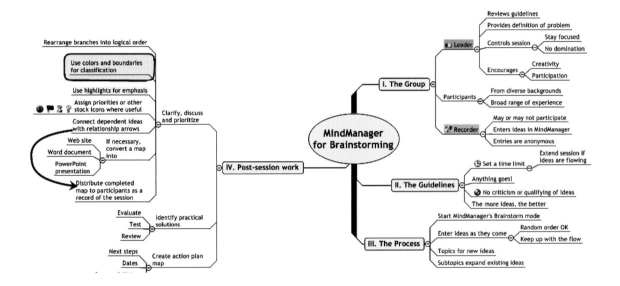

Business Maps

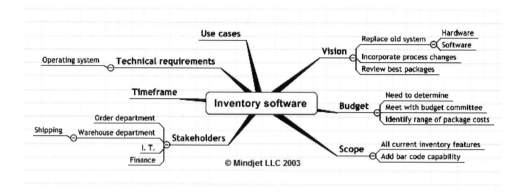

Have you ever sat down to write out an important work-related list, and found you were stuck on the second or third item? Research shows that the linear nature of traditional listmaking tends to shut the brain down from its creative thinking abilities. In contrast, the process of writing in a radial fashion, with the main idea in the middle of the page, works dramatically better. Placing subordinate ideas branching in all directions from the main idea opens up the creative juices of the brain. This is called mind mapping (though recently the term "business mapping" has been used instead). Theories abound on why this approach works so well, including the suggestion that a radial graph tends to activate both sides of the brain in contrast to linear listmaking which apparently activates only the left brain (if you're interested in the various theories, I list a book in the Appendix that goes into some detail).

Business Mapping Really Works

Whatever the reason, business mapping really works; it really does lead to much more fruitful and successful brainstorming. I've been making business maps by hand on paper regularly since 1990 when I first read a book on the subject. Then when the company Mindjet released its software called Mind-Manager in the mid nineties, I added computer-based business mapping to my quiver of tools. In spring of 2003, Mindjet added a Tablet PC version of MindManager, which has gained popularity among the Tablet PC community. Note that in October 2003 Mindjet released a major redesign of their nontablet software, called X5, and the tablet version of X5 is due for release soon after this book hits the bookshelves in February 2004.

The MindManager software greatly helps your ability to make and modify business maps. But before I describe this software, let me point out that you can do basic business mapping on a piece of paper, or in any simple drawing program such as Windows Journal.

Try a Simple Exercise

Here, let's give this a try. Put your Tablet PC in landscape mode, open up Windows Journal, and in the middle of the page write in moderately small lettering the words "To-do This Week," stacking the words and drawing a tight circle around the words as shown below.

Now draw a short line at about two o'clock and write the word "chores," and do the same at four o'clock with the word "family," at six with the word "car," and at nine with the word "work" (see Figure 11-1).

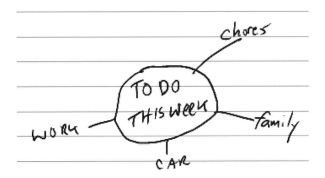

Figure 11-1. Start of a simple business map drawn using Windows Journal.

Now, with whatever category you feel inspired to start with, draw lines from the individual word for that category, and place any to-do topics that come to mind, making branches to add multiple words against one subcategory. If nothing comes to mind quickly for a particular subcategory, move your attention to the next subcategory and stop and think there for a moment. Write anything that comes, and when your thoughts stop flowing quickly, move to the next category. Here's one example (see Figure 11-2).

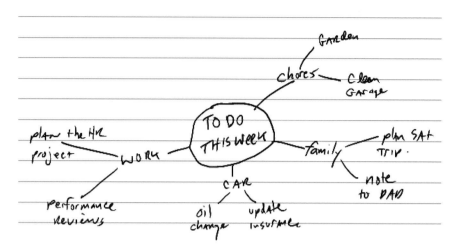

Figure 11-2. Completion of our simple business map.

Keep Brainstorming

This is brainstorming, so the idea is to not judge or evaluate the items as you think of them, rather just write them down as they come. If while writing on one category you think of something for some other category, quickly jump over to the category and write the word. If you think of a whole new category, insert that in any space you can find off the main circle. The key is to move from category to category so that as creativity dies in one area ideas are provoked in other areas. It's good to stop every so often and gaze at the whole diagram; this often leads to new inspirations for things to add to the business map.

Rapid Generation of Ideas

You will be amazed at how much information you can generate in a short length of time using this technique. If you aren't at first amazed, keep practicing; this technique is almost foolproof. The key is to write quickly, do not judge your thoughts as you write them down, and jump around the map from point to point quickly. If you ever stall out on a particular category for more than a few seconds, draw your attention away from that category and take a look at the whole map for a moment; you'll be inspired to start placing ideas next to some other subcategory. See Figure 11-3 below for the learning map MindManager includes for brainstorming.

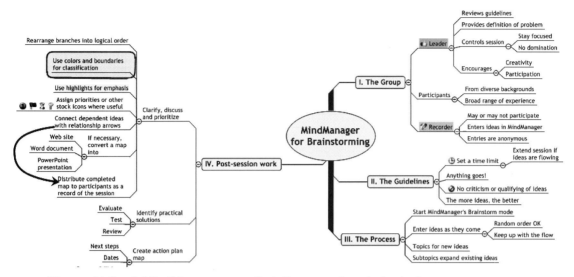

Figure 11-3. A MindManager map that discusses how to brainstorm.

There's something about seeing the whole picture at a glance that leads to much greater creativity, to a greater flow of ideas. Seeing multiple parts of the picture at once allows you to visualize interrelationships, which create new items to write on the business map.

I use business mapping quite consistently and for a variety of purposes. For example, this entire book, prior to writing, was outlined as a business map. This was done nearly down to the paragraph level in some chapters. Large business maps like this are one place software helps, as we'll see in a moment.

Beyond Brainstorming

There are many uses of business mapping other than for brainstorming. For instance business mapping is a great way to summarize on one page the key concepts of a difficult subject. It's a way to present a vision statement of a complicated subject or to present a corporate or departmental strategy (see Figure 11-4 below). It's also a good way to take notes, organize projects, and formulate meeting agendas.

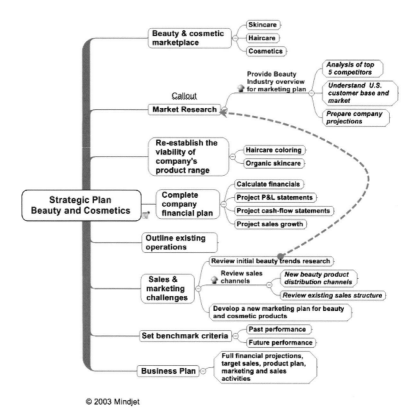

© 2003 Mindjet

Figure 11-4. In addition to brainstorming, business mapping can be used for creating formal business plans, as in this strategic plan business map.

Business Mapping Speeches

Business mapping is particularly useful for creating the notes to use to present a speech; I've done this many times with fantastic success. Many speeches do not need to be delivered in a strictly linear fashion. Rather, the primarily goal is to cover all aspects of the topic during the speech with only a high-level order of topics needed. If you choose a traditional linearly ordered notes format to deliver a speech from, you'll inevitably find yourself inspired to stray from that preconceived order of delivery, which often will cause you to lose your place in the notes during the speech.

In contrast, creating a business map of a speech topic ahead of time and using the printed business map to deliver the speech from works better. This allows you to easily jump around during a speech, from subtopic to subtopic, as inspired by questions or by the spirit of the moment during the talk. It allows you to see the whole of your topic while you speak. And it helps you focus when needed on the main topics, and drill down when needed on any of the subtopics. I highly recommend this approach.

Task and Project Planning

But, by far, I use business mapping most regularly for brainstorming the planning of new tasks or projects. If I'm given a new task that will obviously take a bit of thought to plan out, and I'm at a loss on how to start, the first thing I'll do is find a quiet moment, write that task topic in the middle of a page, and brainstorm using business mapping. This never fails to generate a long stream of ideas regarding scope, actions, possible solutions, next steps. This gives me enough of a start to hang my hat on for more detailed planning.

The business map is often not the end product of a project planning process. Rather it is usually an early or intermediate step which then leads to key deliverables. After such a business map is created, I then take the items generated from the business map and insert them into a more traditional project planning format. The choice of format depends on which stage of the project I am in; it might be a vision statement, a requirements document, or a Gantt chart. And MindManager contains tools to export business maps directly into a variety of endpoint applications, including Microsoft Project.

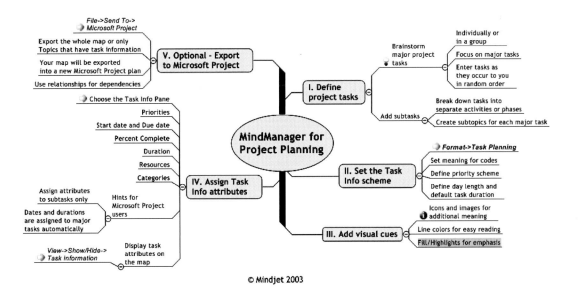

© Mindjet 2003

Mindjet MindManager Software

If business maps can be created so easily on paper or in Windows Journal, one may ask: "What are the advantages of the MindManager software?"

MindManager Advantages

Two Main Advantages to Using a Software Approach

- Paper-based and Windows Journal–based business maps are limited by the size of the page. In contrast the MindManager software lets you create business maps that can expand to an unlimited size, with the ability to collapse and expand portions for easy viewing. Nothing is worse than being constrained by physical space during a brainstorming session.

- With software-based business mapping, you can easily edit as you change your intentions during creation of the map (a likely scenario). It is easy to delete or insert new topics and subtopics and to move the branches and topics around the map.

General Software Advantages

Compared to paper-based business maps, you have all the advantages of any computer-based application, such as:

- Having all your business maps stored electronically

- Easy text-searching through old business maps

- Sharing documents electronically

- Using older business maps as templates for new business maps

- Projecting your business maps on a conference room wall

- Formatting your business maps for formal presentation

Added Advantages

There are tens, even hundreds, of less critical but significant advantages to using the MindManager software compared to hand-created maps, and here are some that I've found most useful.

- The ability to create hyperlinks to other business maps

- Easy placement of symbols on your maps

- Integration of the business map with Microsoft Project so that brainstorming in MindManager can be imported into a project plan

- Conversion of business maps to outline format and back

- Conversion of business maps to PowerPoint presentations

Easy Presentations

This last point is a key one. One excellent use of the MindManager software is to quickly create a professional-looking PowerPoint presentation. Let's say you are asked on very short notice to create a presentation on a topic that you are familiar with but don't have time to create a good set of slides for. To accomplish this, sit down and create a business map of the topic in MindManager. Once the map is done, take time to rearrange the main topics and branches around the central topic to match the set and order of slides that you would like to present. Then use the export to PowerPoint function in MindManager. This export function intelligently creates slides based on the hierarchical relationship of the topics. The first time you get a chance to do this exercise you'll be amazed at how quickly you can create an effective PowerPoint presentation on short notice. We'll go over this topic in more detail in Chapter 12.

You can also create and give presentations from within the MindManager software itself; the software includes a special presentation mode to facilitate this. One advantage of this approach over conversion to PowerPoint is that MindManager enables you to immediately integrate group feedback into the presentation.

Software Versions

X5 and MindManager for Tablet PC

The current MindManager release is called X5. Initially released in October 2003, it offers a dramatically improved user interface over previous versions. The tablet version of MindManager was first released in spring 2003. A tablet version of X5 is due to be released shortly after this book is published in early 2004. A preview of that version is included in this chapter.

Downloading the Software

Like many software companies, Mindjet allows a free trial download from their website, in this case a twenty-one-day license. This is a simple and straightforward install, no complications; just follow the online instructions.

Creating Business Maps in Nontablet Mode

Remember the 80/20 rule discussed in the Introduction? For purposes of this chapter we're definitely going to focus just on the simplest parts of Mind-Manager, probably even less than 20 percent. It's a rich and multifeatured application, but you can gain nearly all the benefits listed above by using it in its simplest form, by just creating simple business maps. In fact, that's the best course of action: get started using this book as a guide to simple uses, decide if you like the approach, and then self-teach yourself the more advanced portions of the software when you are ready.

Start in the Nontablet Mode

The primarily advantage of using the tablet mode (called Pen mode in the software) is that it allows you to use the pen to write tasks in handwriting on your business maps and to either leave them as handwriting or convert them to text later. All the other more traditional aspects of the software are still present in the tablet version, thereby maintaining the easy editing and other benefits of the software.

If you're new to MindManager, I recommend you start in the nontablet mode or Mouse mode as they call it. Doing this in my opinion makes using the software in Pen mode later easier. And furthermore, it is likely that you'll be doing much of your brainstorming at the privacy of your desk where you will have access to a keyboard, and therefore you may not want to work in Pen mode.

If you have not already done so, please now attach the keyboard to your Tablet PC, or put your convertible in laptop mode for the following exercises.

Launching the Software

After starting the X5 version of the software for the first time, you may be presented with a window giving you a chance to run product overviews; instead click the button that says Start MindManager. After taking the startup lessons included in this book, I will show you how to run some very good tutorials built into the software. They will give you deeper training and show you some ideas on other ways to use the software.

After starting MindManager you'll see the following screen (see Figure 11-5).

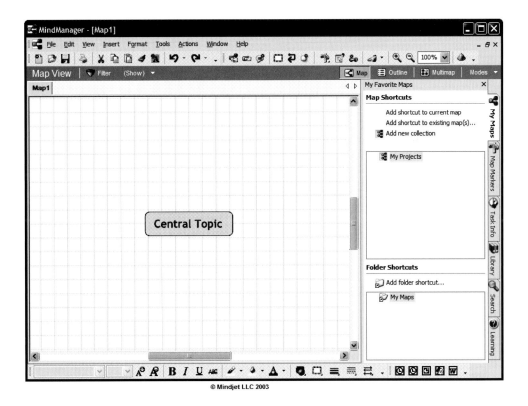

Figure 11-5. The MindManager initial screen.

Also, for now, close the task windows to the right (probably marked Short-cuts) to give you more desk space to work in. Click in the small x in the upper right corner of that shortcut window to close it. You'll be left with a blank business map, ready for you to enter the new map title.

If at any time during this tutorial you want to throw your sample document away and start a new one, you can create a new document by using the New Document icon in the upper left corner of the toolbar.

Entering Topics

For now, I'm just going to have you enter a precreated partial map by copy-ing from this book into the MindManager software. This is so that you can get used to using the software without actually needing to brainstorm at the moment. Let's use the map shown at the beginning of the chapter, repeated here (see Figure 11-6).

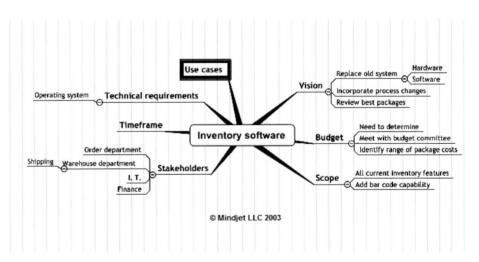

Figure 11-6.   Sample business map to use in the exercise.

To get started, if you're using the tablet version, first make sure that Mind-Manager is in Mouse mode. The way to do this is to confirm that the words in the upper right corner of the software screen that say Pen Mode are not high-lighted in orange. If they in fact are highlighted you are currently in Pen mode, so click once on those words, and the software will switch back to Mouse mode (see Figure 11-7).

© Mindjet LLC 2004

Figure 11-7.   You know you are in Mouse mode when the words Pen Mode are not highlighted.

Next, let's set the zoom factor to 75 percent. Working at 100 percent creates items too large for most of us, particularly on a small Tablet PC screen. To do this, find the Zoom icons in the middle of the upper toolbar (see Figure 11-8):

Figure 11-8.   Setting the zoom factor in MindManager.

Click on the arrow to the right of the number 100, choosing 75 from the drop-down list.

Now, with your mouse, left-click once on the block labeled Central Topic in the center of the new map to select it. Now type in the title as displayed on the map above, and hit Enter.

Once entered, with the Inventory Software block still selected (there's a big blue border around it) now hit the Insert key on your keyboard to create a new main topic branch, which appears above and to the right of the central topic. The Insert key always inserts a subtopic to whatever topic is currently selected. Your map should now look like Figure 11-9.

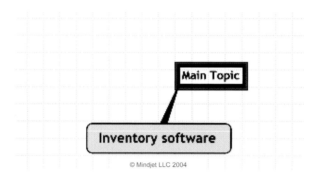

© Mindjet LLC 2004

Figure 11-9. Creating the first main topic.

Note that the new main topic is highlighted (selected) so you can now immediately start typing the text for that topic; your typing will overwrite the
placeholder text that says Main Topic. Type the word Vision and hit Enter to
lock the text entry in.

Click once on the central topic Inventory Software to select it again. Hit the
Insert key again to create another new main topic. Type in the word Budget
and hit Enter.

Now let's try a different way to create the third main topic, this time using the
toolbar.

Click once on the central topic Inventory Software to select it. The toolbar
equivalent to the keyboard Insert key is to click the Insert icon which is at the
middle part of the business map toolbar area and looks like this:

Click that button and a new main topic will form. Type the next title Scope for
that topic and hit Enter once.

Now let's try yet another way to insert a topic; instead of clicking on Inventory Software to select it, leave the last main topic selected (Scope). With the
Scope topic selected, hit the Enter key; immediately another branch will form
off the central topic ready for your entry of the next main topic. The lesson
here is that you can always create sibling topics (topics or branches created at
the same level are called sibling topics) just by hitting the Enter key. Type the
word Stakeholders within this new topic and hit Enter.

Use the Enter key approach now to continue entering the rest of the main topics; keep hitting the Enter key twice in between each topic to create the next one (you hit Enter once to lock the topic name in, and a second time to create the next topic). Note by the way that of the three ways you now know to insert topics, using the Enter key is probably the quickest way to insert a large number of sibling topics.

After typing the remaining topics, this is how the business map should look (see Figure 11-10):

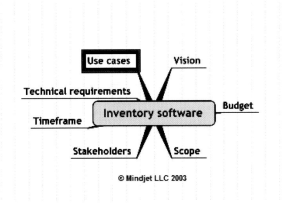

Figure 11-10. Results of exercise with the first level of topics entered.

We are now ready to enter some subtopics around these main topics; let's start with the word Vision. Again use the map in Figure 11-6 as a guide. Click on the word "Vision" and hit the Insert key or tap the Insert toolbar button. Type in the topic: Replace Old System.

Finish the rest of the business map in this fashion.

Expanding and Collapsing Topics

One thing to note is that MindManager allows you to collapse subtopics by clicking on the minus sign at the junction with the main branch. Try this now on any main topic. As you might expect, clicking the plus sign that forms in its place will reexpand that topic.

One reason you may want to collapse a topic is to get its multiple branches out of the way. This allows you to work on one particular topic without distraction. So for instance if you wanted to work on and then complete the Vision subtopic without distractions from the other expanded topics, you could collapse the other topics by clicking the minus sign next to each one, and your screen will look like this (see Figure 11-11):

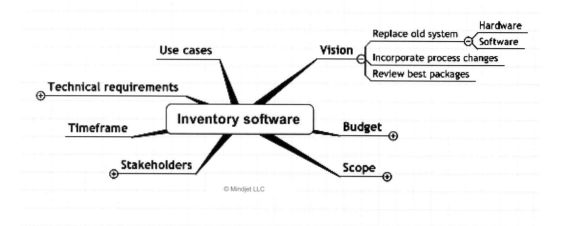

Figure 11-11.   Result of collapsing all main topics except for Vision.

There's another, easier way to do this rather than clicking each minus sign one at a time. Instead click once on the Vision topic and then from the Actions menu choose Focus on Topic. This has the same effect, plus it centers on the screen the topic you are focusing on.

Expanding All Topics and Branches

You can view the fully expanded business map again also in one step, without having to click on all the plus signs one at a time. Rather, first select the central topic Inventory Software, then choose from the Action menu the Level of Detail command, and pick Show Whole Topic from the submenu. The whole map is now expanded.

If you want to expose the full depth below only a specific topic, you can use the same Level of Detail command to completely expand individual topics. Do this by clicking once to select a main or subtopic first, and then use the Level of Detail command.

As your map gets larger and deeper, you may not want to expand all topics and branches to their full depth using Show Whole Topic; that's where the other choices on the Level of Detail command submenu come in. Pick an appropriate level of detail to show from the submenu (indicated by numbers with 1 showing the least detail) and the map will be expanded only to that level.

You can also use a toolbar equivalent of the Level of Detail command by clicking on the down arrow attached to the icon shown below.

Like the Action menu using the down arrow on this icon gives you a choice of various levels of detail. Also note that if you repeatedly click on the icon itself rather than on the arrow next to it, you will cycle through all the level of detail choices, one at a time. In other words your map will, step by step, open to deeper and deeper levels.

Editing Your Business Maps

And now for perhaps the primary reason to do your business map creations in a software package rather than by hand on paper. There is a nearly 100 percent probability that after you get a few minutes into creating a business map, you will want to change it. You will want to change some of the names of your topics, you will want to change the hierarchy, and you will want to move the spatial relationship of branches. This is the beauty of a software-based approach—you can do this easily.

Editing Text in a Topic

You can change the text in any topic at any time. Simply click the topic to select it (a blue square forms around it), and type the new text. Simple.

Instant Floating Topic

You may notice that if you click on a blank space in the MindManager document a small blue arrow forms. If at that point you start typing, you will create a floating topic. This is simply text that is not attached to the branches of the map itself. Use this to create labels or titles or to temporarily record ideas that do not yet logically fit into your current topic list. If the floating topic is later dragged to the map, it will automatically attach as a branch.

Rearranging Topics

You may want to change the order of topics at the same level. Or you may want to change the hierarchical relationship of topics, by moving topics (and all their subtopics) from one topic to another.

Moving main topics around the central topic

If you wish to rearrange the position of the main topics around the central topic without changing their hierarchical level, just select the topic and drag it to its new location (avoid dropping in on top of another topic; this changes the hierarchical relationship). As you drag the topic, and before you "drop" it, the new location of the branch holding that topic will display in red and the new location of the topic will show as a ghost image. For instance in Figure 11-12, the scope topic is being dragged up to a new location in between Vision and Budget.

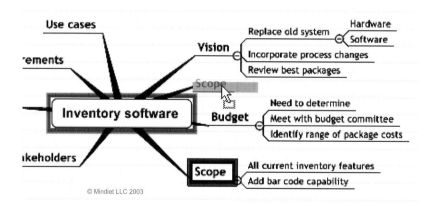

Figure 11-12.   When you drag a topic, before you release the mouse, a ghost image of the topic will form at its new location.

When you drop the item (release the mouse button) at its new location, the topics and branches holding them rearrange themselves cleanly (see Figure 11-13 where Scope and Budget are now reversed in position).

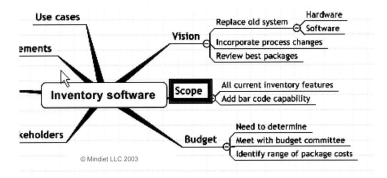

© Mindjet LLC 2003

Figure 11-13.   Once you release the mouse, the dragged topic will reposition, and other topics will move aside to make room for it.

MindManager will attempt to keep the position and layout of topics arranged in an orderly fashion. So the branch may not drop exactly where you position the mouse, but the order will be as you intended it.

Changing the hierarchical relationship of topics

If you want to move a subtopic to a different main topic, or change the level within its own branch, just a little more skill is required.

Let's say you decided that the Scope main topic is more logically placed as a subtopic under Vision. To do this you just drag it there, sort of. The easy part is getting it to be a subtopic of Vision. However a little finesse is required to control which *position* it falls into within the subtopics of Vision.

Two visual clues are provided by the software to make this happen easily. The first visual clue confirms that you've selected Vision as the new main topic to which Scope will be a subtopic. This one is easy: when you click on Scope and start dragging it slightly you'll see a dim red box appear around Inventory Software. This is making the visual statement that "Scope is currently a subtopic of inventory software." Now continue to drag Scope until it starts to touch the Vision main topic. When it does you'll see the dim red box around Inventory Software instantly disappear and reappear around the Vision topic box. This is telling you Scope is now a subtopic of Vision. Don't release the mouse yet because there's more.

You now need to indicate what position within the subtopics of Vision you want this Scope branch to sit. Let's say you want it to be placed between the subtopics Incorporate Process Change and Review Best Practices. Here's how you do that.

As soon as the destination main topic becomes highlighted (the Vision topic in this case) you'll see a dim ghost of a rectangle appear somewhere in the list of subtopics of Vision. This rectangle tells you where the moved topic will be inserted if you release the mouse at that point (see Figure 11-14).

Side Note: If by chance you are using the pen right now as a mouse, and are right handed and working on the right side of the map, you may need to lift your hand a little bit to see this ghost rectangle.

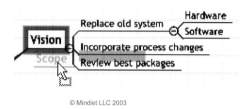

© Mindjet LLC 2003

Figure 11-14. When demoting a topic to a subtopic, the new parent topic will take on a red highlight (Vision above), and the new position of the demoted topic will appear as a dim unlabeled ghost rectangle. This is where the moved topic will drop if you release the mouse.

Keep dragging the scope topic up and down and watch how this ghost rectangle changes position within the list of Vision subtopics; when you get it where you want it, in this case between the subtopics Incorporate Process Change and Review Best Practices, release the mouse and that's where the Scope topic will move to (see Figure 11-15). You'll notice the subtopics of Scope moved as well.

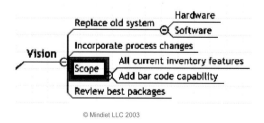

© Mindjet LLC 2003

Figure 11-15. Final subtopic layout after demoting Scope.

Highlighting a Topic and Adding Map Markers

Highlighting

I generally leave formatting instructions out of a book like this, because formatting is usually not a highly valued skill, and it is usually something you can study easily on your own time. However one formatting action that I recommend you learn early is how to mark a topic or branch with a yellow highlighter. This is similar to taking a yellow highlighting marker and drawing it across the text of a printed map. It is a great way to draw attention to a particular topic. Doing this is very simple: you merely select the topic, and click the fill/highlight icon on the formatting toolbar at the bottom of the screen as shown below (see Figure 11-16). Note that the icon is different from what you might expect from a highlighting icon; it is actually a picture of a paint bucket. Because of its small size you might have to use your imagination to see it as a paint bucket.

© Mindiet LLC 2003

Fill/Highlight

Figure 11-16.   Fill/Highlight icon.

You can choose colors by clicking on the arrow to the right of the icon. Keep in mind if you add highlighting to your document that the results may look interesting on a noncolor printer.

Map Markers

The other formatting lesson I urge you to learn now is how to add Map Markers to topics. Map Markers are simply small icons that are added to a branch, next to the text on the branch, to represent some category or classification. The ones I use the most are the checkmark and the number markers. The first I use to mark topics as I complete them, and the second to indicate priority of a topic (see Figure 11-17).

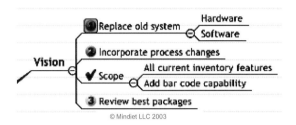

© Mindiet LLC 2003

Figure 11-17. Map Markers are symbols you can place next to the text of topics.

The way to add a Map Marker to a topic is very simple: select the topic, and then click on the Map Marker icon on the main toolbar (it looks like an old-style signpost). Then choose the marker from the drop-down menu (see Figure 11-18).

© Mindiet LLC 2003

Figure 11-18. The Map Marker icon choices.

The menu itself displays relatively few markers. The key here is using the More Icons... button at the bottom of that menu to open a task panel on the right. This panel displays a much larger selection of marker choices (see Figure 11-19).

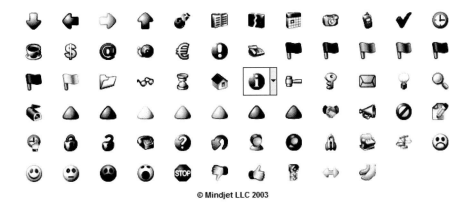

© Mindjet LLC 2003

Figure 11-19.   The complete selection of Map Markers.

You can add as many markers to a specific topic as you wish. To remove only a specific marker from a topic, select the topic and click the marker you want to remove on the marker toolbar menu. To remove all markers from a topic, select the topic and choose the Remove All Markers choice at the top of the marker toolbar menu.

Advanced features

There are a whole slew of more advanced features within MindManager that, in keeping with the 80/20 rule, I will leave to you to study on your own time. The best way to do this is to choose the Learning tab from the right-hand tab bar and follow all the tutorials there. Those tutorials are well designed and implemented (note the Learning tab is the one at the bottom and may not be visible if your business map screen is sized too small; resize it larger if needed).

Creating Business Maps Using MindManager for the Tablet PC

What Is Pen Mode?

Pen mode is an optional mode of MindManager that allows you to use the pen to write tasks in handwriting on your business maps and to either leave them as handwriting or convert them to text later. All the other more traditional aspects of the software are still present when in Pen mode, thereby maintaining easy editing and other benefits of the software. Some toolbars and submenus are enlarged while in Pen mode to make picking them with a pen easier. But, in general, all menus and toolbars remain the same in both modes.

Pen mode also enables use of a number of custom gestures in MindManager. I usually avoid gestures on the Tablet PC, but the ones I use in MindManager are intuitive and simple to remember. I will cover some of those in a moment.

When to Use Pen Mode

I use Pen mode when away from my keyboard and mouse. And even when the keyboard and mouse are nearby, I find I enjoy using the Pen mode of MindManager when creating new business maps, particularly when creating brainstorming business maps. This is because I find that there's something more natural about handwriting ideas than typing them. I can record ideas faster in my handwriting than when typing. And I think I brainstorm more successfully when able to sit in a comfortable chair with the Tablet PC in my lap and write with one hand as I consider the topic. I'm sure this is related to the research that says writing with one hand, compared to typing, leaves more of the brain available for other duties, presumably thinking about the brainstorming topic at hand in this case.

Whatever your preference, there are times when the pen is your only method of input, in meetings for example. So learning the Pen mode of MindManager is a requirement if you wish to brainstorm on the fly. Furthermore, many Tablet PC users use MindManager for note taking in meetings, which would require the Pen mode.

Your X5 Pen Mode May Appear Different

If you are still using the previous tablet version of MindManager and have not yet upgraded to X5, the new tablet software is quite different. In addition to the X5 changes, a number of the command gestures have changed.

And even if you have upgraded, the X5 Pen mode of the copy you have now may appear and function somewhat differently from what you see in this chapter. Reason: in order to meet publishing deadlines, this chapter was written based on a pre-beta version of the X5 Tablet software, and some features will probably have changed by the time of production release. Check the book website (www.seizetheworkday.com) for updates to this and other chapters.

Entering Text in Pen Mode

The way to enter Pen mode in MindManager X5 is, as described in the last section, to click on the Pen Mode button in the upper right corner of the MindManager window (see Figure 11-20).

© Mindjet LLC 2004

Figure 11-20. The Pen Mode indicator and control.

You'll know you've succeeded when you see the button highlight and take on an orange color as shown in the upper right corner of Figure 11-23. Tap it again if you wish to change back to Mouse mode.

Creating a New Document

Creating a new document in Pen mode is nearly identical to creating one in Mouse mode. In both modes, a new document opens with the central topic highlighted. In Pen mode, however, you must tap once inside the central topic area to start editing it.

Tapping inside the area indicates that you are ready to enter handwriting and opens the Handwriting entry window shown in the right side of Figure 11-21. This is a special Handwriting input box, unique to the MindManager software. Write into that box as you would into the Tablet PC Input Panel.

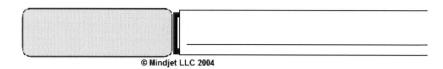

© Mindjet LLC 2004

Figure 11-21. When you tap on the central topic, the MindManager Handwriting input box opens to the right.

When you are finished writing, tap outside the entry window to close it; doing so transfers the title to the central topic area (see Figure 11-22). You can leave the handwriting there as is, or do as I often do, which is to convert the title to text immediately so you can save the file with a clean title. More on converting to text below.

© Mindjet LLC 2003

Figure 11-22. The central topic, with a handwritten title.

Entering Topics in Pen Mode

A nice feature of Pen mode is the ability to create a new topic using a simple gesture. You create a new main topic simply by drawing a horizontal line across the page. To create a new main topic to the right of the central topic, draw the line from left to right. To create a new main topic to the left of the central topic, draw the line from the right to the left. Either gesture signals MindManager to create a new topic and presents the same handwriting entry window as used for the central topic (see Figure 11-23).

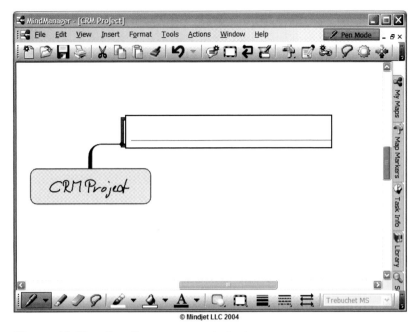

Figure 11-23.   Creating a new main topic.

After entering your handwriting, the ink is copied to the topic branch as shown below (see Figure 11-24).

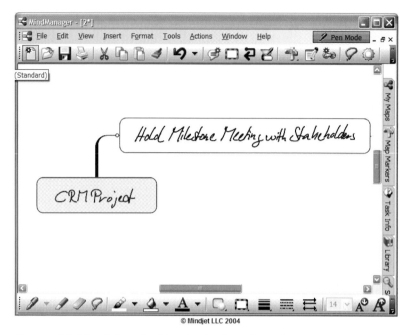

© Mindjet LLC 2004

Figure 11-24.   A handwritten topic placed on the map.

Note that you are not writing or drawing directly on the document, rather MindManager (like many other Tablet PC software packages) requires an input window to enter handwriting.

You can continue to create main topics by drawing new horizontal lines (from left to right or right to left depending on where you want to position the new topic). Just be sure to draw the lines in an open area outside of any existing topics. MindManager will automatically position each new topic below the existing topics.

Instead of using gestures, if you like you can use menu commands or the toolbar tools described for the Mouse mode of X5 to create new topics and subtopics.

If you don't like the default placement of new topics, after they are created you can drag the topics to a new ordering of positions, just like in Mouse mode.

Creating Subtopics

To create subtopics, you need to use a different gesture. Rather than drawing a horizontal line, draw a line that goes down, then turns 90 degrees to the left or to the right. This opens a writing entry window off the currently selected topic (see Figure 11-25). MindManager offers the left or right gesture option in order to accommodate both left-handed and right-handed users.

© Mindjet LLC 2004

Figure 11-25.   Entering a handwritten subtopic.

You can create entire mind maps with multiple hierarchical levels completely in ink (see Figure 11-26).

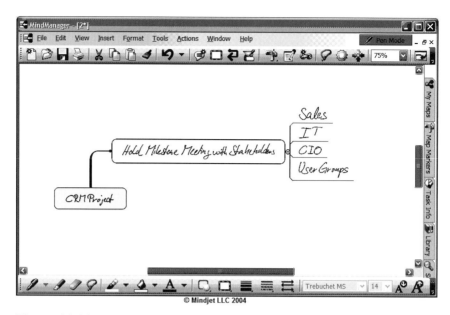

Figure 11-26. You can create an entire handwritten business map.

Editing Ink Topics

Once you've entered ink and left a topic, you can reopen it for ink editing by tapping once on the topic. This opens the ink entry window again, ready for editing.

To erase ink while in the ink editing window, press the pen shaft button, and the cursor will change to an eraser cursor. To perform other operations, such as to select multiple text elements and move them, or to change the pen color or thickness, use the tool bar at the lower left of the screen.

Creating Handwritten Floating Topics

You can create handwritten floating topics simply by tapping in an open space and drawing a horizontal line. Once you have entered handwriting, you can create another floating topic by immediately drawing another horizontal line outside the entry window. MindManager will automatically position the new topic below the previous one.

The Hand Tool

In Pen mode a very useful operation is to drag the viewing position of the map around the screen, to see off-screen portions of the map. Do this by positioning the pen over a blank portion of the screen and depressing the button on the shaft of the pen. The cursor turns into a Hand icon, and if you drag the pen the map moves with it.

Inserting Sketches

You might think that you could draw sketches directly on the document. You can, but you must indicate first that you want to insert a sketch. The easiest way to do this is using the Insert Sketch gesture. This is accomplished by simply drawing a triangle shape on the screen. A box will open up into which you can draw. If a topic is selected at the time you create a sketch, that sketch becomes part of the topic. Otherwise it becomes a free-floating sketch. To edit your sketch, single tap on the sketch. When you are finished drawing, single tap in an open area to stop editing.

Other Gestures

The three gestures taught above are the ones I routinely use. Eleven other MindManager commands can be accomplished with gestures. The Shortcuts pane at the right side of the MindManager window has a guide to them all.

Converting Handwriting to Text

Converting handwriting to text is something you do after handwriting, using a Tools menu command. Keep in mind that conversion to text is purely optional; refer to Chapter 5 for recommendations on when it is best to keep ink versus converting to text. Also note that MindManager, like many other Tablet PC applications, converts all ink to text in the background, whether you explicitly convert or not. So you can search for handwritten text in maps, just like in Windows Journal or OneNote.

When considering converting to text, I recommend that you wait until you have completed a burst of writing and are no longer producing ideas. This is a good time to start text conversion and edit the text you have put down. Or wait until you are back at your desk and a keyboard, to make the text correction steps slightly easier.

To start the conversion process, select the topic where you would like to begin. MindManager will convert that text, and then continue around the map in a clockwise fashion until it is finished or until you tell it to stop. If you do not select a topic, MindManager will first convert the central topic, then move to the upper right quadrant of the map and move clockwise.

To start conversion, choose from the Tools menu the first item: Convert Handwriting to Text. You'll be presented with the following dialog box (see Figure 11-27):

© Mindiet LLC 2003

Figure 11-27. When converting to text, you have a choice of converting the whole map at once or stepping through and confirming each branch one by one.

I always use the first choice in this dialog so that I can edit the text conversions one topic at a time. With this choice, once you click OK, MindManager will select the first topic and present its first attempt at text conversion, ready for editing. If all the text in that topic has been converted correctly, you merely click the Accept button just below the converted text (see Figure 11-28).

If a word is incorrect, you can either key in the correct text or use the input panel to rewrite the text. MindManager presents its own version of the Tablet PC Input Panel so that you have a way to input edits. There's little difference between this input panel and the one provided by default by the Tablet PC.

You can also choose from the drop-down list of other guesses that MindManager has made in converting your text. If you use the drop-down list, note that the more words you have written, the less likely it is that one of the choices will have them all correct. So experiment with the drop-down list a few times to get a feel for when it may be helpful. Once your text is corrected, click Accept.

© Mindiet LLC 2003

Figure 11-28. During text conversion, MindManager presents a first estimate of conversion. Clicking the arrow at the right enables a drop-down list of other possible converted text choices.

Once accepted, MindManager inserts the converted text into the business map. And then MindManager moves to the next topic and once again presents its estimate at text conversion in the same way, waiting for you to make any immediate corrections and then for you to accept.

During conversion to text MindManager does a good job of positioning the various input and edit boxes so that you can see the original handwriting as you examine and change the converted text. The handwritten text and converted text are shown clearly adjacent to each other, and the tools to accept it or correct it are placed just in the right spot.

I find this clear positioning, and the topic-by-topic method of converting text, to be among the best text conversion implementations on the Tablet PC.

During this topic-by-topic conversion process, you can click the Close button (shown in the right side of Figure 11-28) at any time to cease the process. Or you can allow MindManager to cycle through all of the unconverted topics until complete. Once complete, MindManager will proudly tell you so (see Figure 11-29).

© Mindiet LLC 2003

Figure 11-29. At the end of text conversion you are notified.

The business map is then presented with a clean and evenly spaced layout (see Figure 11-30). You can then reposition these topics just as you would in Mouse mode.

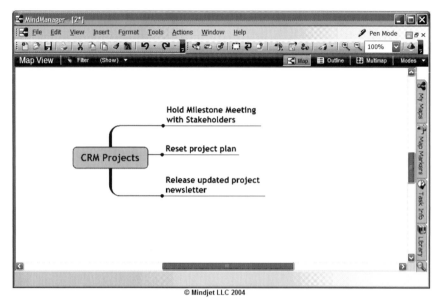

Figure 11-30. A business map once converted from handwriting to text.

Next Steps

At this point, you've learned enough to make business maps using a keyboard and mouse and using the pen. There are a lot more features to learn, but we'll stop here to give you a chance to do some real business maps, without distracting you with features probably not yet useful to you. I've taught you the key points needed to create brainstorming business maps easily and quickly.

Take this business mapping seriously; it really does work. Get ten or twenty maps done, and then come back to the learning center portion of MindManager and teach yourself the more advanced features. By that time you'll be motivated to dig through the tutorials. These tutorials are well designed and implemented and truly useful.

A good excuse to create a business map daily is first thing in the morning to create a To Do Today map, just writing whatever is on your mind. You don't even need to look at your official task list if you do not want to. The idea is to get nagging thoughts off your mind and down on "paper," to make them visible so you can assess and prioritize them. Then move anything that qualifies over to your real task list. It's an excellent way to clear the mind and start measuring the day.

Brainstorming Using Other Tablet PC Software Packages

As mentioned at the beginning of this chapter, you should be able to create a simple business map in virtually any drawing program. However MindManager is such a superior approach, you should at least try it out.

But there also are some kinds of brainstorming that don't really lend themselves to business mapping; some brainstorming exercises lend themselves more toward other graphical approaches. For instance brainstorming through business processes is better accomplished starting with a sketch of the left to right or top to bottom business process flow itself and making notes on that sketch. Architectural brainstorming is better done on a floor plan. With anything that already has a dominant graphical theme, it's better to use that theme during brainstorming. And this is where the other drawing programs come in.

Windows Journal, Sketch Pad, Corel Grafigo—all are software packages optimized for drawing and sketching on the Tablet PC. Each has its strengths. Corel Grafigo looks promising for process drawings and architectural brainstorming. Sketch Pad looks great as a powerful free form sketching tool. And Windows Journal is good just because it's simple and always available; it's the Swiss Army knife of the Tablet PC.

In all these cases, in addition to the specific features of each software package, the main additional advantages these packages bring overall are the same advantages as any computer-based documents:

- Easy editing compared with paper documents

- Having all your documents stored electronically

- Easy text-searching through old documents

- Sharing documents electronically

- Using older documents as templates for new projects

- Projecting your brainstorming on a conference room wall

■   Formatting your documents for formal presentation

And keep in mind the best way to start such a process brainstorm document may be to import an existing process diagram into a program like Windows Journal and sketch on top of it.

You could use both approaches: the process map to think through the process, and the business mapping to brainstorm alternatives uncovered during process map examination. That is probably the best of both worlds.

Chapter 12 Mark Up and Edit Using the Tablet PC Pen

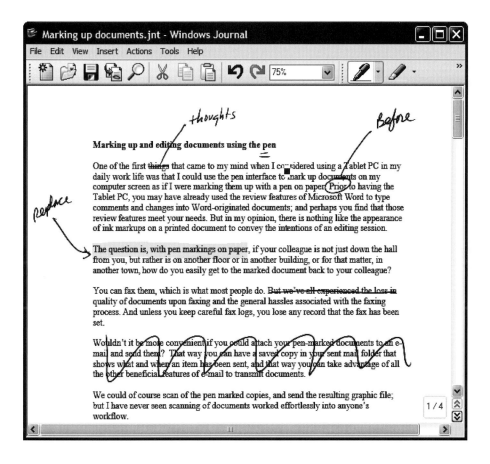

The Business Case

Are you required to edit business documents—memos, presentations, manuals? If so you are going to like the tools the Tablet PC gives you to do this.

One of the first things that occurred to me when I considered using a Tablet PC in my daily work life was that I could use the pen interface to mark up documents on my computer screen as if I were marking them up with a pen on paper. Prior to having the Tablet PC, I had already used the review features of Microsoft Word to type comments and changes into Word-originated documents. These features clearly mark text changes and additions, a feature that is needed with any editing approach. Perhaps you have used this feature of Word and find that it meets your editing needs. But in my opinion, there is nothing like the appearance of ink markups on a printed document to convey the intentions of an editing session.

So why make the pen edits on the Tablet PC when you can print out the document and use your ballpoint pen? One reason is you may start your editing session away from a printer; perhaps you are in a meeting while you're editing. Or perhaps you are like me and prefer to avoid paper when you can.

But the more important reason for marking up documents on the computer is this: what if the colleague who needs to receive these edits is not just down the hall from you, but is on another floor or in another building, or for that matter in another town; how do you easily get the marked document back to your colleague? You can fax them, which is what most people do. But we've all experienced the loss in quality of documents upon faxing and the general hassles associated with the faxing process. And unless you keep careful fax logs, you lose any record that the fax has been sent.

Wouldn't it be more convenient if you could attach your pen-marked documents to an e-mail and send them? That way you can have a saved copy in your sent mail folder that shows what has been sent and when. That also allows you to take advantage of all the other beneficial features of e-mail to transmit documents.

We could scan the pen-marked copies and send the resulting graphic file; but I have never seen scanning of documents worked effortlessly into the average office workflow. And, in general, whenever I can easily get away from creating and handling paper documents, I do.

Marking up soft copies of documents with a pen is a functionality for which the Tablet PC really shines. Research shows there is a 27 percent increase in efficiency for those who mark up documents using the Tablet PC versus paper or traditional computer methods. And since as a Tablet PC owner you are already using a pen interface and are accustomed to writing and drawing on the computer screen, using these skills to mark up documents only requires a small additional effort and self-training.

Your Document Annotation Software Choices

There are eight software packages that you might use for annotating office documents in ink with the Tablet PC.

- Microsoft Office 2003

- Microsoft Office XP (Office 2002)

- Windows Journal

- FranklinCovey PlanPlus

- FranklinCovey TabletPlanner

- Adobe Acrobat

- Microsoft OneNote

- Microsoft Office Document Imaging (ships with Microsoft Office)

By far, Microsoft Office 2003 is the best way to annotate office documents, hands down. If you plan to do pen markups of office documents, get this software.

The older Office XP (with Office Pack for the Tablet PC installed) is of moderate value; you can create pen-written comment boxes and text within the margins but you can't easily write directly over existing Word text with the pen. The exception to this limitation is with PowerPoint 2002 documents where writing directly on the copy does work well, and Excel 2002 where limited ink overlay capability is available.

The next three software choices in the list—Windows Journal, PlanPlus, and TabletPlanner—are of nearly equivalent value for annotating documents and use similar approaches to each other. They allow you to write over existing text. However they are less effective at annotating Microsoft Office documents than Office 2003 is. This is primarily because a document import step is required to prepare for the editing, and once imported the document text is frozen.

Adobe Acrobat comes in near last place for pen editing, primarily because its ink tools are very limited. Microsoft OneNote has some possibilities but has limited document import capabilities.

Microsoft Office Document Imaging is an interesting approach that has some advantages.

Let's go into some details on these solutions.

Microsoft Office 2003: The Best Solution

The best way to approach annotating documents is to use the latest version of Microsoft Office, namely Office 2003. This version (and this version only) has been enabled for true pen markup of Microsoft Office–created documents right from within the Office programs.

We'll cover how to do this immediately below, but note that as of this writing, this new version of Office has just been released and your company may not have upgraded yet. This is fairly common among large organizations: due to the cost and effort of upgrading an entire workforce, the IT departments of many organizations delay purchasing or distributing the new versions of Microsoft Office to their workers, often for months or even years after their release. And the recent reviews of Office 2003 by the computer press have generally recommended holding back on upgrades unless the new collaboration features of Office (SharePoint server for example) are needed by an organization. So it is likely that many organizations will not upgrade for some time.

And even if you do have the latest version because either you or your department has upgraded, you will need to be alert to what software the receiving party has. You need to ensure that the colleagues you are sending the marked-up documents to also have software that can view the ink. Remarkably, versions of Microsoft Office as far back as Office 97 (and perhaps earlier; I have not tested earlier versions) can display your markups, so there's good news there. But if your colleagues are not using Microsoft Office software you'll have to test this ability with whatever software they are using; just because the software claims to be able to import Microsoft Office documents does not ensure that it will work with ink.

Marking Up Office 2003 Documents

The beauty of using Microsoft Office 2003 for pen markups is that you can use your standard Office software to also add ink annotations right on top of text;

the other solutions require a document import step to do that. And more importantly, with Office 2003:

- The underlying text in the documents remains editable.

- The ink markups actually link to (in the case of Word) the paragraph that they are written on; so if subsequent editing above or below the paragraphs causes paragraphs to move, the ink annotations follow with them.

Side Note: There are still limitations with ink annotations. Later text changes made inside a paragraph that is marked up using ink annotation in Word 2003 will lead to alignment problems between the text and the markings; this problem and strategies to work around it are discussed later in this chapter.

The practical value of being able to edit annotated documents is that the workflow of annotating with ink using Office 2003 is much simpler:

- You use one tool to create and annotate.

- The recipient of your comments can read your comments on their screen and make changes in the same document.

With Windows Journal, PlanPlus, and TabletPlanner the underlying imported documents are not editable. So anyone implementing your comments would need to print out the marked-up page and then open the original Office document separately to make the edits.

Ink Annotations versus Ink Comments versus Ink Drawing and Writing Tool

To describe the capabilities of Microsoft Office 2003 for marking up documents in ink let's first focus on Microsoft Word. In Word 2003, there are three distinct ways to add ink with a Tablet PC: ink annotations, ink comments, and ink graphic objects (inserted using the Ink Drawing and Writing tool); each has a different best usage.

Ink Annotations

Ink annotations are marks made right on the text: circling, underlining, scratching out, writing on top of other text. This is the primary added ink capability within Word 2003 over the previous release. It is this functionality that in my opinion represents the true meaning of "marking up a document." It allows expressiveness in your markups, it is closest in appearance to paper markup, and it is easy to do in a meeting without a keyboard. See Figure 12-1 for an example of an ink annotation.

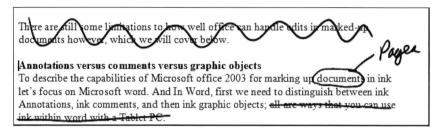

Figure 12-1. Example of using ink annotations in Word 2003. The underlying text remains editable.

This generally works as advertised and makes the upgrade to Word 2003 worthwhile. However some of the "older" ink solutions still have their place in Word 2003. A weakness of ink annotations is that if you want to insert extensive added or replacement text with your pen, you need to find blank areas on the page to do the writing. You can run out of blank areas fast if you have lots of inserts; that's where the other approaches come in.

Comments

Comments in contrast are callout boxes that sit in the margin of the document with a dotted line pointing to where the comment applies in the document. Comment boxes have existed since early versions of Word. In early versions text was added to these boxes using a keyboard. With Office Word 2003 (and Word for Office XP, with the Microsoft Office XP Pack for Tablet PC installed) these comment boxes can be populated with ink as well (see Figure 12-2).

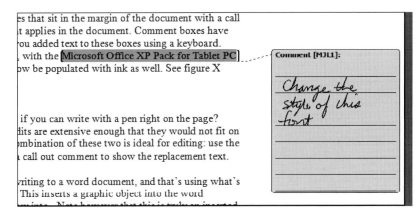

Figure 12-2.   Using Ink Comments box in Word 2003.

Why would you use a comments box if you can write with a pen right on the page? Again, they are useful if your intended ink additions are extensive enough that they would not fit on blank spaces in the page. Actually a combination of these two can be ideal for editing: use the pen to cross out and circle, then use a callout comment to show replacement text.

Ink Drawing and Writing Tool

A third way you can add ink writing to a Word document is using what's called the Ink Drawing and Writing tool. This inserts a graphic object into the Word document ready for you to write or draw into. Note however that this is truly an inserted object that moves existing text aside while you are working with it; it's good for adding a large block of comments but not useful for marking up words within the text (see Figure 12-3).

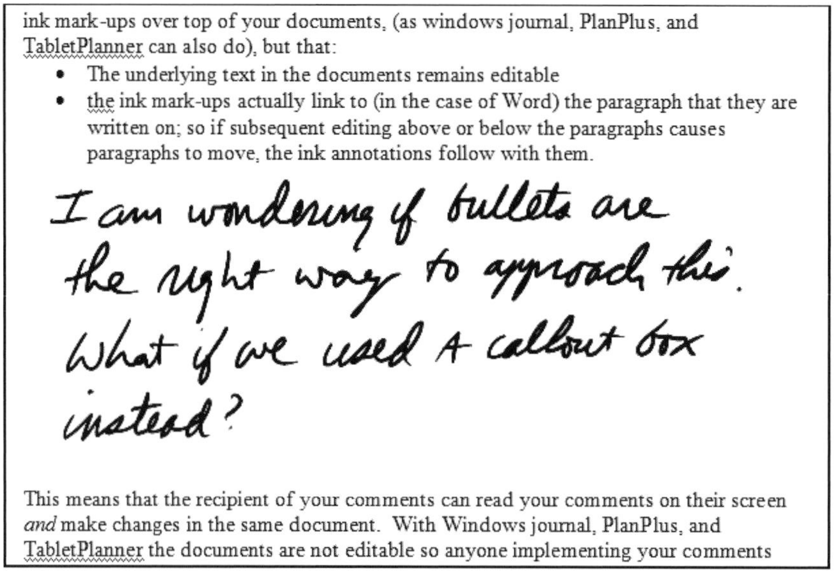

ink mark-ups over top of your documents, (as windows journal, PlanPlus, and TabletPlanner can also do), but that:

- The underlying text in the documents remains editable
- the ink mark-ups actually link to (in the case of Word) the paragraph that they are written on; so if subsequent editing above or below the paragraphs causes paragraphs to move, the ink annotations follow with them.

I am wondering if bullets are the right way to approach this. What if we used a callout box instead?

This means that the recipient of your comments can read your comments on their screen *and* make changes in the same document. With Windows journal, PlanPlus, and TabletPlanner the documents are not editable so anyone implementing your comments

Figure 12-3. Placing ink in a graphic object inserted with the Ink Drawing and Writing tool.

Where would one use the Ink Drawing and Writing tool? While the Annotation tool and Comment tool are designed for review and editing purposes, the Ink Drawing and Writing tool in contrast is intended for inserting original document content during the document creation stage. It certainly can be used for adding review comments as well, but with limits. You cannot use the Show/ Hide Comments and Markups controls to show and hide any ink you add with this tool. Rather the added ink becomes part of and indistinguishable from the original document.

In terms of original content the Ink Drawing and Writing tool is probably most useful for inserting hand sketches and script into the document. This is also the shared tool that Microsoft uses to create ink messages in Outlook.

Regarding using it for document markup, you might use it as above in Figure 12-3 to make extensive ink comments about an entire paragraph or page; you could place the object above or within that paragraph (it appears as a large blank rectangular frame) and write your comments within it. And while comment boxes may seem more appropriate for this, if you print a page with these boxes shown, it causes the rest of the text to print smaller. And ink comment boxes are only available in the Word module of Office 2003; they are not available in Excel or PowerPoint. So the Ink Drawing and Writing tool can have a place in the commenting workflow.

How to Insert Ink into Word 2003

Let's cover the mechanics of using these three kinds of ink markup capabilities.

How to Make Ink Annotations

You start ink annotations in Word by clicking on the Ink Annotations tool within Word's Standard toolbar; this tool appears as follows.

Clicking that button does two things: it changes the pen tip to a red felt tip marker ready for marking up your document, and it adds the Reviewing toolbar to the Word toolbar set, below the Standard toolbar (see Figure 12-4). The Reviewing toolbar has been expanded from previous versions of Word. It now includes a number of commands you'll need when working with Word 2003 ink annotations. For example you can delete all ink annotations using the reviewing Reject Change/Delete Comment tool. You can also hide and show all ink annotations using the Show command on the toolbar. Note that it also has the Ink Annotations tool included.

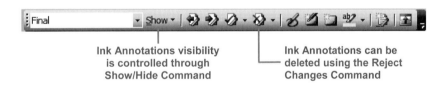

Figure 12-4.   In Word 2003 the Reviewing toolbar includes Ink Annotations controls.

Once you actually start drawing or writing on the document with the Ink Annotations pen, yet another floating toolbar appears on the screen called the Ink Annotations toolbar (see Figure 12-5). This toolbar gives commands you may need while the felt tip pen is active, such as changing colors, changing pen tips, and erasing ink. The Stop Inking button at the right end of this toolbar is how you exit the ink annotation mode.

Figure 12-5. The Ink Annotations floating toolbar is added while inserting ink annotations.

Alignment issues with Word 2003 Ink Annotation

All is not perfect with Word 2003 Ink Annotation; alignment problems can arise when you change the text in the document after the ink marks have been applied. Everything is usually fine if you change text in the paragraphs above and below the marked-up paragraph; in such cases if the annotated paragraph moves, the ink marks move with it. Problems arise when changes are made to the text in the *same* paragraph that the ink annotations are applied to. In this case as you add or delete words, and the paragraph text slides to compensate, the markings do not move with the moving text. As a result it may appear that different words have been commented. And even if you are careful to make text edits to a different paragraph there are occasional issues when a paragraph moves to the next page and the ink stays on the first page.

One strategy to avoid the impact of this during subsequent text editing is to advise your writer, when reacting to your annotations in any given paragraph, to make edits from the bottom of the paragraph up, deleting the annotations as he or she goes. Or the author could be instructed to print out a copy of the annotated document and to delete all on-screen annotations before the actual editing work begins.

How to Use the Ink Comments Box

None of these issues are present when using the Ink Comments tool. Adding ink comments is easy: you merely select the text you want to comment on and then from the Insert menu choose Ink Comment. If the Reviewing toolbar happens to be present you can also tap the Insert Ink Comment tool on that toolbar (see Figure 12-6).

Insert Ink Comments ——

Figure 12-6. The Insert Ink Comments tool on the Reviewing toolbar.

Either of these actions opens a comments window like that shown previously in Figure 12-2; into that window you simply write with your pen. Later you can use the Show command on the Reviewing toolbar to hide or show all of your inserted comment boxes.

Since comments display in the margin, if you print a document with comments, Word needs to automatically scale the document text smaller so that there is room in the margin to display the comments on the printed page.

How to Add Ink Using the Ink Drawing and Writing Tool

Using the Ink Drawing and Writing tool is a little more complex. Recall that it inserts a drawing canvas into your text. There are a couple of steps needed to activate this.

1 Select a point in the document where you want the Ink Drawing and Writing canvas box to appear; note that if this happens to be in the middle of the line that line will be split when the canvas is inserted; if in the middle of a paragraph that paragraph would split.

2 Go to the View menu, choose Toolbars, and add the Drawing toolbar to your collection of toolbars displayed within the Word window; it should appear at the bottom of the document window (see Figure 12-7).

Ink Drawing and Writing tool ──┐

Figure 12-7. The Drawing toolbar is used to activate the Ink Drawing and Writing tool.

3 From the Drawing toolbar tap on the Ink Drawing and Writing tool shown in Figure 12-7. A large blank canvas frame will appear within your document into which you can write and draw. A floating toolbar will also appear that gives you some control over your pen while you are writing in this frame (see Figure 12-8). Notice the similarity with the Ink Annotations toolbar in Figure 12-5.

Figure 12-8. The Ink Drawing and Writing floating toolbar is added while using the Ink Drawing and Writing tool.

4 After you finish writing, you can format the drawing canvas by right-clicking on the canvas and choosing Show Drawing Canvas Toolbar. This displays tools that allow you to apply changes to the frame as a whole (see Figure 12-9). Changes to the frame include resizing, scaling, and controlling how text wraps around the graphic.

You can even use the Text Wrapping tool at the right end of this Canvas toolbar (shown as the icon with the dog on it in Figure 12-9) to cause the writing box to overlay the text, which gets you pretty close to ink annotation capabilities. But keeping alignment correct can be difficult with this approach and it is not recommended for overlay annotations.

Figure 12-9. The Drawing Canvas floating toolbar can be added to adjust the canvas properties.

Inserting Ink into Excel 2003 and PowerPoint 2003

Both Excel 2003 and PowerPoint 2003 have the ability to insert ink annotations and to use the Ink Drawing and Writing tool, and both these tools behave the same as described above for Word 2003. For example ink annotations can be shown and hidden with the Reviewing toolbar, but marks added with the Ink Drawing and Writing tool become part of the drawing. However neither Excel nor PowerPoint allow inserting an Ink Comment box (both have text-based comment box capabilities only).

With PowerPoint 2003, ink can be added in all views except the Slide Sorter view; however the mode of ink entry is dependent upon which view you are in. This makes choosing your approach a bit confusing. For instance Slide Master view only allows use of the Ink Drawing and Writing tool. The Normal view (the editing view) allows use of that and use of the Ink Annotation tool. The Slide Show view has its own Pen tool that works essentially the same as the PowerPoint XP/2002 Slide Show Pen tool (see that section later in this chapter for details). Marks added in the Slide Show view are treated like annotations once back in the Normal view; they can be hidden and shown using the Show/Hide Markup controls on the Reviewing toolbar.

If that seems confusing, this should simplify things: assuming you will be working in the Normal view, which is the common editing view in Power-Point, ink annotations are probably your best choice for markup purposes. The tools look and act identical to those in Word 2003.

Using Microsoft Office XP (2002) with the Microsoft Office XP Pack for Tablet PC

If you are currently using Microsoft Office XP (also called Office 2002) Microsoft did make a moderate effort towards adding pen editing capabilities to this software suite. With the release of the Tablet PC, Microsoft released an add-on for Office XP to enable pen markups of documents. This add-on software, called Microsoft Office XP Pack for Tablet PC, installed some limited pen capabilities into the Office suite of software. Tablet PC users can take advantage of these capabilities for their editing needs.

Should you choose to install this add-on software pack (available as a free download from the Microsoft website) the good news is that this add-on allows you to place pen marks and writing on your Office documents. The bad news is you cannot annotate on top of existing text, which I feel is a minimum requirement for marking up text. Rather with this add-on pack you are limited to the Ink Drawing and Writing tool, and the Ink Comments tool. These two features are described fully in the Office 2003 section above.

These approaches are still effective for use when the pen is all you have to work with (such as in meetings), just not as interesting as using true ink annotations.

There is one exception to this: Microsoft Office XP Pack for Tablet PC does add the ability to overlay pen mark-ups anywhere on PowerPoint presentations; this capability is truly useful and is discussed below.

Marking Up PowerPoint XP Documents Using the Microsoft Office XP Pack for Tablet PC

While the Microsoft Office XP Pack for Tablet PC falls short of providing true pen markup capability to most Office XP applications, it does succeed with PowerPoint documents. No need to import PowerPoint documents into Windows Journal for markup, you can do this right from the PowerPoint application.

The trick however is that you need to do this from the Slide Show mode to be successful; ironically, you cannot do it from the document editing mode (called the Normal view in PowerPoint). The reason: this marking capability was originally envisioned for use *during* a presentation, to emphasize the message of slide elements. Luckily any marks you make in that mode can be saved, and so this becomes an effective markup capability.

Assuming you have the Microsoft Office XP Pack for Tablet PC installed, launch the PowerPoint document you intend to mark up. Then choose View Show from the Slide Show menu, and navigate ahead to the slide you want to mark up. When ready to apply marks, activate the PowerPoint in-context menu button by hovering your pen near the lower left corner of the Power-Point slide. In PowerPoint XP/2002 it looks like this:

And in Office PowerPoint 2003 the set looks like this:

Click on this button (in 2003 click on the pen symbol), and the following popup menu appears (see Figure 12-10):

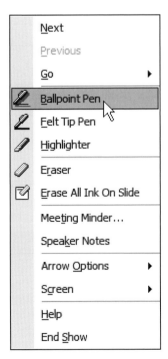

Figure 12-10. In PowerPoint, from the Slide Show mode, you can activate various writing tools.

All of the choices in this menu that have an icon next to them are useful for pen markups of the PowerPoint slides. After you choose one of the three drawing tools, you can simply draw on the slide, right on your screen.

While you have one of the drawing tools selected in the PowerPoint XP version, a small Ink toolbar will appear in the lower left corner of the PowerPoint screen (see Figure 12-11):

Figure 12-11. PowerPoint XP Ink toolbar, visible while drawing in the slide show mode.

The right button on this window allows you to change the color used for the currently selected drawing tool. The left button allows you to get the arrow cursor back, which you may need to do in order to progress to the next slide. In PowerPoint 2003 you right-click anywhere on the presentation screen to reach these same tools

Note that if you are actually in the middle of giving a PowerPoint presentation to a group, say using a projector, these marks appear on the projected image. This is an effective way to emphasize portions of your slide (especially using the yellow highlighting tool) or to add contextual information during the presentation.

Once done with the markups, when you finish the slide show PowerPoint XP presents you with the following dialog box (see Figure 12-12).

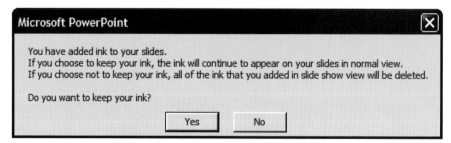

Figure 12-12. After marking up a PowerPoint presentation, you will be asked if you want to save that ink.

A similar message is presented in PowerPoint 2003. If you truly made the drawing marks on the slides as a way to pen-edit the document, you'll want to answer yes to this question; if these were just marks made as emphasis during a presentation, you'll probably want to answer no.

Marking Up Outlook Messages

In both Outlook 2003 and 2002 (the latter with the Tablet Pak added), if you have specified Word as your e-mail editor you can add ink to messages. You can in fact handwrite your messages. However the Ink Annotation tool is not available; rather the Ink Drawing and Writing tool is your main approach.

What to Do if You Have Earlier Versions of Microsoft Office

If your organization is really behind the times, and the only Office software available for installation on your tablet is pre–Office XP, there is still one possible solution. An add-on product called PenOffice for Microsoft Windows (www.paragraph.com) advertises an ability to add ink annotations to versions of Word as early as Word 97. I have not tested this, but it is an option worth researching.

Also note that Word 2003 documents are supposed to be backward compatible with versions of Word as early as Word 97. You do not need do a "Save As" to earlier formats (though there are some features you may need to block if passing to Word 97). So if you would like to use Word 2003 on your tablet, that should not cause major disruptions when exchanging files with colleagues using older software. However if you will be tracking changes or using Word's Compare and Merge Documents command, I have had trouble merging Word 97 documents into Word 2003; so anticipate some issues.

Using Windows Journal to Mark Up Documents

If you do not own a copy of Office 2003, or if the documents you are marking up were not originated in Microsoft Office, are there other easy ways to use your Tablet PC and pen to mark up and share edited documents? Of course, and the solution is your favorite application: Windows Journal.

In the chapter on note taking we mentioned the ability to import documents into Windows Journal and use them as background templates to write on top of. And in the chapter on power documents we mentioned document import into Journal as a basis for a document binder approach. You can use this same import capability to easily import and mark up documents.

Once the documents are imported into Windows Journal, you can mark them up with any of the drawing or highlighting tools. You can scratch through text, you can circle text, and you can highlight text in yellow or other colors. And furthermore, once the documents are imported into Windows Journal, you can search on the text within the imported document. This is useful if the edited document is many pages long and you need to find segments via text search. It is also useful if you want to locate a repeated word so you can mark every instance of it.

And once marked up, you can print the document with the markings or e-mail the marked document to your colleague for review. Your colleague does not need to have a Tablet PC or any special software other than Internet Explorer (5.0 or greater) to view the document with its pen markings.

Importing Documents into Windows Journal by "Printing"

The easiest way to import a document into Windows Journal is to open the document in its originating program, and then "print" the document into Windows Journal. This approach is covered in several of the previous chapters; for example in Chapter 10 see the section titled Importing Documents into Your Windows Journal Document System on page 383.

Marking Up Documents in Windows Journal

Once opened, you can use all of Windows Journal's writing devices to mark and add content to the imported document. There's virtually no limitation. Here's an example of a Word document imported into Windows Journal and marked up using Journal's pen and highlighter tools (see Figure 12-13).

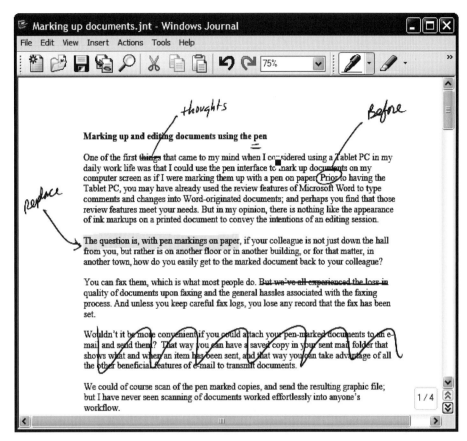

Figure 12-13. Windows Journal page with markups.

Some Limitations

Compared to Office 2003 there are some limitations. Note that once the file is opened in Windows Journal the imported document becomes a nonchange-able background image. All you can do is add to the document image by marking on top of it with the drawing, and highlighting tools. You could even add text using a text box. However this added material exists in a layer above the original text. So you cannot actually *remove* original text using the Eraser tool, nor *change* original text using the Text tool. If changing text is your goal, you will need to do this using a traditional editing approach within the original program that created the document.

Nor can you insert space in the document text using the Insert/Remove Space tool in Journal. For example, suppose you want to add space for more comments in among what you have written. If you attempt this after doing some pen-based editing, watch out. This has the highly undesirable result of sliding all your document markings down the page away from the text that you had intended to mark up. Not recommended.

Sharing Windows Journal Marked-Up Documents

Once done editing, you should save the file. And if your colleague has a Tablet PC you can now e-mail the document to the colleague as is. The colleague can simply open the document in Windows Journal to view or print. Using the Send To command from the File menu makes this a one-step process.

If the colleague does not have a Tablet PC, you can do one of two things. You can send the Microsoft Windows Journal Viewer application to your colleague. This is a free application that opens Windows Journal documents on any Windows computer. This application can be downloaded from the Microsoft.com/downloads web site (see the Appendix).

Or you can use the Export As... command under the Windows Journal File menu to save the document as a Web Archive file (.mht, see Figure 12-14). This enables the document to open as a graphic image within Internet Explorer once it reaches your colleague. Version 5.0 or later of Internet Explorer is required, for both Macintosh and PC.

Figure 12-14. The Windows Journal Export command gives you two file formats to choose from.

You'll notice in Figure 12-14 you are offered another file choice when exporting the file (.tif); I do not recommend using that format, however. It allows a higher resolution image, but when used in the Windows Journal Export command it loses color information in the translation.

Another Way to Import

By the way, an alternative method for importing documents into Windows Journal is to use the Import command under the File menu. The equivalent of this is to tap the Import icon on the standard Windows Journal toolbar. Once you do, the Import dialog box is presented. Using that dialog you must find the document you want to import by navigating through its view of your folder system (see Figure 12-15).

Figure 12-15. Using the Windows Journal Import command to import documents is an alternative to using the print method.

Once the filename is found and selected, you click the Import button in the lower right of this dialog box. Windows Journal then briefly launches the original program that created the file and automatically executes the print to Journal Note Writer step we saw in Chapter 10 (Importing Documents into Your Windows Journal Document System, page 383). It then opens the imported file in Windows Journal ready for your markup steps.

I do not use this import command method of importing documents as often as the print method. This is because I often find it difficult to navigate through the folder system in search of a file using the Import dialog box. To locate the file that I want to import it's usually easier for me to just launch that file and use the Print command. In fact, I usually have the file open at the moment I decide I want to mark it up, so printing from there is a natural next step.

Marking Up Documents Using PlanPlus 2.0

Marking up documents using PlanPlus 2.0 is easy. You merely import the document as an eBinder document as if you are adding it to your power documents collection (using the by-now familiar virtual printer approach described in Chapter 10). Once opened you can then use any of the drawing tools to write on top of the document (see Figure 12-16).

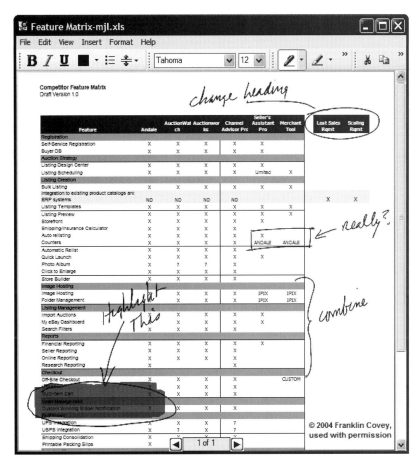

Figure 12-16.   Marking up documents in PlanPlus.

After editing you can then, from the PowerNotes window, use the File menu and choose the Send To command to either e-mail the document back to the author or save it as a file on your own computer. As with Windows Journal you need to be alert as to what file format you send or save this as. You have three choices presented to you in the Save As... dialog box (see Figure 12-17):

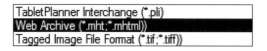

Figure 12-17. Three file formats are available for sharing PlanPlus documents.

If you're sending it to another PlanPlus user or a TabletPlanner user, you can save it in the TabletPlanner Interchange format (which allows later editing). Otherwise choose the Web Archive format so that your recipient can open it within Microsoft Internet Explorer 5.0 or later. Or choose .tif to enable a wider variety of file viewers.

Most of the same limitations apply as are true with Windows Journal:

- You cannot edit the underlying document when you mark it up.

- Recipients do not get back an editable version of the document. They will need to print out your marked-up copy and then launch the original document for editing.

Unlike with Windows Journal, the .tif choice retains color information.

You can also send the edited note file from the PowerNotes file list view, which causes the notes to be copied into the body of the Outlook mail message (see page 281 for instructions). This is an included image, not an attachment, so your recipient will see the full page of notes within the e-mail when they open it in Outlook or Outlook Express. This approach is the simplest way to send notes if you know your recipient uses Outlook; results could be unpredictable with non-Outlook users.

Marking Up Documents Using TabletPlanner 3.0

Like PlanPlus, The FranklinCovey TabletPlanner software can also be used to mark up documents. Again, you simply insert the document as an eBinder document. We have reviewed how to import documents into TabletPlanner in Chapter 10 of this book.

Once imported you then use the FranklinCovey PowerNotes drawing tools to mark it up (see Figure 12-18).

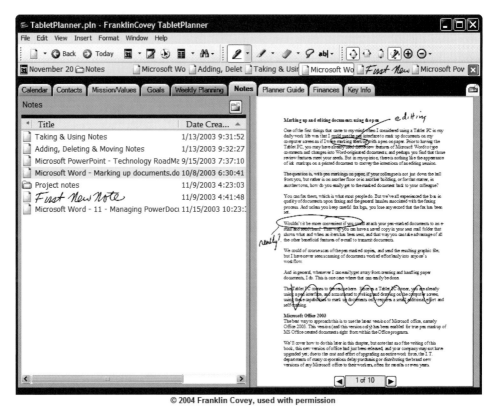

Figure 12-18. Marking up documents in TabletPlanner.

And again, once marked up, just like PlanPlus you use the File, Send To command to export the document, and you have the same three file format choices. Same limitations described immediately above for PlanPlus apply.

Marking Up Documents Using Adobe Acrobat

In Chapter 10 we described how to use Adobe Acrobat to create an electronic binder of documents. We also mentioned that if needed you could mark up documents using the Pencil tool within Adobe Acrobat. In earlier versions of Acrobat, the Pencil tool was poorly optimized for the kind of writing that the Tablet PC does. As of recent updates to version 6, however, the writing is much better but still far short of the other applications. It is also limited by only having two writing tools—the pencil and the highlighter—and of course an eraser tool. And the pencil offers only one color (red) and one thickness (fine). Because of these limitations Adobe Acrobat is not my favored method for marking up documents.

If you do decide to use Acrobat version 6, you'll need to add the relevant toolbars to the document window using the View, Toolbars menu. The Highlighting tool is found on the Commenting toolbar, and the Pencil and Eraser tools are found on the Advanced Commenting toolbar (see Figure 12-19).

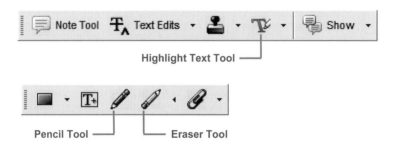

Figure 12-19. The Commenting and Advanced Commenting toolbars in Acrobat version 6 contain tools useful for pen-based mark up.

Adobe Acrobat also includes a full range of review input and tracking tools similar to Microsoft Word, but you'll need to use a keyboard to take full advantage of them. And all participants will need to own a full copy of Acrobat.

Marking Up Documents Using Microsoft OneNote

One of the criticisms of Microsoft OneNote is that you cannot import a document into it as a background object as you can with Windows Journal and the FranklinCovey PowerNote approach. This is true; there is no background image import capability with OneNote. And so it would seem that there's no way to use OneNote for annotating documents.

But after a little experimentation I have found you can import and annotate some documents, although not as cleanly as you can with the other applications.

Ink Annotations

While you cannot import a document as a background image within One-Note, you can easily import the contents of a document from an application like Word, retaining all the formatting and graphics. All you do is select the text in Word, copy it, open a OneNote document, choose the Selection tool, and choose Paste. The text is copied into one large OneNote container, with text formatting and images intact. The only difference is that margins may act differently and the text may wrap at a different point in the sentences. Otherwise the document is complete.

Once the document is imported like this, all you need to do now is to click on the Pen tool and start making your annotations in ink on top of the text document.

Below is a sample of such a document imported out of Microsoft Word with ink annotations applied on top (see Figure 12-20).

The advantage of this approach over say Windows Journal is that the underlying text remains "editable." However if you actually make edits that change the underlying text significantly, and the words move, the markings will be misaligned with the text. So the best way to use this is to print the document with the markings, remove the markings from the OneNote document, and then edit the text. This approach at least keeps the editable text and edited markups transmitted in one document, even if you do need to split them to make changes.

Not all documents will copy into OneNote cleanly though, so use this with caution. And the recipient needs to own a copy of OneNote.

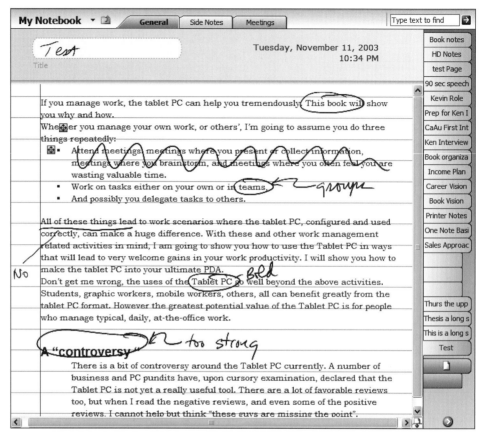

Figure 12-20.   Marking up documents in OneNote.

Audio Annotations

Here's another good use for the audio recording capabilities of Microsoft OneNote that we reviewed in Chapter 9. Import a document into OneNote using the steps above and then, at points within the document that you have comments, click with the Selection tool and record an audio comment. These audio comments are clearly marked wherever they occur and can be played back by your recipient by clicking on the recorder symbol. (Clearly your recipient needs a copy of OneNote.)

Why use audio annotations? Speed and large volume of notes are the main reasons. It's often easier just to dictate thoughts than to write them down clearly, especially if you have lots of ideas. This is most useful if each of your comments is fairly long; single word edits would not be practical with this approach.

Following is a sample of a document imported into OneNote with an audio note added in the middle of it; see the audio time stamp about one-third down the page (see Figure 12-21).

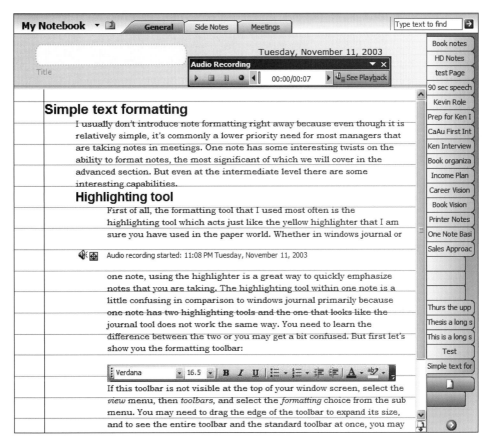

Figure 12-21. Using audio notes in OneNote.

Marking Up Documents Using Microsoft Office Document Imaging

One more solution deserves mentioning, and that's the Microsoft Office Document Imaging tool. This separate application ships with Microsoft Office. Once Office is installed this application can be found under the Microsoft Office Tools menu, within the All Programs portion of the Windows XP Start menu. This software behaves very much like Windows Journal and Franklin-Covey PowerNotes for document import and markup. Just like these software packages, the document to be marked up is printed to a file using a virtual printer driver (called Microsoft Office Document Image Writer within your printer list). And like these packages, the resulting file is opened in an editing environment that allows drawing tools to be used to annotate over the top of the text (see Figure 12-22).

Advantages

The advantage when compared with Windows Journal and PowerNotes becomes apparent when sharing the documents with non–Tablet PC users. Since this tool is part of the Office installation, recipients who own Office can open the document in the document's native Microsoft Document Imaging format. There's no need, prior to sending, for conversion of the document to TIFF or Web Archive formats, as is needed when exporting from Windows Journal or PowerNotes. Because Microsoft Document Imaging is the native format, recipients can add more ink or text annotations and, surprisingly, they can extract the text from the underlying document. This is in contrast with Windows Journal and PowerNotes where the underlying document is completely frozen and its contents unavailable.

This latter capability, to extract text, is made possible by an optical character recognition (OCR) engine built into the Microsoft Document Imaging solution. The OCR engine allows recipients to select text-graphics from the underlying document image and convert the selected image to editable text as it is copied into other applications. Or recipients can export the entire underlying document to Microsoft Word with text converted and with formatting and embedded graphics retained. Such an export is subject to the inaccuracies of OCR, so a better solution if access to original text is needed is to also send the original document to the recipient. But the capability is a handy backup in case the two documents become separated.

If you have a scanner you can scan documents directly into the Microsoft Office Document Imaging application, mark them up with your tablet pen, and then send them out as native documents or as faxes. This latter capability is useful for document markup by tablet users when only the printed copy of a document is available.

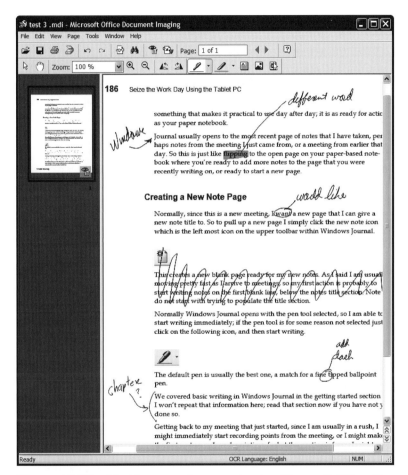

Figure 12-22. Marking up a document using Microsoft Office Document Imaging.

Complications

One complication with using Microsoft Office Document Imaging for sharing marked-up documents is that with the release of Office 2003, Microsoft created a new file format (.mdi) to use with Microsoft Office Document Imaging documents. This new format creates a much cleaner and sharper text document when compared with the previously used format (.tif). The new format is so much better that I do not recommend using the earlier .tif format. If you want to exchange files with recipients who do not have Office 2003, however, you'll need to save and distribute the files in the old, less clear .tif format. Because of this, this solution is really only useful if all your colleagues have standardized on Office 2003.

Original Intended Use of This Software

By the way, the reason this Microsoft Office Document Imaging solution exists in the first place is not because of the Tablet PC, but rather because Microsoft sees this as a tool to be used with faxed and scanned documents. This tool gives fax recipients who can receive faxes directly to their computer as computer-based images (many can these days) a way to mark up the fax and distribute it, without having to print the fax out first. It also gives them a way to extract text from the fax image.

Should You Use Microsoft Office Document Imaging?

So should you use the solution instead of Windows Journal or PowerNotes for marking up and sharing documents? It's really a toss-up. When you export a marked-up document from Windows Journal or PowerNotes for a non–tablet-using recipient, you will probably be using the web archive format (.mht) as described earlier in this chapter. This means that your recipient will be viewing the marked-up document with Microsoft Internet Explorer. If the recipient is only going to view or print the document then this is fine, and the Microsoft Office Document Imaging approach offers no advantages. If there's a chance however that the recipient may want to do further markups on the document or extract underlying text, then the Microsoft Office Document Imaging approach is clearly the way to go. But only if your recipient owns Office 2003.

And if you have a paper document that you want to scan, mark up electronically, and e-mail out to other Office 2003 users, then this application combined with a scanner is an excellent solution. Adobe Acrobat competes with this latter business case, by the way, and is not limited to Office 2003 users. But Acrobat is not a free application and has limited ink markup tools.

Chapter 13 Better Presentations

The Tablet Advantage

Presentations are now a regular part of a work manager's day. Whether for sales purposes or for internal communications, using PowerPoint to create and show presentation slides is a skill the work manager needs to quickly master. Compared with a laptop and desktop, the Tablet PC can give you a significant advantage while giving, creating, and editing your presentations.

■ **While giving presentations**: The greatest improvements show up in your ability to give interactive presentations in which you can write on and highlight slides for emphasis during the presentation. Writing on slides during on-screen brainstorming in working sessions is also effective. This can be done in PowerPoint, but Windows Journal offers an even better presentation capability that takes greatest advantage of these features.

■ **While creating presentations**: The MindManager software covered in Chapter 11 provides a phenomenal capability to create PowerPoint presentations quickly. Presentations that may normally take a day to create can be created in hours.

■ **While editing presentations**: Pen-based editing of PowerPoint presentation documents is an effective way to edit others' work. Given the mixture of graphics and text in the typical PowerPoint document, typed edits can easily get lost on the page. Marking them in ink solves this problem — and it is easy to do while in a meeting.

Of these three, the most impressive is the second item: creating presentations quickly using Mind Manager's PowerPoint export feature. Step-by-step instructions are given in this chapter.

Giving Presentations

The tablet gives you the ability to write and draw on the presentation while you are speaking:

■ Highlight key text with a yellow highlighter as you talk about it (see Figure 13-1).

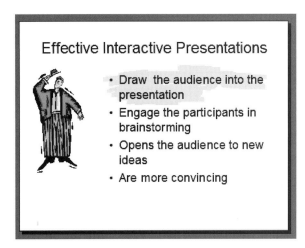

Figure 13-1. Highlighting text during a presentation draws the audience into the point you are making.

■ Circle text, draw arrows, and underline—all for emphasis during the presentation (see Figure 13-2).

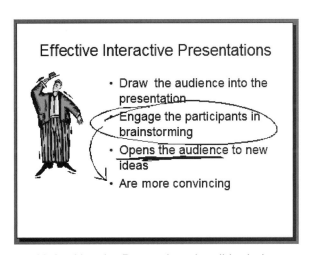

Figure 13-2. Use the Pen tool on the slide during a presentation to emphasize relationships.

Handwritten text might look a little tacky during a formal presentation, but it has its place:

- Short words with arrows drawn to key portions of the presentation are appropriate (see Figure 13-3).

- Recording notes or suggestions from your audience is also appropriate — it shows you are engaged.

- Editing during an informal review of the presentation makes sense.

- And entering text while brainstorming in a working session is useful.

Figure 13-3.   Handwritten text can be effective if used in small amounts.

See Chapter 12 again for instructions on how to write and draw on a slide within a PowerPoint presentation. Remember, with Office 2003 you can mark up within all the views of PowerPoint. In Office XP you can only mark up a slide within the Slide Show mode.

The Tablet PC Also Changes the Dynamics of the Presentation Environment

Think Creatively, Out of the Box

To fully appreciate the benefits the Tablet PC brings to presentations, you need to think creatively.

■ Imagine being able to walk around the room with the Tablet PC held in your arm while giving a presentation; projectors are available with wireless adapters that make this possible.

■ In a one-on-one sales presentation, without a projector, imagine holding the tablet in your hand as you show a presentation to a sales prospect right on the screen of the tablet. This provides a more personal touch then a laptop does. Consider handing the tablet to the prospect and letting him or her flip the pages using the hardware buttons. The high-tech impact of holding and using a Tablet PC for the first time can be impressive.

Tips for Giving a Presentation with the Tablet PC and PowerPoint

The projector connections required with your Tablet PC are essentially the same as using any other Windows XP laptop. However, remember for a slate tablet it is likely that you'll not have a keyboard plugged into the tablet. So be sure to practice on your own before your first audience presentation to learn how to do various activities:

■ Practice switching between the tablet screen and the projector screen.

■ If you need to display previous slides you will likely use the cursor hardware buttons on your tablet for navigation. Be sure you become accustomed to using these buttons before your first presentation.

■ For any other keyboard uses you have been accustomed to, consider how you might accomplish these. Mapping some keys to your tablet hardware buttons is one option.

■ Be sure to switch the tablet to primary landscape mode before starting your presentation. If you project on the wall while in portrait mode, the presentation will be projected sideways. And if you use secondary landscape, the presentation will be projected upside down!

Using Windows Journal as Your Presentation Tool

What I do after creating a presentation in PowerPoint is import the presentation into Windows Journal, and then give the presentation from within Windows Journal. After doing this once, I will now never go back to Power-

Point as the primary presentation mode. I suggest you try this at least once also. Why is this approach so much better than a straight presentation from PowerPoint? Here's why:

- I like to use the highlighting marker during presentations for emphasis. Windows Journal has more usable and flexible pen and highlighter tools than PowerPoint for marking up during the presentation. For example the yellow highlighting pen in PowerPoint XP with Tablet Pack has only one width. It's too narrow for the large fonts normally used within PowerPoint; with Windows Journal you can choose much larger markers. This feature alone made up my mind. The other pens and tools have more options as well.

- With Windows Journal I can have multiple presentations available at once and switch easily between them. With PowerPoint you have to exit the view Slide Show mode, which puts you in the rather busy normal (edit) mode, before you can switch to other presentations.

- The PowerPoint Slide Show mode, while it nicely blanks out the rest of the screen during the presentation, removes access to all other Windows applications and Tablet PC tools. Windows Journal gives you freer rein with this.

- The Windows Journal Page Bar (see Setup section below) is a nice way to have a subtle tool constantly on-screen that allows you to jump quickly to pages. It is also useful to indicate how far you have progressed in the presentation and how many slides remain.

- With Windows Journal you can at any time bring up a blank page to do some free-form brainstorming, perhaps in reaction to spontaneous thoughts in the meeting. You can't do this in PowerPoint.

- While presenting a Journal-created slide in Windows Journal, you can edit and move Journal text and graphics around. You need to return to PowerPoint's normal (edit) mode to do that with PowerPoint objects, and the PowerPoint normal mode is not the friendliest-looking presentation mode.

- And, as an on-screen free-form brainstorming tool, Windows Journal projected on a wall during a working meeting is unbeatable. Think of all the tools you have for drawing sketches, org charts, and process flows and for taking notes. Unlike with a real whiteboard, everything you draw or write is instantly recorded in your computer for later editing and distribution. It is instantly shareable with remote meeting attendees.

How to Set Up Windows Journal as Your Presentation Tool

Chapters 10 and 12 give instructions on how to import documents into Windows Journal. The same approach should be used for presentations. With your presentation open in PowerPoint, use the Print command from the File menu, and from within the printer list choose Journal Note Writer, then click OK. You will then be asked what name to use and where to save the new Journal document. Then Windows Journal will launch with your presentation displayed. Very easy.

Setup

To set up Windows Journal for ideal presentation format, do the following just before your presentation:

- Within Windows Journal, switch to full screen mode (View menu, Full Screen). This is similar to the view slide show mode of PowerPoint in that it hides all applications other than Windows Journal but it is less restrictive. Note that Windows Journal menus and toolbars are still visible, which is good because you'll need access to these to mark up the document. You may consider customizing these toolbars so that everything you have is available for your presentation and nothing else. Commands to access highlighter and pens are still available through menus so you may even consider removing all toolbars to remove distractions.

- Activate the page bar (View menu, Page Bar). As mentioned above, this relatively innocuous on-screen tool enables you to jump to selected pages in the middle of the presentation.

- Turn Reading View on (View menu, Reading view). This enables you to use the physical arrow buttons on your Tablet PC to flip through pages one at a time.

- Close the Tablet PC Input Panel; you won't need it and it will just be a distraction.

- And make sure the appropriate screen orientation is on your Tablet PC; landscape is required if you are using a projector.

Creating Presentations Quickly on the Tablet PC Using MindManager

The Tablet PC combined with MindManager gives you the ability to create PowerPoint presentations very quickly. The technique to do this was alluded to in Chapter 11, and a full description is provided here. I have under very tight timeframes created formal-looking presentations in a matter of minutes. Imagine being halfway through your 10 AM meeting and suddenly realizing that you need to prepare a PowerPoint presentation for an 11 AM meeting. Using this approach, you could pull this off.

Overview

Here's a brief overview of how to do this: Launch the MindManager software; using the Pen mode of MindManager, draw out your business map and convert it to text (refer to Chapter 11 for instructions on using MindManager). Once the map is done, take time to rearrange the main branches around the topic title to match the set and order of slides that you would like to present. During export, MindManager will begin reading the map from the upper right quadrant, so that's where you should place your first topic. Then use the Export to PowerPoint function in MindManager. This export function intelligently creates and formats slides based on the hierarchical relationship of the topics.

The key to why this works so well is that you are likely to find that Mind-Manager allows you to do a very rapid topic brain dump, often in a matter of minutes. This is due to the way business mapping opens the creative channels and avoids the writer's block so common when creating presentations. And a business map provides a better tool to rearrange and structure the relationship and flow of your topics.

Once the topic text is in the map, the subsequent export to PowerPoint is nearly fully automatic. Very little manual intervention is required to create a completed, formatted presentation. How good is the appearance of the presentation that's created? I wouldn't use the first result for a formal sales presentation, but I have no problem using an unedited presentation for an internal meeting.

Exporting into PowerPoint

From the previous chapter you already know how to create a business map using MindManager, so let's assume that you have one ready. I'm going to use an actual business map that I created in my previous role running an IT department of an eCommerce firm. We were having some operational issues and I needed to very quickly create a presentation on those issues for an internal meeting. That business map is below (see Figure 13-4); it's a little complicated and compressed, so don't mind the details. I show it here just to demonstrate how much can be created in less than an hour, initially using a pen interface on MindManager for the Tablet PC and then converting to text within the MindManager application.

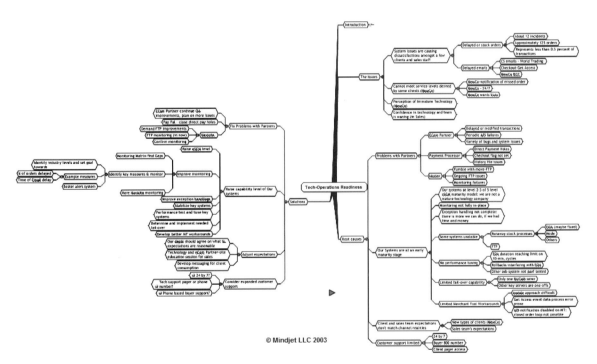

© Mindjet LLC 2003

Figure 13-4. A business map created in less than one hour, to be converted to a PowerPoint presentation.

Then, with virtually no editing or intervention, I created a full set of Power-Point slides using MindManager's Export to PowerPoint function. The first few slides of that presentation I will show below.

Export Steps

1   An early optional step of running this export function is to choose a PowerPoint design template from PowerPoint's standard templates. This is to give the slides a little color and to guide the format of the text portions of the slides. If you want to do this, before you start the export process, open PowerPoint, examine the design templates available, and identify the name of the template you're interested in. That way, when MindManager displays a scrolling list of PowerPoint template names to choose from, you know which to pick. To prepare for this, in Power-Point choose New from the File menu, and click on From Design Template in the task pane. PowerPoint will display a list of template thumbnails; memorize the text name of the one you like. Then exit PowerPoint. A simple template was chosen in the slides below.

2   With your business map open within MindManager click on the Export to PowerPoint tool in the lower right corner of the MindManager screen (see Figure 13-5).

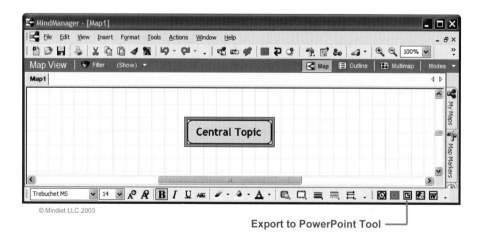

Figure 13-5.   The Export to PowerPoint tool.

3   You'll be asked where to save it and what name to use when you save the resulting PowerPoint document. You'll then see the following dialog box (see Figure 13-6). This is where you have a chance to choose a PowerPoint design template. If you wish to use one, select the second radio button at the top. The wording of the choice between the first and second radio buttons is a little deceiving; even if you choose the second radio button the topic styles in your business map will still be carried to the presentation, which is normally what you want. The second bullet adds PowerPoint template themes to those map styles.

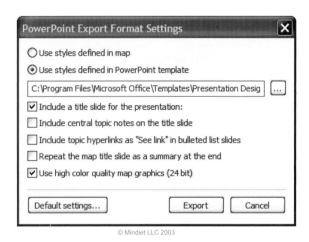

© Mindjet LLC 2003

Figure 13-6.   Select the second bullet and then pick a PowerPoint Template using the Browse button (...) that shows at the right side of the screen.

4 After clicking the second radio button, click the Browse button to the right (the small button with three dots in it) and find the template name you memorized earlier.

5 Once you've chosen the PowerPoint design template, click the Export button on that window. You'll see the software work for a few seconds as it lays out your slides behind the scenes. When it is completed you'll see the following dialog box (see Figure 13-7); choose Open to launch Power-Point and display your new presentation.

© Mindiet LLC 2003

Figure 13-7. At the end of export you are notified. Click the Open button to launch PowerPoint.

The Results

Looking at your newly created presentation you will see, after the optional title slide, an overview slide that gives the title of the map and the root level view of the business map (see Figure 13-8). This slide is a great way to set a context and give a high-level view of the presentation. If you do not like the particular look of the map's graphic elements, MindManager has a nearly unlimited number of design elements to choose from. You make this change in the original business map prior to exporting (from the Format menu choose Topic Shape and Color..., and also choose Topic Layout...). And you can choose not to use the MindManager graphics at all; you can use only a traditional PowerPoint outline view (from the MindManager Format menu, choose PowerPoint Export Settings..., more on that below). But I find the business map images to be very powerful.

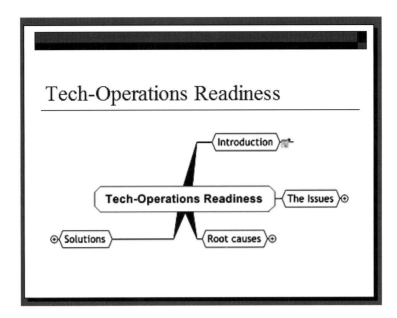

Figure 13-8.   The automatically created Overview slide.

The next slide (see Figure 13-9) takes the topic notes from the first topic (upper right quadrant) and displays it along with the name of the topic (Introduction). I had purposely made the first topic on my business map an introduction topic and placed some topic notes there. In MindManager you use the Topic Notes button to add a virtually unlimited amount of notes to any topic:

These notes are normally hidden in MindManager unless you choose to display them in your business map. They are a handy way to create an introduction slide in your PowerPoint presentation.

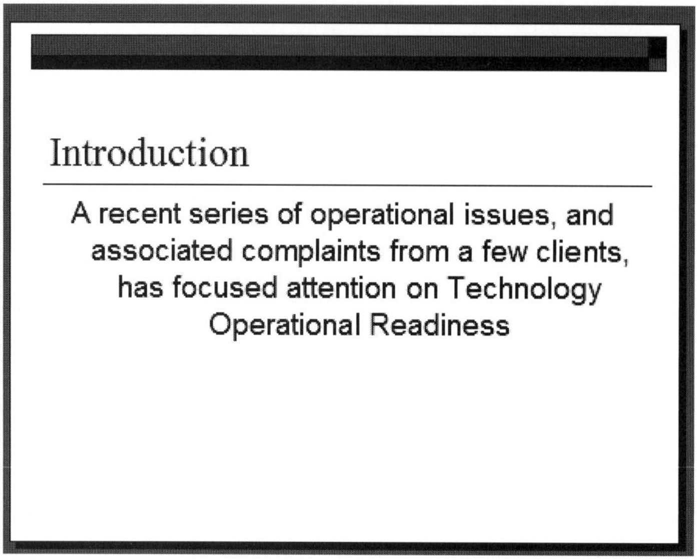

Figure 13-9. The text on the introduction slide comes from the "topic notes" stored with that topic in the business map.

The next automatically created slide takes the next topic along with its sub-topics, and it shows those subtopics while maintaining the central topic view (see Figure 13-10); this allows the audience to continue to see the context of the overall presentation. This is a good way to step through a complicated set of topics while keeping the audience clear about the place of each slide within the overall presentation.

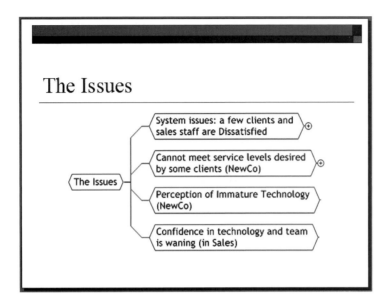

Figure 13-10. Using automatic settings, the first-level topics are displayed in map format.

Below that level, if using automatic settings, the export starts using bullets and subbullets. As you can see, the title comes from that of the first subtopic in the slide before it (see Figure 13-11).

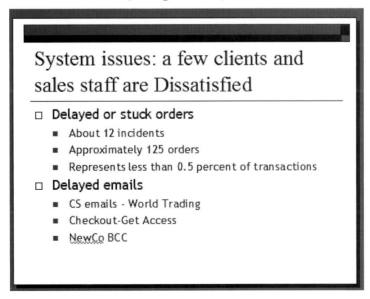

Figure 13-11. A bulleted list is created automatically during the export.

In a matter of seconds, a total of seventeen slides just like these were automatically created with no editing. Note that while this would not be suitable for a sales presentation, this is not bad for an automatically created presentation generated from a quickly created set of brainstorming notes. It is certainly good enough to use in an internal meeting. And, in fact, if you did have time to edit the slides, you could turn this into a first-class presentation.

Modifying Export Settings

The formatting above was achieved using the default (automatic) settings. If you want to vary which topics appear as outline slides and which as graphic, or change other settings that MindManager uses during this export, do this: First select the topic(s) within MindManager that you want to influence. Then under the MindManager Format menu, choose PowerPoint Export Settings... and alter the settings for that topic. I recommend trying out each of the Slide Layout settings available (see Figure 13-12). After some experimentation you can set the export rules to create a variety of formatted maps.

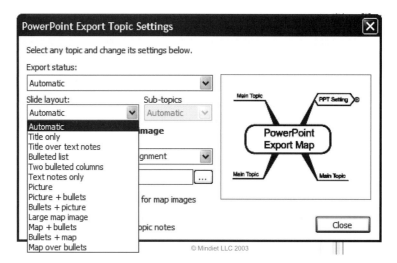

Figure 13-12. The Slide Layout drop-down menu on the PowerPoint Export Topic Settings dialog box provides a wide range of customizations to your export process.

Also note that the best strategy for *editing* these presentations is to go back to the business map within MindManager and make the necessary changes there, and then reexport into PowerPoint. There is no way to import Power-

Point slides back into MindManager so be sure you are done with the business map before you start editing the slides themselves.

Using the Presentation Mode of MindManager

MindManager also has a very nice built-in presentation mode which allows you to present your business maps in a step-by-step fashion directly from the MindManager application. This is ideal for projecting on a screen directly from the MindManager application. This presentation mode automatically starts at an overview level. And then as you advance through the presentation, it displays a slidelike view of topics, marching around the entire map. The software focuses on and expands subtopics as it goes. This provides an excellent set of speaking notes while maintaining the big picture view for the audience.

If your presentation is being made as part of a working group session, this presentation mode has the added advantage of enabling you to capture group feedback on the fly into the map. When group members see their ideas and input reflected in the meeting map, they tend to get much more engaged in the process and committed to its success.

Presentation mode is available under the Modes menu of MindManager.

In Conclusion: Do All This within a Meeting

The benefits listed above are the direct advantages that Tablet PC has for creating presentations. There are many *indirect* benefits as well. For example all the advantages that the Tablet PC offers you to leverage free time within meetings can be applied toward creating presentations within those meetings. All the steps described above for creating a presentation could've been done while sitting in a meeting. Imagine starting a problem-solving meeting at 10 AM and by 11 AM, as the meeting ends, having a fully formatted PowerPoint presentation of your solutions completed. This is yet another reason why the Tablet PC allows you to more effectively leverage your work day.

Chapter 14 Goal Setting on the Tablet PC

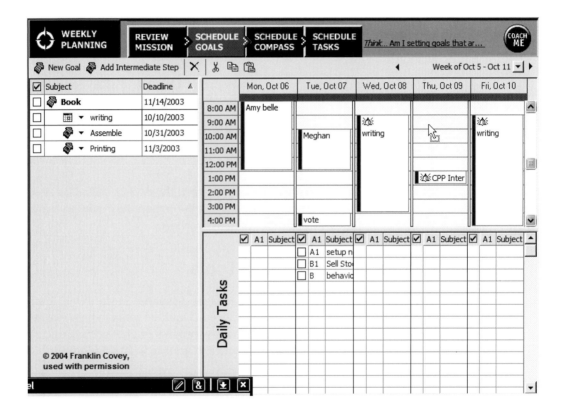

We All Put This Off, Right?

Establishing clear goals is a prerequisite to really effective task planning and work. There's no doubt about that, and no one questions it. Yet we all usually put this activity off.

This is probably because setting goals requires quiet time away from a busy schedule and inspired motivation to commit that time. It's also because, if you have not yet fully mastered the lessons in Chapter 6 on task management, you are perhaps buried in the minutia of your daily tasks. You probably cannot imagine coming up for air long enough to think broadly about your higher intentions.

My recommendation is to use the lessons of Chapters 6 and 7 for awhile and dig yourself out from your avalanche of tasks. When you have that system smoothly in place, return to this chapter. This is why I have deprioritized this activity by placing this chapter near the end of the book. You need to be fluid with the task assignment and execution methodology before attacking this last chapter.

That said, if you are trying to decide between the two FranklinCovey software packages compared throughout this book, you may want to scan this chapter now for some additional decision criteria.

Software-Based Goal-Setting Tools

The two FranklinCovey software packages discussed in this book, PlanPlus 2.0 for Outlook and TabletPlanner 3.0, each include tools to help you set goals. They both attempt to automate the process of goal setting, and they automate linking the resulting activities to your task and appointment data. They both accomplish this relatively well.

I hope you have taken my advice and adopted, or plan to adopt, one or the other of these two FranklinCovey software packages for task management purposes. If so you are likely using the same package for note taking and power document management. There is little to differentiate these two packages relative to built-in goal setting tools. PlanPlus has a stronger help system. TabletPlanner maintains its consistent emphasis on using digital ink. Other than this, I would let the other functionalities guide your choice between these packages.

Let's now cover how these same packages can help you to plan, set, and execute goals.

FranklinCovey Goal-Setting Principles

FranklinCovey as a company has gone further than any organization I know in promulgating the need for, and methods of, setting goals and applying them to work and life. It has succeeded in spreading its theory and practice due to the success of its best-selling books on the topic (*The Seven Habits of Highly Successful People* by Stephen Covey being the best known), due to its workshop series, and due to the success of its line of personal organizing portfolios and software. You are probably aware that there is a chain of FranklinCovey retail outlets that sell these portfolios and software located in shopping malls throughout the world.

I have been casually studying goal setting on and off for over twenty years, and only in the last five years have I come across the FranklinCovey method. My opinion is that the FranklinCovey approach is at least equivalent in effectiveness to competing approaches and probably better. Mix that with its widespread acceptance and easy access to tools to implement it, and it's probably the best choice to use for goal setting and goal follow-up.

Common to both software packages is an underlying set of FranklinCovey principles to guide life and work that can be summarized as follows: all people have a core set of values that guide their individual decisions. Once our own values are identified, clarified, and properly prioritized, we can and should consciously use them as a basis for prioritizing and scheduling activities in our work week and daily life.

Steps to Identify and Implement Goals

The steps promulgated in the Covey books and in the FranklinCovey software packages are these:

■ **Step 1. Mission statement**: Identify and write a mission statement for your work and life that summarizes your core values.

■ **Step 2. Goals**: Use that mission statement to identify life and work goals, and list intermediary steps needed to reach those goals.

■ **Step 3. Roles**: Identify important roles in your work, family, and community that represent responsibilities, relationships, and areas of contribution.

■ **Step 4. Weekly assignment of tasks and appointments**: Take planning steps to ensure that as you plan your week and enter tasks on your task list and appointments on your schedule, you review your mission statement, your goals, and your important roles. Ensure that you balance your time and activities across all three within your week plan.

The Four-Quadrants System

Inherent in all the steps above is the concept of finding what's really important to you at any given point in time. As a tool to facilitate this prioritizing process, Covey in his books focuses on four quadrants for classifying activities:

- I. Important and urgent

- II. Important but not urgent

- III. Not important but urgent

- IV. Not important and not urgent

Stephen Covey's suggests you arrange your life so that you can focus as much of your time and energy as possible on quadrant II activities. This will lead to the greatest benefit and to the greatest likelihood of achieving your life's goals.

There is no way in the few pages I've allowed here to do justice to the depth of thinking that Covey puts into this approach to prioritizing activities in life. Again I encourage you to spend some time reading one of the two Covey books, *The Seven Habits of Highly Successful People* or *First Things First*, to fully appreciate and benefit from his thinking. You may also want to consider taking one of the FranklinCovey workshops. Let's briefly review how each of the software packages implements the Covey approach.

How the Tablet PC Fits In

Considering the theory that using a pen to work in a graphical format leads to activation of both sides of the brain and greater creativity, what tasks could be more needful of a fully activated and creative mind than those associated with personal goal setting? The TabletPlanner software is structured in a way that encourages you to use the pen when following the goal-setting activities.

The PlanPlus for Outlook software in contrast was originally designed to be used on a standard computer. A pen can be used, however, and the same principles above apply; working with a pen and the tablet in your lap leads to more creative and more thoughtful planning than typing away on a computer.

Also, a primary advantage of the Tablet PC is its ability to be everywhere you are and its suitability for use in places a laptop or desktop should never be. Goal setting requires a broad perspective and an open mind. I have done some of my best goal setting while sitting on a ridgetop overlooking the Pacific Ocean. Typing on a laptop feels quite out of place in such a setting, but writing with a Tablet PC perched in my lap works fine.

FranklinCovey Software

Each of the two FranklinCovey software packages takes a different approach toward deploying the above steps to identifying and implementing goals and to ensuring that quadrant II activities make it onto your busy schedule.

PlanPlus 2.0 for Microsoft Outlook

PlanPlus 2.0 for Microsoft Outlook takes a guided tour approach to implementing the four-step FranklinCovey planning process. It walks you through each step, using excellent help screens ("Coach Me" screens) along the way. Figuring out where to start, though, can require a little thought.

If you've been working on the task and appointment manager portion of PlanPlus for some days or weeks now, you've probably seen multiple references, in both the folder list view and the PlanPlus toolbar, to words like compass, goals, mission, and weekly planning. If you are not already a student of the FranklinCovey system, browsing these tools may leave you a bit confused. Luckily it is easy to get past that by focusing your attention on the Weekly Planning screen.

Start with the Weekly Planning Screen

You could, using the folder entries and toolbar buttons, jump directly to any of the individual planning steps, but the best place to start to get an overview of how this all fits together is to look at the Weekly Planning screen. To get there, open the Folder List view in the left side of the Outlook window, expand the FranklinCovey folder, and click on the bottom topic labeled Weekly Planning (see Figure 14-2; Chapter 6 provides a navigation overview of Plan-Plus if you need help with this).

In that screen, the four steps listed in the section above entitled Steps to Identify and Implement Goals are actually coded into the software. They "automatically" guide the user through the planning experience and link the outcomes to the task list and appointment schedule portion of Outlook.

On the Weekly Planning screen, the four steps are highlighted at the top as large bold rectangular process steps, clearly identifying what you need to do to accomplish the planning process (see Figure 14-1).

© 2004 Franklin Covey, used with permission

Figure 14-1. The four steps to identify and implement goals are listed at the top of the Weekly Planning screen. Clicking on these rectangles opens tools to help with each step.

The only one that may not seem to link directly to the four steps I've listed above is Schedule Compass; but just remember that this phrase corresponds to the Roles step (step three) in the list.

Clicking on each process rectangle opens the tools needed to accomplish the planning step within the lower portion of the Weekly Planning screen. These tools, and the needed actions to use them, are clearly laid out. And if you understand the FranklinCovey principles they are nearly self-guiding.

Recommendation on How to Approach the Four Steps

If you are not a current student of FranklinCovey, my recommendation is to "seek understanding first and perform action next." In other words, gain a full understanding of what's going on in these four steps and how they are implemented in the software before starting to actually enter data on any of the screens. To do this, starting from the Weekly Planning screen, click on each of the four process steps and walk through each of the screens, referring as needed to the help screens or the referenced books. The help screens provide all you need to know to navigate the four screens, and those help screens are quickly available via the Coach Me button available on each screen.

These help screens include access to some multimedia presentations designed to introduce you to the FranklinCovey concepts relevant to each screen. The multimedia presentations are actually quite good, and they do the job well of getting you in the frame of mind to do the goal-setting and weekly planning exercises. They also visually simulate the proper use of the user interface of each screen. When I first started using this software, I had not extensively studied the FranklinCovey system, but I found the Coach Me help screens sufficient to get good use of the software.

You should study and restudy the four screens and associated Coach Me help screens until you understand the overall flow, what is being accomplished in each step, and how they link together. Once you feel you have a good overall view, then come back to the first step, the Review Mission step, and spend some time on that. That step alone could take you a half day to a full weekend of reflection to get right, so don't try to rush it. Rather set aside some quality time to do this correctly. Find the equivalent of that ridge over the Pacific Ocean, especially for this first step.

Step-by-Step Entry to the Weekly Planning Screens

As mentioned in Chapters 6 and 7, you should stop and review all your open tasks at least once a week in what is best called a weekly review. This is where you examine your master list to see if any items are ready to be escalated to a daily task. This is also where you examine your goal list and place appointments or assign tasks on the week's schedule to meet those goals. The Weekly Planning screen is the tool to do this.

As mentioned, you reach the Weekly Planning screen by clicking the Weekly Planning entry under the FranklinCovey folder list (assuming you display Outlook in its Folder List view as I recommend). (See Figure 14-2.)

Review Mission

This opens the first planning screen, with the weekly planning process steps at the top of the screen and the first of these steps, the Review Mission step, displayed in the lower portion of the screen (see Figure 14-3). If you've entered a mission previously, it is displayed below the four-step guide, ready for your review prior to scheduling goals for the week ahead. If you have not, copy your mission statement into this screen.

There is very little automation in the Review Mission step; this screen merely serves as a place to store your mission statement for periodic review. Creating a mission statement can be a substantial effort, and I would not try to use this screen as a tool to create one. First you need to study what a mission statement is and how to create it. For this I recommend at a minimum reading the Coach Me help screens associated with this screen, but better is to read the FranklinCovey books referenced in the Appendix. And don't restrict yourself to FranklinCovey material for this important action in your life; there are plenty of books and seminars to turn to for this task.

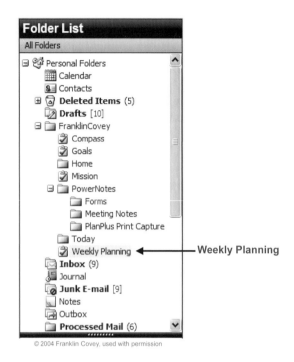

Figure 14-2. Open the Weekly Planning screen from the Outlook Folder List view.

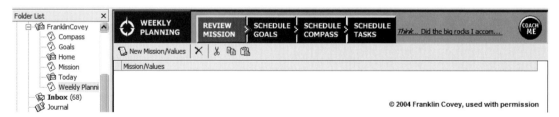

Figure 14-3. The Review Mission screen is the first step.

Regarding Tablet PC tools to use, I recommend MindManager as a brainstorming tool while creating your mission statement. It has an enormous capability to open the flow of ideas, something you want when working through the discovery process of forming your mission statement.

Schedule Goals

Next, you reach the goals screen by clicking on the second step of the four-step guide at the top of the screen (Schedule Goals). Once there, you establish goals on the screen by entering them on the left side (see Figure 14-4). Intermediate steps needed to reach a goal are created below each major goal on the left side also.

These goals are displayed again week to week for you to assign tasks against. The idea is that during weekly planning you review these goals and selectively add them (or intermediate steps needed to reach them) to your schedule or task list for the week. This is done by dragging and dropping the goals or intermediate steps from the left side of the screen to the right side, where a slightly modified week-view of the Outlook schedule and task list resides, ready to receive new items.

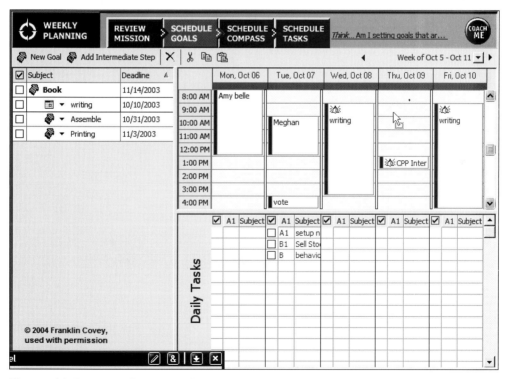

Figure 14-4.   In the Schedule Goals screen you can drag goals and intermediate steps from your goal list to your weekly calendar.

Looking at your long-term goals at the beginning of each week and scheduling time to achieve them in your week's plan is a very important idea within the Covey system. The idea is to lock activities to achieve your key goals into your schedule at the beginning of the week, before your schedule gets too busy with day-to-day work assignments. Then throughout the week you should fit your tactical day-to-day assignments around these activities, giving priority to the goal-based activities. This concept is basic to the FranklinCovey book *First Things First,* and it explains the title well.

Schedule Compass (Roles)

Next is the Schedule Compass screen, which is used for scheduling activities for key *roles and relationships*. It follows the same pattern as above (see Figure 14-5). Attention to roles is one area I find the FranklinCovey approach differs greatly from other goal-setting philosophies and in a very good way. It's an effective way to force balance into one's priorities and weekly activities. Sometimes our goals can be so high minded, or our work so urgent, that we forget some of the more common components of our life that make us who we are. The roles and relationship approach, as applied on the Schedule Compass screen, attempts to correct this. I recommend you spend some time understanding this step. It's a particularly valuable contribution of the FranklinCovey approach.

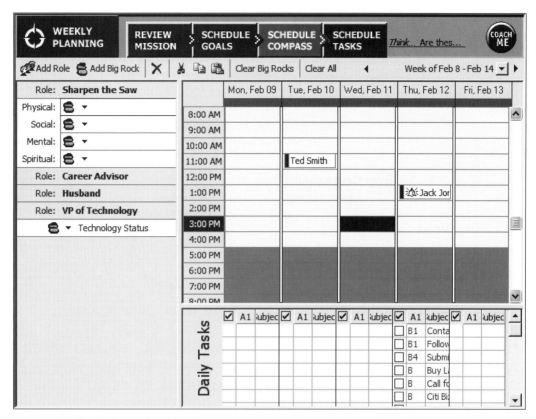

Figure 14-5.   In the Schedule Compass screen you can drag role activities from your roles list to your weekly calendar.

Example roles are Father, Husband, Team Leader, Career Advisor. The idea is simple for this screen: create and present a list of such roles along with typical activities that honor the commitments and intentions of each role. Each week you review that list and in a measured way decide how to express each role during that week. The screen includes a Sharpen the Saw category for activities you schedule to improve yourself (exercise, study, and so on).

The final screen, Schedule Tasks, enables you to view all your master tasks and assign them to days throughout the week. You can drag and convert them to appointments, or drag and convert them to daily tasks. This follows the principles described in Chapter 6 of this book. I recommend you reread the sections in that chapter on daily versus master tasks and on managing tasks, if it's been a while.

PlanPlus Today Screen

PlanPlus 2.0 for Microsoft Outlook also includes a customized Today screen that looks as follows (see Figure 14-6):

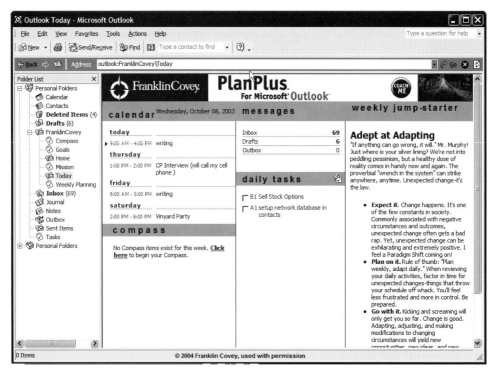

Figure 14-6.   The PlanPlus Today screen.

This is a fully optional view that summarizes all your Outlook items for the current week as well as some of the FranklinCovey items onto one page. It is an executive dashboard of your week's activities. On it your Compass items are shown separately, again, giving balance to your roles in life. Random inspirational and management how-to messages are included on the right side of the today screen.

FranklinCovey TabletPlanner 3.0

FranklinCovey TabletPlanner 3.0 uses the same four-step process as PlanPlus for identifying and implementing your goals. These four steps are presented in the software in nearly the same way as PlanPlus. The actual screens used do differ a little, and the navigation to screens follows the tab approach that by now you are well familiar with on the TabletPlanner.

Because these two software packages implement these steps in such a similar way, please read the section above on PlanPlus; below I'll describe the differences and navigation in TabletPlanner.

Navigating the Goal-Setting and Implementation-Planning Screens

Like PlanPlus, you can directly enter many of the goal-oriented screens corresponding to the four planning steps, or you can go through the weekly planning screen to reach them. Again, I recommend you always use the Weekly Planning screen as your navigation method. In fact it's even more important to use it as your entry point with TabletPlanner, because the method of direct access to the four individual screens is inconsistent across the four screens, which can be confusing. Some screens require menu items to reach, and some require tabs. It's better to unify the approach and just use the Weekly Planning screen and its subtabs. The easiest way to get to the Weekly Planning screen is using the Weekly Planning tab, which is in the middle of the horizontal tab list.

After clicking on the Weekly Planning tab you'll see the following view (see Figure 14-7). Notice that the four planning steps described earlier in this chapter are represented as subtabs at the top of the window, below the main TabletPlanner tabs. And like the process within PlanPlus, the correct way to approach this is to work from left to right across those four tabs. Clicking on each of the tabs opens screens similar to the PlanPlus screens.

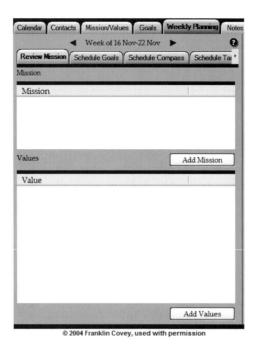

© 2004 Franklin Covey, used with permission

Figure 14-7. Clicking the Weekly Planning tab yields a screen with four subtabs, each corresponding to one of the four steps of the FranklinCovey planning process.

Using Help

You should use the help screens to learn details of each of these four tabs. They are reached by using the questionmark-shaped help button on each page. Like PlanPlus, clicking the button takes you directly to the relevant section of TabletPlanner help. Unfortunately, if you access these four screens through the Weekly Planning screen (as I recommend), the displayed help button returns only the Weekly Planning help page. The information for each screen does not come up. So instead I recommend you open the contents section of that help screen and navigate down to the help book titled The FranklinCovey Planning System. Open that book and you will find subbooks that correspond to principles behind each of these four screens. The principles behind the Schedule Tasks step is found within the Weekly Planning book.

Do not fail to explore every hyperlink exposed within the text of these help screens because they expose other help screens that are not listed in the help contents list, and some of those help screens are key ones. For example the detailed instructions for using the Schedule Compass screen is buried as a link in one such help screen.

Using the Schedule Goals Screen

Clicking on the Schedule Goals tab will show you the following screen (see Figure 14-8). If you are able to see this two-part screen, then good, that's what you want. However I've found that sometimes this screen opens with just the left side goals-list portion of the screen spread across the full width of the TabletPlanner window. If you have this problem, read below on how to fix it. If all is fine, then skip ahead to the section Dragging Goals to Your Week.

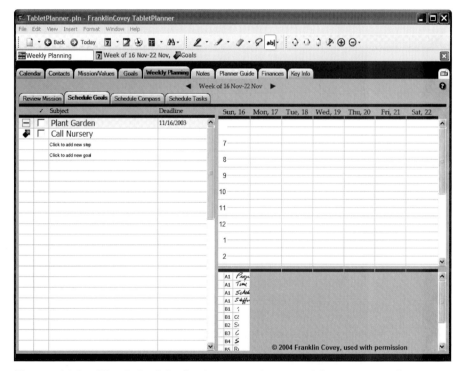

Figure 14-8. The Schedule Goals screen is a special two-pane split screen. You can resize the left and right side by dragging the boundary between the two panes.

Fixing an Unsplit Schedule Goals Screen

If you do have a full goals screen rather than the two-part screen shown in Figure 14-8 above, the problem is that your screen is not split and you need to open up the right pane. Viewing the screen above you might think that this is simply a matter of using the Navigation Bar and the Windows menu for left page right page control, as discussed in the task chapter section on navigating within TabletPlanner (Chapter 6). But in fact if you do try to use that approach, you'll get some very odd behavior.

Rather you need a completely different approach to display the two-part screen. This Schedule Goals screen, and the Schedule Compass and Schedule Tasks screens, are special windows that have two panes (not pages) that must both be displayed across a two-page view.

To open the right side of these two panes, do this: when you are on the full screen view of the goals list, hover your pen just inside the far right edge of the TabletPlanner window; your cursor will turn into a split window cursor:

When it does, click and drag to the left. That should expose the right pane that you see in Figure 14-8 above.

The advantage of having panes rather than pages in these views is that you can adjust the relative size of the two panes to meet your needs.

Dragging Goals to Your Week

Once you've got this view open you can drag and drop goals and intermediate steps from the list on the left page over to your weekly schedule and task list on the right, much as it is done in PlanPlus. Simply click on a goal or intermediate task, and drag and drop it either as an appointment or a task. Note that the software will not let you create a task on a past date.

One other thing about using this goals window. When you create goals on the left side you're given a chance to view a details page for the goal on the right side. This details page allows you to do some detailed goal planning. To see this detail use the same approach you used when creating tasks and editing task details in Tablet Planner (as described in Chapter 6). In the left page hover your pen over the right margin of the subject line of the goal you want to edit, and you will see a right-pointing blue or orange arrow appear. Clicking on the arrow opens a detail screen in the right-hand page for the goal. In this window you can enter additional goal information and intermediate steps to reach that goal (see Figure 14-9).

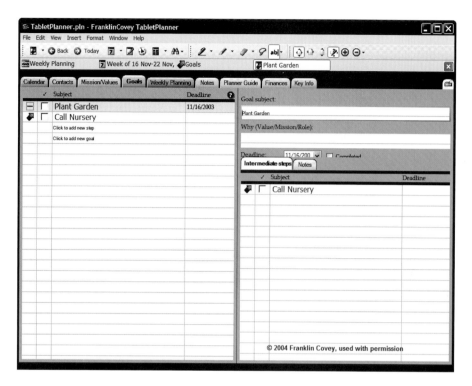

Figure 14-9. Displaying the goal details page on the right.

This details page on the right is a true Navigation Bar page, so when you are done, click the Close box at the right end of the Navigation Bar to close that window and return to the two-pane view shown in Figure 14-8.

The Schedule Compass and Schedule Tasks tabs work essentially the same way.

In Summary

Overall, the FranklinCovey approach to planning and implementing goals is logical and usable. These software packages offer a good way to help you move goals from broad mission-style visions to specific goals to intermediate steps and then to your daily schedules and daily task lists. And this is the key: transfer activities that reflect your important goals onto your daily lists.

Of course this depends on your ability to use those daily lists and actually act on them. But if you have applied the principles in Chapters 6 and 7 on task management and are successfully managing your daily tasks, then this should work to get your important goals where they finally belong: implemented in your life.

The key to making either package work is truly being able to create a discipline of doing weekly planning at the beginning or end of each week, and then following the steps within the software. If you can do that, both packages offer an effective way for moving activities associated with your missions, goals, and roles onto your daily task and appointment lists.

Appendix: **Resources**

Tablet PC Manufacturers and Comparison Web Sites

To research the various Tablet PC models, here are the Tablet PC product pages on the web sites of the major Tablet PC manufacturers:

- www.motioncomputing.com

- www.computers.us.fujitsu.com/www/products_pentablets.shtml

- www.viewsonic.com/products/tablet_pc.htm

- global.acer.com/products/tablet_pc/

- www.eurocom.ca/

- www.hp.com/products/tabletpc/

- www.gateway.com

- www.necsolutions-am.com/products/products.cfm?PageName=Computers

- www.csd.toshiba.com/cgi-bin/tais/pc/pc_tabletPcDetail.jsp?comm=CS

- www.electrovaya.com/

- www.sharpsystems.com

- www.tatung.com/tabletpc/index.htm

Slate or Hybrid List

At the time of this writing, of the manufacturers listed above, the following offered slate or hybrid models: Motion Computing, HP/Compaq, Fujitsu, Viewsonic, Electrovaya, Tatung, and NEC. Remember, a hybrid for the purposes of this book is defined as having a detachable keyboard that, when attached, can support the tablet like a laptop.

Independent Sales Help

The following independent reseller has done a good job of researching various tablet models and identifying and selling models that meet specific needs. Consider contacting them and describing your specific requirements.

www.infocater.com

Comparison Sites, Articles

Here is a link to an informal comparison of current Tablet PC models made and maintained by a Tablet PC enthusiast:

- tabletpc2.com/CompareCentrino.htm

Microsoft's own comparison site can be found here:

- www.microsoft.com/windowsxp/tabletpc/ evaluation/tours/default.asp#

Here are links to magazine articles that review models current at the time of the writing of this book (January, 2004); keep in mind these and other links on this page may not still be active at the time you read this book.

- http://reviews-zdnet.com.com/4520-3126_16-5094267.html?tag=prmo

- www.pcmag.com/article2/0,4149,1438134,00.asp

Accessories

Replacement Tablet PC Pen

- www.wacom.com/tabletpc/accessories.cfm

Software Sources

FranklinCovey PlanPlus and TabletPlanner

- www.franklincovey.com

Microsoft Office, Microsoft OneNote, Windows Journal

- www.microsoft.com

- Windows Journal viewer: www.microsoft.com/windowsxp/tabletpc/downloads/default.asp

MindManager, for creating business maps

- www.mindjet.com

ScanSoft PaperPort Pro 9 Office

- www.scansoft.com/paperport/pro/

Adobe Acrobat

- www.adobe.com/products/acrobat/main.html

Sketchbook Pro

- www.alias.com/eng/products-services/sketchbook_pro/

Monitor Control Software

- UltraMon from realtimesoft.com.

Adding Ink to Older Versions of Office

Office XP: Office XP Pack for Tablet PC

- http://www.microsoft.com/windowsxp/tabletpc/downloads/default.asp

- Pre–Office XP: PenOffice for Microsoft Windows (www.paragraph.com) advertises an ability to add ink annotations to versions of Word as early as Word 97.

Backup Tools

- Iomega Automatic Backup (www.iomega.com)

- FileWare's FileSync (www.fileware.com)

- Syncromagic (www.gelosoft.com/)

- StorageSync (www.azzurri-direct.com/storagesync.htm)

- Drive Image 7 (www.powerquest.com/driveimage/). PowerQuest was recently acquired by Symantec (www.symantec.com).

- Maxtor OneTouch (www.maxtor.com/en/products/external/onetouch/index.htm)

Books

Tablet PC Books

At the time of this writing there were three good reference books written about using the tablet PC. While these books do not dive deep into business usage of the Tablet PC, they each cover a wide range of Tablet PC features and add-on software. Any one of these three books will serve as an excellent overview of the many possible things you can do on the Tablet PC.

- *Tablet PC Quick Reference*, by Jeff Van West

- *Tablet PCs for Dummies*, by Nancy Stevenson

- *How to Do Everything with Your Tablet PC*, by Bill Mann

Windows XP Books

Because the Tablet PC runs on an extended version of Windows XP Professional, answers to nearly all system needs can be found in any good Windows XP reference book. I continue to turn to one book in particular for Window XP assistance, finding the contents complete and insightful. This is not a beginner's book.

- *Microsoft Windows XP Inside Out*, by Ed Bott, Carl Siechert, Craig Stinson

Mind Mapping / Business Mapping

The classic book on mind mapping continues to be the best. It is the original book written by the original inventor of mind mapping, Tony Buzan:

- *The Mind Map Book: How to Use Radiant Thinking to Maximize Your Brain's Untapped Potential*, by Tony Buzan

FranklinCovey Books

FranklinCovey books, and those books associated with the FranklinCovey system, are the classic guides to identifying what matters most in your life, and then using that information to set goals, guide projects, and schedule activities in your week.

- *First Things First*, by Stephen R. Covey, A. Roger Merrill, Rebecca R. Merrill

- *The 7 Habits of Highly Effective People*, by Stephen R. Covey

- *To Do... Doing... Done!*, by G. Lynne Snead & Joyce Wycoff

David Allen Books

I discovered David Allen's books a bit late in my exploration of task management approaches. I have since used his principles for everything from enhancing my FranklinCovey PlanPlus task definitions to reorganizing my physical file cabinets. I cannot recommend his approaches more highly. Start with the first book in the list, read and digest it, and then move to his second book. Also check out David's website for software and ideas: www.davidco.com.

- *Getting Things Done*, by David Allen

- *Ready for Anything*, by David Allen

OneNote Book

- *Complete Guide to OneNote*, by W. Frederick Zimmerman.

Outlook 2003 Book

- *Special Edition Using Microsoft Outlook 2003*, by Patricia Cardoza.

Miscellaneous

- *The Effective Executive*, by Peter F. Drucker

Forums

Great thanks go to the members of the TabletPCBuzz forum for their passion, dedication, and excellent answers to nearly any question:

- www.tabletpcbuzz.com/

Microsoft Tablet PC Official Sites

- www.microsoft.com/windowsxp/tabletpc/

Author's Website

- **www.seizetheworkday.com**

Visit this book's website for access to chapter updates and book corrections as they become available. And as I collect additional insights into Tablet PC business usage, I'll post them at that site.

If you have suggestions for ways to improve future editions of this book, please post them through the Contact Us page on that website.

You can also, at that site, opt to add your name to a mailing list to receive notifications of new editions and new related titles, as they become available. A free newsletter may be forthcoming as well.

Index

P

U

V

W

X